Civil War in South Russia, 1918

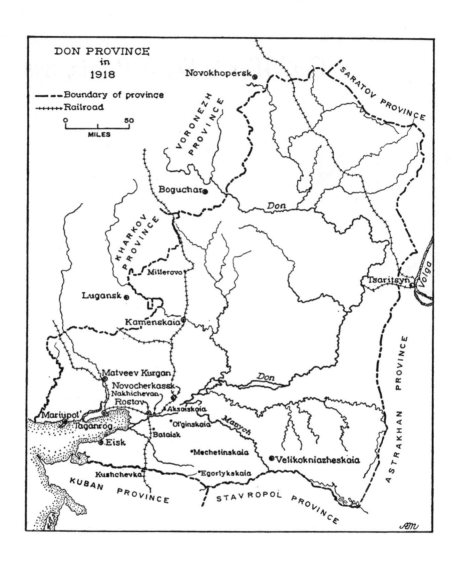

DON PROVINCE
in
1918

— — — Boundary of province
+++++ Railroad

0   50
MILES

Novokhopersk

VORONEZH PROVINCE

SARATOV PROVINCE

Boguchar

Don

KHARKOV PROVINCE

Millerovo

Lugansk

Tsaritsyn

Volga

Kamenskaia

Matveev Kurgan

Novocherkassk
Nakhichevan
Rostov

Mariupol'

Taganrog

Aksaiskaia

Don

Manych

ASTRAKHAN PROVINCE

Ol'ginskaia

Eisk

Bataisk

Mechetinskaia

Velikokniazheskaia

Kushchevka

KUBAN PROVINCE

Egorlykskaia

STAVROPOL PROVINCE

The First Year of the Volunteer Army

CIVIL WAR IN SOUTH RUSSIA, 1918

Peter Kenez

UNIVERSITY OF CALIFORNIA PRESS
BERKELEY·LOS ANGELES·LONDON·1971

University of California Press
Berkeley and Los Angeles, California

University of California Press, Ltd.
London, England

to Dorothy J. Dalby
with Admiration and Affection

Acknowledgments

I am most grateful for the help I received from a number of colleagues. Mr. Hans J. Rogger pointed out to me a large number of major and minor errors and advised me in matters of organization of the material; Mr. William G. Rosenberg read an early version of the manuscript and discussions with him helped me to clarify my thinking on a number of points; Mr. Terence Emmons read the galley proofs and caught some mistakes; Mr. William H. Hill compiled the index.

Within the walls of two major archives I worked in—the Russian and Eastern European Archives of Columbia University, and the Hoover Institution at Stanford, California—I was helped with understanding and kindness. I am especially grateful to Mr. Lev F. Magerovsky, who provided me with much-needed material and gave me useful biographical and bibliographical information. Mrs. Xenia Denikin and Mrs. Olga Wrangel allowed me to use their husbands' archives. It was both useful and pleasant to listen to Mrs. Denikin's reminiscences.

In my research and writing I was supported by the History Department of Harvard University, the Research Committee of the University of California at Santa Cruz, and the Slavic Center of the University of California at Berkeley.

I should like to thank Mrs. Eveline Kanes and Mrs. Dorothy J. Dalby, who corrected many of my grammatical errors and suggested improvements in my writing style. I also thank Miss Jacqueline Crisp, who checked several references, and Miss Jeanine Thompson, who typed the manuscript.

All dates are given according to the Gregorian or Western calendar, except as noted in a few quotations. I have followed the transliteration system of the Library of Congress.

P. K.

Contents

Introduction

The best book on the Russian Civil War, William Henry Chamberlin's *The Russian Revolution*, was published in 1935.[1] That this relatively short study has remained unsurpassed for over three decades, while Russian studies were expanding enormously, shows that the Civil War has received little attention from historians outside the borders of the Soviet Union.

The subject is immensely important. The Soviet Union was created as much by the Civil War as by the revolutions of 1917; indeed, the revolutions and the struggle that followed are inseparable. At the end of 1917, few people knew who the Bolsheviks were and what they wanted, and even Lenin and his followers could not have had very clear ideas about the nature of their future system; it was only in the long and merciless war that the foundations of the Soviet regime were laid. Perhaps Russian Communism would have evolved differently had the bitter necessities of the Civil War not forced the regime to develop some features that had nothing to do with Marxist ideology.

Aside from the obvious historical significance of the Civil War, it is also a subject with great intrinsic interest. The country fell apart and almost every village had its own Civil War, sometimes focused on issues that were unrelated to the ideology of either Whites or Reds. A large variety of socialist and conservative ideologies, mutually exclusive nationalistic claims of people living in the territory of the Russian empire, foreign intervention—all of these had a role in deciding the final outcome. In this period of confusion political institutions collapsed, the values of a civilized society almost disappeared, and in some respects the country reverted to a state of fragmentation that had existed several centuries before.

Modern European history provides no better example of anarchy and its effects on social institutions and human beings.

The complexity of the Civil War, which makes it a fascinating subject, also makes it a difficult one for historical study. In all likelihood this difficulty is the primary cause for its neglect by Western historians. A comprehensive survey of the Civil War can hardly be undertaken until a number of detailed studies of limited areas and periods have been made. Only in such works can adequate attention be given to all or most of the important forces operating in any one area. Extrapolating from one part of Russia to the entire enormous country is perhaps the best way to become aware of the many different issues that were at stake, and of the difficulty of reducing the problems of the Civil War to simple formulae.

South Russia is a particularly good subject for a case study, because it was a microcosm in which one can see most of the ills of Russia, and because of the intrinsic importance of the events that took place there. It was there that the Civil War began and ended, there that the Whites put their most substantial and persistent armies into the field. In this area foreign intervention assumed greater importance than elsewhere; and perhaps nowhere else did the anti-Bolshevik movement suffer more from dissension and the competing claims of national minorities.

The outcome of the Civil War in South Russia, as in other sections, was decided by the struggle of a combination of local and national forces. The aim of the present study is to analyze these forces and their relationships to each other.

The chief actors of the drama were the ex-Imperial officers who came to the Don and the Kuban to take arms against Lenin's regime. For them the choice of a theater of operations was largely accidental; their thoughts were centered on Moscow and Petrograd. (For example, after a stay of almost two years they continued to observe Petrograd, as opposed to local, time.)[2] Who these officers were, how they came to decide to fight the Soviet regime, and how they envisaged Russia's future are among the crucial questions of the Civil War.

The officers formed the general staff of the anti-Bolshevik movement, in both its concrete and its figurative senses. They played a role far out of proportion to their numbers; they provided military and political leadership, and they were a nucleus around which other anti-Soviet groups could unite. However, on their own they would have been impotent. No matter how heroic and determined these few thousand men were, the Bolsheviks would have crushed them without difficulty. From the summer of 1918 on, the overwhelming majority of the White army was made up of Cossacks. The Cossacks cared little about the rest of Russia; for them the Civil War was a struggle against the non-Cossack peasants, the so-called *inogorodnye*, who looked covetously at Cossack lands. Only a partial coincidence of interests existed between officers and Cossacks, and the two groups never understood each other. Consideration of the differences in views within the White camp, and of local circumstances, is essential to an understanding of the Civil War.

The role of the Allies is discussed only to the extent that is absolutely necessary for understanding the Volunteer Army's development. Foreign intervention is the sole aspect of the Civil War that has been adequately treated by historians—Russians and foreigners alike. The motivation of Soviet historians in emphasizing this subject is clear: they have wanted to present the history of the Bolsheviks as a victory not only over their domestic opponents but also over "world imperialism." By describing at different times the Germans, the French, the English, or the Americans as the real power behind the White movement, they have also wanted to serve immediate political goals, which of course, has nothing to do with the search for historical truth. The interest of Western historians in the participation of their countrymen in the Civil War of another nation is easily understandable. However, by stressing only one aspect of a very complex situation, Western historians have unwittingly furthered the aim of Soviet historiography—the casual reader might receive the impression that the war was fought between Russians and non-Russians. This picture, of course, is false: the Reds might have defeated their enemies sooner had they not had outside help, but the Allied contribution to the White Cause was far from being of critical importance.

The delineation of the topic has been a difficult task. Obviously, events in the South took place in a larger national and even international context. The Volunteer Army came to have an increasingly large influence on the Civil War in the Ukraine and in the Crimea, for example, and to appreciate that influence some understanding of the complex events in those areas is necessary. Also, to evaluate the performance of the Whites one must have some knowledge of the strategy and quality of the Red armies.

This study is devoted to the first year of the Civil War, the year of developing programs, of envisaging alternatives, of improvisations and enormous confusion. The end of the war in Europe altered the character of the struggle in Russia. Allied aid began to arrive at Black Sea ports and influenced the course of operations. But more important, the outlook of the participants changed. Not only Europeans but also White Russians had believed the Bolsheviks to be merely German agents, and they consequently regarded the fighting in Russia as an extension of the war in Europe. Now the Volunteer Army had to reconsider its *raison d'etre*. The German defeat was soon followed by the withdrawal of occupation forces from a large part of the country, which then came to be contested by Whites and Reds. The scale of the war was ever widening: the size of the armies grew and the theaters of operations were enlarged, but the most important qualitative change had occurred by the end of 1918.

Civil War in South Russia, 1918

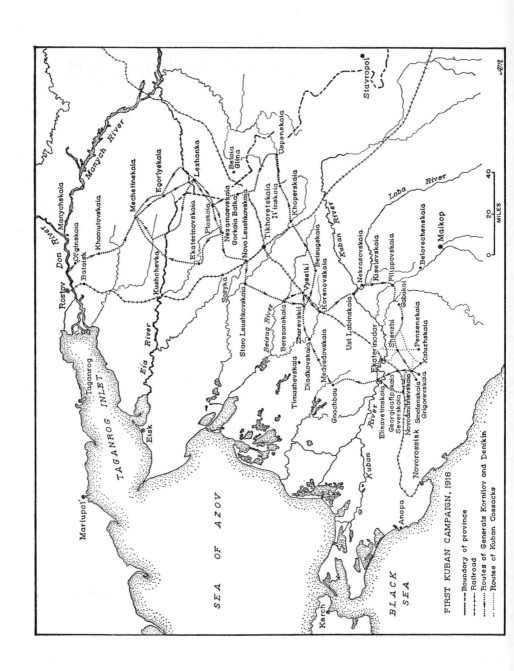

FIRST KUBAN CAMPAIGN, 1918

——— Boundary of province
+++++ Railroad
········· Routes of Generals Kornilov and Denikin
········· Routes of Kuban Cossacks

CHAPTER 1

Dramatis Personae: The Officers and the Cossacks

1917

The Russian Revolution of March 1917 was a spontaneous one, as all great revolutions inevitably must be. The unorganized populace, exasperated by the privations resulting from an increasingly unpopular war, overthrew the 300-year-old Romanov dynasty with remarkable ease. The government fell practically without defenders because it had become isolated from the public and was capable neither of appeasing nor suppressing the opposition, an opposition that called attention to the appalling incompetence of the leadership without fear of punishment. Nicholas II, the last Tsar, neither could nor wanted to attract better men; the last Russian imperial government was clearly below the standard of civilized governments of the world, and obviously incapable of coping with the enormous problems of the country at war.

The Revolution, which had long been expected even if in a different form, was greeted with great enthusiasm and optimism. The public believed that it was possible to wipe the slate clean, that all the ills of the country would magically disappear once its outdated institutions were removed. The Russians even regained some of their former enthusiasm for the war, for it seemed that the Germans could not resist revolutionary soldiers fighting in the defense of their free country. For a short time the country enjoyed if not true national unity at least the appearance of it.

The opponents of autocracy, consisting of liberals who had

made their reputation in the Duma (the Russian Parliament) and socialists who had worked mostly underground, inherited power and authority. In their commitment to democratic institutions, the socialists and liberals shared a great deal and this augured well for the future. For the moment they were in complete control of the situation. The monarchist right was nonexistent as a political force, for the collapse of tsarism left it discredited and in disarray, without a political program. Nor did the extreme left appear as a serious danger. The Bolsheviks had perhaps fewer than ten thousand adherents in the entire country.[1]

The Imperial Duma, which was elected in 1912 on the basis of restricted suffrage, disobeyed the tsar's command to disperse and elected an Executive Committee, which in turn named a Provisional Government. In purely legal terms, therefore, the legitimacy of the government was not beyond question, and in fact the ministers were largely self-appointed. However, in the revolutionary situation this government was as representative of the articulate public as one could expect and it was immediately recognized, both at home and abroad, as the successor to the tsarist government. The government was dominated by members of the Constitutional Democratic (Kadet) Party, a moderate, liberal group that was trying to implant the principles of constitutionalism in inhospitable Russian soil. The Kadet Party boasted the support of the majority of Russian professional people, the bourgeoisie, and a large segment of the enlightened nobility. In the first months, the leading figure of the government was not the rather self-effacing Premier, Prince G. E. Lvov, but foreign minister P. N. Miliukov, who was the best-known Kadet leader, a famous historian, and an outstanding intellectual. The government was also supported by the Octobrists, a moderately conservative party named after the 1905 October Manifesto, which established constitutional limits for autocracy. A member of this party, A. I. Guchkov, an industrialist and ex-President of the Duma, received the important portfolio of defense.

However, the Provisional Government was never the unchallenged master of the country. Even before it was established, the Petrograd Soviet of Workers' and Soldiers' Deputies was formed. That the Soviet (council) was founded so quickly, and without any previous planning, was the result of the experience of the 1905 Revolution, in which councils of workers, peasants, and soldiers played important roles. Although the Soviet in the capital remained by far the most important, Soviets were soon formed all over the country, in factories, in villages, and in regiments. The Soviets were led entirely by socialists, mostly intellectuals, who claimed to speak for the peasants and the workers. The largest party in the Soviets was the Social Revolutionary Party, a populist, peasant organization. The other socialist party, the Social Democratic Party, was divided into moderate Menshevik and extremist Bolshevik wings. The Petrograd Soviet and the Provisional Government were connected in the person of A. F. Kerenskii, a leading figure in the Soviet, who took the post of minister of justice.

It soon became clear that the constitutional situation was impossible; the moderates, socialists, and liberals were not able to provide the country with an effective government. They failed not so much because they made mistakes (which they certainly did), nor because they were bad politicians (which they may have been), but because their political philosophy was irrelevant in Russia in 1917. Perhaps they could have governed the country had there been no war; but in that case tsarism might not have collapsed either. What brought the moderates to victory also condemned them to defeat: the unmanageable problems of an underdeveloped country engaged in a modern war.

The system under which the Provisional Government shared power with the Soviets was called dual power. This is something of a misnomer, for while the Provisional Government had all the responsibility, most of the control was in fact in the hands of the leaders of the Soviets, who had veto power over every act of the government. This power was based on the fact that the Petrograd Soviet of Workers' and Soldiers' Deputies could always call on workers and soldiers to demonstrate in its behalf. Since the Provisional Government possessed no comparable organized force, it existed merely at the toleration of socialist politicians. But the socialists had an ambivalent attitude toward power. On the one hand they were fascinated by it, and on the other they were afraid of the responsibility. As the general situation deteriorated, the soldiers and workers became increasingly radicalized. The leaders of the Soviets, in order not to lose touch with their followers, were forced to take an ever more radical course. The radicalism of the Soviets made it impossible for the Government to govern, yet the socialists did not draw the necessary conclusion and take the task of governing into their own hands.

Of all the issues that divided the public, such as land reform and the type of government Russia should have, the most immediate one was that of the war. Patriotic enthusiasm, rekindled by the March Revolution, was short-lived. The peasant soldiers were tired of fighting: the war was dragging on for the third year without any appreciable results, causing them great suffering for goals they only dimly understood. The concept of Russia's national interests, however, made sense to the politicians of the Provisional Government, to the middle and upper classes, and to the intelligentsia, who therefore believed that Russia must remain faithful to her allies. The politicians understood the depth of dissatisfaction with the war as little as the tsarist government had understood the mood of the people.

The history of the era of the Provisional Government was a history of a series of crises of ever-increasing intensity. The government was losing control, anarchy was spreading into every area of national life, and it soon became evident that the national unity of the March Revolution was merely an illusion.

The first serious disturbances took place in the beginning of May, when demonstrators came to the streets in Petrograd protesting Miliukov's policy of continuing the war to a victorious conclusion. The Petrograd Soviet, supporting the demonstration, forced not only Miliukov but also Guchkov to resign. The new government, in which Kerenskii was the leading figure as minister of defense, included several socialists, and endorsed the principle of peace without annexations and indemnities.

The second major crisis was triggered by Kerenskii's error in encouraging the General Staff of the army to start an offensive in July. Kerenskii's desire for the offensive was at least partially motivated by the conviction that military victories would halt the process of disintegration. But the failure of the Russian armies, which could have been predicted, led to demonstrations and street fighting, not only in Petrograd but all over the country. This time the government was able to re-establish order, and it used the opportunity to jail some of the Bolshevik leaders, who were implicated in the disturbances of the so-called July days.

On July 21 Kerenskii became Premier. In September he called a state conference in Moscow, in which all important groups except the Bolsheviks participated. But the efforts to attain unity were quashed, this time by the attempt of the right, in the Kornilov Mutiny, to displace the Provisional Government and destroy the system of Soviets. Kerenskii could overcome the challenge of his commander-in-chief only by calling on the Soviets to help him. Even though the government succeeded in defeating first the left and then the right, this was achieved at the price of alienating its support. The government was so weak that when the Bolsheviks explicitly announced their intention of taking power in October, it was unable to prevent them from doing so. The Provisional Government disappeared, as had the tsarist government some months before, without defenders.

It was the obvious failure of the liberal and democratic regime to cope with the problems of the country that made many Russians accept either rightist or leftist solutions. Thus the forces that were to fight a three-year-long Civil War came into being. The reasons for the growth of the left and right were closely interrelated. The Bolsheviks gained followers by emphasizing the danger of military counterrevolution, and by accusing the government of not taking strong enough measures to prevent it. The military men, on the other hand, justified their mutiny by pointing to Bolshevik treachery in time of war, and to Bolshevik influence in the Soviets and consequently in the Provisional Government.

Until Lenin's return from Switzerland in April, the small group of Bolsheviks in Petrograd was hardly different from its Marxist colleagues, the Mensheviks. Indeed, some of the Bolsheviks contemplated healing the split, which had occurred in 1903.[2] In the first weeks the Bolsheviks did not oppose the Provisional Government because as Marxists they believed that Russia was not yet ripe for a socialist revolution, and therefore they could not offer an alternative to what they regarded as a bourgeois regime. When Lenin proposed a radically new policy, he had a difficult time convincing his own followers of its merits.

The essence of Lenin's evaluation of the political situation was that the revolution could and should be "deepened," and that therefore there could be no compromise with the bourgeoisie. This meant that the Bolsheviks had to fight the system of dual power and advocate giving all power to the Soviets. Lenin's analysis may have been faulty from a theoretical Marxist point of view; however, he cared far more for the conquest of power than for doctrinal purity. When Lenin convinced his immediate followers that the Party had to aim at taking the government, the Bolsheviks were still a small minority, not only in the country but even in the Soviets. Consequently, to take power the party had to gain followers and allies. To win the soldiers and peasants to his side, he promised them what they wanted: land and peace. Without hesitation Lenin adopted the agrarian platform of the Social Revolutionary Party, which he, like most Marxists, had attacked in the past as bourgeois because it encouraged a desire for private property ownership among the peasants. In the past the Bolsheviks had advocated nationalization of large estates rather than distribution of land. In the summer of 1917, however, as forcible occupation of noble land by the peasants became more and more frequent, the Bolsheviks supported the peasants and welcomed the developing anarchy.

But it was Lenin's unconditional denunciation of the war that was politically most beneficial. As dissatisfaction with the continued struggle deepened, the Bolsheviks, the only major political group advocating immediate peace, were bound to gain. For Lenin, opposition to the war implied no reversal. Since 1914 he had advocated turning the fighting into a civil war. He regarded himself as an agent of the world revolution, one who had come to lead the Russian proletariat only by an accident of birth. From his point of view, it simply did not matter which group of imperialist powers gained more. Without hesitation he accepted German help in getting home from his Swiss exile and gaining financial support for his Party.[3] It seemed to him that the short-term interests of the

German empire and the long-term interests of the world proletariat would both be served by a new revolution in Russia. Since he thought that events in Russia would start the chain of world revolution, German gains in the war did not seem important to him.

This aspect of Lenin's tactics determined his opponents' view of Bolshevism. To many Russians, understandably, collusion with the enemy in time of war was treason. In 1917 and in the first year of the Civil War, the anti-Bolsheviks tended to look at the Bolsheviks not as misguided utopians and social visionaries but as paid German agents. In their mind fighting Germans on the front and fighting Bolshevik agents in the cities of Russia was one and the same task.

The government's energetic action against the Bolsheviks following the July days momentarily slowed down the growth of Bolshevik strength. However, following the failure of the Kornilov mutiny, they succeeded for the first time in gaining majorities in the crucial Moscow and Petrograd Soviets. From that time on, the destruction of the powerless Provisional Government was only a matter of timing. On November 7 Lenin finally achieved his goal.

THE ARMY AND THE REVOLUTION

As anarchy spread and the danger grew that the tottering Provisional Government might fall to the Bolsheviks, a rightist opposition led by officers of the army came into being.* The same men who wanted to destroy the Soviets and who came into conflict with the Provisional Government in 1917 were the ones who

---

*It is difficult to find a value-free term to describe the anti-Bolshevik side in the Civil War. The officers frequently referred to themselves as counter-revolutionaries, but in the modern world "counter-revolutionary" has definite negative connotations. Also, it is debatable whether it would be logically correct to use this term. For Soviet historians this is no problem. According to their interpretation, the real Revolution occurred in November 1917, and all those who opposed that revolution were counter-revolutionaries by definition. On the other hand, if one maintains that the Revolution occurred in March, then all enemies of the political order born out of that revolution, officers and Bolsheviks alike, should be called counter-revolutionaries. To avoid this difficulty, the innocuous term "White" will be used in this study. The terms White and Red are part of international usage, and were adopted very quickly by both sides after the outbreak of the Civil War.

founded the Volunteer Army and led the anti-Bolshevik resistance in South Russia during the Civil War. For them the events of November 7 were not a turning point but something they had expected, something that required only a change of tactics in the continued struggle. The special characteristics of the Russian officer corps, and the peculiar circumstances of the period in which they began their struggle, left their mark on the course of the Civil War.

When it entered the First World War, the Russian army was based on the military laws of 1874, which formed an essential part of the great reforms of Alexander II's reign. The essence of these laws was to extend the obligations of military service to everyone, without regard to social status. The standing professional army became an army of cadres for the nation in arms.[4]

Introducing the principles of universal military service was a great step toward the creation of a modern society in Russia, and the replacement of a standing army by a potentially much larger national one was essential for defending the country. But legislation alone could not make the Russian army as efficient as a Western European one. This was so partly because the democratic principles of the legislation were not altogether realized. Men of higher classes found numerous ways to avoid joining the army, and even if they served they did so only for short periods. The main cause of the army's weakness, however, was the backwardness of Russia. Peasants had no experience in handling modern machinery, the few existing factories could not produce enough war material, and the transportation system of the country could not move troops quickly.

The Russian aristocracy of the nineteenth century did not exhibit the same taste for a military career that the German and French aristocracy did; an army career and life in high society had not become identified in the public mind, so the officers did not enjoy as much social prestige. They also received such notoriously small salaries that Denikin called them an "intellectual proletariat."[5] A low standard of living, little prestige, and the antimilitarist ideology of the intelligentsia made recruiting so difficult that the army never had enough officers. According to the British military attaché to Russia, Sir Alfred Knox, in January 1910 there were 5,123 commanding posts vacant.[6] The situation improved somewhat in the years preceding the war, but even in July 1914 the estimated shortage was 3,000.[7]

The perennial need for officers made it possible for men from the lower classes to rise to the top and for the Russian army to become an instrument for social mobility. The army especially attracted sons of soldiers, who could rise to the highest positions. The social composition of the officer corps did not differ much from that of the bureaucracy, which was also not a socially exclusive institution, or from that segment of the Russian intelligentsia that actively opposed the regime. Consequently, neither in 1917 nor in the Civil War was the social background of the competing leaderships as different as is commonly supposed. The casual observer is frequently surprised that the founders of the Volunteer Army, Generals M. V. Alekseev, L. G. Kornilov, and A. I. Denikin came from poor families. However, there is nothing strange about it when one considers that there were dozens of others in high position in the tsarist army with similar backgrounds. The fact that the leaders of the Whites did not come from aristocratic families could have had an enormous significance in the Civil War. A Kornilov or a Denikin could have appealed to the peasants by emphasizing his background.[8] That neither did so, thus allowing the Bolsheviks to portray them as representatives of the exploiting classes, was a political failure of the first magnitude.

Those officers who came from poor families very soon had nothing in common with the ignorant peasants who made up the army. As officers, they were considered educated men, and education was such a scarce commodity in tsarist Russia that it sharply separated the few from the many. Army regulations emphasized that men and officers lived in different worlds: officers used the familiar form of address with their soldiers, soldiers were not allowed to travel in the inside of streetcars, and officers were not supposed to travel third class on trains.[9] The officers constantly humiliated their inferiors, who reciprocated by nurturing a hatred that surfaced with elementary force in 1917.

While there was a great deal of social mobility in the army, it would be an exaggeration to say that social origins and connections were unimportant for quick advancement. The Imperial Guards, for example, were for all practical purposes reserved for the scions of the nobility. Service in the Guards was more pleasant than in other regiments, and guardsmen advanced much more rapidly than others. Understandably, many resented this.[10] The hostility between guardsmen and regular officers was so strong that it survived the revolutions of 1917. In the anti-Bolshevik army of Denikin the privileges the guardsmen continued to receive through their contacts enraged their opponents.

The education of officers had improved a great deal in the decades preceding the war. In the last decades of the nineteenth century there had been two kinds of officer's schools: "military" and "junker." The military schools admitted young men with secondary education, the junker schools those without. The military schools had a more advanced curriculum, were more prestigious, and promised quicker advancement. In the 1880's these schools produced only 26 per cent of the graduates.[11] The curriculum of the better schools was gradually introduced in more and more junker type schools and finally, in 1911, the distinction disappeared.

The Nicholas Academy, or Staff College, gave the highest military education in Russia. The Academy was organized, as were many institutions of the Russian army, on the German model. Only the best officers, after some years of service in regiments, could enter this Academy. Of the annual 150 graduates, the 50 best students received appointment at the General Staff and the others returned to their regiments.[12] Practically the entire high command of the Russian army in the World War and of the Volunteer Army in the Civil War were graduates of the College of the General Staff. These graduates developed an esprit de corps and secured important commanding posts for fellow graduates. Unquestionably, the officers of the General Staff were the most talented in the Russian army; nevertheless the rank and file officers resented their rapid advance.[13] Since the highest posts were invariably filled by officers of the Staff or of the Guards, the regimental officers felt that good service was not rewarded.[14]

Aside from military subjects, students in junker schools, military schools, and the College of the General Staff studied a variety of disciplines, among them history and literature. The regime made a great effort to keep subversive ideas from military schools, and the precaution of authorities sometimes went to ridiculous lengths. For example, in junker schools contemporary Russian literature was not taught at all because its ideas were considered dangerous.[15]

In spite of the fact that students in army schools came from the same social background as students in other gymnasia and universities and studied some of the same subjects, the atmosphere in military schools differed very much from that in other educational institutions. By the turn of the century, the term intelligentsia could not any more be regarded as synonymous with radicalism, for other competing intellectual currents had appeared; nevertheless, interest in social and political issues among the students remained very great, and revolutionary and antimonarchist agitation continued to play a role in the universities. Of course, this agitation had no place in a military institution. The cadets, unlike their compatriots of similar age, showed no interest in politics. This was perhaps due to a process of natural selection: those who felt most hostile to the regime were least likely to join the army, which had the explicit purpose of defending the tsar.

It would be incorrect to say that the schools inculcated the officers with the spirit of legitimism, or rightist ideologies: the officers merely became apolitical. Denikin, an acute and sympathetic observer, wrote:

At their parties the young people [officers] used to solve in passing all the problems of the world, but they did so in a highly elementary way. After all, everything basic had been decided from time immemorial. . . . The structure of the state was, for the officers, a foreordained, unshakable fact, arousing neither doubts nor differences of opinion. "For faith, Tsar and Fatherland." Criticism rarely went beyond a court anecdote, although such anecdotes—often well-founded and venomous—while not shaking the idea [of autocracy] in the slightest, were even then undermining the mystique created around our relationship with the Imperial Court. The fatherland was accepted ardently, completely, as the entire complex entity of the country and people—without analysis, without knowledge of its life, without delving into the murky realm of its interests. . . . The young officers were hardly at all interested in social questions, which touched their consciousness as something strange or simply dull. In life they hardly noticed them; in literature pages discussing social right and wrong were flipped over as something irritating, obstructing the development of the plot. . . . And, indeed, generally they did not read much.[16]

The hostility between the officers corps and the radical and liberal intelligentsia—which had existed for decades—was deepened by the experiences of the war and revolution. It harmed the cause of both and it was irrational and needless; it resulted not so much from different ideologies and goals, since the officers were rather apolitical, but rather from prejudices and misunderstandings. The intelligentsia, well-acquainted with Western European history, drew faulty parallels between Russian and European officers. Because French and German officers frequently stood for reaction, the intelligentsia approached Russian officers with distrust. The military men resented this and reciprocated in kind. Since in the tsarist regime politics usually denoted opposition to the regime and was the pastime of the intelligentsia, the officers, disliking the intelligentsia, came to disapprove of politics altogether. Lack of the most elementary understanding of politics and distrust of politicians—that is, of intellectuals—characterized every action of the White leaders in the Civil War. The results were disastrous.

Two months after the beginning of the war, in October 1914, the Russian army had 2,711,000 soldiers and 38,000 officers.[17] By May 1917 the number increased to 7,292,600 soldiers and 133,000 officers.[18] The losses of the army were enormous: according to the estimate of General N. N. Golovin, the number of captured, wounded, and dead was 7,917,000; out of this 107,000 were officers.[19] These numbers show that the composition of the army and the composition of the officer corps changed radically in the course of the war. In the campaigns of 1914 and 1915 the major part of the regular officers had already been killed: in the spring of 1915 only one-third to two-fifths of the officers were regulars in the infantry.[20] Officers of the reserve and soldiers—mostly educated ones—who had attended some special courses filled the enormous need for officers created by the high casualty rate and the expansion of the army. The reserve officers had received an inferior training before the war; the one year spent in active service was insufficient to turn a young man into an officer.[21]

The new officers absorbed to a very great extent the spirit of the officer corps. The generals, who naturally set the tone, came from the ranks of the regular officers. But the large influx of new men caused perceptible changes in the character of the officer corps; these men were closer to educated society and they possessed less esprit de corps. When the generals embarked on a political venture during the period of the Provisional Government, the new officers showed little inclination to follow them. The leaders of the anti-Bolshevik armies during the Civil War found the response of the officers disappointing: few men who had become officers after 1914 wanted to fight under Alekseev and Kornilov. Perhaps one explanation of this unwillingness is the lack of cohesion of the officer group existing after the revolutions.

It is difficult to evaluate the quality and training of the Russian officers on the basis of the performance of the army in the World War. When a Russian unit faced a German one of about equal size, almost invariably the Russians suffered defeat. Obviously the quality of leadership was only one factor, and surely not the most important one, in deciding the outcome of battles. Given the lack of equipment, the inferior education of the Russian soldier (who was frequently unable to handle simple machines), and the enormous problems of logistics, no military genius could have competed with the Germans on equal terms. But the difficulties of existing conditions cannot excuse all the errors of leadership. Especially at the beginning of the war, Russian generals committed blunders inconceivable in a Western European army of this time. The famous disaster of the Second Russian army in August 1914 comes to mind. General A. V. Samsonov, the commander of the army, who had been a cavalry leader in the Russo–Japanese war, wanted to use his old tactics in a new and totally different situation. Eager to see the battle with his own eyes, he got into a Cossack saddle and rode forward, leaving behind wireless apparatus and all other "modern" paraphernalia; he cut himself off not only from his base but also from half of his command. The defeat that ensued ended the Russian advance into Prussia.[22]

Perhaps no other senior Russian commander again acted as foolishly and with as tragic consequences as Samsonov did; but his type of blunder was characteristic of the Russian commanding staff, which frequently wanted to substitute bravado for strategy and planning. While this impulse had unfortunate consequences in the World War, it suited the much more primitive conditions of the Civil War, when officers performed acts of unparalleled bravery without which the White cause could not long have survived.

* * *

The officers, from the High Command down, accepted the March Revolution with great equanimity. General M. V. Alekseev,* the Tsar's Chief of Staff and de facto leader of the Russian armies, helped to persuade his sovereign to abdicate. The Commanders of the five fronts, Grand Duke Nikolai Nikolaievich, Gen-

---

*Mikhail Vasilevich Alekseev, the son of a re-enlisted soldier, was born in 1857. After attending officer's school, he became a junior officer in 1876 and received his first fighting experience in the Turkish campaigns of 1877-1878. Alekseev passed the examination to get into the Academy of the General Staff only in 1893, but he soon distinguished himself there and in 1896 became a lecturer at this prestigious institution. In the Russo-Japanese war he served as Quartermaster General of the Third Army. But after the fighting he returned to the Academy as Professor of the history of military science. At the outbreak of the War, he became chief of staff to N. I. Ivanov, Commander of the Southwestern Front. Ivanov, a kindly and modest soldier but lacking in decisiveness and intelligence, came completely under the influence of his energetic chief of staff. When on September 5, 1915, the Tsar himself assumed the post of Commander-in-Chief, he chose Alekseev as his chief of staff. Nicholas, who had no previous military experience, of course could not direct the enormously complicated operations of a modern army of several million men, and the entire responsibility fell on his chief of staff.

Alekseev was not prepared for such a difficult task. He found that knowledge of military matters did not suffice in leading a large army, and political considerations were frequently more important than military ones. The son of a poor soldier was a stranger in court circles, but in his new position Alekseev proved himself a man of intelligence, and his advice to the Tsar frequently transcended purely military matters. Alekseev supported the idea of a responsible cabinet and tried to counteract Rasputin's influence.

erals A. E. Evert, V. V. Sakharov, N. V. Ruzskii, and A. A. Brusilov expressed support for Alekseev's arguments.[23] General L. G. Kornilov,* who, in one of the last official acts of the Tsar, had been named Commander of the Petrograd military district, exhibited little loyalty to the Imperial family: as the highest ranking soldier in the capital it was he who carried out the arrest of the tsarina.[24] The unity of the High Command in refusing to resist was so great that two instances of loyalty were conspicuous: General Count Keller and Khan Nakhichevanskii, two corps commanders, offered their troops to suppress the revolution. After the victory of the revolution, General Keller resigned rather than swear loyalty to the Provisional Government.[25]

Although preferring a monarchy, the officers accepted the revolution. They did so not out of republican principles but because after three years of war the issue did not seem worth fighting for. To attempt to suppress the revolution for the sake of the unpopular Imperial family clashed with their notion of patriotism, since they believed that a civil war, which would have been inevitable, would have destroyed Russia's ability to resist the enemy. They sacrificed the Tsar in order to continue the war.

Had the Tsar chosen to carry on the fight, it is likely that he would have found many supporters among the officers, even if resistance was futile. (Every indication had shown that soldiers

---

*Lavr Georgievich Kornilov was born in Ust Kamenogorsk, in Siberia, in 1870. He had some Buriat-Mongol blood in his veins, which explains his oriental features. He always remained proud of his Eastern heritage, and the East came to play a large role in his life. His father was a Cossack who rose to junior officer rank, but his salary was so meager that he had to leave the army and take a position in local administration to support his large family.

Lavr Georgievich attended officer's school and served in Turkestan for a while before he could enter the Academy of the General Staff in 1895. Later he returned to the East and participated in some explorations: in the summer of 1899, he explored the area of Kushki and later Chinese Turkestan and some provinces of Persia. From 1907 to 1911 Kornilov was military attaché in China, and at the outbreak of the World War he commanded a brigade in Brusilov's Eighth Army.

Kornilov possessed unusual courage, which inspired his soldiers, and a

coming in contact with the revolutionaries would refuse to fight.)
But the Tsar made the task of accepting the new regime easier by
giving an apparent legality to the changes. After his abdication he
appealed to his troops:

> Fulfill your duty, defend our glorious Fatherland, obey your com-
> manders, submit to the Provisional Government. Remember that all
> weakening of discipline of the service plays into the hands of the
> enemy.[26]

In spite of the officers' quick acceptance of the revolutionary
changes, the prospects for successful cooperation between them
and the new regime were gloomy from the beginning. Unlike the
officers, the socialist leaders of the Soviets, who acquired an increasing influence in the Provisional Government, regarded the
revolution as a value in itself. The "revolutionary democrats," as
they called themselves, believing both in the continuation of the
war and in a genuine social and political revolution, wanted to
reorganize the army on the basis of democratic principles. In this
reorganization they hoped to find a remedy for the ills of the army,
which had become increasingly evident. They naively believed
that the Russian soldier, as a free man, would fight better. The
officers, on the other hand, quickly forgot that the disorganization
of the army had begun before the revolution and attributed it entirely to the acts of the new regime. They took each evidence of

---

charismatic personality, but he was insubordinate. Soon after the outbreak
of the war, on September 10, 1914, contrary to orders he did not retreat and
his insubordination endangered the entire Eighth Army. Three months later,
without permission or planning, he conducted a raid which led to the capu-
ture of 2000 of his men. In the spring of 1915, at the time of an enemy offensive, again contrary to orders, Kornilov did not withdraw and was wounded
and captured. He achieved a national reputation when in the autumn of 1916
he became the first Russian general to escape from an enemy prison.

The daring nature of the escape made him one of the heroes of the war:
the Emperor gave him a reception and awarded him the Order of St. George,
Third Class. On March 15, 1917, in the name of the Duma, Rodzianko appointed Kornilov commander of the troops of the Petrograd military district. One of the last official acts of the Tsar was the approval of this appointment.

further decline in the fighting capacity of the army as proof of the baneful influence of the new regulations. Those who regarded the destruction of the monarchy as a necessary price to pay for the successful continuation of the war felt cheated. As the army deteriorated, relations between officers and representatives of the new regime worsened; they blamed each other.

A day before the abdication of Nicholas, on March 14, the Petrograd Soviet of Workers' and Soldiers' Deputies issued Order No. 1.[27] Although the Order was addressed only to the Petrograd garrison, its impact was soon felt throughout the entire army. It called on the soldiers to form councils (Soviets) in every military unit down to the size of companies. It asked soldiers to obey the orders of the Military Commission of the State Duma only if they did not contradict the orders of the Petrograd Soviet (the Provisional Government had not yet been formed). It abolished old forms of address of officers and conferred on soldiers all rights of citizenship, including full participation in politics, when off duty.

Of all the acts of the Petrograd Soviet this one was the most controversial. Trotskii regarded it as the "single worthy document of the February Revolution,"[28] while the officers believed that publication of the Order contributed substantially to the destruction of the army. The significance of the action of the Soviet can be exaggerated. No doubt the Order was conceived in a spirit hostile to the officers; however, it merely registered and expressed—it did not create—the hostility of the peasant soldiers. It was simply that in the revolutionary events in Petrograd the officers lost control over their soldiers and could not re-establish their authority. No one could do it for them.

Order No. 1 was only the first step toward changing the old order in the army and was soon followed by others. On March 28 the Soviet promulgated the Declaration of the Rights of Soldiers, which further developed the reforms: officers lost their right to have orderlies and their right to discipline was curtailed, whereas soldiers were allowed to wear civilian clothes off duty and to receive mail and literature without censorship.[29]

The next step in the democratization of the army was taken by the Provisional Government, which set up a commission under ex-minister of war General A. A. Polivanov to study the reforms. The Commission accepted most of the reforms initiated by the Soviet. To make the introduction of changes easier, the government purged the high command: in the course of a few weeks 150 senior officers retired. The purge had contradictory results: the ministry dismissed the untalented and many who had not wanted to cooperate with the government, but at the same time the Stavka (General Headquarters) and Front commanders conducted their own purges. Frequently, generals and colonels were dismissed because they had too friendly relations with the newly elected committees and the Stavka regarded them as "opportunists." It is fair to say that the composition of the officer corps after the purge remained basically the same as it had been before.[30]

In the search for remedies, constant changes were made in the highest command. Before his abdication the Tsar had appointed Grand Duke Nicholas Commander-in-Chief, but as the revolution in Petrograd took a radical turn it became evident that the Grand Duke would not be able to assume his office. Under the circumstances, Prime Minister Prince Lvov asked General M. V. Alekseev to accept, formally, the duties he had been carrying in fact. Alekseev accepted reluctantly: he was in poor health, and he evaluated the situation realistically and was pessimistic. The Provisional Government named General A. I. Denikin* as his chief of staff, which insulted Alekseev, because the government acted without consulting him. In spite of this unpromising beginning, Alekseev and Denikin came to like each other and worked well together.[31] Denikin

---

*Anton Ivanovich Denikin was born in Włocławek, Warsaw province, in 1872. His father, Ivan Efimovich, was born a serf and was given away by his lord as a recruit at the age of 27. He spent the rest of his life in the army, in which he learned to read and write, and eventually became an officer. Although he spent 43 years in Poland and married a Polish woman who spoke only broken Russian, Ivan Efimovich never learned Polish. Young Anton Ivanovich passionately identified himself with his father, with Orthodoxy, and with Russian nationalism, and in the Civil War he became one of the most uncompromising defenders of the unity of the Russian state, showing little sympathy for the nationalist aspirations of small nations.

Anton Ivanovich entered junker school in 1890 and the Academy of the General Staff in 1895. He fought in the war against Japan and by the out-

wished only that the Commander-in-Chief would give greater responsibility to his subordinates.

Kornilov found his duties as Commander of the Petrograd military district distasteful. He commanded the most disorganized, ill-disciplined troops of the Russian army, among whom the Petrograd Soviet of Workers' and Soldiers' Deputies had far greater authority than he had. He soon came into conflict with the leaders of the Soviet and took an intense dislike to them. When in the beginning of May demonstrators demanded the resignation of Miliukov, Kornilov wanted to disperse the crowd with his soldiers, but the Soviet countermanded his order. After this incident Kornilov did not want to remain in Petrograd and asked A. I. Guchkov, the Minister of War, to transfer him. Kornilov left the capital with bitter memories and with the conviction that only radical methods could clear up what he regarded as anarchy.[32] Alekseev had just relieved General N. V. Ruzskii of his post as Commander of the Northern Front—according to Denikin, for "opportunism," by which he probably meant that Ruzskii showed himself too eager to cooperate with elected committees and commissars.[33] Guchkov wanted Kornilov to take Ruzskii's place, but Alekseev objected to this appointment with great passion, even threatening to resign. Since Alekseev knew Kornilov only slightly, his objection could not have been based on personal grounds; he merely did not think that the younger general was a good enough commander or had had enough experience. There can be no doubt that this incident made the future cooperation of the two generals much more difficult. Kornilov, a vain man, could never forget this slight. He took command of the Eighth Army, whose commander, General Kaledin, had been dismissed by General Brusilov, the Commander-in-Chief of the Southwest Front—ironically because Kaledin had objected to democratization.[34]

In early June the Provisional Government dismissed General

---

break of the World War he was a major general, serving in Brusilov's Eighth Army. He became commander of the "Iron Brigade," one of the best units of the Russian army, which in the course of the war became the Iron Division. Denikin proved himself to be an excellent officer, a leader of men, and a humane and prudent person. His job, however, did not require making strategic decisions involving large armies.

Alekseev as Commander-in-Chief and appointed as his successor General Brusilov, who among the senior generals was most optimistic about the fighting capacity of the revolutionary army. But neither the government's acceptance of the reforms nor the frequent changes in leadership could arrest the process of the army's disintegration. Discipline continued to deteriorate to such an extent that at times entire units refused to obey orders and the desertion rate increased enormously.

The ill-conceived offensive which began on July 2 represented the most significant episode in the Russian army's gradual demise.[35] The offensive was at least partially inspired by the idea that a victory would raise the morale of the army. The offensive failed, partly because of misplanning and lack of coordination but largely because the Russian soldier refused to attack. After some initial successes achieved by superiority in numbers, the army soon had to retreat, and the retreat became a rout. The Provisional Government lost the gamble; instead of halting the disorganization of the army, the great offensive accelerated it.

Relations between soldiers and officers became more and more embittered. The age-old hatred of servants for their masters, of peasants for their social superiors, was vented on the officers. Neither the Soviets nor the Provisional Government agitated the soldiers against their commanders; the hatred needed no promoters. From the first day of the revolution soldiers mistreated and sometimes murdered their officers, and these occurrences became more and more frequent. The soldiers—peasants in uniform—saw in their commanders the epitome of the exploiters, the protagonists of an unpopular war, and opponents of a revolution which promised salvation. The officers were regarded as counter-revolutionaries even before they objected to the achievements and goals of the revolution. Under the circumstances the Bolsheviks had no difficulty persuading the soldiers that their officers wanted to reestablish tsarism.

How could the officers fight back? How could they defend themselves? To blame the ignorance of the peasants, and the tsarist mismanagement of the war which caused untold suffering and bitterness in Russia, would have required great political sophistication and an almost saintly acceptance of the unjustified hatred of the soldiers. Instead the officers held the Provisional Government and the Soviets responsible for all their troubles.

This was unfair, for the "revolutionary democrats" were anxious to save the army, and they merely envisaged different methods than the officers had in mind.[36] It is true that the ideas of the socialist leaders did not work, and that only idealists with little knowledge of armies and wars could have thought that such methods would work. These men wanted to gain the confidence of the soldiers by accepting some of their demands. But to say that their methods were impractical is not the same as saying that the officers had a better solution. The "strong arm" method, advocated by the officers from the very beginning, was just as unrealistic as the method of giving in to every demand of the soldiers. It was unrealistic because it presupposed the existence of a "strong arm," when in fact this did not exist. If the officers could have made their soldiers execute their commands, there would have been no March Revolution. The illusory nature of the officers' solution became most evident at the time of the Kornilov affair: then a "strong man" proved just as ineffective as any socialist agitator; only some of the officers followed him and this was not enough.

For the socialists the revolution was as much of a value as victory in war. It became more and more obvious that the two values were mutually exclusive—victory in war and the deepening of revolution required different policies—but the socialists could never agree on their priority. The officers did not understand the socialists' dilemma; in their eyes anything that compromised the interests of the war efforts was treachery. From their point of view the Bolshevik position made more sense than Kerenskii's. Brusilov wrote:

> I could understand the attitude of the Bolsheviks when they preached "down with war," "peace at once and at any price;" but I could not comprehend the tactics of the Social Revolutionaries and the Mensheviks, who on the one hand wished to destroy the Army for fear of counter-revolution—which does not say much for their understanding of the mentality of the troops and of the masses —and on the other wished to carry the war to a successful conclusion.[37]

An affinity between the thinking of officers and Bolsheviks is shown by the fact that many officers of the Imperial Army, among them General Brusilov, found it possible to join the Red Army in the Civil War. After the November Revolution many officers came to regard Bolshevism as a threat to the future of Russia and therefore joined the White armies; but even when fighting Lenin's army most of them did not develop the hatred for Lenin and his comrades that they held for Kerenskii and his ex-government. When General Alekseev wrote to Bruce Lockhart, in the spring of 1918, that he would rather cooperate with Lenin than with Savinkov and Kerenskii, it was not entirely a figure of speech.[38]

In the revolutionary atmosphere of 1917 it was perfectly natural for the officers to form a pressure group; every other kind of profession had its own organization. The officers were slower to organize than other groups, merely because forming councils reminded them of the methods of "revolutionary democracy." The need for coordination, however, became more and more obvious. General Alekseev called together a national conference of officers which then proceeded to set up a permanent institution. The Cossacks, the Union of the Cavaliers of St. George (the holders of the highest Russian military decoration), and prisoners who had escaped from enemy camps also set up pressure groups.[39] At the time of the Kornilov affair, all these organizations supported the Commander-in-Chief; later they were all to play a role in the forming of the Volunteer Army.

In the course of 1917, because of their disappointments, the officers moved to the right. They did not become counter-revolutionaries in the sense that they advocated a complete return to tsarism, but they opposed the order born with the revolution. The heroes of these officers became the generals, who took the most uncompromising stand against the Provisional Government. Denikin, the future leader of the Whites, first achieved prominence for his sharp attacks on the policies of the government. In June Denikin became Commander-in-Chief of the Western Front. In this capacity he participated in the meeting of the Commanders-in-Chief held on July 29 in the presence of Kerenskii. Denikin's long speech on this occasion was perhaps the most daring and most comprehensive attack on all the changes which had taken place in the army since March. He wanted to re-establish capital punishment, which had been abolished, do away with the institution of committees and commissars, restore the former power and standing of the officers, and forbid politics in the army. Kornilov, who was not present at the meeting, wrote Denikin afterwards:

> I have read the report you made at the Stavka on July 19 (O.S.) with deep and sincere satisfaction. I would sign such a Report with both hands; I take off my hat to you, and I am lost in admiration before your firmness and courage. I firmly believe that, with the help of the Almighty, we will succeed in accomplishing the task of reconstructing our beloved Army and of restoring its fighting power.[40]

But it was General Kornilov who became the greatest hero of the dissatisfied officers, as well as of all conservatives. His rise to prominence was amazingly rapid: he commanded the Eighth Army for only a month, he headed the Southwest Front for only ten days, and on July 31 he replaced General Brusilov as Supreme Commander-in-Chief. In the perspective of later events the constant support he received from politicians is a curious phenomenon: at first Guchkov and then Kerenskii supported the general in spite of the protests of professional military men. The generals insisted that if Kornilov had genuine military talent, which they questioned, he certainly had had no chance to prove himself.

The most important reason for Kornilov's appointment to the highest post in the Russian army was that Kerenskii, who came to understand the extent of disorganization after the ill-fated offensive, agreed with him about the necessity of taking strong measures to improve the army. At the July 29 meeting of the Stavka, the Premier heard nothing but bitter criticism. After the harsh speech of Denikin, Kerenskii, with his characteristic theatricality, shook hands with him and said: "Thank you, General, for your outspoken and sincere speech."[41] The fact that Brusilov had served the revolutionary authorities too eagerly became a major cause for his dismissal. Kornilov, on the other hand, precisely because he was one of the most outspoken and determined opponents of the new regime, seemed to be the right person to undo the earlier reforms. His

aversion to politics and his immense political naïveté appeared as
an advantage to Kerenskii, who regarded these qualities as proof of
earnestness and typical traits of a "strong man." The Premier was
not afraid of the ideas of the new appointee: it was well known
that he was not a monarchist and did not want to re-establish the
old order. Indeed, when disagreements came, they were caused
much less by ideology than by differences in style and deep-seated
prejudices.

That Kornilov was an unfortunate choice from Kerenskii's point
of view became clear immediately. Quarrels started on the very
first day, for Kornilov had accepted the post stipulating various
conditions, among which the most curious was the first, which
claimed responsibility only to his own conscience and to the whole
nation. Denikin, unlike the less sophisticated Kornilov, understood
perfectly what this meant:

> When in due course I read this telegram [Kornilov's telegram to
> Kerenskii] in the newspapers, I was not a little surprised at the first
> condition, which established a highly original form of suzerainty
> on the part of the Supreme Command until the convocation of the
> Constituent Assembly.[42]

The Provisional Government, hestitating to take issue with the
new appointee, simply disregarded this statement. But when soon
after Kornilov threatened to resign over the appointment of General V. A. Cheremisov as Commander of the Southwest Front,
Kerenskii was ready to accept the resignation. He was only dissuaded by B. V. Savinkov, the ex-terrorist Social Revolutionary
who served in the government as assistant minister of war. Under
Savinkov's influence Kerenskii gave in, and Cheremisov did not get
the post.

Kornilov appeared on the national scene at a time when there
was great need for a man like him. A heterogeneous group of people was increasingly dissatisfied with the order born of revolution:
landowners were afraid of losing their land, factory owners worried for the safety of their factories, but above all many patriotic
Russians believed that the spreading anarchy would endanger the
country's ability to resist the foreign foe. Those who believed that

the "deepening of the revolution" would imperil Russia looked to Kornilov, who was a colorful hero of the war, not prominently connected with the old regime and therefore not discredited, and a man with a reputation for decisive action. As a symbol, he played a role even before he undertook any action against the Provisional Government.

Kerenskii was ready to adopt many of Kornilov's demands: after all, he had appointed Kornilov precisely because he hoped that the latter would take energetic steps to pursue the war. But the General had no understanding whatever of the political difficulties the Provisional Government had to face. A gradual, unannounced return to the pre-revolutionary military order was not enough for him; instead he wanted a radical elimination of the revolutionary reforms in the army. The sudden national prominence, even the hero worship, which he came to enjoy from some circles strongly influenced his behavior. He came to believe in his personal mission and claimed the right to speak also on non-military matters. Worst of all, he seriously overestimated the forces which supported him.

Not even Kornilov's apologists claim that their hero had an understanding of politics and a coherent political program. Denikin wrote:

> He, the stern and straightforward soldier, deeply patriotic, untried in politics, knowing little of men, hypnotized both by truth and flattery, and by a general longing expectation of someone's coming, moved by a fervent desire for deeds of sacrifice—he truly believed in the predestined nature of his appointment.[43]

There was no dearth of people to advise the general in political matters. In the group of adventurers who took advantage of his political naïveté, the most notorious was V. S. Zavoiko, an ex-marshal of the nobility, who continued to play a significant role in Kornilov's entourage during the Civil War. It was Zavoiko who composed Kornilov's orders, manifestoes, and even correspondence; he had a florid style, which the General for some reason greatly admired, describing it as "artistic."[44]

The exact date when Kornilov decided to attempt a violent change in the status quo cannot be established. It is not unlikely that weeks before the first conspiratorial move, the Commander-in-Chief had made up his mind that it was necessary to suppress the Bolshevik Party, and since he hardly discriminated between the socialist majority of the Soviets and Lenin's party, he wanted to disperse the Soviets too. The first conspiratorial move took place on August 19 or 20 (Lukomskii did not remember the exact date), when Kornilov ordered General A. I. Krymov to concentrate the Third Cavalry Corps in an area from which Petrograd could be attacked. According to A. S. Lukomskii, the Stavka expected a Bolshevik rising to take place early in September.[45] It is impossible to establish whether these intelligence reports were genuine or invented later by the generals to justify their behavior. Lukomskii quotes Kornilov in his memoirs:

> It is time to put an end to all this. It is time to hang the German agents and spies, with Lenin at their head, disperse the Council of Workmen and Soldiers' Deputies and scatter them far and wide, so that they should never be able to come together again! You are right. My chief object in moving the Cavalry Corps is to have it at hand in the vicinity of Petrograd, at the end of August, and, if this demonstration of the Bolsheviks takes place, to deal with the traitors of Russia as they deserve to be dealt with. I intend to place General Krymov at the head of this operation. I know that in case of necessity he will not hesitate to hang all the members of the Council of Workmen and Soldiers' Deputies. As to the Provisional Government, I have no intention of going against them. I hope to come to an agreement with them in the last moment. But now is not the moment to speak of it to anyone, for Mr. Kerenskii and especially Mr. Chernov will not consent to my plan, and all will be spoiled. If I do not come to an agreement with Kerenskii and Savinkoff, I may have to deal the blow to the Bolsheviks without their consent. But afterwards they will be first to thank me for this, and it will be possible to form a strong government in Russia, independent of all kinds of traitors.[46]

These words by Lukomskii leave no doubt that Kornilov was planning to disperse the Soviets even without the consent of the Provisional Government and thereby change the political system which had emerged from the March Revolution. Since Lukomskii was a major participant in the plot it is likely that he wanted Kornilov to appear in the best light. Therefore one reads with skepticism of Kornilov's intention of leaving the Provisional Government alone after the success of the coup. Indeed, this would have made little sense; the General had a very low opinion of the Prime Minister, who would have remained powerless after the coup. There is evidence that in fact the Stavka was planning the murder of Kerenskii.[47]

A self-appointed intermediary between the Stavka and the government, Prince V. N. Lvov, helped bring the issue out into the open. Lvov, who had heard about the plans of the Stavka, wanted to reconcile Kerenskii and Kornilov and started negotiations with them both. At Kornilov's headquarters he was regarded as an emissary from Kerenskii, which he was not, and he created the impression that Kerenskii would be willing to give up power without a fight. This, of course, would have been preferable from the point of view of the conspirators.[48] Lvov wrote down the Commander-in-Chief's demands in Kornilov's presence in order to present them to Kerenskii. A coincidence further increased Kornilov's optimism about the success of his venture. Savinkov, another advocate of cooperation between the Commander-in-Chief and the Prime Minister, handed to Kornilov Kerenskii's request for a cavalry corps to defend the Provisional Government from the Bolsheviks. This way Kornilov's troops could enter the capital without bloodshed. Kerenskii, however, specified that the command should not be given to General Krymov. Kornilov promised Savinkov that another general would lead the troops, but at the same time had no intention of recalling Krymov.[49]

Lvov presented Kornilov's demands to Kerenskii on September 8. Immediately after the interview, Kerenskii had a conversation with Kornilov on the Hughes teletape machine. In the course of this conversation the Prime Minister impersonated Lvov in order to get confirmation that the demands, which Kerenskii rightly construed as an ultimatum, really originated with the Commander-in-Chief.

During the same night, Kerenskii called a cabinet session in which the Kadet ministers resigned and Kerenskii assumed exceptional powers to suppress the mutiny. He dismissed the Commander-in-

Chief by telegram and ordered the cavalry corps, which was moving toward Petrograd, to stop all troop movements.

The conspirators at the Stavka felt betrayed. After the messages through Savinkov and Lvov and the Hughes teletape machine conversation, they believed that Kerenskii, seeing the Bolshevik danger, was willing to entrust power to the Commander-in-Chief without fighting. Kornilov had no intention of resigning, and instead ordered Krymov to proceed. Meanwhile, the non-socialist politicians, and some of the socialist ones, too, urged Kerenskii to resign in order to effect a compromise. Kerenskii, however, leaning on the Soviets, who promised and gave him support, refused to give up his office. Both sides took their cases to the people by issuing appeals.

Kornilov's movement collapsed with amazing rapidity. Troops approaching the capital, under the instigation of agitators from the Soviets, Bolsheviks among them, refused to fight; railroad workers stopped trains and post office workers did not forward Kornilov's telegrams; his allies in the capital found themselves impotent and abandoned him; *agents provocateurs* failed to stage a mock Bolshevik rising.[50] Kornilov must bear a large share of the responsibility for the ignominious failure. It is questionable whether he had the strength, even with the support of the Provisional Government, to suppress the Soviets in the army and everywhere in the country, but he could have made his position much stronger. He assumed responsibility for a civil war by instructing Krymov to proceed even when it was obvious that he would meet with strong resistance, and Krymov's detachment was small and insufficiently equipped. Undoubtedly, the officers and perhaps some of the Cossack units would have been more ready to fight if their hero himself had assumed personal command.

When everyone abandoned Kornilov, only his colleagues, a handful of generals, remained firm. Lukomskii refused Kerenskii's request to take command of the entire Russian army, and remained loyal to his commander, as did the other prominent members of the Stavka, including General I. P. Romanovskii, the Quartermaster General. The commanders of the four European fronts announced their solidarity with the Commander-in-Chief: General V. N. Klembovskii of the Northern Front refused, as Lukomskii had done, to take Kornilov's place. Denikin, typically, wrote a sharp, uncompromising letter to Kerenskii in behalf of Kornilov. But the senior leaders of the army could not affect the course of events; their action merely increased the soldiers' hostility to their officers.

The task of restoring order in the Stavka by removing the mutinous generals fell on General Alekseev. Alekseev obviously sympathized with Kornilov's desire to restore discipline in the army and order in the country by applying strong methods, but he did not publicly associate himself with Kornilov at any point, presumably because the cautious old general was skeptical about the possibility of success. Alekseev's caution undoubtedly added to the bitterness Kornilov felt toward him, and it was yet another reason why the two men would find it so difficult to collaborate as leaders of the Volunteer Army. Alekseev may have kept aloof in order to be able to become a compromise leader between Kerenskii and Kornilov. Indeed, for a time it seemed that Kerenskii would resign in favor of General Alekseev. But by September 12 it became obvious that Kornilov was thoroughly beaten, and Alekseev accepted the post of Chief of Staff under the new Commander-in-Chief, Kerenskii, in order to make the removal of the conspirators as painless as possible. The old general went to Mogilev and personally arrested the leaders of the coup. This was the end of the "Kornilov affair."

Some aspects of the conspiracy are still unclear. Kerenskii's role is one of the debated issues. His enemies claim that he must have had advance knowledge of the plot and either had changed his mind at the last moment or had deliberately tricked Kornilov in order to get rid of him. Many historians blame Kerenskii today for his failure to cooperate with the general, and regard the suppression of the Soviets by Kornilov as the only defense against the Bolsheviks.[51]

We know little about the political and financial support Kornilov received during the organization of his coup. It is clear that while most non-socialist politicians knew about the preparation, and tacitly supported them, they were not anxious to compromise themselves by open participation in this questionable venture.[52]

But however one evaluates Kerenskii's role and performance,

the behavior of foreign powers which might have given Kornilov some aid and encouragement, and the politicians who allowed but did not help Kornilov's plot, it is clear that Kornilov showed little political acumen. He inexcusably overestimated his forces, and he did not organize his conspiracy properly; he failed not only as a politician, by offering nothing to the Russian people at the crucial hours save the continuation of an unpopular war, but also as a military leader.

The effects of the Kornilov movement were immediate and disastrous for the anti-Bolsheviks. Lenin's warnings about the danger of counter-revolution suddenly gained credibility. In the weeks following the suppression of the plot, the Bolsheviks gained majorities in the Petrograd and Moscow Soviets for the first time, and they increased their strength almost everywhere in the country. The soldiers' irrational hatred of officers increased; even those officers who had absolutely nothing to do with the conspiracy were mistreated by the soldiers, who came increasingly under Bolshevik influence.

The legacy of the Kornilov affair was to play an important role in the entire Civil War. The anti-Bolshevik socialists and the officers always distrusted each other, and the events during the era of the Provisional Government made this distrust more profound. But it was Kornilov's conspiracy which caused the final and irremediable break. Neither side was willing to forgive and forget the imagined and real insults, or as they expressed it, the "treachery." Undoubtedly, a major cause of the victory of the Reds in the Civil War was lack of cooperation in the camp of their enemies.

The conspiracy separated the officers even from Kadet and Octobrist politicians who, by and large, had wished success to Kornilov. The officers alone acted openly, and after their failure they felt betrayed by the would-be supporters who escaped unscathed.[53] This is perhaps one reason why on the White side in the Civil War civilians played a comparatively small role.

The conspiracy also created the general staff of the anti-Bolshevik struggle, for it brought together a group of people who could start the organization of the fight immediately after Lenin's conquest of power in Petrograd. Kornilov's arrest was followed

General Alekseev shortly before his death

Kornilov in Moscow

The men in uniform are (from left to right) Captain Fouquet (the head of the French delegation to Ekaterinodar), Denikin, Lukomskii, Colonel Shapron. Dragomirov and Romanovskii

General Kaledin (his last photo)

by the arrest of Denikin and his colleagues at the headquarters of the Southwest Front at Berdichev. Denikin was falsely charged with participation in the conspiracy. In fact, his only "crime" was the declaration of sympathy with the Commander-in-Chief. The Provisional Government set up a Commission of Inquiry under Military Prosecutor I. S. Shablovskii, who was favorably disposed toward the prisoners. The prisoners from Mogilev and Berdichev were brought to a monastery in Bykhov, near Mogilev, where they were accommodated in reasonable comfort.[54] Almost all the prisoners at Bykhov were to play leading roles in the Volunteer Army. One might say their seniority in the Army began on the day of their arrests.

Kornilov's conspiracy predestined him to be the leader of the Whites: he became the best known anti-Bolshevik in the country. The White struggle had its hero even before the struggle began.

THE DON AND KUBAN COSSACKS IN 1917

The Volunteer Army was an organization of officers. They created the Army, set its tone, determined its ideology, and always retained leadership in it. However, it was neither officers nor Russian soldiers but Kuban and Don Cossacks who made up the majority of the fighting men. The Cossacks, men who differed in background and ideology from the officers, came to fight the Bolsheviks for reasons of their own.

The Cossacks are the descendents of free men, escaped serfs, and adventurers who gathered in the border areas between the Slav states of Poland and Muscovy, and in the Tatar khanates. As early as the fifteenth century, they posed a threat to the political and social order of the Russian south. The tsars, however, by combining force with clever diplomacy, soon gained control over the marauding frontiersmen. Once in the hands of the central power the Cossacks, who were excellent fighting men, became a valuable tool for guarding and expanding the frontiers.

In the late eighteenth century the Cossacks lost their former autonomy. The central government no longer allowed them to choose their chief executive officer, the ataman; instead an elderly general with non-Cossack background was usually appointed by the Tsar.

However the Cossacks retained self-government on the village
(*stanitsa*) level. Their rudimentary knowledge of political organization stood them in good stead in the Civil War.

The Cossacks, reliable servants of the Tsar against internal and
external enemies, formed a privileged estate: they had to serve
twenty years in the army, but in compensation they received land-
holding and tax privileges. They organized themselves into eleven
communities (*voiska*), among which the Don and the Kuban were
by far the most important.[56] The standard of living of the Cossacks was much higher than that of the Russian peasants; they were
also better educated and, perhaps most importantly, they were
proud of their way of life.

In no province of the Russian empire did the Cossacks make up
the majority of the population. Only 49 per cent of the four million
inhabitants of the Don, and only 44 per cent of the three million
inhabitants of the Kuban, were Cossacks.[57] Since the Kuban and
the Don were among the richest agricultural areas of Russia, they
attracted a large number of peasant settlers. Even though some of
the settlers had lived on the Don or Kuban for generations, they
could not become members of the Cossack estate, and they could
not even acquire permanent residence in the area. They had to retain passports from the districts from which their ancestors had
come. Because these Russian peasants always remained aliens in the
Cossack *voiska*, they were named *inogorodnye*, which means
people coming from other towns. According to 1914 figures the
inogorodnye formed 48 per cent of the population of the Don and
53 per cent of the Kuban. (The non-Cossack remainder consisted
of the original inhabitants of the area, Kalmyks on the Don and
different Caucasian tribes on the Kuban.)[58] The Cossacks were
much wealthier than the *inogorodnye*. On the Don the *inogorodnye* owned only 10 per cent of the arable land and on the Kuban
27 per cent.[59] The *inogorodnye* holdings were small: the average
size of an *inogorodnyi* plot on the Don was 1.3 *desiatina*, on the
Kuban 1.5 *desiatina* (1 *des.* equals 2.7 acres).[60] A large majority
of peasants had to rent land from the Cossacks, and rising rents became increasingly burdensome. Even though, as Soviet authors like
to point out, stratification was increasing among Cossacks and non-

Cossacks alike, and many peasants were richer than the average Cossack, the hostility which developed was not between the poor and the rich but between Cossacks and *inogorodnye*.

There was a sizeable working class on the Don, but not on the Kuban. However, the industrial towns of Rostov and Taganrog, and the mining district of the Donets, did not become integrated into the life of the Don *voisko*. Characteristically, it was not Rostov, one of the largest Russian cities, which was the capital of the *voisko*, but Novocherkassk, the insignificant and Cossack-controlled village. A large percentage of the workers of the industrial cities of the district came from *inogorodnye* families: as land rents constantly increased the *inogorodnye* were forced off the land. Understandably, during the Civil War the cities of the *voisko* became the centers of anti-Cossack, most often Bolshevik, activities.

The existence of a privileged military estate was an anachronism in the twentieth century, and the two revolutions of 1917, which aimed at the destruction of the old order, created favorable conditions for those who wanted to abolish this remnant of the past. The *inogorodnye* above all wanted Cossack lands, and the Cossacks, understanding the ambitions of the *inogorodnye*, soon realized that the defense of their way of life depended above all on their ability to keep the Russian peasants of the province under control. Consequently, the Civil War which developed on Cossack territories differed markedly from the war in the rest of the country: on the Kuban and on the Don the war became a life-and-death struggle between the two sections of the population. Both sides were only remotely interested in national issues; in the search for allies it was natural that the Cossacks turned to the Whites and the *inogorodnye* to the Bolsheviks, but the alliance remained a limited one.

The March Revolution found the young Cossacks on the front. (The Cossack soldiers, in distinction from their elders who had remained at home, were called *frontoviki*.) The Cossack soldiers maintained discipline longer than the others. Their regiments were commanded by Cossack officers, men of similar social and cultural background, and therefore the hostility between men and officers, which so deeply impaired the fighting capacity of the Russian army, did not develop in Cossack units. The Provisional Government used the better disciplined Cossacks for police purposes; for example, they were instrumental in putting down the disturbances in July.[61] Their activity on behalf of the government added to their reputation as obedient servants of the existing authority.

While the Cossacks maintained better discipline than the other soldiers, they did not entirely escape the influence of the revolutionary atmosphere. War weariness and disenchantment with the policies of the government spread even among them, and Bolshevik propaganda effectively exploited discontent. The radicalization of the *frontoviki* created a rift between them and the older Cossacks, who retained their traditional loyalties. The serious differences of opinion between the old and the young Cossacks were discovered only after the November Revolution, as one regiment after another returned from the front. This lack of unity among the Cossacks very much hindered the ability of the governments in Novocherkassk and Ekaterinodar to resist the Bolshevik onslaught.

The inhabitants of the Don *voisko* received the news of the March Revolution enthusiastically. Events in Petrograd created a hopeful mood all over the country, and the Cossack territories were no exceptions. Momentarily the enmity between the two segments of the population was forgotten.

Representatives of various social and political organizations formed the Don Executive Committee. Ataman Baron Grabbe, who had assumed his office only in 1916, refused to cooperate with the Executive Committee, which therefore removed him from office and named E. A. Voloshinov instead as provisional ataman.[62]

The ataman and Executive Committee represented only the better organized and politically more articulate part of the population, namely the Cossacks. Representatives of the *inogorodnye* met for the first time in May, when it was already clear that the truce between the two parts of the population was ending. The conference was dominated by extremists, and it accepted a resolution calling for the abolition of all Cossack privileges. However, the belligerent resolution had no immediate consequences and the conference disbanded without even forming a permanent body or electing a responsible leader. When the Cossack parliament, the so-called *krug,* met soon afterwards, it elected an ataman and a government, without paying any attention to the wishes of the Russian peasants. The March Revolution then, brought no change in the status of the *inogorodnye*, who remained second-class citizens.

The *krug* elected ataman Aleksei Maksimovich Kaledin, who thus became the first democratically chosen leader of the Cossacks since 1723. He was an excellent choice. Kaledin, who at the time of his election was 55 years old, had attended the Mikhailovskii Artillery Academy and the College of the General Staff. During the World War he had gained a reputation as one of the best leaders in the Russian Army, and became General of the Cavalry.[63]

Kaledin was a conservative; he had opposed the reforms introduced into the life of the army by the revolution more outspokenly than most of the other senior leaders. Because of his uncompromising attitude, Brusilov, then commander of the Southwest Front, decided to dismiss him. Kaledin returned to his native Don, and as highest ranking officer living in Novocherkassk became a candidate for the post of ataman. That the Cossacks chose to elect a man who had just lost his position because of his opposition to the reforms of the revolution shows the temper of the older Cossacks, who remained at home.

Kaledin was not a good administrator; he was too concerned with details to be able to present a comprehensive program.[64] Nor was he a charismatic politician: on public occasions he spoke deliberately and rarely aroused his audience; there was nothing of the demagogue about him. Yet, he was an outstanding leader, and one of the most appealing figures of the anti-Bolshevik movement. His dedication, high ideals, and selflessness inspired genuine respect. The conservative Kaledin exercised his leadership in introducing a radical and necessary change after the November Revolution: he persuaded his Cossacks to accept the representatives of the *inogorodnye* as partners in the government of the *voisko*. His policy ultimately failed; the bitter antagonists were in no mood to compromise. Nevertheless, in trying to bring together Cossacks and *inogorodnye*, Kaledin showed himself to be a more farsighted leader than his fellow politicians.

Ataman Kaledin participated in the Moscow State Conference and created a sensation by delivering the most conservative speech.[65] He encouraged the government to free itself from the pressure of "party and class organizations," by which he meant the Soviets, and he called for the removal of defeatists from the government. Most important, he wanted the institution of commissars and Soviets in the army abolished, in order to raise the army above politics. Kaledin's speech made him a hero of the anti-Bolsheviks. When Kornilov decided to move against the Soviets and the Provisional Government he counted on Kaledin's support. No doubt, Kaledin wholeheartedly sympathized with Kornilov's program and wished him success, but he was not in a position to offer effective help. He was the leader of a divided district and hardly master of his own house; the Don was surrounded by cities in which the workers were hostile to Kornilov and would have prevented Kaledin's Cossacks from attacking Moscow or Petrograd. After the collapse of the Kornilov conspiracy the Provisional Government wanted to arrest Kaledin together with the other rebellious generals. The *krug*, however, decided to come to Kaledin's defense, and instead of surrendering him to the justice of the Provisional Government it insisted on the ancient right of the Cossack Assembly to be the exclusive judge of its elected leader.[66] The ensuing trial was a formality: it was a foregone conclusion that the representatives who had elected the Ataman a few months before would take his side against Kerenskii. The Provisional Government was too weak to enforce its decision on the Don. The Don government and the *krug* continued to pay lip service to the central authorities in Petrograd, but by defying the Provisional Government the Don in fact became independent, a state within a state.

Relations between the *inogorodnye* and the Cossacks continued to deteriorate. The most uncompromising leaders among the *inogorodnye* gained increasing popularity; the anti-Kaledin movement was especially strong in the cities. Mensheviks and Social Revolutionaries dominated the Soviets, but Bolshevik strength, as elsewhere in the country, rapidly increased. The "July days" were a defeat for the Bolsheviks, but the failure of the Kornilov affair helped them to recoup their losses and to gain new followers. Among the workers of Rostov and Taganrog, the Mensheviks remained the strongest party, but the miners of the Donets came under predominantly Bolshevik influence. Even more important from the point of view of the Bolsheviks was the support they received from the regiments stationed on the Don. A majority of the soldiers came to support the Bolsheviks, and since a regulation of the Provisional Government had allowed the soldiers to vote, wherever they happened to be, Bolshevik voting strength in the cities of the Don greatly increased.[67]

In November, 1917, the Don, like the rest of the country, was on the verge of Civil War.

The social and economic structure of the Kuban was very similar to that of the Don, and political developments in 1917 also followed a similar pattern. However, the situation in the Kuban was further complicated by disunity among the Cossacks.

The Kuban *voisko* was of relatively recent origin; it had been formed in 1860 from the Black Sea Cossacks and the *lineitsy*. The Black Sea Cossacks were the descendants of the members of the Zaporozhe Sech.* When the Sech was destroyed in 1775, some of the Cossacks escaped to Turkey, but others were settled by Catherine II on the shores of the Black Sea, in the Kuban. These warriors formed their own *voisko* and remained conscious of their Ukrainian background. At the end of the eighteenth century, Catherine settled some Don Cossack regiments in the Upper Kuban to act as a defensive force against the Mountain tribes of the Northern Caucasus. Because these Cossacks were placed on the "line" between the settled territory and alien tribes they acquired the name of "line men," *lineitsy*. Unlike the Black Sea Cossacks, who spoke a Ukrainian dialect, the *lineitsy* spoke Russian.[68] The two Cossack communities did not integrate.[69]

Following the March Revolution, political life in the Kuban had a more auspicious beginning than on the Don. Ataman Babich resigned his post and left Ekaterinodar.[70] In April an assembly gathered in the capital of the province, in which both Cossack and *inogorodnye* representatives participated. The Cossacks recognized that the *inogorodnye* must have a role in the government; and the *inogorodnye* showed conciliatory sentiments when they supported

---

*Zaporozhe Sech was an Ukrainian Cossack *voisko* existing between the 15th and 18th centuries.

a resolution according to which the land question had to be resolved in such a fashion as not to hurt the interests of the "working" Cossacks. The Assembly elected an Executive Committee, in
which representatives of both parts of the population participated.

The spirit of compromise aroused by the March Revolution did
not survive long. *Inogorodnye* came to demand the abolition of
more and more of the privileges of the Cossack estate, while the
Cossacks came to fear a genuine democracy, which would give
decisive political power to the more numerous *inogorodnye*. The
compromisers gradually lost ground among both parts of the population. The break occurred during the July session of the province
Soviet, when the Cossack delegates walked out of the meeting and
formed their own *voisko* Soviet, while withdrawing recognition
from the District Executive Committee.

The destruction of existing organizations gave political power to
that part of the population which was better established, namely
the Cossacks. The Cossacks had already formed their government
in Ekaterinodar, which originally had the task of dealing only with
special Cossack matters. The abolition of the Executive Committee
made this government the only effective central organ in the district. The Cossack leaders, instead of giving concessions to the
inogorodnye, wanted to preserve their privileges and saw the best
hope for this in cooperation with the Cossacks of other *voiska*.
Cossack federalism quickly gained followers on the Kuban.

The Kuban had no elected ataman until October 1917. The
election campaign led to increased rivalry betwen the *lineitsy* and
the Black Sea Cossacks. The head of the Kuban government, A. P.
Filimonov, a *lineets*, was elected ataman on October 25. He had
nothing of the vision and moral authority of Ataman Kaledin. By
his own admission, his chief aim always was to save as much as
possible from the institutions of the old regime.[71]

The Kuban had practically no industry and therefore no working class. But the short-sighted policies of the Cossack leaders created favorable conditions for Bolshevik propaganda among the
peasants. On the eve of the Bolshevik revolution, relations between
inogorodnye and Cossacks on the Kuban were even worse than on
the Don.

CHAPTER 2

The Beginnings of the White Movement

The significance of the events of November 7 is obvious only in retrospect: to weary contemporaries the Bolshevik uprising represented merely another crisis. Indeed, one could argue that politically the conquest of majorities in the Petrograd and Moscow Soviets, which isolated the Provisional Government, was a more significant event, and that the uprising did not solve the central issue, which was the ungovernability of Russia. It was easy to remove the powerless Provisional Government, but it was extremely difficult to replace it successfully. The Bolsheviks still had to prove themselves.

Even from a purely military point of view the fighting of November 7 was far less severe than what was shortly to follow. In the battle for Moscow between November 10 and 15, some 500 Bolsheviks died. On November 11, the students of the military schools, the cadets, staged an uprising in Petrograd in the course of which they managed to capture a telephone station and the co-commissar for war, V. A. Antonov-Ovseenko. The uprising, which had about 200 victims, collapsed because it was badly planned, and because the Social-Revolutionary politicians, who stood behind it, failed to attract support from workers and soldiers in the capital.

For the Bolsheviks, Kerenskii's efforts to bring troops from the front were even more dangerous. The deposed Premier first turned to General Cheremisov, his ex-protégé who served as Commander of the Northern Front, which, being closest to Petrograd, was strategically situated. But Cheremisov refused to help. Perhaps he hoped to bargain with the Bolsheviks; perhaps he realistically understood that his soldiers would not fight; perhaps he had been so disillusioned with the Provisional Government that he saw no reason to help it against the new authorities. Whatever the reasons were, Kerenskii's chances of regaining his position diminished daily.

The last soldiers to fight for Kerenskii were the 700 Cossacks of General P. N. Krasnov. That Kerenskii had to turn to Krasnov, to the man who was profoundly implicated in the Kornilov mutiny, showed the utter bankruptcy of the policy of the Provisional Government. Krasnov obviously had other aims aside from the restoration of the deposed government, and whatever the outcome of the fighting was, Kerenskii was hardly likely to emerge victorious. But there was not even much fighting. The Cossacks slowly advanced on the capital, meeting much larger and hostile forces everywhere. As the Cossacks increasingly felt their isolation, their doubts about their mission grew and morale dissolved, and when they encountered more than token resistance from Bolshevik sailors they retreated and the retreat sealed the fate of the venture. Kerenskii was forced to escape and Krasnov fell into the hands of the Bolsheviks. The Bolsheviks were prudent enough not to alienate the Cossacks, and Krasnov, who promised not to fight the new regime, was therefore allowed to go. Krasnov was soon to violate his word, and we have no evidence that he did so after much mental anguish. After this success, the Bolsheviks safely possessed the capital for the first time, although in most of the country their rule was not yet established.

In view of the bitterness of the Civil War, the question arises: What, in the crucial hours, was being done by those who were soon to oppose the Bolsheviks with so much self-sacrifice and determination? They could not have been taken unaware: the Bolsheviks had made no secret of their intentions, and army officers and politicians alike had been talking about the Bolshevik danger for months. Why, then, did they give their enemies time to establish themselves?*

---

*It should be emphasized that these remarks refer to that small minority

The paralysis had many causes. Kornilov's followers as well as Kerenskii's were bitterly disappointed in the Russian people. They understood that the workers and peasants, and most important, the soldiers with weapons in their hands, if they did not become Bolsheviks, were at least sufficiently influenced by propaganda not to fight the new regime.[1] The feeling of isolation momentarily discouraged resistance. Paradoxically, their enemies' exaggerated optimism also played into the hands of the Bolsheviks. Everyone in Russia—and outside of Russia, for that matter—was convinced that the new regime could not last. The anti-Bolsheviks believed that the people would be disillusioned soon and that the party which was chiefly responsible for anarchy would be the least able to control it. The Tsar and the democratic parties could not govern Russia; how could a group of adventurers holding outlandish ideas maintain themselves in power? Why struggle against a regime which was bound to collapse soon anyway?[2]

Perhaps the most crucial cause of inaction was the general misunderstanding of the nature of Bolshevism. It would be anachronistic to blame contemporaries for errors of judgment: Bolshevism, as we know it, did not yet exist; the party was in the process of adjusting to a totally new and unexpected situation in which the leaders themselves had only hazy ideas about the future of their regime. The two wings of the future anti-Bolshevik movement, the socialists and the officers, both misjudged their opponents. The greatest error of the socialists was to underestimate the differences which separated them from the new leaders. Mensheviks and Social Revolutionaries thought of the Bolsheviks as another socialist party. They placed great faith in the results of the coming general election, for they assumed that the Russian people would repudiate the party which has seized power, and it seemed unthinkable that a socialist party would not abide by the will of the people.[3]

Those who belonged to the right wing of the political spectrum, on the other hand, were so blinded by hatred of Kerenskii and

---

of the Russian population which, in a short time, would voluntarily fight the Bolsheviks. The great majority of the people, including the officers, did not want to fight, either immediately after the uprising or later.

"revolutionary democracy" that they saw no reason to defend the Provisional Government against any usurpers.[4] It took some time before they realized that they would find the new regime even more odious than the old one. A mistake frequently made by this group, especially by the officers, was to regard the Bolsheviks merely as German agents.[5]

Today we know that the Bolsheviks received aid from the enemies of their country. Yet the fact that the short-term interests of the Bolsheviks and the Germans coincided, in as much as they both wanted to bring down the Provisional Government, was almost irrelevant in judging the character of Bolshevism. The Bolsheviks had plans that went far beyond helping the Germans.

The psychological origin of the officers' misconception, however, is easily understandable. They had fought a most bitter war for three years, and had found it necessary to sacrifice literally millions of their countrymen. In order to be able to fight the war, they had to believe that the outcome would be crucial for their country. Under the circumstances they came to subordinate everything in their minds to the needs of the war; they looked at events exclusively from the point of view of the Russo-German struggle; they attributed all the ills of the country to the machinations of a fiendish enemy.

Those men, who would shortly be leading the military anti-Bolshevik movement, were momentarily bewildered and confused: their two aims, fighting the foreign and the domestic enemy, required different behavior. Ingrained habits made them believe that it was the continuation of Russia's participation in the World War which was more important. How could they leave the front in order to confront the Bolsheviks, when the Russian armies were still defending the motherland, at least nominally? How could they set a bad example of insubordination for their soldiers? Why should they turn against the agents, the Bolsheviks, and allow the real enemy to conquer? The dilemma of choosing between two enemies was to remain with the Volunteer Army for the entire duration of the World War. Events soon made it impossible for White officers to fight the Germans. Nevertheless, in theory at least, the Army always remained an anti-German organization.

It is important to remember that not all, perhaps not even a majority, of the Russian officers were anxious to continue the war against the Germans. Many shared the general war weariness and would have been happy to end the fighting on almost any terms. But these were the officers who used the opportunity created by the Bolsheviks to return to their families, who wanted nothing more than to be left alone, and who therefore lost political significance. Those who were most determined to fight the Bolsheviks were also the ones most determined to fight the Germans.

It was Lenin's decision to occupy the General Headquarters of the Army, while preparing armistice negotiations with the German, which provided the crucial turning point in the thinking and behavior of the officers. The obvious impossibility of continuing the war against Germany marked the beginning of the White movement and led ultimately to the formation of the Volunteer Army.

THE FALL OF THE GENERAL HEADQUARTERS AND THE PRISONERS OF BYKHOV

How tentative Bolshevik authority was in the first weeks, and how cautiously the Bolsheviks played their weak hand, was best shown by their behavior toward the Stavka. Lenin and his colleagues clearly understood that an eventual showdown with the leaders of the army would be inevitable. They knew French revolutionary history well and feared that Mogilev might become a Russian Versailles. Yet in spite of evidence pouring in substantiating their fears, for two weeks Lenin was unwilling to dismiss General N. N. Dukhonin, the Chief of Staff, who also acted as Commander-in-Chief during Kerenskii's absence. Lenin postponed the final break as long as he could.

Bolshevik suspicions about the Stavka were not unfounded: Mogilev attracted the enemies of the new regime. Kerenskii had turned to Dukhonin for help; the general was willing to give it, but his orders were not executed. The well-known leaders of the Social Revolutionary Party, V. M. Chernov, N. D. Avksentiev, and A. R. Gots, came to Mogilev and toyed with the idea of forming a government under Chernov. But they decided that such an action would be premature, for they hoped that the Constituent Assembly, which was to be convened in January, would simply dismiss the Bolsheviks.[7] They feared that an ill-considered action might compromise the party's position at the coming assembly.

As one discouraging report followed another, the political and military leaders remained inactive. They spent their last days at Mogilev in an endless series of inconclusive meetings trying to decide what to do.[8] The man chiefly responsible for the indecision was General Dukhonin, who, as the leader of the Russian armies, was in the best position to organize resistance. Dukhonin, an honest and intelligent officer, completely lacked the charisma and decisiveness necessary for leading a national movement. Like most officers, he was paralyzed by the illusion of the possibility of continued fighting against Germany, and he considered that aim so important that he was unwilling to endanger it by starting a civil war.

A problem which weighed especially heavily on Dukhonin's mind was what to do with the prisoners at Bykhov. When the Provisional Government had arrested the officers implicated in the Kornilov affair in September 1917, it detained them in a monastery in the small village of Bykhov, near Mogilev, entrusting their guarding and safety to the Stavka. By the time of the November uprising, all but the five most prominent generals—L. G. Kornilov, A. I. Denikin, A. S. Lukomskii, I. P. Romanovskii, and S. L. Markov—had been freed. Dukhonin knew well that letting the last prisoners go would have been tantamount to declaring war on the Bolsheviks, who dreaded Kornilov; and, on the other hand, it was unthinkable to hand over his colleagues to a merciless enemy, who, most likely, would have executed them. Dukhonin, as was his wont, procrastinated in this difficult situation.

The imprisonment, however, was ficticious from the very beginning. The Tekinskii regiment, which was stationed in Bykhov, was so fiercely loyal to Kornilov that it would gladly have allowed the escape of the generals, and on command would even have attempted to arrest Kerenskii.[9] The prisoners had remained in prison, believing they would be exonerated by an investigating commission. Interestingly enough, they hesitated to leave even after the Bolshevik take-over.

Even the veteran anti-Bolshevik prisoners of Bykhov failed to understand the magnitude of the political change caused by the November Revolution. For a while they continued to believe in the possibility of fighting Germany and therefore refrained from disobedience, which, it seemed to them, would further undermine the morale of the army. The generals wasted valuable days waiting for the permission of their superior to leave: the idea of insubordination was repugnant to them.

The relationship between the generals at Bykhov and the Stavka was ambiguous. Theoretically, of course, Dukhonin was Kornilov's superior, but Kornilov, and to a lesser extent his fellow prisoners, possessed a prestige in Mogilev with which Dukhonin could never compete. The officers at the Stavka continued to refer to Kornilov as *Verkhovnyi* (supreme leader), an honor which Kerenskii, the nominal Commander-in-Chief, or Dukhonin, had never received.[10] On the one hand, the incarcerated men were awaiting permission to leave, and on the other they repeatedly gave unsolicited advice, which sounded like instructions to their superiors. Kornilov insisted that the Stavka should not be given up without a fight, and made the following recommendations to Dukhonin:

(1) Bring to Mogilev immediately one of the Czech regiments and the Polish Ulan regiment. (2) Occupy Orsha, Smolensk, Zhlobin, and Gomel' with detachments of the Polish corps, strengthening them with Cossack batteries from the front. (3) Concentrate on the line Orsha, Mogilev, Zhlobin all detachments of the Czecho-Slovak Corps [of the Kornilov regiment] under the pretext of taking them to Petrograd and Moscow, and one or two Cossack divisions among the better ones.* (4) Concentrate in the same district all the English and Belgian armored cars and man them entirely with officers. (5) Concentrate in Mogilev and in nearby locations, under strong guard, a supply of rifles, munitions, machine guns. . . . (6) Establish close ties and precise agreements with the Atamans of the Don, Terek, and Kuban. . . .[11]

---

*The Imperial government formed fighting units from Polish and Czech prisoners of war. The Czechs and the Poles, unlike the Russians, did not lose their desire to fight the Germans.

The letter is interesting, for it shows that Kornilov was out of touch with the situation, and did not understand that many of the units he pinned his hopes on would not fight the Bolsheviks. It is also significant that at this time Kornilov contemplated only military moves and had no political weapons with which to combat the Bolsheviks.

Lukomskii sent sounder advice to Dukhonin and to Diederichs, the Quartermaster General. He suggested that the Stavka should be moved without delay to Kiev, where the personal safety of the officers would be assured and the fight against the Bolsheviks could be continued by using units of the somewhat more stable Southwestern Front.[12] Indeed, this idea was considered and supported by Diederichs, but ultimately there was no consensus and the Stavka remained inactive in the crucial days.[13]

The break between the Stavka and the Bolsheviks came over the issue of peace negotiations with the Central Powers. On this issue Dukhonin could not afford to compromise, and Lenin could not afford to procrastinate. On November 20, Lenin instructed the Chief of Staff to begin peace negotiations with the enemy. Dukhonin, who still wanted to avoid giving a blanket refusal, gained two days by asking a series of questions. But then he finally declared that he could not participate in the proposed peace conference, and by this open defiance made his removal inevitable. Lenin named Ensign N. V. Krylenko Commander-in-Chief, and Krylenko immediately gathered a small force consisting mostly of sailors and started toward Mogilev to take possession of the Stavka.[14]

Krylenko left Petrograd on November 24. The next day, the local Bolshevik Military Revolutionary Committee arrested General Baluev, Commander of the Western Front in Minsk, where the Stavka was located.[15] Krylenko and his soldiers were approaching Mogilev slowly, but without much danger of being stopped. Up to the very last day Dukhonin could not make up his mind whether to take a stand. However, resistance seemed more and more futile, for his troops did not obey his orders. In spite of his instructions, a bridge leading to Mogilev was not blown up. Foreign representatives, politicians, and some of the officers decided to

leave Mogilev on December 2, one day before the arrival of Krylenko. Dukhonin decided to stay at his post.

The question of what to do with the Bykhov prisoners became
more urgent. The elected Commissar of the Cossack units, V. V.
Shapkin, went to Diederichs and suggested that Kornilov should
be taken to the Don where he would be safe.* Diederichs wrote
out an order allowing Kornilov to leave, and together with Shapkin
took it to Dukhonin for his signature. Shapkin described the incident: [16]

> We found Dukhonin alone in the office. Without saying a word
> Diederichs gave him the order he had written regarding taking the
> prisoners to Kamenskaia on the Don. Having read it, Dukhonin
> contemplated for a moment, then took a pencil decisively and
> signed the order. Giving the paper back to Diederichs, Dukhonin
> said: 'With this I have signed my death warrant.'

In the course of the next day Dukhonin changed his mind twice.
Only one day before the arrival of the Bolsheviks did he send
Colonel Kusonskii to Bykhov with the message that the prisoners
should leave their place of confinement immediately.[17] For this decision he was to pay with his life: on December 3 revolutionary
soldiers pulled Dukhonin out of his train and murdered him. Krylenko, who was unable to prevent this excess, maintained that the
anger of his followers was caused by Dukhonin having allowed
Kornilov to escape.[18]

The five leading figures of the coming White movement continued to wait for the formality of their superior's decision. Kornilov, who was the least patient, ordered his loyal Tekinskii regiment
to prepare for a march but Denikin pleaded with Kornilov in the
name of his fellow generals to postpone departure for at least two
more days. Kornilov gave in.[19] Under the circumstances the prisoners had nothing to do but to make plans: false papers were prepared and the route of the Tekinskii regiment was decided on. The
generals agreed without debate that they should go to the Don;

---

*Among the changes introduced by the Provisional Government into the
life of the army was that army units were allowed to elect commissars who
acted as political officers. Even Cossack units used this privilege.

no one even thought of an alternative. They fully expected the Don government, which had defied Kerenskii, to be sympathetic to the enemies of Bolshevism.

Owing to careful planning, the generals could leave the same day the permission came. Markov, Lukomskii, Romanovskii, and Denikin traveled incognito, but Kornilov refused to hide his identity, and chose to lead the Tekinskii regiment personally. This was an impetuous and ill-considered gesture. The Bolsheviks, who soon found out that their feared enemy had eluded them, had such loose control over the country that they could not possibly have found a man traveling incognito. But the General obliged them by taking with him a few hundred soldiers whose route was easy to trace.

The journey of the regiment was extremely difficult.[20] The soldiers started a forced march in order to get as far away from Bykhov as possible; they rested only four nights out of seven. The weather was cold and the soldiers were poorly equipped. They had only vague ideas of what was ahead of them. When, after seven days of marching, a Red armed train caught up with them, it was too much even for the loyal Tekinskii regiment. The battle was not very serious—even though Kornilov's horse was killed under him—for the Reds only fired from a distance and soon departed. Nevertheless, Kornilov could barely reassemble the regiment. He pleaded theatrically and even threatened to commit suicide, but to no avail: the soldiers refused to go any farther. On the next day Kornilov boarded a train in the garb of a Rumanian peasant with a passport in the name of Larion Ivanov. Without further difficulties, the future leader of the Volunteer Army arrived in Novocherkassk on December 19.

The journey of the other generals was safer. Lukomskii, dressed as a German colonist, traveled through Mogilev and Moscow. His only inconvenience was that he had to cut off his mustache and beard.[21] Romanovskii became an ensign and Markov a common soldier.[22] Colonel Kusonskii took these two on his train to Kiev, and they continued their journey from there. Denikin pretended to be a Polish nobleman and set off on his journey alone. He had become a general at the beginning of the war, and since that time he had lost touch with the thinking of the average man. Having spent his time in the army, he knew little about the problems which occupied the attention of most Russians at this time. But for the short duration of this journey people talked to him as they talked to one another. He sensed the hatred of the poor for the rich in its full intensity for the first time. In his memoirs, he noted that this hatred could not entirely be the result of Bolshevik propaganda; the conditions of the Russian peasants in previous centuries and the travail of the war years must also be responsible. Perhaps this short but close contact with the Russian people made Denikin's attitude toward the old regime more equivocal than it otherwise might have been. He blamed the Russian people as a whole, rather than the Bolsheviks in particular, for the country's misfortune. None of the other important White leaders wrote sentences like these:

> Now I was simply a "burzhui," who was shoved and cursed, sometimes with malice, sometimes just in passing, but fortunately nobody paid attention to me. Now I saw real life more clearly and was terrified. First of all, I saw a boundless hatred of ideas and of people; of everything that was socially or intellectually higher than the crowd, of everything which bore the slightest trace of abundance, even of inanimate objects, which were the signs of some culture strange or inaccessible to the crowd. This feeling expressed hatred accumulated over the centuries, the bitterness of three years of war, and the hysteria generated by the revolutionary leaders.[23]

Denikin, Markov, and Romanovskii arrived in Novocherkassk on December 5; Lukomskii came the next day.

THE BEGINNING OF THE ALEKSEEV ORGANIZATION

When the generals from Bykhov arrived in Novocherkassk, they found an anti-Bolshevik organization of officers which ultimately became the Volunteer Army. The name of the group, the Alekseev Organization, properly reflected the fact that it was entirely the fruit of one man's labor—General Alekseev.

The origins of the Organization go back to the period of the last months of the Provisional Government. Very little is known about the first stages of Alekseev's work: he died in 1918 and unlike most generals had no time to write his memoirs. After the Kornilov Affair, the Provisional Government did not trust its officers, and so Alekseev's organizational activities had to be conspiratorial to a large extent, which may explain the dearth of available source material.

In all probability, the general started his work as a purely charitable activity; he wanted to help the families of those who were detained in connection with the Kornilov affair, and the needy officers who had turned to him for help.[24] As a result of his past position at the Stavka, he had excellent contacts with politicians of various persuasions, and he used his contacts to obtain funds. His letter to Miliukov, dated September 1917, is interesting because in it he subtly threatened some industrialists that he might reveal the degree of their participation in the Kornilov affair unless they contributed money to help the families of the imprisoned:

> I have yet another favor to ask you. I do not know the addresses of Mr. Vyshnegradskii, Mr. Putilov, and others. The families of those detained are being reduced to starvation. In order to save them it is necessary to collect and to hand over to the Officers' Union Committee up to 300,000 rubles. I urgently request these men to come to their help. They cannot leave to their fate the families of those to whom they were linked by a common ideal and common endeavor. I earnestly request you to take upon yourself this task, and advise me of the results. We, officers, are more than interested in the matter.
>
> It should be said that if the honest press does not immediately start an energetic investigation of the case, then in five to seven days our politicians will bring the case to the revolutionary court martial, in order to hide the truth and conceal the true circumstances of this case. Then General Kornilov would be compelled to give before the court a broad picture of the whole preparation, of all his negotiations with individuals and groups, of their participation [in the action], so as to show the Russian people, with whom he was proceeding, what were the true purposes which he pursued, and how he, abandoned by everybody in a moment of hardship, had to appear with a small group of officers at a hasty trial, in order to meet this fate for his perishing homeland.[25]

We do not know how much money Alekseev collected, but his appeals could not have been entirely unsuccessful since he was able to give assistance to hundreds. The organization gradually acquired functions other than the distribution of charity, some of them illegal according to the laws of the Provisional Government. For example, contrary to regulations, Alekseev helped officers stay in Petrograd by persuading his industrialist friends to employ them as workers.[26] In a revolutionary period, an organization of officers inevitably had political significance. Some politicians, for example the reactionary V. M. Purishkevich, hoped that Alekseev would use his officers to put pressure on the Provisional Government to pursue more conservative policies.[27] At that time Alekseev participated a great deal in the political life of the country: he corresponded with such anti-Bolshevik leaders as Ataman Kaledin, maintained ties with various military schools—perhaps for coordinating activities in case of an expected Bolshevik rising—and founded another "Alekseev Organization" in Moscow.[28]

But in spite of all the previous planning and talk about the Bolshevik danger, when the uprising occurred on November 7 the old general was just as stunned as most of his countrymen. Boris Savinkov, the Social Revolutionary politician and a determined enemy of the Reds, called on him on the day of the Revolution; to his disappointment he found that Alekseev had no plans for the immediate future.[29] The military force available to him, his group of officers, was far too weak to mount armed resistance.

Alekseev left Petrograd on November 13 incognito and arrived in Novocherkassk two days later. Before leaving Petrograd he instructed his aide, Colonel Vedeniapin, to send officers to the capital of the Don province as soon as he had received notice of his arrival;[30] Alekseev was the first to recognize that in order to fight the Bolsheviks it was necessary to form a new army rather than try to save units of the old one.

The Alekseev Organization in Petrograd and Moscow provided people with money, false documents, and civilian clothes to make the not very dangerous trip to the South even safer. Another organization, the Association of Officers and Soldiers, representing those who had escaped from enemy prison camps, likewise played an active role in smuggling officers to the South. A nurse, M. A. Nesterovich, who was connected with this organization, traveled seven times between Moscow and Novocherkassk in November and December, taking hundreds of officers with her. The unsuspecting authorities in Moscow gave permission to travel to nurse Nesterovich and her companions.[31]

How Alekseev envisaged his task in this period can best be seen from a letter he wrote to Diederichs, the Quartermaster General of the Stavka, on November 21, six days after his arrival on the Don.[32] Unlike Kornilov, he did not regard his undertaking as chiefly a military one. He reported to Diederichs that he was already in touch with journalists and other professional propagandists, and maintained that it was necessary to spend more money on propaganda than on building an army. Above all, Alekseev wanted South Russia to become a base of anti-Bolshevik operations under a strong government.

The main purpose of his letter, however, was to coordinate his military plans with those of the Stavka. Like Kornilov, he wanted to use the Czech corps against the Bolsheviks but considered the formation of a new army to be the most important military task. Alekseev realistically understood that this future army would have to be made up principally of officers, and that it must be a voluntary organization. He turned to Diederichs for help in equipping his troops.

It soon became clear that even the realistic Alekseev was too optimistic about the forces available for the anti-Bolshevik movement. One disappointment followed another: very few officers answered his call; the movement suffered because of the lack of funds; and perhaps most disappointing of all, the population of Novocherkassk and the entire province proved hostile.

THE DON AND THE NOVEMBER REVOLUTION

The Bolsheviks and their enemies paid great attention to the Cossacks' attitude toward the November Revolution. Many believed that if a force to defend the Provisional Government still existed it had to be the Cossack troops, who had come to the defense of authority in Russia many times before. However, in the crucial hours even they were unwilling to oppose the Bolsheviks. Their leaders in Petrograd understood that the Cossacks could not fight alone, for they needed artillery and infantry support which was not available.[33] Furthermore, Bolshevik propaganda had met with some success even among the Cossacks, and the officers could not be sure of the loyalty of their men. Consequently, the Council of Cossack *voiska,* the most powerful Cossack organization, which had given support to Kornilov against Kerenskii, was forced to remain "neutral" at the time of the Bolshevik uprising.

Yet many still placed high hopes in the Cossacks. They believed that while the Cossacks were not able and willing to fight alone for law and order everywhere in the country, they would at least defend their own territory. They would maintain stability in their *voiska,* so they reasoned, and this would give the anti-Bolsheviks a respite and refuge, as well as time and a place to organize. Naturally the hopes of the future White leaders were focused on the largest of the Cossack territories, the Don, whose Ataman, General Kaledin, was a man of well-known conservative convictions.

Indeed, Ataman Kaledin did not disappoint his friends. He did not hesitate in his opposition to Bolshevism, but it turned out very soon that he was powerless because he had no forces to rely on. On November 9, immediately after receiving news of the Petrograd revolution, and acting in the name of the *voisko* government, he invited the members of the Provisional Government to Novocherkassk to join him in organizing the anti-Bolshevik struggle. In a telegram to them he guaranteed their personal safety in the Don.[34] Perhaps because of his telegram, the Don capital was full of rumors about the presence of ex-Prime Minister Kerenskii. The rumors were false, for Kerenskii decided not to accept the hospitality of his previous political enemy, Kaledin.[35] A military directive issued by Kaledin on November 13 also showed over-estimation of his strength. He ordered the 7th Cossack Division to occupy Voronezh as a first move toward overthrowing Bolshevism.[36] However, the division never left the Don district because the Cossacks, influenced by soldiers returning from the front, decided to disperse. After this incident Kaledin limited his aim to the defense of the *voisko.*

In the Don, as everywhere else in Russia at this time, the masses of soldiers returning from the front could not be controlled. It was particularly unfortunate for the Don that the route of the soldiers returning to Russia from the collapsed Caucasian front led through that province. Since the railroad system could not take care of the traffic, many of the returning men had to wait in Rostov and Novorcherkassk for extensive periods, contributing much to anarchy. Cossack regiments from the West also soon arrived. Kaledin was at first encouraged to see that these regiments by and large maintained better discipline than non-Cossack ones, and he hoped to use them against the local Bolsheviks to restore the authority of his government. This hope, too, proved to be illusory for the Cossacks saw no reason to fight the Bolsheviks, who had promised to end the war. Kaledin, who had left the front after the March Revolution, did not understand the changes which had occurred in the thinking of his men. The arrival of each regiment was a new disappointment to him, and he only gradually realized how much power he lacked.

The returning non-Cossack Don units were inclined to favor the Bolsheviks.[37] This does not mean that they were anxious to fight, but rather that if they had to choose they preferred Lenin to Kaledin. An interesting and characteristic situation arose early in December, when some local Bolshevik leader decided to try to end the defiance by the Novocherkassk government of the central authorities and ordered the 156th Infantry Regiment of the 39th Division, stationed in Stavropol district, to proceed against the provincial capital. Kaledin entrusted the defense to the 35th Cossack regiment of the 8th Division. But Cossacks and non-Cossacks refused to fight each other. They set up a neutral zone by agreement and neither side listened to the officers who ordered them to shoot.[38] This incident, of course, illustrates the impotence of the Bolsheviks as well as the weakness of the Novocherkassk government.

In a situation in which soldiers wanted to avoid fighting, units which continued to obey orders acquired special value. Undisciplined as the Black Sea sailors were, they gave the Bolsheviks a nucleus of strength which the Whites did not possess. Red Guard units, formed from workers and miners of the Don district, also played a significant role in spite of their inexperience.

The political importance of miners and workers was far out of proportion to their numerical strength. This was because only the proletariat took to arms at this time while the peasantry—Cossack and *inogorodnye*—remained inactive. The workers of the three industrial areas of the Don (Rostov, Taganrog, and the Donets Basin) had been hostile to the Cossack government since the March Revolution. The miners followed the Bolsheviks. Among the workers of Taganrog and Rostov the Mensheviks, almost as hostile to Kaledin as the Bolsheviks, were the strongest party before November. After November Bolshevik influence became dominant.[39] The results of the November election showed a great increase in Bolshevik strength in the Constituent Assembly, especially among the workers. In Rostov the Bolshevik Party emerged as the largest with 25,569 votes. The Cossack slate got 14,248 votes, the Kadets 13,677, the Social Revolutionaries 7,565, and the Mensheviks 4,615.[40]

In the *voisko* at large the Cossack candidates received the largest number of votes (640,000), but their victory was illusory: the *inogorodnye* divided their votes among the Social Revolutionaries (480,000) and the Bolsheviks (250,000), both parties hostile to Cossack privileges.[41] If the lines were drawn between Bolsheviks and Cossacks, the *inogorodnye* unquestionably would have preferred the Bolsheviks. Until the peasants had first-hand experience with the Red Army they found little to object to in Bolshevism. In November 1917 many *inogorodnye* turned to the Bolsheviks in the hope of getting Cossack land.

Kaledin could have maintained himself in the face of the workers and *inogorodnye* opposition had the Cossacks been willing to give his government full support, but he could count only on the older Cossacks; the *frontoviki*, who were armed and therefore more important, deserted him. The Cossack government had hoped to challenge the Lenin regime, but it soon became obvious that this government could not even suppress the local revolutionaries.

The *voisko* had been de facto independent since the day it had defied the Provisional Government by refusing to extradite Kaledin. On November 20, the government formally declared its independence until the formation of a lawful Russian national government. The same declaration convened the third session of the *krug* for December 15 to discuss the organization of an independent administration.[42]

In this unstable, unfriendly political environment General Alekseev started to build his army. It was inevitable that the presence of Alekseev's Organization would soon become an issue in local politics, and also that the officers themselves would start to play a political role by supporting Kaledin against the Bolsheviks and the compromisers.

Kaledin permitted the arriving officers to stay in a hospital at 39 Barochnaia Street.[43] While there were no patients at this hospital, the medical staff stayed behind and shared the building with the officers. To avoid friction with the local population, Alekseev ordered his followers to pretend to be wounded or ill, and not to leave the hospital without his permission. On November 17, the army consisted of 40 men.[44] These 40 men composed the first officers' squadron and the date, November 17, was later regarded as the beginning of seniority in the Volunteer Army. Official enlistment, however, started only at the end of the month. Then the volunteers signed up for four months; they received no salary, only the promise of food.

The small force grew very slowly and by the end of November it had about 300 members.[45] However, the very existence of the organization was endangered by Kaledin's request to move the army outside Don territory within two weeks.[46] Kaledin, of course, agreed with Alekseev's aims, but he was pressured by his Cossacks, who believed that the Bolsheviks would attack the Don because it was giving refuge to their enemies. Kaledin suggested to Alekseev that either Stavropol or Kamyshin become the new headquarters. But the population of these cities would have been even more hostile, and it is unlikely that the army could have survived in non-Cossack territory.

Alekseev, instead of making preparations to leave, continued his organizational work. He asked for assistance from General Shcherbachev, commander of the Russian armies on the Rumanian front, which, probably because of its distance from the main industrial centers of Russia, was somewhat less disorganized than the others. Shcherbachev refused to help the White movement at this time.[47] Nor were Ruzskii and Radko-Dmitriev, two other well-known generals from the World War who were living in the Northern Caucasus, anxious to cooperate. Through nurse Nesterovich, Alek-

seev was in touch with ex-Minister of War Guchkov, who regarded
the developing anti-Bolshevik movement in Siberia as more important, and contrary to numerous promises he had made to Nesterovich, he sent only insignificant sums to the South.[48]

Lack of funds was among the most serious of Alekseev's numerous problems. In spite of his excellent contacts with the Moscow
and Petrograd rich, he received only a few thousand rubles in the
first month of the army's existence.[49] The officers lived in poverty.
A colonel complained to Nesterovich that officers had been coming
to him for fifty kopeks for cigarettes and he had not been able to
help them.[50]

So great was the confusion prevailing in the Don province that
by the time the army had 300 fighters it was considered to be a
significant force. Kaledin could not maintain order among his
troops and he was forced to ask for Alekseev's help. Volunteer officers performed the role of policemen. In small detachments, under
the command of a Cossack officer, they were sent to various trouble
spots: at railroad stations they restrained disorderly soldiers who demanded that their train should have preference over others; in
stanitsy the volunteers defended the population from hungry de-
serters who wanted to take food by force. For these services the
Don government paid the officers, and what was perhaps even more
important, it gave them rifles.[51]

The army was badly equipped; at the beginning of December,
when it already had about 600 officers, it still possessed only 100
rifles and no machine guns at all.[52] Kaledin would have liked to
give more help but could not because the storehouses were controlled by regimental committees hostile to the Whites. The volunteers acquired rifles and munitions mostly by disarming demoralized regiments.

These regiments were dangerous both to the embryonic volunteer movement and to the government of Ataman Kaledin. The
Ataman's proclamation of independence was regarded as a declaration of war by the Bolsheviks in the Don, and this led to a series
of increasingly bellicose moves on both sides. The first response
came from the miners of Makaevka district, who, on November
29, countered Kaledin's announcement by proclaiming the Don

Soviet Republic. The declaration had no practical significance, but the strike of miners which accompanied it did: coal production was diminished to such an extent that the Don could not even produce enough coal for its own needs.[53]

On December 1, the 272nd Infantry Regiment (non-Cossack) passed a resolution refusing to recognize the authority of the Don government. Since the regiment was stationed in Novocherkassk, this was an immediate challenge. Two days later, Kaledin disarmed the rebellious regiment with the aid of Alekseev's officers. It was characteristic of existing conditions that this regiment, which had so resolutely defied the *voisko* government, allowed itself to be disarmed and dispersed without firing a single shot.[54] This action had significant consequences for the future of the volunteers. The Ataman realized that he depended on the support of Alekseev's organization, and he therefore allowed the officers to stay on Don territory beyond the two-week deadline.

The news that the Soviet regime was sending Red Guard detachments to occupy the area created an atmosphere of crisis in Novocherkassk. Under the pressures of external attack and internal disorder, Kaledin declared martial law on December 5. In his declaration the Ataman pleaded especially with the workers, promising that existing Soviets would not be disturbed if they limited their work to matters which concerned them directly. The same manifesto also promised that Cossack troops would not go beyond the boundaries of the Don.[55]

The Bolsheviks were preparing for battle. In November, with the participation of Social Revolutionaries and Mensheviks, they formed a Military Revolutionary Committee in Rostov.[56] The Bolshevik Central Committee of Rostov-Nakhichevansk sent a delegation to the Black Sea sailors at Sevastopol asking for their assistance against Kaledin.[57] As usual the Bolsheviks could count on the sailors. A convoy of ships came to Rostov, and the organization of Black Sea sailors sent a telegram to Novocherkassk demanding the abolition of martial law in Rostov. The sailors attacked Kaledin in their telegram for suppressing the peasants (presumably the *inogorodnye*), persecuting the miners, and not delivering enough coal and food for Soviet Russia.[58] The Rostov Military Revolutionary

Committee, encouraged by the sailors' support and counting on local Bolshevik regiments and workers' battalions, decided on December 9 not to recognize the authority of the *voisko* government.[59] This was rebellion. The non-Bolshevik members of the Revolutionary Committee, who disagreed with this step, left the Committee. General Pototskii, commander of the only non-Bolshevized battalion of the city, wanted to disperse the Committee but was unable to do so.[60] His Cossacks, who did not want to fight, were disarmed and escaped to Novocherkassk.[61] Pototskii was jailed, however, along with other prominent followers of the government. The Bolsheviks controlled the city for five days. Their rule was moderate; politicians who had escaped from Bolshevik Russia were not disturbed.

Kaledin's military position was difficult nevertheless; after fruitless negotiations with the Military Revolutionary Committee he decided to take Rostov. The operation, begun on December 9, can be regarded as the beginning of the Civil War. It was the day of St. George, the patron saint of Russia, and many attributed great significance to this coincidence.

The first battle of the Civil War established a pattern: Kaledin called on the Cossacks and they refused to obey.[62] Then the Ataman sought help from the Alekseev Organization.[63] Alekseev sent all the men at his disposal: between 400 and 500 officers went from Novocherkassk to Rostov to fight the Bolsheviks. This force was much smaller than the Red Guard; nevertheless, the officers seized the initiative and won. The victory was accomplished by determination and military ability. The White officers' success gave courage to some Cossack units, who also participated in the second part of the operation, but the main task was undoubtedly accomplished by Alekseev's men. Bolshevik resistance stopped on December 15; the most important Communist leaders escaped, the soldiers went back to their barracks, and the Red Guardists became "peaceful" citizens again.[64]

Kaledin entered Rostov on December 15. He placed greater emphasis on reconciliation than on exterminating Bolshevism. He asked the workers to give up their weapons and a large number of them obeyed.[65]. A part of the population greeted him as a savior.

Kaledin, however, had too much moral sensibility to assume the pose of a victor. He said:

> I need no ovations. I am not a hero and my arrival is not a holiday. I come to your city not as a fortunate conqueror. Blood was shed and we have nothing to be glad about. My heart is heavy. I fulfilled my civic duty and I need no ovations.[66]

The victory in Rostov gave a new lease on life to the Cossack government. The Ataman gained prestige, and it was a propitious time for him to introduce reforms: the third session of the *krug* opened as Kaledin entered Rostov.

Among the issues discussed by the *krug* the most important was giving parity to the *inogorodnye* in the government of the Don. As long as the Don had been an integral part of Russia, the Cossack organs of self-government could be regarded as agencies responsible only for Cossack affairs, and this was a legitimate reason for excluding non-Cossacks. To continue this exclusion after the government's declaration of independence would have meant instituting a dictatorship of one half of the population over the other. Bolshevik influence was strong among the non-Cossacks, and as long as they had no say in the government it was difficult to combat this influence.

The question was hotly debated. The most convinced advocate of parity was the Cossack socialist politician P. M. Agaev, and he was supported by S. G. Elatontsev, a member of the government. The *frontoviki* favored Agaev's position, if for no other reason than that they believed that this compromise would assure peace.[67] The opposition was strongest among the representatives of Cherkassk district, which was the richest in the Don, and where the average Cossack landholdings were larger than elsewhere.[68] Presumably the wealthy Cossacks were afraid that giving a voice to the *inogorodnye* in the government would bring land reform closer.

The Ataman, having returned from Rostov, addressed the *krug*. His prestige was sufficiently great at the time that his opinion on the question of parity was decisive. He pleaded for bringing the *inogorodnye* into the government.

The *krug* decided: (1) to give all power to the government of the *voisko* until the formation of a legal all-Russian government; (2) to give half of the posts (eight) in the government to the representatives of the non-Cossack population; and (3) to convene the Constituent Assembly of the district on January 11.[69]

CHAPTER 3

The Birth of the Volunteer Army

By defeating the Bolsheviks in Rostov, their most important stronghold on the Don, Alekseev's army saved itself from immediate danger. It also won the gratitude of the Cossack government, at least to the extent that the government came to tolerate Alekseev as a defender of the Don. Nevertheless, the existence of the army remained precarious for three reasons. In the first place, Alekseev had too few volunteers and not enough money. Secondly, bitter infighting greatly weakened the Alekseev Organization. Thirdly, in spite of the fact that the army saved the Don from the Bolsheviks, the local population remained hostile.

From mid-December to mid-January an average of 75 to 80 volunteers per day came to the Don.[1] By the end of this period the Volunteer Army had about three thousand members—a small number considering the fact that the Russian Army had several hundred thousand officers and non-commissioned officers at the end of the World War.[2]

The lack of response by officers was a bitter disappointment to the leaders of the White army, and something they found hard to explain even in their memoirs. Perhaps the most frequent explanation to be found in emigré memoir literature is that travel to the Don was dangerous, and those officers who wanted to come were simply not able to get to Novocherkassk.[3] This argument is not convincing. If well-known generals could come and go, sometimes even without bothering to assume an incognito, the average officer surely could have done the same. It is noteworthy that there is not a single known incident in this period in which a famous military leader was arrested only because he was suspected of wanting to join General Alekseev. Bolshevik control was weak even in the capitals, and the Reds could hardly have prevented a larger movement of officers even had they been aware of the danger which threatened them. If the Bolsheviks freed General Krasnov, who had led an army against Petrograd, after only a short time in captivity, it would have made no sense for them to prevent other officers from traveling. It is not that Lenin and Trotskii were overconfident; they simply did not know from which direction to expect danger.

We must remember that the great majority of officers who lived on the Don and the Kuban, where travel was not difficult, did not want to join the army either. The history of the Rostov enlistment bureau is interesting because it illustrates this point.[4] The bureau grew out of a self-defense unit which was formed by the officers living in Rostov during the brief period of Bolshevik rule in December. After the defeat of the Reds, about two hundred officers banded together and elected General Cherepov as head of the detachment to coordinate the work of the unit with that of the Cossack government. According to the understanding between Alekseev and Kaledin, by which the Novocherkassk government was in charge of the Cossacks and the organization of refugee officers was left to Alekseev, Kaledin sent Cherepov to his comrade. In this way the Rostov unit became part of the Alekseev Organization and an enlistment bureau was set up in that city. Because many members of the Cherepov group were only interested in local defense, they left the unit at this time.

Enlistment progressed slowly in Rostov. The bureau recruited fewer volunteers than the number of officers who left the Cherepov group when it became part of the Alekseev Organization. The leaders of the army in Novocherkassk had planned a Rostov regiment, but there were hardly enough volunteers to form a squadron. When the Volunteer Army started on the Kuban campaign in February, only one-third of the 200-man Rostov squadron followed.

The enlistment drive in the second largest city of the Don, Taganrog, was even less successful. There were hundreds of officers
here, but during the month when the enlistment bureau was open
only fifty joined.[5] There were thousands of officers in the Don,
and in the Kuban, and especially in the Mineral Waters district of
the Northern Caucasus, but Alekseev issued one appeal after another in vain. He traveled to Ekaterinodar twice to attract support,
but without success.

In explaining the failure of the recruitment drive, Denikin attributed great significance to the fact that the Don authorities,
guarding the autonomy of the district, would not permit Alekseev
and Kornilov to issue a mobilization order.[6] Denikin seems to have
forgotten that Kornilov, disregarding the wishes of the Don government, did issue such an order on January 11, 1918. Even though
the order threatened those who did not respond with "indelible"
disgrace, it had no appreciable results.[7] Although it is impossible
to disprove Denikin's argument completely, and though it is con-
ceivable that if Kornilov had issued his order a month earlier it
might have made some difference, it appears unlikely that an un-
enforceable command could have broken the inertia of the Russian
officers.

Some observers believed, then and later, that officers did not join
because the leaders of the White army had not developed a positive
ideology.[8] Statements concerning human motivations are necessarily tentative and perhaps an attractive program would have induced many officers to sign up. But even in the perspective of time
it is difficult to see what this program could have been. One might
argue, as the leaders of the army did, that the endorsement of any
concrete political program would have weakened the army by
limiting its base of support; a conservative program would have
alienated the progressives and vice versa.

The appeals by Alekseev and Kornilov remained unanswered
for the same mixture of reasons for which the Cossacks refused to
fight the Bolsheviks. After months of political upheaval Russian
officers still wanted peace at any price. The Volunteer Army, however, asked them to continue the war against Germany, and as a
precondition to overthrow Bolshevik rule. It seems that both sol-

diers and officers disagreed with the leaders of the Volunteer Army in assessing the desirability of continuing the war against the foreign enemy. Perhaps the army would have gained more recruits if Alekseev and Kornilov had recognized that Russia could not resume her role in the World War, and that it would be better to concentrate their efforts in fighting the Bolsheviks. But to ask the generals to give up fighting the foreign enemy was to ask them to be something other than what they were. Alekseev and Kornilov saw the Bolsheviks as agents of Germany, and from their point of view it would have made no sense to struggle only against the agents.

The officers, like the Russian people in general, had no clear idea who the Bolsheviks were and exactly what they wanted, and since they were tired of the political disorders of the Provisional Government, they were susceptible to the idea that the new rulers could not be as bad as they had seemed a few months earlier. The officers in Rostov must have been typical of officers in the rest of the country: they lived through five days of Bolshevik rule during which most of them remained neutral and were not disturbed. From this experience they deduced that the Bolsheviks would not harm those who did not oppose them.[9] The Russian officers waited passively for the storm of the Civil War to blow over their heads.

The inadequate response of the Russian officers profoundly affected the character of the developing White army. Since the overwhelming majority of the officers kept themselves out of the Civil War, the element which dominated in the White army was unrepresentative not only of the Russian people, but also of the Russian officer class; only the young and the most embittered joined. The first volunteers in Novocherkassk were painfully aware of their isolation, and this awareness lowered their morale and increased their bitterness. Their growing frustration, in turn, made them eager listeners to extremist, monarchist, and reactionary agitators.

Since only a few men volunteered, by the middle of 1918 the Army had to follow the example of the Bolsheviks and depend upon conscription. At that time the army occupied almost entirely Cossack territories and consequently Cossacks were conscripted. The Volunteer Army became an army largely made up of Cossacks, and this fact severely limited its maneuverability; the soldiers wanted to go no further than the boundaries of their own *voisko*.

Among the first three thousand volunteers there were perhaps only a dozen soldiers; the rest were officers, cadets (junkers, as the Russians called them) and students. When General Cherepov came to report about the work of the Rostov enlistment bureau, Kornilov looked at the list of volunteers and burst out: "These are all officers, but where are the soldiers?"[10] The soldiers did not come, then or later. Observers were impressed by the low average age of the volunteers; even sixteen and seventeen year-olds were allowed to enroll. If we can take the word of the journalist B. Suvorin, Alekseev complained to him in these picturesque terms: I see a monument which Russia will erect for these children: on a bare rock a destroyed eagle's nest and a murdered eaglet [with the inscription] "But where were the eagles?"[11]

The relations of the first volunteers with the officers in Rostov, Novocherkassk, and Taganrog—who, in their opinion, shirked their duty—were uniformly hostile. The volunteers resented the officers, who spent their days in the cafés of the Don cities, and the officers in turn were contemptuous of the volunteers, calling them "toy soldiers."[12]

If Alekseev was disappointed by the weak response of the officers, he had even more reason to be disappointed by the behavior of the Russian rich, who were no more willing to give money than the soldiers were willing to give their lives. Insufficient enlistment and lack of money were connected problems: poverty of the members of the army frightened away many who might have joined, and one of the impediments to getting money was that the army seemed to small to be taken seriously.

Unfortunately, entries in Alekseev's account book begin only in January 1918, so that details of the army's finances during the first months of its existence are not known.[13] We do know, however, that an illegal, anti-communist organization in Moscow sent between 500,000 and 800,000 rubles to the South during these months.[14] From private contributions Alekseev received perhaps another 100,000 rubles.[15] M. M. Fedorov, a Kadet ex-minister in the Provisional Government and one of the first politicians to come to work for the White army, negotiated an agreement with the Don government by which Alekseev received 25 per cent of the *voisko's* income.[16] It was this money which assured the army's survival and with which it was able to pay its members, however modestly, from December 1917.[17]

When Alekseev started to organize his army, he counted on financial aid from the Allies. That this aid did not materialize was a bitter disappointment to those anti-Bolshevik Russians who remained faithful to the Allied cause under very trying circumstances. However, one should not blame the Western governments for their lack of desire to help. Even in the period preceding the Brest-Litovsk treaty, when Allied diplomats still hoped to persuade the Bolsheviks to continue the war against Germany, these diplomats attempted to establish ties with the Whites. As early as November the British had considered giving aid to Kaledin, and on December 14 the British government approved a grant of 10 million pounds.[18] The French at the same time planned to send 100 million francs. It was not the Allies' fault, but because of the general confusion prevailing in Russia at the time very little came of all this. Alekseev received only 300,000 rubles from Colonel Hucher, a French representative. Another agent, Captain Bordes, was sent from Jassy by General Barthelot, the Allied Commander on the Rumanian front, to deliver 7 million francs through Hucher, but by the time Bordes arrived at Novocherkassk the Volunteer Army was already in the Kuban. Bordes sent 3 million francs to Moscow with Hucher, and he himself continued his unsuccessful search for the Whites in South Russia with the rest of the money.[19]

At the end of 1917, Novocherkassk was becoming one of the political centers of Russia. Among the dozens of well-known public figures who came to this city, most of them were members of the Kadet Party (or People's Freedom Party, as it was also named). P. N. Miliukov, an ex-foreign minister and the man who came closest to being the "leader" of the Party, A. I. Shingarev, another ex-member of the Provisional Government, and Prince G. N. Trubetskoi were in Novocherkassk. For some Kadet leaders, like M. M. Fedorov, the jurist K. N. Sokolov, and V. A. Stepanov, an ex-member of the Provisional Government, this was the beginning of their association with the Volunteer Army, and it was to last as long as the army existed. Among the well-known politicians who came to Novocherkassk were: M. V. Rodzianko (an Octobrist and Speaker of the Fourth Duma), P. B. Struve (who had established his reputation as a socialist, but gradually moved to the right and by 1917 considered the Kadets to be too radical), and B. V. Savinkov, the Social Revolutionary ex-aide to Kerenskii.[20]

Since the lives of prominent opposition leaders in Bolshevik-ruled Russia were not yet endangered (the murder of Shingarev and F. F. Kokoshkin in January 1918 must be regarded as exceptions), the men who came to the South came not to escape danger but to take part in the anti-Bolshevik struggle. The chief role of politicians in Novocherkassk was to help the incipient army maintain connections with Russian society and use their influence to secure financial aid.

The White army had yet to establish its identity. Major questions remained unresolved, and the politicians, of course, were anxious to make their influence felt. The important questions were who would lead the army and what role civilians would play in the White movement. The resolution of the second question depended largely on the outcome of the struggle for leadership in the army between Generals Kornilov and Alekseev.

Kornilov arrived on December 19. As Denikin remarks, it was obvious from the first moment that cooperation between Alekseev and Kornilov would not be easy.[21] Their backgrounds, personalities, and followers were very different, their past associations had left bitter memories, and they disliked each other.

Alekseev's views were closest to those of the Kadets. As Chief-of-Staff in the Stavka he had made valuable contacts with statesmen; understandably, the Kadet politicians who had great respect for the older general would have liked to see him as leader of the army. These statesmen had much less confidence in the political ability of Kornilov, whom they blamed for mismanaging his coup. Nonetheless, it was Kornilov who emerged victorious from the political battle because he had support where it counted, among the officers. The Russian army as a whole, and perhaps even the officer group, would have preferred Alekseev, but the army gathering in Novocherkassk was composed of very unrepresentative elements, the most vociferous enemies of Bolshevik rule. The junkers and officers who cared enough to fight the Reds respected Alekseev, but they idolized Kornilov.

On December 31, an important meeting took place between the politicians and the generals to decide who would lead the army.[22] Kornilov presented an ultimatum: if unlimited power was not granted to him, he would go to Siberia and start his organization there.[23] Everyone at the meeting knew that this was a serious threat because if Kornilov left, the majority of the officers would follow him and this would be the end of the Alekseev Organization. The politicians present at the conference worked for a compromise which would allow Alekseev and Kornilov to share power. Accordingly, unlimited power over the army was offered to Kornilov and the direction of political and financial matters was to be retained by Alekseev.[24] Kornilov hesitated. He turned down Alekseev's suggestions that he should go to Ekaterinodar and organize the officers in the Kuban, and he continued to talk about going to Siberia. He finally accepted the original proposal when representatives of Moscow anti-Bolshevik organizations threatened the withdrawal of financial aid if the two generals did not cooperate. A week later Kornilov formally assumed command of the army and the Alekseev Organization was renamed the "Volunteer Army."

Denikin was entrusted with working out the "constitution" of the Volunteer Army on the basis of the agreement of December 31. This document, accepted and signed by Generals Alekseev, Kornilov, and Kaledin, was the first attempt at establishing formal authority on the territory controlled by the White army. Denikin's proposal was as simple as one would expect from a statesman-soldier:

(1) Civil authority, foreign affairs and finances [are entrusted] to General Alekseev.

(2) Military power [is entrusted] to General Kornilov.

(3) The government of the Don district [is entrusted] to General Kaledin.

(4) The highest authority [is entrusted] to the triumvirate. It decides all matters of the highest significance. At meetings that triumvir will take the chair into whose competence the matter under discussion belongs.[25]

At the same time, at the initiative of M. M. Fedorov, a council of public figures was formed for the purpose of helping General Alekseev with his work of maintaining contacts with foreign governments and Russian anti-Bolshevik organizations, and above all for the purpose of raising money. Apart from Fedorov, other illustrious members of this council were P. N. Miliukov, P. B. Struve, A. S. Beletskii, and Prince G. N. Trubetskoi. The Don government had already formed an organization with rather similar functions, and in order to avoid working at cross purposes, two of their representatives—the well-known Kadet politician N. Paramonov, and M. P. Bogaevskii, Ataman Kaledin's closest aide—joined the council.[26]

The division of power among the triumvirs did not work. The line between military, financial, and political matters was hard to draw, and Kornilov increasingly usurped Alekseev's powers. The civilians soon realized that in a movement dominated by Kornilov, they could play no significant role. Kornilov had a deep-seated dislike of politicians and politics, a feeling characteristic of simple-minded soliders, especially of those with rightist convictions. Kornilov's distrust of politicians preceded the revolution. As a prisoner of war in Austria in 1915-1916 he had frequently expressed his wish to his fellow prisoners to "string up all these Miliukovs."[27] Now he treated politicians in Novocherkassk with contempt, shunned their advice, and avoided contact with them as much as possible. Kornilov's Chief of Staff, General A. S. Lukomskii reported that one of the reasons for moving the headquarters of the Army to Rostov in January 1918 was Kornilov's desire to get away from the public figures gathered in the Cossack capital. Since Rostov was closer to the front at that time, he believed that politicians would not follow the headquarters into the danger zone.[28]

There was constant friction between Alekseev and Kornilov and their respective staffs. On January 22, Captain Kapel'ka, a member of Alekseev's staff, informed his superior he had heard Kornilov was planning a coup in connection with moving the army to Rostov. According to Kapel'ka's information, Kornilov wanted to use this opportunity to declare himself dictator.[29] Alekseev hurriedly convened a meeting of politicians and senior generals, and invited Kornilov to explain the situation. Kornilov was insulted and refused to appear. Denikin and Kaledin had great difficulties in reconciling the two men. Kornilov was willing to continue cooperating only when Alekseev apologized, and it was agreed that the civilian council would be limited to an advisory capacity.

A few days later another incident occurred which further exacerbated the relations between Kornilov and Alekseev. Prince Devlet Girei, a Circassian leader, came to Rostov to propose to Kornilov the formation of an army by his people. He asked for a million rubles for this purpose. Kornilov liked the idea and approved of the plan, but Alekseev flatly refused to give the Prince so much money for such a risky venture. In an effort to placate Kornilov, however, he offered to give 200,000 rubles, but Devlet Girei would not accept this sum.[30]

By this time relations were so bad between the two leaders that they talked to each other only when it was absolutely necessary. Routine communications were made through messengers, although their Rostov offices, in Paramonov's house, were next to one another.[31]

Continuous quarrels between the highest leaders of the army poisoned the atmosphere in Rostov and Novocherkassk. Finally the army, down to the lowest ranks, split into two camps. Roman Gul' describes his enlistment which illustrates the depth of this rift:

> In a small room a male and female ensign signed up people and took their documents; the man asked, Who can recommend you? I named a close relative of General Kornilov, Lieutenant Colonel Kolchinskii. The ensign made a grimace, shrugged his shoulders and said through his teeth: "Look, he does not really belong to our organization. . . ." I was surprised and understood nothing. Only later Lieutenant Colonel Kolchinskii explained to me that the officers of the enlistment bureau were partisans of Alekseev, but he was a Kornilovite; between these two tendencies there is covert discord and secret struggle.[32]

It is tempting to seek ideological differences for the disagreements between Alekseev and Kornilov. Indeed, most of those writers on the White movement regard this as a fight between republican and democratic elements on the one hand and conservatives and monarchists on the other. The difficulty is that while some writers think Alekseev represented conservative ideology, others connect him with republicans and democrats. Miliukov, for example, who knew both generals, believed that the monarchists followed Kornilov, while Alekseev always remained a supporter of the March Revolution.[33] Denikin, whose personal knowledge of the people concerned was more intimate, thought it was the other way around.

The solution to the puzzle is this: there were really very few ideological differences between Alekseev and Kornilov. If the two ex-Commanders-in-Chief had been pressed—as they were not—Kornilov might have revealed a greater commitment to the republican form of government, and in this sense Denikin was right. But Kornilov's attitudes were determined not so much by his political ideology, which was confused and unsophisticated, as by his temperament, and by temperament he was a radical. His propensity for radical solutions endeared him to the most vociferous enemies of Bolshevism, which was why Miliukov associated him with the extreme right.

In their attitude toward radical solutions, however, there was a genuine difference between the two leaders. Nesterovich, a messenger between various anti-Communist organizations and the army in the South, describes an incident which illustrates this difference. She was asked by a secret officers' organization to discover Alekseev's attitude toward a terrorist attempt. The plan was to blow up the Smolnyi, the Bolshevik headquarters, when important leaders held a meeting there. By chance, Nesterovich talked to Alekseev in Kornilov's presence:

> General Alekseev, as always, talked in a quiet, calm tone: "No, one must not do this, because innocent people would suffer. Terror would begin and the population of Petrograd would pay for it."
> But General Kornilov had a different opinion; he said that having eliminated the chief leaders of Bolshevism, it would be easier to overthrow the present regime. "Even if we have to burn half of Russia"—he said passionately—"shed the blood of three fourths of the Russians, nevertheless, it is necessary to save Russia."[34]

Alekseev's word carried greater weight with the organization and the attempt on the Smolnyi was never made.

Kornilov instituted the policy of taking no prisoners, and the Volunteer Army adhered to this in the first months of its existence. Referring to the Red Guards, he said: "Do not capture these criminals. The greater the terror the greater our victories."[35]

Much as Kornilov and Alekseev disagreed about practical policies, they shared the same general ideological outlook with all senior officers and politicians. This unanimity was based on the acceptance of the fundamental ideas of the March Revolution. There were very few convinced monarchists in Russia at the time—they had been so embittered by the experiences of the past year that they had retired from public affairs entirely. Both Alekseev and Kornilov had been discredited in the eyes of the monarchists: Alekseev because he had helped persuade the Tsar to abdicate, and Kornilov because he had arrested the imperial family.[36]

Under the circumstances, it was relatively easy to agree on the first manifesto of the Volunteer Army, which was published on January 9. It declared that the army would fight the Bolsheviks and the Germans alike. Beyond defeating the Bolsheviks the manifesto said only this about the aims of the army:

> The new army will defend civil liberties in order to enable the master of the Russian land—the Russian people—to express through the elected Constituent Assembly its sovereign will. All classes, parties, and groups of the population must accept that will. The army and those taking part in its formation will absolutely submit to the legal power appointed by the Constituent Assembly.[37]

The politicians of the Volunteer Army had learned the technique of avoiding controversial issues in 1917 under the guise of respect for the Constituent Assembly; the approach of the Provisional Government had been exactly the same. The army was to adhere to this tactic during its entire existence. This document seems to refer to the Constituent Assembly, which was about to convene in Petrograd. Undoubtedly, the Assembly, which had a Social Revolutionary majority, would have been almost as hostile to Kornilov as it was to Lenin. Not surprisingly, the Volunteer Army later modified its position by demanding new elections, because it maintained that delegates to the Assembly had been unfairly elected. Whether or

not there should be new elections to the Constituent Assembly became the major bone of contention between the army and the anti-
Bolshevik socialists, who had been completely satisfied with the results of the elections.[38]

On February 5, Kornilov issued his own manifesto.[39] It was somewhat more explicit than the previous one, but the basic thoughts
were the same. Kornilov advocated the Kadet program: the war
should be continued to a victorious end, the land question should be
dealt with by the Constituent Assembly, the civil liberties achieved
by the March Revolution should be preserved. Two points of the
manisfesto deserve special consideration. Kornilov wanted to continue the war with an army re-established on a volunteer basis—a
highly unrealistic proposition. His manisfesto also stated explicitly
that the Constituent Assembly, dispersed by the Bolsheviks on January 18, should be restored.

Shortly after Kornilov composed his manifesto the Volunteer
Army was forced to leave Rostov; therefore, Kornilov's program
was never distributed and had no political importance. That Kornilov composed it at all, however, is significant. It was in fact inspired
by I. A. Dobrynskii, an adventurist and an unsavory character whom
the other leaders distrusted.[40] According to the agreement signed by
Kornilov a month earlier, political matters were to be dealt with by
General Alekseev. Not only did Kornilov fail to consult the older
general before composing his political program, which was intended
for wide distribution; he did not even bother to inform him. One
can imagine that General Alekseev was insulted and angered by this
treatment. He dispatched a messenger to the next room requesting a
copy of the manifesto. Kornilov sent a copy of the document, along
with a short letter in which one can detect a note of irony:

> In answer to your letter of February 1st, No. 13, about the informa-
> tion given to you by Doctor N. S. Grigoriev about my political
> program, I wish to inform you that it is not clear to me which
> program Doctor Grigoriev had in mind. If he had in mind the
> Bykhov program—this was printed in the newspapers. The "Pro-
> gram of General Kornilov," which is enclosed, is the outgrowth of
> the earlier one. This is still not refined and I will publish it when
> the time is right in my opinion.[41]

Alekseev showed the manifesto and letter to Miliukov. The Kadet politician was even more indignant than the general. He stated his views in a letter to Alekseev, which shows the bitterness of the conflict among the leaders of the Volunteer Army better than any other document:

> This political tactic of General Kornilov, unfortunately, does not appear to be either an accident or a first manifestation. The tactic is based on the rejection of political parties in general, which is rather common among political dillettantes. [General Kornilov considers all political parties bankrupt because 'they are bound by the dead letter of their programs' . . .] At the same time, again like these dilettantes, General Kornilov constructs his *own* political program, and apparently, some kind of party. . . . [As in August 1917, when General Kornilov had bitterly disappointed the people:] Russia turns out to be in the hands of a similar group of leaders. Using the expression of General Kornilov's program [Russia is] again in the hands of an adventurist.[49]

Miliukov noted that in composing his program alone, Kornilov had violated the agreement which formed the basis of the Volunteer Army. He predicted that if Kornilov published this program, the broad front of support which had been given to the Volunteer Army would disintegrate. Far more important than the composition of political manifestos was the issue of the army's relations with the socialist opposition to Bolshevism. This issue was to plague the White movement until its collapse.

It would be wrong to search for the causes of disagreement between officers and anti-Bolshevik socialists merely in their conflicting ideologies. In fact, the programs coincided in many ways. Under the circumstances, one is forced to conclude that it was prejudice and the memory of past struggles which kept the two groups apart—ultimately with disastrous results for both. It must be admitted that the great majority of the socialists showed little more wisdom than the officers, and that they failed to recognize how wide the gap was between themselves and the Bolsheviks. However, among the socialists there were exceptions, and none more notable than B. V. Savinkov, who was willing to swallow his pride and make extraordinary efforts to bring unity to the anti-Bolshevik camp.

Savinkov had had a most unusual career. As a terrorist Social Revolutionary, he participated in the assassination of Minister of the Interior Plehve in 1904. In exile he won acclaim as a novelist; later, during the First World War, as an enthusiastic advocate of the Allied cause, he joined the French Army. After the March Revolution he returned to Russia and served as one of the closest aides to Premier Kerenskii, in which capacity he tried to reconcile the Prime Minister and the Commander-in-Chief, Kornilov. Whatever one thinks of Savinkov's past and personality, it must be admitted that after the November Revolution he showed a statesmanlike understanding of the need for cooperation between all the enemies of Bolshevism, and that he was willing to make personal and ideological sacrifices for this cause. After the fall of the Provisional Government, Savinkov established contact with the organization of Cossack *voiska*, and with an officers' organization, and he even advocated cooperation with the Ukrainian nationalists as enemies of Bolshevism, though he disapproved of Ukrainian separatism. From Petrograd he traveled through Moscow and Kiev to the Don.[43] He tried to convince other socialists to help the White generals, arguing that otherwise these generals would become even more conservative. Savinkov had not expected to win cooperation easily, but the hostility he found in Novocherkassk surpassed his worst fears.[44]

Savinkov and his associate, Vendziagolskii, arrived in Novocherkassk at the end of December. Kornilov at first refused to meet him, and even the sensible Kaledin kept Savinkov and Vendziagolskii waiting before informing them that he was too busy to see them.[45] Kaledin later relented and persuaded Kornilov to receive the socialist politicians. However, Kornilov delivered a harangue blaming and threatening communists, socialists, and democrats alike; he held the entire intelligentsia—democratic revolutionaries, soviets, and commissars—responsible for Russia's troubles.[46] Savinkov's interview with Alekseev was more successful. He argued that the Volunteer Army would not be able to gain broad support without the participation of socialists and would inevitably be associated with blind counterrevolution.

The generals disagreed about what form, if any, Savinkov's participation in the Volunteer Army should take. Kaledin and Alekseev thought that the inclusion of socialists in the army's leadership would allay the Cossacks' distrust. Kornilov at first opposed all cooperation, but he finally accepted Alekseev's argument that if Savinkov started organizing alone, it would harm the army.[47] Unlike Kornilov, Denikin did not relent; he did not even appear at meetings where Savinkov was present. When he met Savinkov's associate, Vendziagolskii, he refused to shake hands.[48] Although Lukomskii shared Denikin's dislike for Savinkov, on one occasion he asked the Social Revolutionary what he thought of the possibility of cooperation. Lukomskii gives Savinkov's answer in his memoirs:

> General, I know well that our political views are not similar. But now we have the same aim and the same road—that is, to overthrow the Bolsheviks and save Russia. In the future, of course, we will again become political enemies, but for the time being I definitely declare and promise that from my side there will be no action against you which would be based on our personal relations.[49]

Savinkov grew tired of the long debates about his personal role and submitted an ultimatum: if in two hours the meeting of generals and politicians did not accept his conditions, he would regain his "freedom of action."[50] By this he probably meant that he would create a military organization of his own. The ultimatum was effective and Savinkov's conditions were accepted. As a result, four socialists entered the council: Savinkov, Vendziagolskii, and two Don socialists who had been instrumental in working out the agreement about parity—P. M. Agaev and S. P. Mazurenko.

The agreement with Savinkov was less significant than it seemed. The council had vaguely defined rights and purposes and it could do nothing over Kornilov's opposition. When the army moved to Rostov two or three weeks after the founding of the council, it was disbanded altogether. At this time Alekseev entrusted Savinkov with the organization of foreign propaganda and Vendziagolskii with the direction of matters relating to nationalities. However, the officers' hostility toward the socialists was so strong that they were unable to fulfill their tasks. Even their lives, especially Savinkov's, were in constant danger. Dobrynskii and Zavoiko organized an attempt on Savinkov's life, and the revolutionary saved himself only by his own courage.[51] General Romanovskii, who according to Vendziagolskii, was the only man in the military who understood the importance of collaboration with the socialists, suggested to Savinkov and Vendziagolskii that they leave, because "here your enemies are stronger than your friends."[52] When, in the middle of January, Alekseev asked Savinkov to go to Moscow and represent the Volunteer Army there, Savinkov accepted. At the same time Vendziagolskii was sent to Kiev.

Savinkov's short stay with the Volunteer Army showed how deep were the wounds caused by the "Kornilov affair." The officers did not want to work with the socialists, even with those as far to the right as Savinkov. In his memoirs Denikin blames Savinkov for not having won over the socialist circles in Moscow for the Volunteer Army. From the history of Savinkov's stay in Novocherkassk it is clear that he was not the only one to blame.[53]

The small Volunteer Army, weakened by internal dissension, had to operate in a hostile atmosphere. Workers, peasants, and Cossacks, for different reasons and in varying degrees, disliked the officers who gathered in Novocherkassk. The majority of the Cossacks did not sympathize with the Bolsheviks and many simply tried to wish away the Civil War. They argued, not without reason, that without the presence of a counter-revolutionary army the Bolsheviks would leave the Don alone for the time being. The hostility between the Cossacks, concerned with neutrality and local autonomy, and the White officers, interested in the Don as a basis for military operations against Russia, had started as early as the beginning of the Alekseev Organization and it was to persist until the end of the Civil War.

Kaledin, a faithful officer of the Imperial Russian Army, gave full support to Alekseev and his fellow officers, even at the price of increased hostility among his constituents. To avoid embarrassing the Ataman, and also for the sake of self-preservation (the small army could not defend itself against the Cossacks), the Alekseev Organization operated in semi-secrecy until the Rostov expedition in the middle of December. Even that victory only slightly strengthened the army's position in the Don. Although the generals, who came from Bykhov at the time when the fighting in Rostov had already begun, were well received by the Ataman, nevertheless, he felt compelled to ask them to leave the Don, at least temporarily.[54]

Romanovskii was allowed to stay in Novocherkassk either because he was less well-known than the other generals or because he was considered more liberal. But Lukomskii had to go to Vladikavkaz, and Denikin and Markov to Ekaterinodar, at least for a brief period. After they returned, they still tried to attract as little attention as possible and therefore did not wear uniforms. Kornilov's arrival was kept secret even from the officers for over ten days.[55]

General Alekseev understood the importance of good relations with the Cossacks and frequently asked his soldiers to use extreme tact. Alekseev's warnings, however, were not effective. Soldiers of the White army felt bitter that the burden of the defense of the Don fell entirely on their shoulders, and this bitterness frequently resulted in aggressive, provocative behavior. The worst example of this was the scheme of General Kornilov's aide, Zavoiko, who prepared the overthrow of Ataman Kaledin in order to elect General Kornilov in his place. The feverish atmosphere of Novocherkassk produced no more infantile scheme than this. Zavoiko did not understand that the Cossacks were opposed to the anti-Communist struggle and that Kaledin was a friend without whom the army could never have been started. Kornilov found out about Zavoiko's plan and ordered Zavoiko to leave the Cossack capital within twenty-four hours; however, rumors of Zavoiko's enterprise reached the Ataman and caused understandable indignation.[56]

The *inogorodnye*, not surprisingly, were even more hostile than the Cossacks to Alekseev's organization. Kaledin, who wanted to unite the population of the Don against the Bolsheviks and bring the *inogorodnye* into the government, found that the most important obstacle to cooperation was the objection of their representatives to the presence of an anti-Bolshevik army in the Don. To overcome this hostility Kaledin's second in command, M. P. Bogaevskii, arranged a meeting between General Alekseev and representatives of the *inogorodnye* on January 31.[57] From descriptions of this meeting by participants it appears that Alekseev made a very favorable impression on his political enemies. He emphasized that the army was cooperating with socialist politicians and mentioned the names of Plekhanov, Argunov, Savinkov, and Vendziagolskii as friends of the Army. Alekseev answered questions like these patiently:

> If you have, General, as you say, contact with democratic circles— continued Brykin [an *inogorodnye* representative]—then why do members of your organization never restrain themselves in their suspicion of democratic organizations and use expressions like "Council of Deputies of Dogs?" [*Sovet Sobachikh Delegatov*].[58]

Alekseev asked indulgence for the behavior of his soldiers, stressing their past sufferings, and emphasized that the Volunteer Army would not interfere in local politics, so that the socialists and the *inogorodnye* in general had nothing to fear. Alekseev's diplomacy may have gained the sympathy of some of the *inogorodnye* leaders, but the great majority of the population remained irrevocably hostile.

One of the reasons for moving the army to Rostov was to get away from the interference of the Don government. But whereas in Novocherkassk the army had faced only covert hostility, in Rostov the workers' hatred for the White army was so strong that it became a major problem simply to maintain the security of officers.

The army moved to Rostov on January 30.[59] By this time the population of the city knew that the arrival of the Red Army was only a matter of time, and the workers waited for the communists as liberators. Prophecies were rife in the city of the "good things" which were bound to happen upon the arrival of the Bolsheviks.[60] As the defeat of the Whites was increasingly taken for granted, the hatred of the workers for the officers was more and more openly exhibited. It was dangerous for officers to walk in the streets at night. On one occasion, at a political rally, the workers of Bataisk, a suburb of Rostov, lynched four unarmed officers. More than once Rostov was close to massacre.[61]

The Volunteer Army could not even count on the support of the wealthy inhabitants of the town. It is true that they collected 6.5 million rubles (of which the Volunteer Army received only two million) for the fight against the Bolsheviks, but they were unwilling to do anything more.[62] The committee formed for the defense of the town was completely inactive, and this angered the White officers, who felt misunderstood and neglected.[63]

DEFEAT

The anti-Bolshevik movement on the Don was living on borrowed time. There were three sources of danger: first, the workers of the Don, who had suffered a setback in the defeat of their uprising in Rostov, but were far from crushed; second, the dissatisfied Cossacks who had rejected Kaledin's government and formed their own; and third, the Red Army, victorious in the Ukraine, was now approaching the Don. Any one of these forces was numerically superior to the combined strength of the Volunteer Army and Kaledin's reliable soldiers; a coordinated attack of the three pro-Soviet forces made the defeat of the Whites inevitable. Only lack of discipline and cooperation among its enemies saved the Volunteer Army from total annihilation. The Red commanders who could not believe that the anti-Bolshevik forces were as weak as they seemed were excessively cautious. Their error is excusable for no one in the country, either the Bolsheviks or their enemies, knew how little determined support there was for anti-Bolshevism.

The fate of the Volunteer Army on the Don and the survival of Kaledin's government were inextricably tied to each other. The Don would have been overrun by the Bolsheviks much more easily without the Volunteer Army—the Red Army progressed much faster in the Ukraine than on the Don—but the small Volunteer Army could not defend the Don without substantial help from the Cossacks.[64]

The formation of the parity government did not reverse the tide which was running against the Kaledin regime. Parity existed for less than two months, under very unfavorable circumstances, and this short time was not enough to diminish the mutual distrust of Cossacks and *inogorodnye*, which was the legacy of many decades.

The projected Constituent Assembly of the Don did not materialize, partly because the northern part of the *voisko* was already occupied by the Bolsheviks and therefore could not send delegates, and partly because the meeting of the *inogorodnye* which took place in Novocherkassk on January 11 and 12 was hostile to the idea of parity government and to Kaledin. The *inogorodnye* were reluctant to fight the Bolsheviks because they feared that fighting would merely help to set up a Cossack dictatorship. It showed the temper of the *inogorodnye* that 40 of the 150 delegates were Bolsheviks, and that the socialist Mazurenko brothers, two of the chief architects of parity government, did not get elected because they were regarded as too moderate.[65] The meetings were extraordinarily stormy. The Bolshevik delegates kept interrupting the speeches of Kaledin and M. P. Bogaevskii with shouts of: "executioners!" and "down with counter-revolutionaries."[66] As a result of Cossack concessions (the most important among them was the promise of three million *desiatin* land for the *inogorodnye* and general amnesty), the majority of the delegates conditionally accepted the necessity of fighting the Bolsheviks. However, Bogaevskii and Kaledin were not able to prevent the passing of a resolution hostile to the Volunteer Army.

In spite of the good faith of both Cossack and *inogorodnye* leaders in desiring cooperation, the parity arrangement did not work. The major cause of the failure was that the ministers of the new government were leaders without followers; they could do nothing to persuade either the *inogorodnye* or the Cossacks to fight the Bolsheviks. Meetings of the government were more like political gatherings than business sessions. The *inogorodnye* representatives were responsible to a radical electorate and therefore on many issues they had to take positions vastly different from the Cossack ministers. The latter regarded this as sabotage. Before every session of the government the *inogorodnye* and the Cossacks decided separately what positions to take on each individual issue.[67] The civil servants, almost all Cossacks, continued to report to Cossack ministers. The *inogorodnye* ministers had no real political experience and the Cossack ministers consequently made most of the important decisions.

The government was gradually losing control over events. The Bolsheviks organized undisturbed even in Novocherkassk. In mid-January, a revolutionary committee was formed in the capital which maintained relations with the other Red forces.[68] The disintegration reached such proportions that the Bolsheviks were able to print their newspaper, *Maidan*, unhindered on the government press.[69]

Kaledin had to recognize that existing Cossack units were more of an avant-garde for the Bolsheviks than a defensive force. The government still had sixty regiments, but they were valueless.[70] When the soldiers began selling their weapons, and at times even their officers, to the Bolsheviks, the wisest thing to do was to disperse existing units.[71]

The only units remaining available to the government were voluntary partisan formations which, like the Volunteer Army, were made up of officers and schoolboys. The best partisan unit, about 150 men strong, was the first, formed by Esaul V. M. Chernetsov on December 13, in connection with the Bolshevik uprising in Rostov.[72] Chernetsov had led a partisan detachment which had operated behind the German lines during the World War.[73] During the term of the Provisional Government he had commanded a Cossack unit which maintained order among striking miners in the Donets basin. Since his detachment was the main force at Kaledin's disposal, its short existence was an active one. It was sent to different parts of the voisko, wherever the authority of the government needed to be defended.

The nearly powerless Kaledin government could survive only as long as it did not have to face an organized opposition. Spurred on by the approach of Soviet troops, the soldiers of anti-Kaledin Cossack regiments, and the Cossacks of the northern, poorer districts of the voisko decided to form a military revolutionary committee on January 20. The meeting of the committee on January 23 in stanitsa Kamenskaia at which 21 regiments were represented, declared Ataman Kaledin's government deposed and elected Podtelkov as president of the Military Revolutionary Committee and M. Krivoshlykov as his lieutenant.[74]

The new revolutionary committee was not a Bolshevik organization—both Podtelkov and Krivoshlykov were Left Social Revolutionaries—and it did not have firm ties with either Petrograd or the approaching Red Army. Its successes and popularity can be explained by the fact that it expressed the widely shared feeling that once the Kaledin's "counter-revolutionary" regime was overthrown and Kornilov's army chased out of the Don territory, then Soviets and Cossacks could coexist. Interestingly enough, the politics of the Revolutionary Committee were rather less progressive than the politics of the "counter-revolutionary" Novocherkassk government: unlike Kaledin, Podtelkov said nothing about giving Cossack lands to the *inogorodnye;* unlike Kaledin, Podtelkov made no effort to win over the *inogorodnye* and the miners in the armed struggle. In fact, the Revolutionary Committee turned down the miners' offer of military help, saying that this would have a bad effect on the Cossacks.[75] From the point of view of the Bolsheviks there was only one real difference between the Kamenskaia organization and the Novocherkassk government: Kaledin refused to recognize Soviet power.

Realizing the weakness of his position, Kaledin initiated negotiations with the Military Revolutionary Committee, which began in Novocherkassk on January 28. Podtelkov, who headed the Kamenskaia delegation, demanded complete power, the dissolution of the *krug* and of partisan units, and the expulsion of the Volunteer Army. In his reply the Ataman disputed the Committee's claim to represent the Don, but he promised to negotiate with leaders of the approaching Red Army and asked the Revolutionary Committee not to attack while these negotiations were in progress.[76] While Podtelkov, Krivoshlykov, and four of their comrades were debating with Cossack members of the Novocherkassk government, the report came in that Chernetsov had driven the Revolutionary Committee from Kamenskaia and also reoccupied the town of Milerovo. Since the two sides had agreed on a cease fire for the duration of the negotiations, the delegation from Kamenskaia with good reason regarded Chernetsov's action as treachery. Kaledin was not the kind of man to violate his word, and it seems very likely that Chernetsov acted without the Ataman's knowledge, but however it was, after this event there could be no more bargaining.[77]

With the renewal of hostilities against the Revolutionary Committee two fronts developed: the Don Cossacks—that is, Chernetsov's detachment—defended Novocherkassk from the North against the troops of the Revolutionary Committee, and the Red Army approaching the Don from the West confronted the Volunteer Army. In spite of occasional victories by the Whites on both fronts, the numerical superiority of the Reds was so great that they could not be stopped. Kornilov and Kaledin frequently turned to each other for help, each believing that the situation on his front was more threatening.

The Soviet troops had the initiative. After their victory in the Ukraine, the Don became the primary theater for the Bolsheviks. Early in January, Antonov-Ovseenko, the conqueror of the Ukraine, began to execute his plans. He first wanted to unite the indigenous anti-Kaledin forces of the Don and then meet an invading small Red force under Petrov, which was coming South from Voronezh; finally he planned to turn to the South and join with the 39th Infantry Division, which was in the North Caucasus. This division was under Bolshevik influence and Antonov-Ovseenko hoped to use it in further battles. On January 8 Antonov-Ovseenko divided the Soviet troops into two groups: the main forces under Sivers turned to the South and threatered Taganrog and Rostov, while another unit under Sablin moved to the East to unite with Petrov.[78]

In spite of the enormous superiority of the Red Army, the Don invasion bogged down. Red troops everywhere fought with little enthusiasm and on one front they did not fight at all, as had happened in the beginning of December with the 39th Division and the 8th Cossack Division, the Cossack regiments at Cherrkovo and the soldiers of Petrov agreed on a truce and neither the Bolshevik nor the Cossack leaders could prevent it. Among the Red armies only Sivers' army was still advancing.[79]

It was the formation of Podtelkov's Military Revolutionary Committee and then Chernetsov's violation of the truce which reactivated the fronts. At first Chernetsov's Cossacks performed well. With the aid of battery from the Volunteer Army, Chernetsov succeeded in expelling the Military Revolutionary Committee from its headquarters, and on January 31 at Likhaia he inflicted serious casualties on Sablin's troops. But this was Chernetsov's last victory. On February 3 he was surrounded and his hundred partisans had to surrender. At nightfall he attacked the Red Commander, Podtelkov, with his bare hands; in the confusion many of his partisans escaped, but Chernetsov was killed on the spot.[80]

After the dispersal of Chernetsov's unit, Sablin and Petrov could unite without opposition. Kaledin now had only small, uncoordinated partisan bands, and they could not form a front again. Novocherkassk remained unprotected.

While the headquarters of the Volunteer Army were in Novocherkassk, the leaders of the army lived up to their stated policy of non-interference in the internal affairs of the Don. The move to Rostov changed this. In the district of Rostov-Taganrog the authority of the Ataman was only a formality, and here the Volunteer Army deliberately adopted policies different from those of the Ataman. While Kaledin persisted in his effort to reconcile all segments of the population, the Volunteer Army suppressed workers' organizations.[81] Neither policy could have been successful at this time: the workers and a large segment of the *inogorodnye* were irreconcilably hostile to Kaledin. The Volunteer Army was not strong enough to suppress the opposition, and lack of coordination between Army headquarters and the Ataman made matters worse.

In the second half of January, Sivers' army of 10,000 approached the territory controlled by the Volunteer Army. In the first skirmishes the Whites did well: at Matveev Kurgan on January 25, a small, well-disciplined unit under Colonel Kutepov made the Reds temporarily withdraw.[82]

However, the Volunteer Army's hope of holding the front was shattered by the Taganrog workers' uprising on January 27.[83] Since production in the factories had stopped and wages had not been paid, the atmosphere among the workers was explosive. When a White soldier killed a worker of the Baltic factory, a Bolshevik stronghold for months, the funeral became a political demonstration in which 50,000 workers participated. The Volunteer Army authorities wanted to prevent the demonstration, but they lacked the strength. The fighting which began in the city was unlike anything that had occurred since the beginning of the Revolution. The workers and soldiers were not reluctant to shoot at each other. The ferocity of the fighting was the first indication of the nature of the Civil War, which was getting under way. Here there was no question of negotiations. When twelve armed workers ran out of ammunition and were captured, the junkers put out their eyes, cut off their noses, and buried them alive with dead dogs. The other side did not lag behind in savagery. White soldiers who were surrounded in a wine cellar were burned alive. No one was allowed to escape.[84]

Kutepov, facing Sivers, had to send reinforcements to Taganrog, but the city could not be saved. The Volunteer Army could spare only 500 soldiers and this was not enough to subdue 5,000 determined, armed workers. The only hope for the Army was that the workers would run out of ammunition; therefore, the fate of the city was decided by the battle for the arsenal. When the insurgents took the arsenal, the 200 soldiers who survived withdrew.[85] Taganrog was in the hands of the insurgents on February 2 and Sivers renewed his advance on February 3. Five days later the Red Army units and the workers of Taganrog joined forces.[86]

The disastrous military developments induced the leaders of the Volunteer Army to prepare for the evacuation of the Don. From the point of view of the cause they represented—liberation of Russia from the Bolsheviks—sacrificing the army for the defense of Rostov and Novocherkassk would not have made sense. Kornilov's and Alekseev's decision to leave the Don was the direct result of the 39th Division's attack on Bataisk. The division, which had been under Bolshevik control since the November Revolution, was engaged in a struggle against the Kuban Cossack government, nevertheless in the first half of February it was strong enough to threaten Bataisk and thus cut off the line of retreat for the Volunteer Army.

Kaledin, perhaps understandably, saw the situation differently from the generals in Rostov. He was bitterly disappointed when he first heard of the possibility that the Volunteer Army might retreat from the Don.[87] He asked Alekseev and Kornilov to come to his headquarters to discuss what should be done, but by February 8 the military situation was so uncertain that neither of the leaders wanted to leave the army and so General Lukomskii was sent in their stead. Kaledin learned from Lukomskii that the final decision had been taken. The envoy of the Volunteer Army tried in vain to persuade the Ataman to join the march to the Kuban.[88] On February 12 Kaledin convened his government, observed that the situation was hopeless, and recommended resignation of the government and surrender to the Novocherkassk city Duma. Two hours later Kaledin shot himself through the heart.

Perhaps the suicide of their Ataman impressed the Cossacks, for there was a new flicker of enthusiasm for the anti-Bolshevik cause. The city Duma proved incapable of governing, but the Cossacks of

Novocherkassk *stanitsa* elected as Provisional Ataman A. M. Nazarov, who, unlike Kaledin, believed in the possibility of continuing the fight.[89]

The *krug* was scheduled to meet on February 17. The larger part of the Don territory was already under Bolshevik occupation and therefore there could be no question of new elections. Since only those representatives of the three previous *krugs* who were still in Novocherkassk participated in the meetings, it came to be called "little *krug*." There was to be a Congress of *inogorodnye*, but this did not take place because the delegates did not come to the meeting; the idea of parity died with Kaledin. The *krug*, adopting an irreconcilable attitude toward the Bolsheviks at the first meeting, introduced general mobilization and the death penalty, sent a delegation to the Volunteer Army asking it to remain and help fight the Bolsheviks, and confirmed Nazarov in the post of Ataman.[90]

When the 6th Cossack Regiment arrived from the front it was regarded as a miracle; the regiment marched in the streets of Novocherkassk with complete discipline; it had no commissars and no committees, and the soldiers announced their willingness to fight. Against the undisciplined Red troops a single such regiment might have saved the Don. After much speech making and celebration the regiment was sent to the front.[91] Under the impact of newly found enthusiasm the Volunteer Army was reconsidering its departure and again sent General Lukomskii to Novocherkassk as permanent representative.[92]

What many took for the first signs of life in the new Don were in fact the last convulsions of the old. The volunteer units which had been formed a few days before by old Cossacks soon fell apart. The 6th Don Cossack Regiment, the pride of the *voisko*, went to the front on February 19 but two days later refused to fight. The *krug*, which had opened in such an uncompromising mood, soon sent a delegation to Sablin, asking why the Soviet armies had come to the Don, and why the fighting should continue now that Kaledin was dead and the *inogorodnye* had a role in the government (which was already untrue).

On February 20, Nazarov notified the Volunteer Army that the Cossacks were incapable of continued resistance. Kornilov decided to evacuate his army on the night of February 21. The evacuation took place in perfect order; on February 23 the army marched through Aksai to Olginskaia, where it regrouped. There was no need to make a decision about the direction of the march because the Bolsheviks left only one route free.

Lukomskii tried to persuade Nazarov, as earlier he had tried to persuade Kaledin, to join the march of the Volunteer Army, but the Ataman thought the Bolsheviks would not harm the elected representative of the Cossacks.[93]

Sivers entered Rostov on February 23. Sablin could have taken Novocherkassk on the same day, but he waited for the troops of the Revolutionary Committee to take the city. While the *krug* was discussing Sablin's answer on February 25, the soldiers of the Military Revolutionary Committee under the command of Golubov occupied Novocherkassk. The President of the *krug*, Voloshinov, and Ataman Nazarov were arrested and executed six days later.

Under Field Ataman Popov, 1,500 Cossacks left Novocherkassk to start on a march which was to last for two months. The evacuation took place in great disorder: many Cossacks and officers who would have liked to join the march realized too late that the small army had already left.[94]

With the occupation of the Don the Bolsheviks completed the conquest of the country: by the end of February 1918 Soviet authority was recognized almost everywhere in Russia. The salvo from the battleship *Aurora* signaled the beginning of the November Revolution; the execution of Nazarov and Voloshinov marked its completion.

CHAPTER 4

The Ice March

The period of the Ice March was the heroic age of the Volunteer Army. Bolshevik successes had been uninterrupted and the White forces had been steadily weakening, yet the few thousand men who left Rostov at the end of February 1918 kept their morale. United by a boundless hatred of the enemy, the soldiers performed miracles of military accomplishment; the world had seen few armies of comparable size with greater fighting ability.

In spite of terrible privations suffered at this time by the army, and in spite of the hostility of the surrounding population, the soldiers who participated in the Ice March were keenly aware of its drama. The immense sufferings and incredible victories of this period quickly became legends, and later played an important role in the development of the White movement, binding together the army's leadership and giving pride to its soldiers. Even in exile, White Russians drew strength from remembering these moments of greatest heroism.[1]

DECISION AT OLGINSKAIA

In retrospect it is clear that the Bolsheviks made a great blunder in allowing the Volunteer Army to escape from Rostov. The city had been surrounded on three sides, and with better leadership and discipline the Red Army could have closed the circle. V. A. Antonov-Ovseenko, the Commander-in-Chief of the Southern forces, ordered the 112th Regiment to occupy Olginskaia and thereby cut the Volunteer Army's line of retreat, but instead of carrying out the order the regiment marched to Stavropol province and dispersed there.[2] The fifteen hundred Cossacks belonging to Field Ataman P. Kh. Popov also succeeded in escaping from Novocherkassk because of the lack of discipline among their enemies; V. S. Golubov disobeyed the order of the Rostov Military Revolutionary Committee to pursue Popov.[3] Since Antonov-Ovseenko was most concerned at the time about the German invasion of the Ukraine, he could not pay sufficient attention to eliminating the remnants of the White forces.[4] He hoped that a strong Soviet regime would be established on the Kuban and that the Volunteer Army, unable to find a base in either Cossack *voisko*, would simply fall apart.[5]

The bulk of the Volunteer Army left Rostov marching east on the northern side of the Don, but a regiment under General Markov crossed the Don at Rostov and marched on the other bank. Even at the very beginning of the march the Army could not help being aware of the hostility of the population. Kornilov chose *stanitsa* Aksaiskaia as the first rest place, and Denikin and Romanovskii had to negotiate for two hours with the Cossacks, who, fearing the anger of the Bolsheviks, did not want to allow the army to spend the night there.[6] Before permission was finally given, the generals had to promise that there would be no fighting in the *stanitsa* under any circumstances, and that the army would move on the next morning.

On February 23 the army crossed the Don at Aksaiskaia. The Reds did not pursue, but two airplanes harassed the long thin line of soldiers as they marched across the ice. The airplanes flew very high and the bombs they dropped fell harmlessly wide of the mark.[7] The greatest danger was the thinness of the ice at spots, but the crossing took place without incident.[8]

On the afternoon of February 23 the entire army arrived at *stanitsa* Olginskaia. The spirits of the soldiers, which had been very low when they left Rostov, rose somewhat because of the successful river crossing.[9] For the time being they could rest at Olginskaia safe from unexpected attack. The army remained there for four days, waiting for the Cossacks of Ataman Popov, drawing up plans and being reorganized for an extended march.

The Cossacks of Olginskaia, a rich settlement as yet untouched by war and revolution, received the army much more hospitably than had the inhabitants of Aksaiskaia. A delegation of five older Cossacks came to see Kornilov, asking how they could help. Pleased with this offer, Kornilov set up a commission under General Bogaevskii to consult with the representatives of the *stanitsa*. The Cossacks promised 100 soldiers and 50 horsemen, an offer which was not particularly generous since it was a very large settlement. The next day there appeared some twenty-odd children of about fourteen, not a single adult among them. Bogaevskii asked why they had come:

> Did your grandfathers tell you that you are going to march with the kadets* and fight against the Bolsheviks? No, we did not agree to do that [they said], and all began to yell at the same time, the happy expression disappearing from their faces. Well [asked Bogaevskii], you have horses, who sent them here? Terrified, they interrupted each other and said that they had brought the horses from the watering place. They had simply met an old man who told them to go to the square, what for they did not know.

As it turned out, the children had expected to march in a parade. Not a single Cossack of Olginskaia joined the Volunteer Army.[10]

Kornilov consolidated twenty-five small units, many of which had only a few dozen soldiers, into larger ones.[11] He formed three regiments and a battalion: The "Officer" regiment under General Markov, the "Kornilov" regiment under Colonel Nezhintsev, and the "Partisan" regiment made up mostly of remnants of Cossack partisan units under General A. P. Bogaevskii. General Borovskii

---

*The Russian peasants, playing on the meaning of the word kadet (a student in a military school) and the abbreviation Kadet (Ka De for Constitutional Democratic Party), called the soldiers of the Volunteer Army kadets. The Army and the politicians were distressed by the confusion of names. The Army wanted to have nothing to do with any of the political parties, and the Party, which had come into being to spread the principles of liberalism and legality, was very much embarrassed by many actions of the Army. The peasants, however, were perceptive; the leaders of the Army and Kadet politicians had a very similar image of the future Russia (see chapter 7).

commanded the "Junker" battalion which included the few officers who had enlisted in Rostov. Besides these four units which comprised the great majority of fighting men, the army had small cavalry detachments, consisting almost entirely of Don Cossacks. Many of these Cossacks joined the army here in Olginskaia, having escaped from Novocherkassk. The Volunteer Army also had a small artillery division with eight guns and a technical detachment which consisted entirely of Czechs and Slovaks who had joined the army while it was still in Novocherkassk.[12]

In addition to its four thousand fighting men[13] the army carried with it a civilian retinue of about a thousand persons. These were politicians (such as V. N. Lvov, L. V. Polovtsev, L. N. Novosiltsev, N. P. Shchetnina), journalists, professors, soldiers' wives, and nurses.[14] This large group of non-combatants hindered the army's progress.

The soldiers did not have enough munitions—each had only a few hundred rounds—and there were only 600 or 700 shells for eight guns. Lacking a radio transmitter, the army became completely cut off from the outside world during the Ice March. General Elsner, who had been entrusted with preparations for the march in Rostov, must have been responsible for some of the inadequacies. He had plenty of time to organize, and the soldiers could have brought a larger quantity of weapons and horses with them.[15] On the other hand, the Volunteer Army did have enough money. General Alekseev brought six million rubles with him, and therefore, at least at the beginning of the campaign, the army paid, and paid well, for the food it took from the population.[16]

It is difficult to form a clear picture of the soldiers' morale. All descriptions, naturally, come from participants, and it is likely that the memorialists looking back are better able to recall the heroism than the grumbling and loss of confidence which must also have been part of the ordeal. Still, there is no reason to doubt that morale was generally high, except, perhaps, during the few days following the evacuation of Rostov. The soldiers had unlimited faith in their commanders and a boundless hatred for their enemies. Most of them preferred death to capture by the Reds—there were several instances when wounded soldiers committed suicide—and such desperation enhances fighting spirit.[17] On the other hand, general uncertainty about the future, the reluctance of some officers to serve as privates, and ever-present political quarrels must have affected morale adversely.

The generals did not communicate to their soldiers the decision taken at Olginskaia to march to the Kuban. Consequently, wild rumors circulated about the destination of the march: some thought they were walking to Siberia, others expected to turn back to Central Russia, and still others believed that their destination was the Caucasus.[18]

The Army was top-heavy, as shown by the distribution of ranks at the end of the campaign: three generals, eight lieutenant-generals, 25 major-generals, 199 colonels, 50 lieutenant-colonels, 215 captains, 251 staff captains, 394 lieutenants, 535 cornets, 688 ensigns, 364 under-officers, 437 junkers, 235 corporals, 15 sailors, 148 medical personnel, and 118 clerks.[19] Many colonels and captains fought as privates, but others refused. For example, Markov entrusted a squadron to a certain Colonel Borisov, but this man considered the command of a squadron beneath his dignity and did not take the assignment.[20]

Even in this fervently anti-Bolshevik army there were political disagreements, because inevitably some were more conservative than othrs. Alekseev had to summon Denikin on the second day of the army's stay in Olginskaia to ask him to prevent a possible fight between students and junkers because the junkers had called the students socialists.[21] And there were quarrels among the men as to whether the Imperial family should be considered responsible for Russia's defeat in the World War.[22]

The senior army leaders held a series of conferences in order to decide in what direction they should proceed. Some advocated going to the Sal'skaia steppe, around the river Sal' on the left bank of the Don, but others wanted to take the army to Ekaterinodar, the capital of the Kuban. The generals well understood that the fate of the White movement might depend on this decision, yet, as so often in war, the decision had to be made on the basis of insufficient information. None knew what the situation of the Cossack government in Ekaterinodar was, or whether the Sal'skaia steppe would be able to provide food for five thousand people for an extended period.

Kornilov, very uncharacteristically, had no firm views. At first he inclined toward going to the Sal'skaia steppe, but he was willing to reconsider. It was Alekseev and Denikin who wanted to march to Ekaterinodar. The Kuban seemed a better choice to them because they hoped that the Cossacks there would join the Volunteer Army, and then Ekaterinodar could become a base for organizing a large scale anti-Bolshevik movement. They maintained that the Sal'skaia steppe could not supply a large army and pointed out the danger of being surrounded by the Bolsheviks who controlled not only the northern bank of the Don but also the railroad line from Tsaritsyn to Tikhoretskaia to Bataisk. Undoubtedly the men who had commanded large armies only a short time before were influenced by the lessons of the World War, where encirclement always had disastrous consequences.[23]

It is likely that at least Alekseev's preference was influenced by prudence. We know from his correspondence at this time that he was deeply pessimistic.[24] He talked to his comrades about building a large army in Ekaterinodar, but in private he must have considered the dissolution of the army. He wanted to take his soldiers to the Kuban to make it easier for them, if worst came to worst, to escape from Russia through the mountains of the Caucasus.

General P. Kh. Popov, who arrived with his Cossacks, five guns, and 40 machine guns on February 26 insisted that his men would not leave their native Don.[25] When the conference accepted the position of Alekseev and Denikin, Popov departed toward the river Sal'. This was a great loss for the Volunteer Army because Popov's detachment consisted mostly of horsemen, which the Army needed very badly. On February 27 the Army and its civilian entourage, about five thousand people in all, marched out of Olginskaia. They marched fifteen to twenty miles a day.[26] The roads were muddy and walking was difficult, but everyone, except the sick, had to walk. Frequently the army was unable to obtain food, even for money.

The army's route led through Stavropol province, a large part of which was controlled by Bolshevik Soviets.[27] The first battle of the campaign took place on March 6, at Lezhanka, on the border of Stavropol province and the Kuban. A local Bolshevik force, assisted by soldiers of the 39th Division, confronted the Volunteer Army. Markov unexpectedly crossed the small river Egorlyk with his regiment and this move surprised the enemy so much that it withdrew. Markov, however, had no cavalry and could not pursue the Bolsheviks.[28] Most of the inhabitants of the *stanitsa* must have sympathized with the Reds, because about half the people fled from the victorious army.[29] The Whites managed to capture dozens of officers of the 39th Division in the battle. Kornilov had them court-martialed, but the court freed them on the condition that they join the Volunteer Army.[30] The first victory of the army greatly improved morale and the speed of the march increased substantially.

On March 9 the army entered the Kuban, where it found that the local Cossacks—unlike the Don Cossacks—were distinctly favorable to the White cause. Frequently they took no money for food, and more important, a sizeable number of Kuban Cossacks enlisted. In *stanitsa* Nezamaevskaia, the army gained 140 recruits and in Vyselok an additional four to five hundred.[31]

The most dangerous moments of the march came when the army had to cross railroad lines. It was especially difficult to cross the main Vladikavkaz-Rostov line, for this had to be done between the Bolshevik-held stations of Sosyka and Tikhoretskaia. The Whites approached the danger zone soundlessly at night while the Czech engineer battalion cut the rails. As the soldiers crossed the tracks, the Bolshevik armored train could be seen in the distance, but it could come no closer.[32]

In the Kuban, the first fighting took place at *stanitsa* Berezanskaia on March 14. Even though the Whites easily forced their enemies to flee, the battle was very disappointing for the volunteers because the enemies were not Bolshevik soldiers of the 39th Division but local Cossacks and *inogorodnye*. The *stanitsa* meeting, upon hearing of the Whites' advance, had decided to fight the "kadets."[33]

The next battle was much more serious. For some time Kornilov had tried to avoid meeting Bolshevik military units because he wanted to arrive at Ekaterinodar as quickly as possible, but now that the Cossack capital was not far away he hoped to help the Cossack government by engaging the main Bolshevik army. Also the Volunteer Army was running out of munitions, and there was no other solution but to take them from the enemy. White intelligence reported that at the Korenovskaia railroad station they would encounter only the rear guard of the Reds, and this report led Kornilov to decide on the attack. The report, however, was erroneous; the Volunteer Army encountered ten thousand Bolshevik soldiers at Korenovskaia. The battle which ensued was the Army's bloodiest to that date: in four days of continuous fighting the Whites lost 400 men. Many times it appeared that they would be forced to retreat by the much larger Bolshevik army. It is very likely that the Volunteer Army could not have recovered from a defeat at this time. Kornilov used all the reserves and did not spare the last rounds of munitions. The gamble paid off and on March 17 the Whites occupied the railroad station and captured large military stores.[34]

The pleasure of victory was spoiled by the bad news the army received in Korenovskaia: the Kuban government and army had evacuated Ekaterinodar under Bolshevik pressure. Since the purpose of the march was to reach Ekaterinodar in order to unite with the Kuban army, the direction of the march had to be reconsidered. Denikin and Romanovskii believed that the army should continue toward Ekaterinodar and attempt to occupy the city.[35] Kornilov, however, decided otherwise. He thought that the army was too weak and tired for such a task; instead he led his army south of the Kuban river into the Circassian villages, where he hoped that the soldiers could rest and wait for the Kuban army.

Kornilov had to make his decision without the benefit of reliable information about the strength and disposition of enemy troops and without knowledge of the whereabouts of the Kuban army. Moving in the direction of Maikop to secure rest was a serious mistake, for that city had become a Bolshevik stronghold[36] and the left bank of the Kuban was occupied by the Reds. At the time when Kornilov was most anxious to avoid battles, the army was forced to fight continuously. The Whites won "victories," but at the price of heavy casualties. By March 22 the exhausted army was near collapse when the volunteers realized from the sound of distant artillery fire that the Kuban Army could not be far away. On the same day at *stanitsa*

Filipovskoe, the army changed direction; instead of continuing southward, it moved west to join the Kuban army of Pokrovskii.

THE KUBAN AND THE NOVEMBER REVOLUTION

Social and political conditions in the Kuban in November 1917 were much like those in the Don, and consequently repercussions of the Bolshevik revolution were similar in the two *voiska*. But the Kuban was unfortunate in having no one of Kaledin's stature and vision to try to bring the different elements of the population together. A. P. Filimonov, who was elected Ataman on October 25, was a rather narrow-minded conservative who believed that the Cossacks should preserve all their privileges.[37] Immediately following the November Revolution representatives of Cossacks and *inogorodnye* tried to reconcile their differences by working out a compromise. It provided (1) that popularly elected organs should govern the Kuban until the convocation of an all-Russian Constituent Assembly; (2) that local organs of self-government should be elected without distinctions between *inogorodnye* and Cossacks; (3) that three *inogorodnye* would join the *voisko* government.[38] However, largely because of the lack of progressive and imaginative leadership, the Cossack parliament, which was called the *rada* on the Kuban, did not ratify the agreement.

It is true that the Cossacks relented later and on January 25 agreed to the formation of a parity government, which included as many representatives of the Cossacks as of the Russian peasants. But by then it was too late, for the government's authority was recognized only in Ekaterinodar and in the surrounding *stanitsy*. Each side questioned the good faith of the other and under the circumstances parity failed even more miserably on the Kuban than it had on the Don. The population of the Kuban came to be even more polarized than that of the Don: *inogorodnye* listened willingly to Bolshevik propaganda, and the Cossacks were a shade more favorable to the Whites here than in the other Cossack *voisko*.

Filimonov and his fellow leaders placed their hopes on the Cossacks returning from the front, the *frontoviki*, believing that they would defend the status quo against the *inogorodnye* and against the armies of Lenin and Trotskii.[40] But, as on the Don, the returning

Cossack units dispersed as soon as they arrived. Here too, there were moments of hope and disappointment. The First Black Sea Regiment, unlike the others, arrived in Ekaterinodar in perfect order. Filimonov immediately sent it to fight against the Bolsheviks with the mission of recovering some strategically important villages. The regiment proved unreliable and soon had to be dissolved.[41]

Very shortly the Kuban was on the verge of anarchy. As early as November 13, the government had had to disarm a Bolshevik-leaning artillery unit in the capital, a move which was accompanied by shootings, demonstrations, and general disorder.[42] In *stanitsa* Gulkevichi the *inogorodnye* set up a Bolshevik regime and Filimonov had to send a detachment to enforce his authority. As the Whites approached, the local Bolshevik leader, Nikitenko, declared himself loyal to the Ekaterinodar government, but when the force withdrew Nikitenko had Filimonov's representatives executed.[43]

The greatest threat to political stability came from the proximity of the Caucasus front. In vain Filimonov implored General M. A. Przhevalskii, the Commander on the Caucasian front, to stop the flow of soldiers. The General was powerless, and one demobilized regiment after another entered the Kuban.[44] The 39th Infantry Division, abandoning the front, became the mainstay of Bolshevism in the entire Northern Caucasus and its regiments helped to set up soviets in Tikhoretskaia, Torgovaia, Stavropol, Kavkazkaia, and Armavir.[45]

Since regular units proved worthless, the Kuban government tried to counter Bolshevik power by forming volunteer units. The Cossacks, however, did not want to enroll and the only units which came into being—and these without the help of the government were formed by Russian officers who had come to the Kuban in large numbers. The government at first hesitated to encourage these formations, because it correctly understood that open reliance on Russian officers would further alienate a large segment of the population, but soon Filimonov decided to support the officers with a grant of 100,000 rubles.[46] The first unit, formed by Colonel Galaev in the middle of December, had about two hundred volunteers by the middle of January.[47] Galaev, a popular and talented officer, was killed in early February fighting the Bolsheviks.

The second volunteer unit of about a hundred men was formed at the end of December by Captain A. Pokrovskii, a man who was destined to play a great role in the White movement. Pokrovskii had been among the very few Russian pilots in the World War; he was an exceedingly brave and decisive man, but also ambitious, cruel, and without moral scruples—the sort of man who finds it easiest to advance himself in troubled times.

The few hundred Russian officers, of course, in spite of occasional successes, could not prevent the growth of Bolshevik power. By January the Bolsheviks controlled all the major railroad lines on the Kuban and had thus succeeded in cutting ties between the Don and the Ekaterinodar government. This was a great loss for Kaledin, because the Kuban had supplied him with munitions and the flow was now interrupted.[48] It was also a loss for the Volunteer Army because it prevented recruitment. The Army command in Rostov sent 60 men to Ekaterinodar under Captain Ben'kovskii to try to re-establish communications, but the Bolsheviks disarmed the Whites at Timashevskaia and put them into a Novorossisk jail.[49]

Novorossisk and Armavir were the two main Bolshevik centers. It was the Novorossisk group which challenged the Ekaterinodar government first: on January 30 the Soviet sent an ultimatum demanding that the *rada* recognize the authority of the Petrograd government and dissolve all volunteer formations or be prepared to see the Red Army occupy the capital.[50] It is ironic that in the first crucial battle Russian officers had to defend the Kuban capital on their own. The Cossacks, who had protected the old order in Russia so many times before, now needed the help of aliens to maintain order in their own *voisko*.

The Whites had 700 volunteers against the 6000 approaching Bolsheviks.[51] The first encounter took place at Enem, about 13 miles from Ekaterinodar, on February 4. The swift manuevers of the Whites surprised the Reds, who were defeated badly. The officers captured and executed the Red commander, Iakovlev, and took a large supply of munitions from the enemy.[52] In the second battle at Georgie-Afipskaia, which followed two days later, the Whites again managed to surprise and defeat their enemies. Seradze, who succeeded Iakovlev, was wounded and captured. According to the

Bolshevik version he was murdered in the hospital; according to White sources he died on the way to the hospital.[53]

Pokrovskii, the architect of the almost miraculous victories over a numerically superior enemy force, received a hero's welcome in Ekaterinodar and was raised to the rank of Colonel. Some of his friends, probably not without his knowledge, started to work for his nomination as Commander-in-Chief of the Kuban army.[54] In the past few months the army had had three different commanders; two had resigned because they lacked faith in the possibility of victory, and the third, I. E. Gulyg, did nothing in the crucial hours and was widely disliked because of his vanity.[55] The two victories gave a new lease on life to the Kuban army. K. L. Bardizh, the well-known Cossack politician, recruited successfully among the Cossacks of the Taman Eisk district.[56] The Whites managed to establish a solid, circular front against their enemies and protect the capital from all directions. Filimonov called a meeting of the representatives of the rada and government on February 27 to decide on a successor to Gulyg. The participants chose Pokrovskii, even though Uspenskii, the minister of war, opposed it so strongly that he resigned rather than cooperate with Pokrovskii.

When Pokrovskii came to Ekaterinodar to accept his commission from the Ataman, he left his troops under the command of I. Kaminskii. The Bolsheviks started a new attack at this time. Kaminskii, while drunk, withdrew without fighting and allowed the Bolsheviks to take Vyselka on March 1.[57] Kaminskii's irresponsible action had disastrous consequences: it endangered the entire front and ultimately led to the defeat of the Cossack volunteer troops, which had been formed only a very short time before. The Whites could afford no mistakes; it was clear that Ekaterinodar could no longer be held.

Filimonov called a meeting of the representatives of civilian authorities and military men in order to decide what to do in the emergency. Some members of the government argued that the rada and government should be dissolved, and that members should return to their stanitsy to work for an anti-Bolshevik uprising.[58] Others, including L. L. Bych, the premier of the government, and N. S. Riabovol, the speaker of the rada, advocated that the army should leave Ekaterinodar and try to unite with the Volunteer

Army, which they knew had left Rostov. The meeting adopted the
second alternative and preparations were made for evacuation. Riabovol formed a detachment from members of the *rada*, about 120
to 130 men strong. On March 13 an army about the size of the Volunteer Army left Ekaterinodar. The government addressed a last
proclamation to the citizens, and its pathetic tone is significant:

> We turned to you more than once; we called on you to fight
> against anarchy and dissolution long ago. But unfortunately, you,
> Cossacks and *inogorodnye*, became confused by lies and provoca-
> tions and were misled by the pretty but false words of fanatics and
> people who had sold themselves. You gave us no help and support,
> when it was needed, in the holy struggle to protect the Constituent
> Assembly, which could save the fatherland. You gave us no support
> in the struggle to win your right to decide independently the fate
> of your native district. It is painful to express it bluntly, but it is
> true: you were unable to defend your own representatives.[59]

THE NOVO-DMITRIEVSKAIA AGREEMENT AND
THE DEATH OF KORNILOV

The Bolshevik conquest of Ekaterinodar marked the height of
anarchy on the Kuban. There were no front lines. While in some
stanitsy the population was favorably disposed toward the exiled
government, in others it passed Bolshevik resolutions. As in medieval
Europe, armies independent of any central authority played blind
man's buff with each other. Kornilov and Pokrovskii knew nothing
of the strength, intentions, and dispositions of the enemy, and it was
more or less accidental that they were ultimately able to unite their
armies. Neither the Cossacks nor the Volunteer Army had long-
range plans; it seemed impossible to them that Bolshevism could be
victorious in the long run and they merely wanted to survive the
immediate difficulties.

For the five thousand refugees from Ekaterinodar, only three
thousand of them soldiers, the march started with a disappointment.[60] The inhabitants of *stanitsa* Pensenskaia ran away because
they feared the "kadets." But the Whites, even in their dejected
mood, were unwilling to negotiate with the Bolsheviks. The "*rada*
on horseback" turned down the peace offers of a delegation from

Ekaterinodar because it hoped to reconquer the capital with the aid of Kornilov's army.[61]

The following days were spent in aimless wanderings from *stanitsa* to *stanitsa*, and in repeated meetings to discuss the direction of the march. At these meetings the Kuban leaders frequently reversed themselves. On March 22, for example, politicians and military men agreed on a march toward Batalpashinsk, to the southeast of Ekaterinodar, and on the next day a forced march was begun; but on the evening of March 23, it was decided at another meeting to turn toward the Black Sea coast. This apparent aimlessness further depressed the low morale of the group.[62] Hundreds left the march in order to return to Ekaterinodar, or to their native *stanitsy*. The Kuban army and *rada* were on the verge of complete dissolution.

The march toward the sea coast started at night because the group hoped to pass unnoticed between two Bolshevik-held settlements. In order to make the march easier, the Cossacks left a large part of their baggage behind. They could not avoid a battle, however; the Bolsheviks attacked at Kaluzhskaia. While the fighting was going on the news came that the Volunteer Army was in the neighboring village. It was this knowledge which gave courage to Pokrovskii's men to defeat their enemy and win an important victory.[63] Pokrovskii was hastily named General in order to have more prestige when negotiating with the leaders of the Volunteer Army, and together with his chief-of-staff, V. G. Naumenko, he was sent to Shendzhii to meet Kornilov.

Both armies had awaited this meeting for weeks, rightly seeing it as their only hope for success. One would imagine that the meeting between representatives of two harassed, desperate armies would be emotional. It was nothing of the sort. "When Pokrovskii approached General Kornilov's house with his convoy, Kornilov came out on the porch and then quickly returned to his room," wrote Naumenko, an eyewitness.[64] Kornilov regarded himself not as the leader of a few thousand desperate men, but as the representative of Russia, the Commander-in-Chief of all Russian armies. Under the circumstances there could be no question of receiving as an equal a man who a few weeks before had been only a captain. The proper protocol had to be preserved. Instead of Kornilov, Romanovskii and

Markov received the Kuban delegation and invited them to dinner. Only after dinner did Kornilov ask for information about recent events on the Kuban and about the Kuban army. General Alekseev submitted to Pokrovskii the conditions on which the unification of the armies should take place: (1) the Ataman should be subordinate to the commander of the Volunteer Army; (2) the Kuban government and *rada* should be abolished; and (3) the Cossack troops should be absorbed by the volunteer units. Pokrovskii, who was a non-Cossack officer, had no sympathy whatever for the claims of Kuban separatism; nevertheless, he was surprised at the excessive severity of these demands.[65] He argued that the Kuban army should maintain its separate identity and should be under Kornilov's command only temporarily.

> Alekseev burst out: "Colonel—excuse me, I do not know how to address you—we know well how the soldiers feel about this question. Only you do not want to overcome your vanity." Kornilov said sharply: "United army and united command. I do not accept any other situation. Please inform your government of this."[66]

Pokrovskii was entrusted by his government to negotiate an agreement, but Kornilov and Alekseev demanded so much that he did not dare take the responsibility alone. Under these circumstances, no decision was made at the meeting.

The leaders in the Kuban camp disagreed among themselves. Some separatists, like N. S. Riabovol, believed that it would be better to take the army into the mountains rather than sacrifice the autonomy of the Kuban.[67] Others thought that even if the two armies united, the *rada* and the government should disperse rather than compromise themselves by cooperating. However, common sense prevailed and three days later, on March 30, the Kuban sent another delegation to Novo-Dmitrievskaia to negotiate with the leaders of the Volunteer Army.

This time the meeting was somewhat more cordial and both sides made compromises. Perhaps the battle which was raging against the Bolsheviks, practically in front of the house in which the negotiations took place, moderated the generals' and politicians' commitment to principles. Agreement was finally reached on three points:

(1) the Kuban army was to be absorbed by the Volunteer Army; (2) the *rada*, the government, and the Ataman were to continue their activities in cooperation with the army command; and (3) the head of the Kuban army was to become a member of the Kuban government and work to enlist Cossacks into the Army.[68]

The unification roughly doubled the size of the army and its stores of munitions. Kornilov formed three brigades out of the six thousand men who were available. He entrusted the brigades to Generals Markov, Bogaevskii, and Erdeli, respectively. Since many of the Cossacks brought their horses, the Volunteer Army for the first time acquired a sizeable cavalry, which under the conditions of the march was especially important.

After unification the Volunteer Army was more successful in enlisting Cossacks, but perhaps as a consequence, it had to face even more bitter opposition from the *inogorodnye*. The Russian officers were fanatically anti-Bolshevik and treated soldiers of the Red Army with extreme cruelty, but they had nothing against the *inogorodnye* as such. This changed after Novo-Dmitrievskaia, when the Cossacks mistreated *inogorodnye* simply because they were *inogorodnye*. In many instances the anti-Bolshevik cause came to be subordinated to a local Kuban civil war.

The Novo-Dmitrievskaia agreement was the most important step toward transforming the army into something very different from what was originally envisaged. While the army had been organizing in Novocherkassk and Rostov it had very few Cossack members. The first large group to join was A. P. Bogaevskii's, which left Rostov together with the Volunteer Army. Then hundreds of Cossacks fleeing from Novocherkassk chose to enroll in the Volunteer Army in Olginskaia rather than join Field Ataman Popov. Consequently, on entering the Kuban, Cossacks made up one third of the army.[69] The casualty rate in the battles of the campaign had been high, but because enlistment cancelled out the losses the size of the army in Novo-Dmitrievskaia was no smaller than it had been in Olginskaia. The new volunteers were almost exclusively Cossacks. While there is no data available, it is reasonable to believe that before unification Cossacks made up half of the Volunteer Army. On the other hand, Pokrovskii's troops included only a few hundred non-Cossacks. Although Russian officers had been the first to enlist in volunteer formations in Ekaterinodar, by the time of the beginning of the march they were only a small minority.

At Novo-Dmitrievskaia Kornilov, Denikin and Alekseev came to head an overwhelmingly Cossack army, but the generals failed completely to appreciate the significance of this fact. They regarded the Cossacks as ordinary Russians and believed that the desire for autonomy was merely the work of a few rabble-rousers. It is characteristic that Alekseev attributed the desire for an independent Kuban army to Pokrovskii's vanity; and it is even more characteristic of their mentality that Denikin chose to quote Alekseev's statement with approval in his memoirs, though after years of experience he should have known better.[70] The generals' inability to understand that Cossack leaders enjoyed popular support led them to make politically disastrous decisions which in the coming years were to hurt the White cause enormously.

As a result of the bitter struggle which followed between Kuban separatists and Russian nationalist officers, both sides came to question or denounce the Novo-Dmitrievskaia agreement. It is clear, however, that neither side could have survived independently, and in fact both armies had been on the verge of dissolution. Nor would temporary cooperation have been sufficient.[71] If, after the end of the Kuban campaign, the Cossacks had separated from the army, the one thousand or fifteen hundred remaining officers could not have formed an army of any consequence. As the Civil War developed, the size of the armies was growing on both sides; at the end of 1917 a few hundred soldiers could accomplish significant strategic tasks, but this was no longer true by the middle of 1918. Worst of all, a non-Cossack army on the Don or on the Kuban had little chance of growing. The White movement in the Russian south had to harness the energies of the Cossacks or face oblivion. But the Kuban Cossacks also needed the superb military leadership of the best officers of the Imperial Russian Army. Without this leadership, the Cossacks would have formed a fighting force only a little better than the much larger and equally committed Red Army.

Neither side understood the degree of interdependence and drew the necessary conclusions from it. The Cossack politicians should have moderated their demands, or at least postponed them until a more propitious time. The generals of the Volunteer Army should have evaluated their strength and the aspirations of their allies correctly, and given concessions to the Cossacks in matters of local autonomy, preferably with good grace. One the other hand, they should have made every effort to avoid being involved in the local struggle between Cossacks and *inogorodnye*, because being labeled as enemies of the Russian peasant in one area of the country was bound to have national repercussions.

The bitterest battle, the one which was to give its name to the entire campaign, took place between the first and second meetings of representatives of the Kuban and the Volunteer Army. The Volunteer Army, marching from Shendzhii to Novo-Dmitrievskaia on March 28, had to fight the Bolsheviks. The day, which started with sunshine, soon became a rainy one, and then the rain turned to snow and it became very cold. The Bolsheviks were firing from the opposite side of a small river, and the only way for the volunteers to silence the guns was to cross through the shallow icy water. The task was accomplished at a great loss: many officers froze to death. The next day the volunteers took revenge on the captured Bolsheviks for the cruelty of the weather by hanging seven of their leaders.[72]

With the size of his army almost doubled, Kornilov considered himself strong enough to attack the main objective of the march, the Kuban capital. The stakes in this battle were enormous: if the White movement could acquire a base on the Kuban, there was a good possibility of forming a strong Cossack army at a time when the enemy hardly possessed a regular fighting organization. However, in case of defeat, the very existence of the Volunteer Army would be endangered. It was an ambitious move to take the offensive against an army which was three or four times larger, but Kornilov's confidence was based on the unbroken line of victorious battles of the Kuban campaign.

Kornilov planned his strategy carefully. As so often before, he managed to surprise the enemy by crossing the Kuban river west of Ekaterinodar at *stanitsa* Elizavetinskaia. General Kazanovich's regiment easily defeated the small group of Bolsheviks who tried to harass the crossing, and Bogaevskii's brigade successfully got to the other side of the river on April 8.[73] At this point Kornilov made an error. On April 10 he impatiently ordered the attack to begin on Ekaterinodar, before Markov's brigade could also finish the crossing.[74]

Bolshevik resistance was unexpectedly furious. There are no reliable data on the size of the Red Army in the city, but White intelligence estimated that there were about 18,000 soldiers.[75] The Volunteer Army had fought against worse odds and won, but this time the Bolsheviks did not retreat. Perhaps it contributed to the fighting spirit of the Reds that while the battle was going on the first Congress of Soviets on the Kuban took place in the city.[76]

The Reds succeeded in beating back the first wave of attackers even before Markov's brigade could cross the Kuban river. Coordination broke down between the various regiments of the Volunteer Army. Kazanovich, for example, fought his way into the city, but then realized that the Kornilov regiment was not covering his left flank, as he had expected, and he had to withdraw.[77] Casualties on both sides were very high. The Volunteer Army lost some of its ablest leaders, among them Colonel Nezhintsev, perhaps General Kornilov's closest friend. But victims among the Bolsheviks were perhaps five or six times as numerous as among the Whites. The ten to fifteen thousand Bolshevik dead would seem to indicate that the difference between the two sides was not in dedication to a cause but in military skill.[78]

Kornilov called his first war conference since Olginskaia on April 12. The participants sat at the table in unusual gloom: the momentum of the attack against a numerically stronger and better equipped enemy had fizzled out. Kornilov opened the conference in a characteristic manner, by declaring, before asking the opinion of others, that he was planning to continue the attack. Denikin, Romanovskii, and Bogaevskii advised caution and retreat, but Bych and Filimonov supported Kornilov's view. Markov did not participate in the debate, but was gently snoring. When awakened he said he had not slept for 48 hours, and if he was so tired that he was unable to stay awake the ordinary soldier must have been even more exhausted.[79] Finally the conference accepted Alekseev's proposal that the attack continue after a day's rest.[80]

According to the independent testimonies of Generals Denikin, Bogaevskii, and Kazanovich, Kornilov did not believe in the success of the operation, but regarded it as a suicidal venture. He said to Kazanovich: "Of course, we may all fall here, but in my opinion it is better to die with honor. To retreat now would bring certain destruction, because we have no supplies and no munitions. It would be a slow agony."[81]

Kornilov was even more explicit with Denikin, who remained alone with him after the council of war. Denikin said:

> Lavr Georgievich, why are you so inflexible in this matter? [Denikin referred to the planned attack.]
>
> There is no other way out, Anton Ivanovich. If we do not take Ekaterinodar there is nothing left for me but to put a bullet through my head.
>
> You cannot do that. That way thousands of lives would be thrown away. Why do we not retreat from Ekaterinodar, have an extended rest, gain strength, and organize a new operation? In case of the failure of the attack, retreat will be hardly possible.
>
> You will lead them out.
>
> I stood up and said with great excitement: "Your excellency! If General Kornilov commits suicide, then no one will lead your army away—it will perish completely."[82]

On the morning of April 13, a chance shell killed Kornilov; it exploded in the farmhouse where he had his headquarters and the rubble buried him. General Denikin, who immediately assumed provisional command, in vain tried to keep the Commander's death secret. The news had a staggering effect on the soldiers, who had, after five days of fighting, just suffered a bitter defeat. The Volunteer Army was on the verge of panic.

Aside from Kornilov, Markov, a man of soldierly virtue and legendary courage, was perhaps the most popular commander.[83] Denikin was relatively little known among the soldiers. If he was known at all, it was not for his most recent performance, but for his role in the World War as the leader of the famous Iron Division.[84] His assumption of command could not immediately calm the soldiers' anxieties over the future of the army.

Alekseev issued an order the same day in which he informed the soldiers of Kornilov's death and appointed Denikin commander of the army.[85] It is interesting that although he had founded the army and had bitterly contested Kornilov's leadership, Alekseev made no attempt on this occasion to take direction of the army into his own hands. This was probably because the march had strained his failing health and he felt physically incapable of assuming the arduous role.

Alekseev fully trusted Denikin. While he had been Commander-in-Chief under the Provisional Government, Denikin had served as his Chief-of-Staff for a time and they got along well. (Indeed, Denikin never disappointed him: in the following months cooperation between the two generals remained smooth, and in spite of occasional differences, they never lost their regard for each other.) The senior officers also had great respect for Denikin. In the previous months Alekseev had been pushed into the background by Kornilov, who never consulted him, and it was Denikin who participated in formulating policy and who became the second most influential man in the army.[86] To the senior officers it seemed perfectly natural that he should take Kornilov's post.

It is likely that Kornilov, had he lived, would have destroyed the army by trying to break the defense of the Bolsheviks at Ekaterinodar. Denikin, who had wanted to retreat earlier, knew that their leader's death had depressed the morale of the soldiers so much that victory was impossible, and he did not hesitate to give up the attack. After consulting with Filimonov, Alekseev, and Romanovskii, Denikin ordered a forced march to begin on the evening of April 13.[87] Since the only route open was to the north, he had no choice of direction. The Bolsheviks again had a good opportunity to eliminate the demoralized Volunteer Army. However, Sorokin, the Red Commander-in-Chief, did not seriously pursue the Whites. As Sukhorukov, a Soviet author, writes: "Instead of continuing the struggle with the counter-revolution which was still dangerous, Sorokin returned to Ekaterinodar for parades and demonstrations, exhibiting the corpse of Kornilov which was burnt after a completely unnecessary spectacle."[88]

Denikin was well aware of the danger which threatened his army and acted with determination to save it by ordering forced marches to get away from the danger zone as quickly as possible. He fought isolated battles with small Bolshevik bands, but the Volunteer Army succeeded in avoiding the main Red forces. To speed up the march Denikin took extreme measures. After the bloody battle for Ekaterinodar the Volunteer Army had a large number of wounded, and the long hospital detachment slowed down the movement of the army. Denikin ordered the 64 severely wounded, with two doctors and three nurses, to stay behind at *stanitsa* Elizavetinskaia. After a few days' march, 119 men were left behind with doctors, nurses, and money to pay for their food in *stanitsa* Diad'kovskaia. On a third occasion, at *stanitsa* Il'inskaia, 28 men stayed behind. The Volunteer Army freed a few Bolshevik hostages who stayed with the Whites in order to win the enemy's sympathy. Leaving the wounded further depressed the morale of the army, but Denikin had no choice. The carts which had carried the wounded were needed for carrying the healthy and for increasing mobility. According to White sources, 136 men out of 211 who had been left behind survived Bolshevik captivity.[89]

At the beginning of May, after several small and large engagements and the crossing of dangerous railroad lines, the Volunteer Army returned to the area from which the campaign had started, the borderlands between Stavropol province, the Don, and the Kuban. The Ice March had ended.

The Army, which had started the march with four thousand soldiers, had five thousand at the end of the campaign. In spite of almost constant fighting, the volunteers had exactly the same amount of munitions in the middle of May as they had at the start of the march; they took as much from the Bolsheviks as they had used.[90] The army failed to achieve the objective of the march, the liberation of the Kuban. It lost many of its first and best soldiers; and above all, it lost Kornilov, the man whom the anti-Bolsheviks would have liked to see as the dictator of Russia.

Yet the Ice March was far from being a failure. Inducing the Cossacks to join changed the character of the army and made further growth possible later. But the greatest achievement of the march was simply survival. No doubt, the chief reason that the army was not destroyed on the Kuban was the incredible lack of discipline of the Red troops, who were much better equipped and numerically ten times stronger. However, to point to the errors of the Bolsheviks is not to denigrate the heroism and accomplishments of the Whites. Only by accepting the most extreme forms of privation could they keep the army together in this most difficult period of the Civil War and take advantage of the turning of the tide when it occurred in the late spring of 1918.

THE DON SOVIET REPUBLIC

When the Volunteer Army returned from the Kuban to the Don, it found a far more hospitable environment there than it had left behind. The Communist experiment, the Don Soviet Republic, had failed, and in its failure it managed to accomplish what Kaledin could not do—turn the Cossacks against Bolshevism.

The Don Soviet Republic, lacking the determined and purposeful leadership of a Lenin, split by hostile factions, threatened by the advancing German army, could not recreate stability. Kaledin was defeated by the combined forces of local Bolsheviks, Podtelkov's insurgent Cossacks, and the invading Red Army. The leaders of the Rostov and Taganrog Revolutionary Committees, and the Cossack leaders of the Kamenskaia group, found that they were pushed into the background by outsiders. Podtelkov, who was made president of the Republic, was obviously a figurehead. It is not that the Red Army simply executed tasks given to it by the Bolshevik Central Committee; ties between Rostov and Moscow were tenuous, and commanders like Sivers were virtually independent. To remedy this situation Antonov-Ovseenko, the leader of the Southern Forces, asked Lenin to send a representative to the Don, but Lenin had no one to send and instead asked Antonov-Ovseenko to be the chief representative of the Council of Commissars, the Sovnarkom.[91] Antonov-Ovseenko could not go himself, but he sent Commissar Voitsekhovskii, who together with Sivers became the real ruler of the district. Voitsekhovskii nationalized the mines and factories, organized forced collectivization of food, extorted money from the bourgeoisie, and introduced a reign of terror. The Rostov Revolutionary Committee, and especially Podtelkov's district Military Revolutionary Committee, which had moved from Kamenskaia to

Rostov, very much disliked Voitsekhovskii's policies and soon relations between the competing sets of leaders were so bad that they
continually threatened each other with arrests.[92]

It is ironic that the declaration of the Don Republic's independence came not during Kaledin's rule, when the Don was virtually
independent, but during communist occupation, when the Don was
ruled by Red Army soldiers, most of whom did not belong to the
region. On February 26 Antonov-Ovseenko notified Lenin in a telegram of the Cossacks' desire for self-rule. Lenin had no objection to
autonomy of the Don district but stipulated that the Congress of
Soviets of the Don must work out its own agrarian reform program.[93] However, events made the local leaders go further than
Lenin had originally intended. The district Revolutionary Committee thought that an independent republic would make it more
difficult for the Germans to occupy the Don in the name of advancing self-determination. The Revolutionary Committee therefore promulgated the Don Soviet Republic on March 23 without
waiting for the Congress of Soviets.[94]

The Bolsheviks tried to create a new civil administration. Beginning with the Rostov city *duma* on March 2, they dissolved all city
dumas and the Military Revolutionary Committee called elections
to local and district Soviets.[95] With the exception of priests, mer-
chants, policemen, and officers, every person over twenty years of
age had the right to vote. But in most *stanitsy* the elections were
never held; and where they were, the Atamans were usually elected
chairmen of the Soviets, and so little changed except in name.

The Congress of Soviets met in Rostov on April 9.[96] It discussed
land reform and nationalization, but the most debated and important
question was whether the Don should accept the peace treaty of
Brest-Litovsk. Since the district was directly threatened by German
armies, the decision of the Congress had national significance. Both
the partisans and the opponents of peace with Germany understood
this, and therefore the Bolsheviks sent Ordzhonikidze to Rostov to
argue for peace, while the left Social Revolutionaries sent Kamkov
to fight against the treaty. After several days of debate the Bolshevik
position was accepted by a vote of 348 to 106 with many abstentions.[97] However, shortly afterwards the Germans invaded the Don

and the Bolsheviks found it necessary to reverse their decision and advocate revolutionary war, so that the peace resolution of the Congress became a source of embarrassment.[98]

The citizen of the Don cared little for the resolutions of the Congress of Soviets, or for remaining Atamans chairmen; for him the Soviet regime meant anarchy and terror. The worst terror occurred where it made the least sense: in the Bolshevik strongholds of Rostov and Taganrog. In the last months of the Kaledin regime the Bolsheviks had gained much support in these two largest cities of the Don. Then the population had waited for the soldiers of the Red Army as if for liberators. But the invading troops destroyed this good will in a short time and sympathy changed into fear.[99] Executions and searches began immediately.

The lives of officers were in the greatest danger. These men had not joined the Volunteer Army in spite of threats, but now they had to hide. For the first time they understood that the luxury of "neutrality" was impossible in the Civil War. Consequently, when the Whites reconquered the Don most of these officers joined the Volunteer Army. The Red general Sivers ordered that anyone who had been a member of the Volunteer Army was to be executed. While that Army had been stationed in Rostov many students of fourteen and fifteen signed up, but most of them, perhaps because of their parents' objections, did not accompany the army on the Ice March. Now these children were liable to be shot.[100] The Military Revolutionary Committee of Rostov dissociated itself from this order and demanded that no one under 17 should be punished.[101] However, this was ineffectual because Sivers' staff simply disregarded the Committee.

Terror was applied even against members of socialist parties and ordinary workers. For example, the prominent Menshevik leader, P. P. Kalmykov, was killed by disorderly soldiers. On March 1 the Bolsheviks closed down the Menshevik paper *Rabochee Delo*.[102] The Mensheviks experimented with starting another one, *Rabochee Slovo*, but this was also closed down within a month.[103] On March 26, the Social Revolutionaries and Mensheviks left the meeting of the Rostov city Soviet in protest and they never returned.[104]

Had Sivers' staff wanted to stop the terror, as it did not, it would have been nearly impossible. No power could discipline the soldiers of disorganized military units who came to Rostov from the Ukraine, escaping the Germans. They looted and killed often simply for the clothes of their victims.[105] But terror was sporadic and unpredictable. While army officers and prominent Kadet politicians, including Miliukov, were able to hide and survive, many were murdered simply "for wearing boots similar to those of the members of the Volunteer Army."[106]

Terror in Taganrog was just as bloody. The cruelty with which the officers had attempted to put down the uprising in January left bitter memories. Dozens of officers were arrested and brutally murdered. Among the officers arrested here was General Rennenkampf, a hero of the Russo-Japanese war and well known for the abortive Russian offensive in August 1914. Instructions came from Petrograd to offer Rennenkampf a command position against the approaching Germans. When Rennenkampf refused, Antonov-Ovseenko himself ordered his execution.[107]

Perhaps nothing the Bolsheviks did caused such widespread indignation as their treatment of the Church. They arrested the Archbishop of Novocherkassk on February 26 and jailed him for ten days. According to an Investigating Commission organized by the Volunteer Army in 1919, there were fifteen cases of the murder of priests.[108] The new authorities abolished church weddings and religious instruction in schools. The Church fought back by anathematizing the Bolsheviks.[109] Although the population of the Don was subdued by terror, on occasion it did come to the defense of priests.[110]

The Cossacks, living in their *stanitsy* more or less out of the reach of the Bolsheviks, suffered much less than the urban population. Yet it was they who turned actively against the new regime and played the chief role in its overthrow. The Cossacks were disappointed because leadership in their native district was taken away from them and usurped by outsiders. More important, Bolshevik policy threatened their privileges. Even before the occupation of Novocherkassk, General Sablin, the commander of one of the invading Red Armies, had announced to *krug* representatives: "Cossackdom as a separate and privileged estate should be eliminated."[111] It seemed that the

Bolsheviks would act on the basis of their announced intentions. Indeed, the Congress of Soviets, which was dominated by the *inogorodnye*, discussed plans for taking away Cossack lands.

The fact that *frontoviki* returned to their *stanitsy* contributed to the diminution of Bolshevik strength among the Cossacks. As long as they belonged to military units Bolshevik leaders could influence them, but when the same young men rejoined their families, it was the view of their elders which prevailed and the older Cossacks never sympathized with the Bolsheviks.

Anti-Bolshevik resistance began in the *stanitsy* around Novocherkassk. This was the richest area and therefore least predisposed toward Bolshevism; it was also the one which marauding Red soldiers and Bolshevik food-collecting parties could reach most easily from Rostov, and therefore it suffered the most. The forced collection of food created great hostility, and Bolshevik agents were murdered by angry Cossacks even during the first weeks of the Soviet Republic.

The first sign of the coming large-scale anti-Bolshevik rebellion was the defection of V. S. Golubov.[112] Golubov was a very brave man and an excellent soldier, but he was also an adventurer and careerist whose chief goal was to become Ataman. He quickly divined the mood of his fellow Cossacks. In January 1918, he deserted Ataman Kaledin and joined Podtelkov, and it was he who led the troops which occupied Novocherkassk. The Bolsheviks never fully trusted him and purposely kept him away from Rostov, the center of power. They had reason to suspect him. Golubov did not carry out the Military Revolutionary Committee's order to pursue Popov's army after Popov and his 1500 Cossacks escaped from Novocherkassk. Instead Golubov captured M. P. Bogaevskii, Ataman Kaledin's closest friend and assistant. He must have had some plans for using his prisoner because he refused to hand him over to the Rostov authorities.

In the first days of April 1918, Golubov openly turned against the Bolsheviks and toured the *stanitsy* around Novocherkassk to enlist volunteers. But by then he was too infamous to inspire trust in anyone. The Cossacks did not respond, and when the Bolsheviks found out about his activities and sent a detachment after him on April 7 he had to flee. A few days later he became one of the first victims of the rebelling anti-Bolshevik Cossacks, who did not forgive his past.[113]

The Cossack rising was entirely spontaneous and therefore disorganized. On April 10, the Cossacks disarmed and killed a detachment of Red soldiers who had come to collect food at *stanitsa* Krivianskaia, which is only a few versts West of Novocherkassk. This time the Cossacks were not satisfied with their "victory" and decided to form an insurgent army. The rebels elected Esaul Fetisov as their commander, largely because he was the only officer present at the meeting. His first act was to send messengers to neighboring *stanitsy* to ask for help. In a few days he put together a small army of 300 to 400 men and decided to carry out a surprise raid on Novocherkassk on April 14.[114] The Bolsheviks knew nothing about Fetisov's army and were taken completely by surprise. Therefore, they withdrew to Rostov almost without fighting.

Fetisov's raid was not well prepared. He had no staff, his soldiers were badly equipped, and he had no plans for the future. Although it was clear from the beginning that the Cossacks could not keep their conquest, the venture was not without benefits. It enabled the officers who were trapped in Novocherkassk during Communist rule to organize and thereby create a movement which was to take the chief part in liberating the Don, and which would serve as the basis for future governmental authority. On April 14, G. P. Ianov, a well-known conservative politician, formed a Council of Defense. Three days later, this Council named K. S. Poliakov Commander of the not yet existing Cossack armies, and S. Denisov his chief of staff.[115]

When on April 17 the Bolsheviks attacked from two directions, Rostov and Aleksandrovskaia, the Cossacks put up as little fighting as the Bolsheviks had a few days before and they withdrew to Krivianskaia.[116] On the next day, April 18, the army moved to *stanitsa* Zaplavskaia and here began the so called "Zaplavskaia sitting" *(Zaplavskoe sidenie)*, which lasted until May 8, the date of the liberation of Novocherkassk. The uprising spread rapidly and Cossacks came from nearby *stanitsy* to join the army. Poliakov's army, which at the beginning of its stay in Zaplavskaia had 4,000 men, had 6,500 by April 23.[117] On April 21 the Council of Defense renamed itself Provisional Government of the Don.[118] Luckily for the Cossacks, the Bolsheviks remained passive and enabled them to carry out their work undisturbed.

The Zaplavskaia army was the largest of the Cossack armies, but it was not the only one. Another army of 1,000 or 2,000 men was forming on the left bank of the Don,[119] and Field Ataman Popov returned with his troops, which had dwindled to 1,000 from the Sal'skii steppe. The mood of the Cossacks had changed, and those *stanitsy* which had been hostile to the Whites two months before now greeted Popov as a hero.[120]

A delegation from the Zaplavskaia army met Popov at Konstantinovskaia on April 23. The meeting was no warmer than the one between Kornilov and Pokrovskii. I. A. Poliakov, a member of the Zaplavskaia delegation, writes:

> To be truthful, it must be said that the meeting was very painful. They received us coldly and dryly. What is more, they tried to interpret our coming as the penitence of a sinner. But what were our sins—we were not told. It was especially striking that the Ataman and his retinue . . . above all were interested in personal matters rather than in the general situation in Zaplavskaia.[121]

In Poliakov's view, which was very likely correct, the Ataman was jealous that an army had been organized without his participation. It is also likely that the leaders of the Zaplavskaia group were unhappy about the idea of giving up their independence by recognizing the authority of the Ataman. Disagreement between the Cossack leaders was to impair the efficiency of their armies and was to last until the occupation of Novocherkassk.

Nevertheless, the leaders of the Zaplavskaia army and the Ataman worked out a compromise. Civil authority was to remain in the hands of the Provisional Government until the election of a new *krug*, "the *krug* of the Saving of the Don." All military powers were given to Popov, who formed three army groups: a Southern group (Zaplavskaia army) under Colonel Denisov and Colonel I. A. Poliakov, now his chief of staff; a Northern group under Colonel Semiletov from the detachment which had executed the Sal'skii campaign; and a Trans-Don army under Semenov.[122]

The Zaplavskaia Cossacks and Popov disagreed about strategy.

The Cossacks in Zaplavskaia wanted to take Novocherkassk as soon as possible; Popov, however, took regiments from the Southern group, added them to the Northern army, and attacked Aleksandrovsk-Grushevsk on April 29 instead. The attack, which was unsuccessful largely because of a lack of discipline among the soldiers, further lowered Popov's prestige in Zaplavskaia.[123]

The Don consisted of three politically different parts. In the Rostov and Taganrog-Donets mines industrial area, where cities and *inogorodnye* settlements predominated, the Bolsheviks could easily overcome internal opposition. The North was the least significant politically. It was cut off from developments in the South, and for a long time the population did not even find out when Bolshevik rule was overthrown in the centers of the Don. The strength of the insurgents was limited to the rural South, where the Cossacks were stronger than the *inogorodnye*, principally because they were better organized.

Popov's three armies, of course, consisted almost entirely of Cossacks. They hardly discriminated between Bolsheviks and *inogorodnye*. Indeed, there were *stanitsy* where the Cossacks saw no reason to join the distant anti-Bolshevik army, but instead fought the enemy which was closest, the nearby *inogorodnye* settlements.[124]

In spite of the rapid growth of the insurgent army and in spite of its success, the victory of the rebellion seemed far from certain. By the end of April the Cossacks were hardly better disciplined than the soldiers of the Red Army. After the smallest setback—and there were many, since the Cossacks frequently ran away at the approach of the Red Army—some regiments wanted to give up fighting altogether and negotiate with the Bolsheviks. For instance, the Krivianskaia Cossacks, who were first to organize, could hardly be persuaded not to stay in their *stanitsa* after the defeat in Novocherkassk.[125] Since the same men who had fought Kaledin now turned against the Bolsheviks, the spirit and ideas of the insurgents were remarkably similar to those of the "revolutionary *frontoviki*" of December 1917 and January 1918. This was a movement of rank and file Cossacks who were fiercely egalitarian. For example, the officers were not allowed to wear epaulets and were called "citizen officer" rather than "Your Excellency."[126] Many officers did not join the army because they had no faith in its success. The most prominent of these was General Krasnov, who was hiding in *stanitsa* Konstantinovskaia at the time. When representatives of the army approached him and asked him to assume command, he answered: "I have no faith in the Cossacks and want nothing to do with them."[127] There were many Cossacks who never forgave the future Ataman for this statement.

The precarious balance of contending forces was tipped by the arrival of two new enemies of Soviet power: the small army of Colonel Drozdovskii, and much more important, the Germans.

By the end of April the Germans occupied almost the entire Ukraine. Lenin's government correctly anticipated that the invaders would not stop at the borders of the Ukraine, but it was absolutely powerless to stop their advance. Chicherin, the Soviet Commissar for Foreign Affairs, sent imploring telegrams to Berlin, but to no avail;[128] German troops entered the territory of the Don from Lugansk on April 26 and threatened Taganrog. Moscow wanted to avoid war at any price, but for the Bolsheviks in the Don it was more difficult to preserve their detachment. They, too, made conciliatory moves, promising the Germans that Red units coming from the Ukraine would be disarmed. In this way the Germans could have no pretext to pursue them. But when fruitless negotiations could not prevent the occupation of Taganrog on May 1, the Bolsheviks made futile and feverish attempts to organize defenses, contrary to directions from Moscow, which was ready to sacrifice the Don.[129]

The Bolsheviks adopted the policy of revolutionary war which had been advocated by the left Social Revolutionaries and Left Communists before. A Council of Defense formed in Rostov and called for general mobilization. The Council planned to draft the "bourgeoisie" for defense work, such as building fortifications, and to collect three million rubles from the Rostov rich. But nothing came of these plans. In the great confusion, when the population knew that the days of the Bolsheviks were numbered, the Bolsheviks could not enforce their will.[130] Podtelkov, unaware of the change of mood among the Cossacks, went to the northern districts of the *voisko* hoping to repeat his feat of organizing a "revolutionary" Cossack army. Instead of answering his call, they captured and hanged him, along with his friend and assistant Krivoshlykov, on May 9. The other members of his mission were shot at the same time.[131]

Obviously the days of Soviet rule on the Don were numbered. The Bolshevik position was hopeless; since the fall of Taganrog, Rostov was defenseless from the West. The Bolsheviks pathetically sent emissaries to the Germans asking why they attacked, the same question the *krug* had asked the Bolsheviks two months before. On May 1 Ordzhonikidze himself went to German headquarters, where he was told that German goals were to "help the Ukrainians to recover their frontiers,"[132] and to occupy Rostov. The Germans' purpose in occupying the industrial areas of the Don district is self-evident: they needed the raw materials produced in the mines of the Donets for their war effort, and they wanted a friendly government in the rest of the district which would be helpful in securing foodstuffs.[133]

The arrival of the Germans radically changed the course of the Civil War in South Russia in favor of the Whites. In overthrowing Bolshevik rule the Germans enabled the Whites to organize at a time when, if left on their own, they could not have survived. The first attack on Rostov, however, was not carried out by the Germans but by the soldiers of Colonel M. Drozdovskii. Drozdovskii organized a unit of about a thousand men (667 officers, 370 soldiers, 14 doctors, priests, and administrators and 12 nurses),[134] and marched with this unit from the Romanian front to the Don to join the White army there. The founders of the Volunteer Army had counted on dozens of Drozdovskiis, but they were disappointed; this march was a unique event in the history of the Civil War. It is possible to find objective reasons why Colonel Drozdovskii succeeded where everyone else had failed, but it is also true that Drozdovskii himself must have been an extraordinary man with charisma and a great determination.

Russian soldiers in foreign territory were protected from revolutionary agitation, and therefore the armies on the Romanian front were far less disorganized and demoralized than elsewhere. With Allied help, the Romanian government succeeded in maintaining discipline not only among its own troops but also among the Russians. As early as November 1917, General Alekseev, who understood the potential importance of Russian officers on the Romanian front, turned for aid to General Shcherbachev, the Commander of the front. Although Shcherbachev sent a trainload of medical supplies to the Volunteer Army, he refused at first to collaborate with Alekseev, because he hoped to organize an anti-German and anti-Bolshevik Ukrainian front with Allied aid.[135] Consequently, the initiative for forming volunteer units to join the officers on the Don came not from Shcherbachev but from Colonel Drozdovskii. However, the political situation changed radically in December, when the Ukrainian *rada* started negotiations with the Central Powers and thereby eliminated the possibility of forming a Ukrainian front. Now the Allies began to regard the Volunteer Army as the only nucleus of anti-German strength, and Shcherbachev, who maintained extremely close relations with Allied diplomats, also changed his attitude. He decided to enlarge Drozdovskii's plan, and on February 6 he entrusted the organization to General Kelchevskii.[136] The formation of military units, however, went slowly. In the beginning of March only 900 men in Jassy and 800 in Kishinev signed up for the march to the Don. At this stage the Romanians, fearing revenge from the Germans, who were gradually occupying their country, forbade further organization and demanded the disbanding of existing units. General Shcherbachev and General Kelchevskii decided to comply. Drozdovskii, however, was of a different opinion. The Kishinev group, commanded by General Belozor, dispersed, but the officers under Drozdovskii, in Sokoly outside of Jassy, decided to follow him in the march in defiance of the Romanians. The significance of a determined leader can be seen from the fact that one group dispersed while the other, of more or less the same size and composition, did not. Drozdovskii and his men challenged the Romanians to disarm them. The Romanian parliament was in session and Drozdovskii aimed his cannons at the parliament building; he threatened to fire at the first hostile action.[137] It was not necessary. Under pressure, the Romanians even gave trains to transport the troublesome army to Kishinev in order to get rid of them as soon as possible. Here some members of Belozor's group joined Drozdovskii and the long march began.

The small army moved quickly through the Ukraine; at times the

soldiers covered 40 to 45 miles a day. Under prevailing anarchic conditions, an army consisting of a thousand men was a significant force,
and they easily defeated the few small Bolshevik groups which happened to be in their way. The marchers, however, were plagued
with uncertainty; they did not know what awaited them on the Don.
Only toward the end of the march did they learn that the Volun-
ter Army was no longer on the Don, and that Kornilov was reputed
to be dead. At this time some lost heart and left the ranks of the
group, but Drozdovskii attracted others.

Drozdovskii was presented with the dilemma which was to become a central problem for the entire Volunteer Army—namely,
what was to be the attitude of the White officers toward the German army? The issue never presented itself more sharply and directly: the German advance and Drozdovskii's march coincided. Because Drozdovskii's attitude was typical of the men who made up
the leadership of the Volunteer Army, it is worth examining.

The group was initially organized to carry on the war against the
Central Powers, but as the march progressed it became more and
more difficult to maintain the myth that the enemy was Germany.
It was embarrassing in its obvious conflict with reality. The "enemy"
knew perfectly well that Drozdovskii wanted to join the Volunteer
Army, an organization which also professed hostility to Germany.
The Germans could certainly have squashed the small unit with
ease, but they not only refrained from destroying the White army,
but even showed sympathy and repeatedly offered it help. In fact,
for all practical purposes the Germans and Drozdovskii collaborated.
For example, German troops and Drozdovskii's men arrived at the
Dniepr at the same time and the two armies agreed not to interfere
with each other's crossing. But then the Bolsheviks began to shell
the Germans; here was a clear case of Russians fighting the enemies
of their country. Without hesitation, Drozdovskii attacked the Bolsheviks and thus helped the Germans to cross the river. Obviously
embarrassed, Drozdovskii saw the need to explain to his soldiers
after the fighting was over that there had been no previous agreement with the Germans, and that the Whites took arms against the
Bolsheviks because they regarded them as German agents.[188] Under the circumstances, this surely made little sense. At another meet-

ing with Austrian troops, the Austrians yelled good luck to the Russians.[139] The Germans even offered to help Drozdovskii take Rostov, but Drozdovskii turned this down. A. V. Turkul, a participant writes: "when we went by with our wounded, short commands were given and the German Ulan regiment gave the Russian volunteers a military salute." He sensibly added: "Then we understood that the war with Germany was finished."[140]

The Germans and the White officers were drawn together not so much by their common military objectives as by sympathy based on a set of common values and norms. It was easy for the Russian officers to discover this affinity; all they had to do was to compare the Germans with the Ukrainians, the soldiers of the *rada*, and the Bolsheviks. It maybe worthwhile here to quote at length from Drozdovskii's diary:

> What odd relations exist between ourselves and the Germans; we behave like acknowledged allies, collaborate, treat each other in a severely correct manner, and in all cases of clashes between ourselves and the Ukrainians they are always taking our side. At the same time one German remarked that those officers who do not recognize our peace are our enemies. Probably, the Germans do not understand our forced alliance against the Bolsheviks, and either do not guess at our hidden aims or consider the realization of them impossible. We respond with meticulous civility. One German officer said: "We try to assist the Russian officers in every way, we feel strongly for them, while they keep away from us, and behave like strangers."
>
> With the Ukrainians, on the other hand, relations are terrible. They are after us all the time with some demand, such as that we take off our shoulderstraps; they are afraid to fight openly—a demoralized band trying to strike from behind. They do not recognize the division of military spoils, a principle acknowledged by the Germans. Their commandant issues severe orders not to insult us, but they do not mind these. Some of them were beaten up, the slaves, the rascals. When we left they pulled down the military station flag (not even strictly national) tore it into pieces, trampled it under foot. . . .
>
> The Germans are our enemies; we hate them but we have some

respect for them. For the Ukrainians we have nothing but contempt, as for renegades and demoralized bandits.[141]

Drozdovskii arrived at Rostov on May 4.[142] He had only the vaguest understanding of the immensely complicated internal situation in the Don and he knew nothing about the plans of the Cossacks to attack Novocherkassk almost simultaneously; nevertheless, he decided to attack Rostov. He wanted to anticipate the Germans in order to capture military supplies which he expected to find.

The foolhardy venture of attacking a large city with a thousand men was almost successful because unaware of Drozdovskii's soldiers, the Bolsheviks expected a German attack. Moscow had directed the Don Bolsheviks to avoid fighting the Germans at all costs; consequently, at the approach of a hostile army the Bolsheviks fell back in disorder. Only on the next morning did they discover their mistake and send reinforcements from Novocherkassk to reoccupy the city.

The Southern Cossack army in Zaplavskaia was planning an offensive against Novocherkassk. On May 1 the Cossacks defeated a Bolshevik army which was sent against them, and this victory gave them courage for a second attack on the capital.[143] This time the battle was carefully planned. The reluctant Popov gave his blessing on May 3, and May 6 was chosen for the date of the attack. Drozdovskii knew nothing of the Cossacks' plans and they knew nothing of his. What was even more remarkable, the Cossacks did not know about the German advance; they merely noticed that the Bolsheviks were nervous "because of some unknown force."[144]

Denisov, who directed operations against Novocherkassk, succeeded in capturing the city, but the Bolsheviks showed unexpected resilience; after a day of fighting it seemed that the Cossacks might not be able to keep their conquest. Only then did Denisov's staff hear about the approaching Germans and Drozdovskii. Chief-of-Staff Poliakov immediately dispatched a messenger to Drozdovskii.[145] Drozdovskii's arrival decided the battle and the Bolsheviks were defeated.

On May 6 the Germans occupied Rostov without opposition.

The Red Army leaders escaped to Tsaritsyn and set up their head-quarters there. The Red Army retreated in great confusion; hundreds of soldiers remained in the town because they lost touch with their units. The Germans disarmed them and let them go. They did everything very calmly and in perfect order, an impressive phenomenon to the Russian observer.[146]

Thus ended the short history of the Don Soviet Republic.

CHAPTER 5

Taking Stock

The late spring and early summer of 1918 was a period of crisis for the young Soviet regime; its very existence was endangered by foreign intervention, domestic opposition, and the rising tide of anarchy.

Of the three dangers, the last was by far the most serious. In 1917 Lenin and his comrades proved themselves extremely able revolutionaries, which meant that they knew how to undermine established authority and how to take advantage of spreading anarchy. But the assumption of power on November 7 changed the nature of the Bolsheviks' task overnight: the same people who had harangued the masses to overthrow the government now had to man the ministries themselves. There is no better measure of Lenin's greatness as a politician than his ability to execute this *volte face* and ultimately carry his followers with him by transforming them from agitators into administrators.

The change of government exacerbated the country's enormous problems. Industrial production fell, the railroad network almost ceased to function, and worst of all, the bread shortage, which had played a major role in bringing down the two preceding regimes, reached crisis proportions in the early summer of 1918.

What distinguished the Bolsheviks from previous governments was not their ability to solve the bread crisis; hunger was to last until the end of the Civil War and beyond. But the Bolsheviks knew how to reduce the political danger to their rule inherent in such a situation. They took energetic measures to equalize distribution as much as possible by encouraging the poor to take from the rich. This method may have alienated a powerful segment of the population, but it created an activist image for the Bolsheviks as men who would not just simply give way to events as their predecessors had done. More important, the Bolsheviks, unlike previous governments, suppressed spontaneous hunger riots with great firmness and brutality.

The introduction of "revolutionary" terror went hand in hand with the disregard of those features of communist ideology which would have hindered consolidation. Lenin, who a few months before had talked about the ability of armed workers to run the government, now turned to experts of the old regime for help.[1] The Bolsheviks used "specialists" not only in reconstructing the economy and the administration but also in the extremely sensitive area of organizing the Red Army.

Yet no matter how energetic and flexible Bolshevik leadership was, the disintegration of the country was so profound that the survival of the regime was very much in question during this period. That Bolshevik rule did not ultimately collapse can be explained only by the hesitation and weakness of its enemies.

Although the Bolsheviks averted immediate German occupation of Petrograd and Moscow by signing the very humiliating Brest-Litovsk treaty, they were conscious that the Germans might change their mind at any moment and that there was no Communist army to stop them. German policy toward Russia in 1918 was extremely complex, and was motivated both by short-range and long-term considerations. For the time being, Berlin could have no better government in Moscow than Lenin's, because no other government would have accepted a Brest-Litovsk type of treaty.[2] Even though there was no serious military force in Russia, the Germans felt they could not spare the manpower necessary for occupying the enormous country. In the long run Berlin was determined to destroy Russia as a major power. Consequently, to make sure that the Russian empire would not be recreated, the Germans tolerated the Soviet regime in the center of the country, but in the peripheries they aided and sometimes even created anti-Communist governments. In Finland, as well as in the Baltic states and in the Ukraine, the Germans made possible the creation of socially conservative and nationalist governments.

From the point of view of the course of the Russian Civil War, the Ukrainian was the most important among the new governments.[3] In the Ukraine, unlike Central Russia, the local Bolsheviks were not strong enough to take power, and therefore the Ukrainian Parliament, the *rada*, could proclaim the independence of the country soon after the November Revolution. The *rada* was not destined to govern the country for long, for it proved inadequate against the combined force of local Bolsheviks and invaders from Russia. However, the Germans were determined not to allow reunification and sent armies which chased out the Bolsheviks with great ease at the end of April. In Kiev, they set up as head of state General Skoropadskii, who assumed the fancy historical title of Hetman. Skoropadskii's regime lacked popular support and was maintained entirely by German arms. In order to justify breaking away from Russia, the regime used nationalistic slogans, but in reality Skoropadskii, the loyal officer of the Imperial Russian army, was totally lacking in desire and ability to satisfy the genuine nationalistic yearnings of the Ukrainians. Skoropadskii's conservative government was anxious to help the various anti-Bolshevik organizations, and Kiev soon became one of the centers of organization for the Whites.

Largely for geographical reasons, the Allies were not in a position to give substantial help to their Russian friends in the first half of 1918.[4] Although a small force of British marines landed in Murmansk as early as March 1918, and the Japanese a month later in Vladivostok, both cities were so far removed from the main centers of the country that the presence of foreign troops there did not make much difference. The situation changed substantially in May, when Czech and Slovak troops turned against the Bolsheviks. These troops had been formed by the Provisional Government from prisoners of war in order to fight the Germans. Unlike the Russians, the Czechs and Slovaks did not lose their enthusiasm for the war, and when it became impossible to fight on the Russian front they wanted to continue the struggle for the independence of their country in Western Europe. The Bolsheviks, the Allies, and the Czechs agreed on the long and difficult route through Siberia. The Czechs, how-

ever, never reached their goal, because while traveling through
Siberia they started to fight the Bolsheviks. Under prevailing conditions, fifty thousand Czechs formed a strong enough army to be
able to overwhelm the Reds and to hold the enormously long railroad line. The possession of that line made them masters of Siberia.
By overthrowing the weak Bolshevik rule in the East, the Czechs
enabled the Whites to form an anti-Bolshevik front there which, in
a short time, was to become the major battlefield in the Civil War.

In the first half of 1918, domestic opposition seemed far less dangerous for the Bolsheviks than foreign enemies. The largest anti-
Bolshevik Russian army, the Volunteer Army, was far away and
very weak. The Bolsheviks had only contempt for their defeated
political opponents, socialists and liberals alike. Oppression was
barely beginning: at the end of April 1918 there were only 38 political prisoners in Petrograd, and the Kadet paper *Rech'* was allowed
to publish until the end of May.[5] Very likely, the government
simply did not yet consider it necessary to take more brutal steps.
In the rather congenial atmosphere of Moscow, a large number of
organizations were formed; these constantly changed and split up,
and were uniformly powerless, inefficient, and irrelevant. The two
most important organizations were the Right Center, a coalition of
liberals and conservatives in which the conservatives predominated,
and the Union for Regeneration, which had some Kadet members
but was led mostly by Social Revolutionaries.[6]

The leading figures of Russian liberalism and socialism had operated in an utterly different environment, and were now incapable
of appreciating the magnitude of the changes around them and of
adjusting their policies accordingly. They spent their time in fruitless debates and their ultimate contribution to the anti-Bolshevik
cause was practically nil.

One of the chief issues which separated the two major anti-
Bolshevik organizations was what attitude to take toward the Constituent Assembly, which had been dispersed by the Bolsheviks in
January 1918. Those who were satisfied with the composition of
the Assembly insisted that after the defeat of the Bolsheviks the
same Assembly should be convened again. The conservative parties
which did badly in the elections of November 1917 wanted new

elections. Neither side appreciated how unlikely it was that Russia soon would have *any* kind of Constituent Assembly. An equally ephemeral yet bitterly divisive issue was who should lead the anti-Bolshevik movement. The Union for Regeneration wanted the movement to be led by a directorate of three men, one of them a general, while the Right Center believed that the country needed the dictatorship of one military man.

All the anti-Bolshevik organizations came into being in the name of continuing the war and consequently had a pro-Allies orientation. However, even on this issue unanimity disappeared in the late spring of 1918. Some members of the Right Center (an organization which came to be increasingly dominated by leading figures of the old regime) considered turning to the Germans for military and financial help. The left wing of the Right Center found the change of policy unacceptable and formed a new organization, the National Center.

Following the initial defections from the Allied cause, an increasing number of politicians were willing to accept help from anyone in order to overthrow the Bolsheviks. It is noteworthy that politicians who had been associated with conservative causes in the past were far more likely to turn to the Germans than were men of the left. The explanation for the correlation between a conservatism and a German orientation must be that the left put far greater value on associating with countries with progressive social and political systems. The split between pro-Allies and pro-German elements in the anti-Bolshevik movement was to have adverse results. Men who had fought the Germans for years, and came to fight the Bolsheviks originally because they wanted to take the country out of the war, regarded those who looked for German help as renegades. There could be little cooperation and trust between the two camps.

By the beginning of the summer of 1918, Moscow lost its importance as a center of anti-Bolshevik resistance. On the one hand, the Bolsheviks tightened their control in their new capital; on the other, more promising arenas for fighting developed in the peripheries of the country, and Siberia, the Don, and the Ukraine emerged as new political centers. In Moscow, though the various groups within the anti-Bolshevik conspiratorial movement did not cooperate they at least kept in touch with one another. When most of the leaders of the conspiratorial organizations moved away from Moscow, geographical distance was added to political distance. Under Czech protection, the socialist politicians, members of the Union for Regeneration, dominated in Siberia, at least for a while, while Kiev, a city under German occupation, attracted the conservative, Germanophile members of the Right Center.

The Volunteer Army, which had maintained some tenuous ties with all the organizations operating in Moscow, continued to receive information from Kiev, but it was ill-informed about developments in Siberia.

THE KRUG FOR THE SALVATION OF THE DON AND THE FIRST MONTHS OF ATAMAN KRASNOV'S ADMINISTRATION

Among the anti-Bolshevik centers which came into being in the middle of 1918, it was the Don which was first to fight the enemy. The Don *voisko*, with German help, succeeded in putting together a strong army, capable not only of liberating the district but also of threatening the surrounding major cities.

The experience of living in the Don Soviet Republic fundamentally changed the political views of the Cossacks. Now they understood that Bolshevism was not only a deadly threat to their estate privileges but also to their very way of life. From this understanding, however, they did not draw the conclusion which Kaledin had drawn a few months earlier—namely, that it was necessary to unite the entire population of the *voisko* and fight the Red Army. After the liberation of Novocherkassk, the Cossacks cared little about developments in Moscow and the rest of Russia; instead, they wanted to suppress the *inogorodnye*, whom they regarded as their chief enemies. The anti-Bolshevik oratory of the Cossack leaders merely hid their fear of living under the rule of the *inogorodnye*. Under the circumstances, the institution of parity was never even mentioned again; the *inogorodnye* became second-class citizens with no role in the government, and with remarkably few exceptions they did not fight in the army of the Don.

The Don Provisional Government which had been formed in April, before the recapture of Novocherkassk, was headed by the conservative G. P. Ianov. This government established amicable relations with the German command in Rostov, set up an embassy in the Ukraine, refused to accept subordination of the Don army to General Denikin, and called an election of the *krug*, from which it excluded the *inogorodnye*.[7] It is worth remembering these acts of Ianov's government, for in them we can find the germs of Ataman P. N. Krasnov's future policies.

The government started its work under difficult circumstances. A large part of the *voisko* was still occupied by the enemy; industry came to a standstill; communications broke down to such an extent that the government had no knowledge of political and military developments in the district; and the Bolsheviks had burnt the documents of almost all departments.[8] It is to the great credit of the Provisional Government that it succeeded in convening the meeting of the *krug* only five days after the capture of Novocherkassk.

The "krug for the Salvation of the Don" opened on May 11. It had but 130 participants, since only the liberated *stanitsy* could send delegates to Novocherkassk. The intelligentsia, which had always been prominent in local politics, was hardly represented this time, and instead simple front-line Cossacks were in the majority. The *krug* earned the name "*seryi*" (grey) for its composition. This time there were no parties, the speeches were short, and the entire session lasted only five days.[9] That it was a conservative assembly can best be seen from its decisions on small but symbolic issues. The Cossacks decided to abolish the new calendar introduced by the Bolsheviks, to reestablish the old form of address for officers, and to permit officers to wear epaulets. The *krug* wanted to undo not only the changes introduced by the Bolsheviks but also the reforms of the March Revolution.

The main task of the *krug* was to organize the anti-Bolshevik war. It ordered the mobilization of Cossacks for six years, it gave *stanitsa* atamans extraordinary powers for the duration of the fighting, and perhaps most important, it established the principle of one-man rule. Only after these decisions did the representatives elect the man in whose hands all power was to be temporarily concentrated.

The recapture of Novocherkassk did not alleviate the disagreements and hostility between the two camps within the Don army;

the leaders of the *Zaplavskoe sidenie,* or Southern army, and the followers of Field Ataman Popov heartily disliked each other. General Denisov and G. P. Ianov advanced the candidacy of General P. N. Krasnov largely to prevent the election of Popov, who very much hoped to get the post.[10] Krasnov was initially reluctant, but he consented to address the *krug* on May 14. The General, an excellent speaker, well understood the mood of his listeners and his speech made a profound impression. He called for the preservation of Cossack economic and political privileges, the construction of a strong army, and the creation of a strong central authority in the hands of the Ataman.[11] Perhaps as a result of seeing the enthusiastic response of the delegates to his speech, Krasnov decided to become a candidate.* On May 16 the *krug* elected him with a great majority (107 for Krasnov, 10 against, and 13 abstentions).[12]

On May 17 Krasnov presented to the *krug* the "Basic Laws of The All Great Don *voisko,*" which consisted of 50 points. These laws gave all power to the Ataman until the convening of the next *krug* and affirmed the principle of inviolability of private property. The most noteworthy point, number 24, abolished all laws and regulations promulgated after the abdication of Nicholas II.[13] This made Krasnov the second White leader (following Skoropadskii, who had done the same things a few weeks earlier), to repudiate the March Revolution and espouse an explicitly restorationist, counter-

---

*P. N. Krasnov was born in *stanitsa* Beshenskaia, on the Don, in 1869. His father had been a lieutenant general. Krasnov attended military school and the Academy of the General Staff. As a young officer he gained a reputation as a journalist in military circles. He also gained many enemies: the future Ataman wrote that Novocherkassk was an insufferably dull place, and many Cossacks never forgot this insult. At the outbreak of the World War he was only a colonel, but was soon promoted to major general and distinguished himself as commander of several different divisions. He commanded one of the divisions during the ill-fated attempt of the 3rd corps, under General Krymov, to secure the capital for Kornilov in September 1917. After Krymov's suicide, Krasnov took command of the corps, which fought the only battles in defense of the Provisional Government at the time of the November Revolution. Because of this, Krasnov was arrested and only freed after a month. He made his way to the Don and lived in relative obscurity until Denisov and Ianov persuaded him to address the *krug.*

revolutionary position. Krasnov submitted these laws with an ultimatum: if the *krug* desired to change anything of substance he
would resign. He put it picturesquely in his memoirs:

> The Ataman answered one of the members of the *krug*, who asked
> whether it would be possible to make changes in the basic laws:
> "Yes, articles 48, 49, and 50, the ones concerning the flag, the
> emblem, and the anthem. You may suggest to me another flag, with
> the exception of red, another emblem, with the exception of the
> Jewish star of David, and another anthem, with the exception of
> the International.[14]

Krasnov started his administration with the support of the great
majority of the Cossacks. Unlike Kaledin, he almost always acted
in unison with the wishes of his electors and unlike Filimonov, the
Ataman of the Kuban, who was a dry and uninspiring man, Krasnov
could preserve the dignity of his office when dealing with other Russians or foreigners. If the policies were not, the style was unmistak-
ably his: the journalist and novelist was always present in the politician.[15] His historical imagination was boundless. He was magnifi-
cently capable of helping the Cossacks to develop their nationalism
by selecting such titles as All Great Don *voisko* (*vsevelikoe voisko
Donskoe*)—a title which had gone out of use in the time of Peter the
Great—and by naming his delegation to the Ukraine "*zimovaia
stanitsa*," which was the title of Cossack representatives in the court
of pre-Petrine Moscow. In encouraging nationalism, Krasnov perhaps unconsciously found an essential weapon against the Bolsheviks. This new preoccupation with the glories of the past allowed
the Cossacks to regard the struggle against their enemies as a war of
national liberation, not merely one for defending their private interests against their fellow citizens.

The main achievement of Krasnov's administration was the successful pursuit of the war against the Bolsheviks. The new Ataman
took over a badly equipped army, only 17,000 strong, which suffered from disagreements between commanders.[16] The Don army
which grew up in individual units still bore the marks of partisan
organization, and Krasnov's first task was to create order and enforce
discipline. Since his election was a victory for the "Southern Army,"

Field Ataman Popov together with his most prominent supporters retired, and General Denisov became Krasnov's second in command. This arrangement removed the source of friction among the commanders. The *krug*'s approval of partial mobilization enabled the Ataman to field a large army which was financed by printing new money, which Krasnov did not hesitate to do.

The tide turned against the Bolsheviks. Even though in May they still had 70,000 soldiers, their forces were uncoordinated, harassed by Cossack guerillas, and continually on the retreat. The Red Army, now fighting on hostile territory, could not make up for the losses and its size was decreasing. On the other hand, by the middle of June, the Don Cossack army more than doubled and had 40,000 soldiers.[17] The Germans covered the *voisko* from the west and the Volunteer Army from the south, and so Krasnov was able to concentrate movements in eastern and northern directions. By the end of August, with the exception of five *stanitsy*, the entire *voisko* was liberated. As a result of Krasnov's successes the government in Moscow for a while came to regard him as the most threatening enemy, and in the summer of 1918 it sent its largest army against him.

A major cause of Krasnov's success was the support he was receiving from the Germans, yet his pro-German orientation soon became the most controversial aspect of his policies. His attitude toward the foreign invader was in sharp contrast to that of the leaders of the Volunteer Army, and the German issue became the chief source of contention between the two White forces. No one criticized Krasnov for trying to find a *modus vivendi* with Germany. Even such a hostile observer as General Denikin recognized that the Don could not have defied the Germans. German armies occupied a substantial part of the *voisko*, including the largest cities and the Cossacks at that time had no desire whatever to fight them. Also, the Ataman had a clear mandate from his constituents to establish ties with the Germans: the Don Provisional Government had negotiated with the local command in Rostov, and the *krug* explicitly approved the conduct of the government in this matter. But Krasnov, lacking experience in politics and diplomacy, was not circumspect in dealing with the embarrassing allies.

Two days after his election, on May 18, the Ataman wrote his first letter to the German Emperor. The letter itself was innocuous —he merely asked for the recognition of the Don as an independent country until the Russian Constituent Assembly could be convened —but it was unwise for Krasnov to attempt to deal with the Emperor rather than with his representatives.

On July 11, the Ataman sent Prince N. N. Leikhtenbergskii and Major General Cheriachukin to Berlin with a second letter.[18] This letter to Wilhelm created a great stir, eliminated much of his domestic support, and evoked the hostility of the leaders of the Volunteer Army. From a practical point of view, the only important part of the letter was that in which the Ataman promised raw material and foodstuffs in exchange for munitions. However, the Ataman said much more. He asked the assistance of the former enemies of Russia in acquiring the cities of Kamyshin, Voronezh, and Tsaritsyn for the Don, and asked the Emperor to support the Don's claim to Taganrog against the Ukraine, thus implicitly accepting Wilhelm's right to decide on Russian territorial matters. Elsewhere he promised that he would not tolerate any force on the territory of the *voisko* which was hostile to Germany, a promise which the Volunteer Army regarded as a threat to its existence. The tone of the letter shows not so much bad politics as bad taste: "The glorious Don Cossacks have been engaged in fighting for their freedom in two months and the fight resulted in our complete victory. The Cossacks have fought with a courage equaled only by that displayed against the English by a people of Germanic stock, the Boers ... " It was surely unnecessary to drag in the English-Boer war at this point. But Krasnov, carried away by his own rhetoric, continued to enumerate other wars:

The All Great Don *voisko* and the other states of the Don-Caucasus Union do not forget the friendly service of the Cossacks to the German people, [they do not forget] the wars in which Cossacks and Germans fought shoulder to shoulder; at the time of the Thirty Years' War Cossacks fought in the army of Wallenstein, and in 1807 and 1813 under Count Platov they fought for the freedom of Germany. And now, after almost three and a half years of bloody war on the fields of Prussia, Galicia, Bukovina, and Poland, Cossacks and Germans have learned to respect each other's courage and steadfastness and now they offer their hands to each other, as two noble warriors, to fight together for the freedom of the native Don.

The letter ends with these lines:

A close alliance, which is cemented by the blood which was shed on common battlefields by the warlike Germans and Cossacks, promises mutual benefits and friendship and will become a powerful force against all our enemies.

It is not a diplomat who is versed in the fine points of international law who turns to your Imperial Majesty with this letter, but a soldier who has learned in honest battles to respect the power of German arms, and therefore I ask your forgiveness for the straightforwardness of my tone, since I am unaccustomed to being cunning and I ask you to believe the sincerity of my feelings.[19]

Krasnov was truthful in saying that he was not a diplomat, but the Emperor should not have believed "in the sincerity of his feelings." The Ataman, while protesting his friendship to Germany, encouraged the Volunteer Army to cooperate with the Czechs, who were avowed enemies of the Kaiser; he talked about the Don-Caucasus Union, which he knew perfectly well did not exist; and, of course, in a few months he was to call the attention of England and France to the battlefields where Englishmen, Frenchmen, and Cossacks died together. While no diplomat could have been more cynical, a good one certainly would have used more tact and taste.

Krasnov was not a German puppet like Skoropadskii, the Hetman of the Ukraine. The part of the Don which was under his authority was liberated by his Cossacks, and therefore he had far greater room in which to maneuver. German troops occupied the Ukraine in order to extort as much food and raw material as possible, but the German high command was wary of penetrating deeper into Russia for fear of spreading their army too thin.[20] Under the circumstances, Krasnov's policy was a pleasant surprise for the Germans, since they gained political influence and economic benefits without the sacrifice of lives. They undoubtedly would have been willing to exchange captured weapons for the food and mineral wealth of the Don without Krasnov's compromising himself by associating too

closely with them. The Ataman apparently never understood the
strength of his bargaining position.

As policy makers in Berlin decided that a permanently divided
Russia would best serve German interests, the Don came to play an
important role in their plans.[21] Among the states to be carved out of
the Russian Empire was the Don-Caucasus Union, in which the
Kuban, the Terek, Astrakhan, and the Northern Caucasus would
have been united under the pro-German government of Krasnov.

The idea of cooperation on the part of Cossack *voiska* had existed
before Krasnov's administration. In Kaledin's time, however, it
amounted to nothing more than planning for mutual aid among the
Cossacks, and obviously had nothing to do with a German orientation.[22] Under prevailing circumstances, Krasnov's plan for the Union
had no chance of success: most of the territory he wanted to include
in his future "independent" state was either occupied by the Bolsheviks or was controlled by governments which did not share his German orientation. While Krasnov must have known that the Don-
Caucasus Union was not likely to become a reality, he nevertheless
kept pretending to Berlin that it was almost an accomplished fact.

Unlike the grandiose scheme of a Don-Caucasus Union, which
had no practical importance, the exchange of weapons for food was
highly beneficial both for Germany and for the Don. The Germans
supplied an enormous amount of war material during the summer
of 1918. In the first month and a half, the Don received 11,651 rifles,
46 cannons, 48 machine guns, 109,104 shells, and 11,500,000 cartridges in exchange for food.[23]

Krasnov quickly established cooperation with the local German
command. On May 31, he negotiated with representatives of General von Knerzer, Commandant of Rostov, and on June 18, received
Major von Stefani, the representative of Field Marshall Eichhorn,
Commander of German forces in the Ukraine. On July 10, Major
von Kochenhausen, who took up permanent quarters in Rostov,
was named liaison officer between the German Army and the Don
government, and after that date all important negotiations took place
through the Major.[24]

Relations remained consistently friendly. The Germans agreed to
evacuate the Donets basin, which they had occupied, and the two

sides even agreed on a common expedition against a Bolshevik force stationed near Bataisk. The nature of the small disagreements between the two armies is interesting, nevertheless. Since boundaries were defined imprecisely, the Germans would requisition in a territory which the Cossacks regarded as their own and vice versa. Ironically, the Germans in many instances appeared as defenders of the population against the unruly Cossacks. For example, Major von Stefani protested to Ataman Krasnov on May 27:

> On May 26, at three o'clock in the afternoon in khutor Russkaia, the starosta and a sixteen-year-old notary were tortured by six officers and nine Cossacks to such an extent that they suffered serious wounds; many other inhabitants were severely beaten with rods. [The Cossacks] did not pay for the requisitioned horses, saddles, fodder, and foodstuffs. . . .

Stefani enumerates two similar incidents and adds:

> I call the attention of Your Excellency to the fact that all these requisitions took place in villages settled by non-Cossacks; the few small Cossack settlements [in the area] remained completely untouched.
>
> In settlements under the authority of the German army the soldiers were warned to preserve the life and property of the inhabitants. . . .[25]

Apparently the Germans were not blameless either. The Ataman wrote to General von Knerzer on May 29: "The Germans stationed in Malyi Nesvetaisk requisition bread, meat and eggs without paying, collect horses, fodder and in general do not behave as is befitting an army. . . . "[26]

Although Hetman Skoropadskii of the Ukraine and Ataman Krasnov pursued very similar policies and regarded each other as allies, and though the substantial trade was mutually beneficial, undecided territorial issues remained an obstacle to friendship and even closer cooperation.[27] The debate over Taganrog, between the Don and the Ukraine, though similar to debates among other White forces, is still one of the most absurd stories of the Civil War. The Bolsheviks possessed not only Moscow and Petrograd but also a large part of the Don at this time; and since they presented a very

real danger to the existence of both "independent" states, it is difficult to understand how Krasnov and Skoropadskii could attribute
so much significance to the issue whether Taganrog belonged to the
Ukraine or to the Don. The only explanation can be that both the
Hetman and the Ataman were amateur politicians, incapable of
separating the important from the ephemeral.

Taganrog, an industrial city with only a small Cossack population, was included in the Don *voisko* only in 1888, and even after
this date the city had little in common with the rest of the *voisko*.[28]
The Bolsheviks started the dispute unwittingly when, at Brest-
Litovsk, they acceded to German demands and recognized Taganrog as part of the Ukraine. Since late April, when the Germans occupied the city, it was the German attitude which was crucial in
the debate. Krasnov and his "minister of foreign affairs," General
A. P. Bogaevskii, understood this well and sent one letter after another to the German commanders in the Don asking for their sup
port.[29] At the same time, they sent General Semenov to organize a
militia in the city, one which would be under the authority of the
Don government. But the population had no desire for Cossack
government and the city *duma* took a hostile position on Krasnov's
plan.

Since Semenov's activities endangered the peace of Taganrog, the
German commandant asked Krasnov to recall the General.[30] Krasnov answered in his characteristic style:

> I ask you not to blame General Semenov too much, even if he took
> thoughtless steps in connection with Taganrog. He is an old sol-
> dier, and not a diplomat; he is a passionate patriot, whose heart can-
> not be reconciled with the claim of the Ukraine to Taganrog.
> How can you think that anyone among the Cossacks could be
> reconciled with this? In 1855 my grandfather defended Taganrog
> from the English and did not allow their unit to get inland, and the
> body of my father lies in the Taganrog cemetery. . . .[31]

Then Krasnov proceeded to blame the Ukrainians for Bolshevik
strength in Taganrog.

At first the Germans wanted to take no sides in the dispute between the Ukraine and the Don. They excluded the officials of both
sides from the government of the city and its administration re-

mained entirely in their hands.[32] Later, however, they came to favor the claim of Krasnov's government. German help might have been the result of the Ataman's better diplomacy, or perhaps the foreigners supported Krasnov because they needed him more than Skoropadskii; after all, the Hetman was merely their own puppet. It is likely that Skoropadskii's recognition of the independence of the Don on August 11, and his renunciation of his claim to Taganrog, were the result of German intercession. As a gesture of good will, the Germans withdrew their troops from Taganrog in October and the city was annexed to the *voisko*.

Aside from Taganrog, Krasnov wanted to annex cities which had never belonged to the *voisko*. General A. V. Cheriachukin, a confidant and admirer of the Ataman, and the Don's envoy in Kiev, wrote in his memoirs:

> No matter how desirable the wider boundaries of the Don would have been, I considered it essential to report that the inclusion of Voronezh, which had never belonged to the Don and was not needed because of strategic considerations, would cause an unnecessary impediment in negotiations and would meet strong opposition from the Ukrainians; aside from this, the annexation of Voronezh would further anger the Bolsheviks and would make it more difficult to defend the boundaries of the Don in general. Not objecting to the annexation of the strategically important Povorino, Kamyshin, Tsaritsyn, or Lugansk, I asked the Ataman to exclude Voronezh from the cities he considered essential for us.
>
> The Ataman agreed; nevertheless, on the map which had been prepared before, Voronezh remained inside of our borders. [The map was prepared for the delegation leaving for Kiev.][33]

As General Cheriachukin foresaw, Krasnov's extreme claims became the source of disagreements with the Ukrainians. When evaluating Don-Ukrainian relations one must remember that Skoropadskii's megalomania was just as bad as Krasnov's. When General N. A. Svechin, another Don envoy, visited the Hetman, he saw in his room a map of the "Ukraine" which included not only Taganrog but also Rostov, the Donets, the entire Kuban, and even Novorossisk.[34] In spite of all these ridiculous disagreements, Krasnov's relations with the Ukraine were smooth and easy compared with his difficulties with the leaders of the Volunteer Army.

THE VOLUNTEER ARMY AND MECHETINSKAIA AND EGORLYKSKAIA

When the Volunteer Army returned from the Ice March it took up quarters in the *stanitsy* Mechetinskaia and Egorlykskaia. Here in the area south of Rostov and Novocherkassk, the army was secure from the enemy because of the Don army's victories and the ineptitude of the Kuban Reds. Although militarily these months were the most passive ones in the entire history of the army, it was still a crucial period, because the relative quiet allowed the leaders to evaluate their political and military goals. In December and January everyone expected the Bolshevik regime to collapse momentarily, and in the course of the Ice March the only important problem was survival, but now for the first time the generals had to face the possibility of a protracted struggle, and therefore had to develop policies on Cossack separatism and on the Allies and the Germans, and had to establish contact with political organizations. The decisions taken in this period had a profound effect on the entire course of the Civil War.

Now that the Don army was much stronger than the Volunteer Army, Denikin could have moved to Rostov or Novocherkassk only on Krasnov's terms. Denikin, however, preferred the inconveniences of staying in *stanitsy* and the handicap in recruiting to compromising himself by open collaboration with the Germanophile Krasnov, and he sent only the sick and the wounded into the Don hospitals. To keep the two armies at a distance from one another would also help reduce inevitable quarrels between the soldiers.

After the great trials of the Ice March, dozens and perhaps hundreds left the army, so that in the beginning the size of the army was reduced rather than increased. Many of the Don Cossacks who had joined at the end of February now preferred to fight under Krasnov. Among them was General A. P. Bogaevskii, the commander of one of the three brigades, who became foreign minister in the new *voisko* government. Others had enlisted at the end of 1917 for only four months and now exercised their right to leave.[35] Also, many of the schoolchildren who had participated in the march now wanted to return to their parents.

But soon new arrivals more than compensated for the losses. The German occupation of the Ukraine and other parts of Russia enabled many to come who previously had thought they could not. But most of the new recruits came from the cities of the Don. These men had wanted to avoid fighting in the Civil War, but during the era of the Don Soviet Republic they had learned that neutrality was impossible. The largest group of newcomers was led by Colonel Drozdovskii, who had participated in the liberation of Novocherkassk. While on the Don, his detachment grew from one thousand to twenty-five hundred men.[36] Krasnov, whose relations with Denikin had deteriorated, wanted to persuade Drozdovskii to organize an independent army which would be coordinated with his units. But the Colonel turned down the suggestion and united his small army with Denikin's troops on June 8.[37] The unification of the forces was a great moment for the White soldiers, and the arrival of twenty-five hundred men gave fresh hope that most Russian officers would eventually join the struggle. Also, the veterans of the Kuban campaign looked with wonder and envy at their comrades: they were dressed so much better and looked so much more like soldiers.[38]

Because of its increased size, Denikin reorganized his army by making divisions of the former brigades. Generals Markov and Borovskii and Colonel Drozdovskii were named to head the infantry divisions and General Erdeli to head the only cavalry division. By the middle of June the army had between nine and ten thousand soldiers.[39]

Supreme authority came to be concentrated increasingly in Denikin's hands. Although Russian society continued to regard Alekseev as the leader of the army, in fact he became more and more of a figurehead. His failing health, caused largely by the hardships of the Ice March, made it impossible for him to take the same amount of work upon himself as he had done a few months earlier. There was no competition for power between the two leaders and they cooperated with each other harmoniously. Denikin respected the older man and always treated him with courtesy.

In the middle of June, Alekseev moved to Novocherkassk, partly because of his health and partly because he hoped to be able to keep in better touch with political developments all over the country. His physical absence and his increasing indecisiveness further sapped his influence in Mechetinskaia. He was almost persuaded to assume monarchist slogans; he changed his mind several times about the wisdom of the second Kuban campaign; and on at least one occasion he even considered cooperating with Germany.[40] Since Alekseev hesitated and Denikin did not, it was always Denikin's policy which prevailed.

For the purposes of attracting political and financial support Alekseev formed a "political department" in Novocherkassk.[41] The department never gained much importance. Since its tasks were never precisely defined, it was inevitable that there would be some duplication of work and some disagreements between it and the army staff. However, the disagreements never became serious enough to destroy the mutual trust between Alekseev and Denikin.

Neither the army staff at Mechetinskaia nor Alekseev's political department had much use for politicians. Mechetinskaia did not attract politicians as Novocherkassk had before the Ice March, or as Ekaterinodar would after its liberation in August—a situation which Denikin found perfectly satisfactory. When Rodzianko, the ex-President of the Duma, suggested that Denikin summon the members of the four *dumas*, the Commander-in-Chief turned down the suggestion instantly.[42] Since he thought of politics and ideology only as divisive forces, he wanted to keep politicians—and as much as possible politics—away from the army.

But the attempt to keep the army apolitical in a civil war was bound to fail. In this period the chief political issue Denikin had to face was whether or not to espouse a monarchist position. From its inception, the army attracted a large number of rightist extremists and reactionaries. The experiences of the Ice March, in the course of which the men almost always lived in a hostile environment, created much bitterness, which is always a potent source of extremism. In the early summer of 1918, it was estimated that 80 to 90 per cent of the non-Cossack segment of the army was monarchist.[43] The monarchists formed secret societies and began to display tsarist medals and flags.

Denikin faced great pressure to come out for monarchism, not only from his soldiers but also from such popular commanders as

Drozdovskii, who belonged to one of the secret societies. Such diverse men as the Kadet leader P. N. Miliukov, the conservative and able V. V. Shulgin (who played an important role in persuading the last tsar to abdicate), and General A. Lukomskii, an old associate, gave the same advice.[44] Alekseev was inclined to listen to the advice of monarchists, but Denikin uncompromisingly continued to maintain that the future form of the state of Russia should be decided by a Constituent Assembly.

By remaining firm Denikin performed a great service to the anti-Bolshevik cause. An explicit identification of the Volunteer Army with the defunct tsarist regime would have further alienated the large majority of Russian peasants, on whose attitude the success of the White cause ultimately depended. As hostile as the Kuban Cossacks were to Bolshevism, they nevertheless objected to tsarism and had the Volunteer Army become a monarchist army, this would have increased separatist aspirations among the Cossacks.[45]

Denikin understood some of the practical arguments against monarchism, but he did not advocate convening a Constituent Assembly merely because of the political advantages of this course. His personal preference was always for a constitutional monarchy, but he never allowed himself to be influenced by this, because he believed that his small army had no right to decide such an important matter for the Russian people.[46]

The cleavage between the leaders and the rank and file of the army increased. Undoubtedly some soldiers left the army because they disagreed with its announced principles, and most of the officers would have fought more enthusiastically under tsarist banners. Had Kornilov lived, the problem would not have arisen. There is no reason to doubt that he would have remained faithful to the principle of sovereignty of the people which he announced in 1917, and his prestige had been so great in the anti-Bolshevik army that the complaints could not even have arisen. But Denikin was a much less charismatic leader, and up to that date his contributions to the White cause were much less conspicuous. He was therefore less able to control the dissatisfaction. To gain support Denikin, in cooperation with Alekseev, published the "Goals of the Army" in the middle of May.

I. The Volunteer Army is fighting to save Russia by (1) creating a strong, disciplined and patriotic army; (2) waging merciless war against Bolshevism; (3) reestablishing unity and lawful order in the country.

II. In attempting to cooperate with all politically–minded Russian people [*gosudarstvenno mysliashchimi*], the Volunteer Army cannot take on a party label.

III. The question of what form the state is to take should be postponed to the last stage [of the fight] and will be the expression of the will of the Russian people after it is freed from tyranny and madness.

IV. [The Volunteer Army will have] no contact either with the Germans or with the Bolsheviks. To us only these positions are acceptable: the Germans must withdraw from the territory of Russia; the Bolsheviks must capitulate and be disarmed. . . .[47]

The two leaders decided to discuss the political issues with their followers and therefore called a meeting of all officers down to platoon commanders in Egorlykskaia on May 18. Alekseev talked about the dangers of a German orientation and Denikin talked about monarchism. Denikin said:

There was a powerful Russian army [whose soldiers] knew how to die and how to be victorious. But when soldiers began to decide questions of strategy, of war and peace, monarchy or republic, the army fell apart. It seems the same thing is being repeated. Our only task is to fight and free Russia from the Bolsheviks, but many are dissatisfied with this position. They demand the immediate raising of the monarchist flag. What for? In order to divide us into camps and start an internecine war? In order that those circles which do not help the army now, but who don't hinder it either, should start an active fight against us? In order that the thirty-thousand-man Stavropol militia, with whom we are negotiating now and who do not desire monarchy at all, should join the Red Army? And finally, what right do we have, as a small group of people, to decide about the fate of our country without its consent, without the consent of the entire Russian people?[48]

Dangerous as was the dissension between monarchists and republicans, the disagreements between the Don and Kuban Cossacks and the leaders of the army was even more threatening. In spite of the substantial influx of Russian officers in May and June, 50 to 70 per cent of the army consisted of Kuban Cossacks, and the officers and Cossacks belonged to different worlds.[49] Denikin handled the issue of Cossack separatism with remarkable blindness: he dissolved Kuban units, he hurt Cossack pride by putting Cossacks almost invariably under Russian officers, and he explicitly opposed any sign of independent policy action from the *rada* and the Kuban government.[50]

But the *rada* was not intimidated: it sent a delegation to Skoropadskii in spite of the disapproval of the Volunteer Army leaders.[51] The negotiations, however, proved fruitless. The Ukrainian government would have supported the Kuban only on condition that the Kuban become part of the Ukraine, and this the delegates did not want to accept, partly because of the German orientation of the Kiev government and partly because they well understood that that government was hopelessly weak.[52]

The Kuban leaders also dealt directly with Krasnov. Because of Krasnov's Germanophile policies, the Kuban representatives did not accept his scheme for a Don-Caucasus Union, and the cooperation between Kuban and Don Cossacks never became close. The Kuban Cossacks never found better allies than the Volunteer Army. But the leaders of the Volunteer Army did not understand that Cossack cooperation was only conditional; the Cossacks fought in the Volunteer Army not because they shared its ideology and goals, but because only this organization promised rapid liberation of their native land.

The short-sightedness which characterized Denikin's attitude toward the Cossacks of his army was perhaps even more obvious in his attitude toward the Ataman of the Don, General Krasnov. The personalities of the two men could not have differed more: Denikin was modest, inflexible, impeccably honest, and somewhat dull, while Krasnov was vain and devious and substituted picturesque expressions for sound reasoning. The two men took an immediate dislike to each other, and to the discredit of both they allowed their decisions to be influenced by these feelings.

It would be wrong, however, to attribute the conflict between the Don and the Volunteer Army entirely to the personalities of the two leaders, for the quarrels had appeared in embryonic form even before the election of the Ataman. When Denikin received news of the liberation of Novocherkassk by the Cossack army at the beginning of May, he sent General Kisliakov to establish contact with the anti-Bolshevik Don. Kisliakov's report disappointed Denikin. The Provisional Government in Novocherkassk politely but firmly rejected Denikin's suggestion of establishing a united command, and it was already clear that the Cossacks would not adopt the same rigidly hostile attitude toward the Germans as Denikin had.[53]

Denikin watched developments in Novocherkassk with increasing dismay. He blamed Krasnov unjustly for the birth of Cossack nationalism, which played a great role in the deliberations of the *krug* for the Salvation of the Don. He was unduly disturbed by the outward manifestations of this nationalism, the new flag and the anthem. With more justification he disapproved of the restorationist atmosphere of Novocherkassk, of excluding the *inogorodnye* from the government of the *voisko*, and of returning to the legal system of tsarist times.[54]

The first meeting between General Krasnov and the leadership of the Volunteer Army took place at *stanitsa* Manychskaia on May 28. The Volunteer Army was represented by Generals Alekseev, Denikin, Romanovskii, and Ataman Filimonov, while Krasnov brought along General Bogaevskii and Colonel Bykadorov. The meeting, which lasted from one o'clock in the afternoon until late in the evening, took place in an atmosphere of hostility.[55] It was obvious to all participants from the beginning that there could be no question of building the same friendly cooperation between Denikin and Krasnov as had existed between Kaledin and Alekseev a few months earlier. Kaledin, who had been ten years older than Denikin, had the reputation of being one of the best generals of the Russian army during the war, and by 1914 had already commanded a division. Denikin, a man with a strong sense of propriety, would have treated Kaledin as an equal, and would have made no attempt to subordinate him to his command. On the other hand, Krasnov was an upstart in his eyes. He never understood that revolutionary times made the principle of seniority an anachronism; even though at this time when he needed Krasnov far more than the Ataman needed him, perhaps

without realizing it, he constantly treated the Ataman as a subordinate, lecturing and reproaching him. Krasnov intensely resented this
treatment. In his memoirs, he mentions that he told Denikin that he
would not tolerate his tone because he was "no little general now,
but a leader of five million people."[56]

The Manychaskaia meeting was not entirely fruitless. Krasnov
promised the Volunteer Army six million rubles from the Rostov
bank, and the continued supply of German munitions; he permitted
Volunteer Army enlistment bureaus to operate in Novocherkassk
and Rostov, and he granted hospital service for the sick and the
wounded. The Volunteer Army, in exchange, promised to protect
the Don from the South against the Bolsheviks.[57] Undoubtedly, it
was the Volunteer Army which gained more by this agreement, for
the Bolsheviks on the Kuban were disorganized and it was quite unlikely that they could manage to stage an attack on the Don.

On all other issues of substance the Volunteer Army leadership
and the Don delegation disagreed. Denikin again brought up the
principle of united command, which in fact meant the subordination of the much larger Don army to the Volunteer Army. The
Ataman, understandably, showed no interest in this proposal. Denikin protested sharply that at Bataisk German soldiers had fought
side by side with soldiers of the Volunteer Army and Don Cossacks.
Krasnov promised that this would not happen again, but he was
irritated by what he considered hypocrisy.[58] On the one hand, the
Volunteer Army accepted weapons which came from the Ukraine
with permission of the occupation forces; on the other, Denikin not
only refused to cooperate openly with the Germans, but also attacked the Ukrainian and Don governments for doing so. As
Krasnov described the situation a few months later at the meeting
of the *krug:* "Yes, yes, gentlemen, the Volunteer Army is clean and
undefiled. But I, the Don Ataman, take the dirty German bullets and
shells, wash them in the quiet Don, and give them clean to the Volunteer Army. The entire shame for this matter rests with me."[59] Krasnov's bitter and sarcastic remark gave a fair picture of the attitude
of the Volunteer Army's leadership. The main purpose for holding
the Manychskaia meeting was to coordinate the strategies of the two

armies. On this issue, which will be discussed in some detail in the next chapter, there was no agreement.

Following the Manychskaia meeting, relations deteriorated further. As the Germans adopted a hostile policy toward the Volunteer Army, they put pressure on Krasnov not only to cease support of the anti-German army, but to disarm and disperse it, or at least to substitute more malleable generals for Alekseev, Denikin, and Romanovskii.[60] It is to Krasnov's credit that he not only disregarded these suggestions, but continued to support the Volunteer Army with weapons and money. However, the Germans' pressure made Krasnov even more irritated by Denikin's intransigence and evident lack of understanding of his difficulties. At the same time Denikin, who held a low opinion of Krasnov, became worried that the Ataman would accede to the Germans' demands and take steps against the Army.

As the Volunteer Army and the Don government came to represent different orientations in foreign policy and different social philosophies, it was inevitable that they attracted followers from each other's camp. A large number of Cossack politicians who disliked Krasnov's conservatism found aid and comfort at the headquarters of the Volunteer Army.[61] On the other hand, the appeal of Krasnov's more conservative line disturbed Denikin, who remembered that the monarchist Colonel Drozdovskii had considered joining Krasnov's army rather than his.

An important source of trouble between the two armies was the quarrels, which were perhaps inevitable, between Cossacks and officers in Novocherkassk. Even though the Volunteer Army as a whole wisely stayed away from the city, many officers found reasons to be there rather than remain in the extremely dull *stanitsy* of Egorlykskaia and Mechetinskaia. The Cossacks resented the rudeness of "aliens," and the officers did not like the manifestations of Cossack separatism.

Denikin had especially bad relations with the thirty-four-year-old General Denisov, the Commander of the Don army. Denisov wanted to treat Denikin as an equal and this the Commander of the Volunteer Army could not tolerate.[62] Denisov constantly made fun of the

Volunteer Army, and of course his words were soon relayed to Denikin. On a social occasion, in the presence of Volunteer Army Don officers, Denisov described the Volunteer Army as "wandering musicians," an expression which for some reason deeply insulted Denikin.[63] Later, when the Don leaders tried to ingratiate themselves with the Allies, Volunteer officers compared this behavior to that of a prostitute who sells herself to those who can pay the most. Denisov retorted, with considerable justice: "if the Don *voisko* is a prostitute selling herself to those who can pay, then the Volunteer Army is a pimp living on her earnings and kept by her."[64]

As at the time of the formation of the Volunteer Army, lack of funds was again one of the gravest problems. A million rubles a week was necessary to support an army of almost ten thousand.[65] Most of the time there was enough money at Alekseev's disposal to support the army only for a few weeks. Alekseev even contemplated the dissolution of the army for this reason, writing to Miliukov on May 23: "Without money—with an aching heart and fear for the fate of those released—I will soon have to dissolve the army.[66]

Lack of money hindered recruitment. The Volunteer Army set up recruiting centers in many large cities which the Germans had freed from the Bolsheviks, but the operation of these offices was severely limited because of lack of funds.[67] Because of its poverty, the army could hardly compete with other anti-Bolshevik organizations (for example, the Southern army and the Astrakhan army), which were well supplied with German money.

The main source of money was the Don government, a source which was politically compromising and personally humiliating to the leaders of the army. Alekseev tried to appeal to the Rostov rich, but the results were meager. Nor was he more successful in his attempt to get money through Miliukov's contacts in Kiev; Miliukov soberly advised him to accept Krasnov's terms for cooperation.[68] In the middle of May, Alekseev sent two emissaries to Vologda to solicit aid from the allied diplomats. Indeed, a few weeks later the army received ten million rubles from the French, which up to this time was the largest donation from the Allies.[69]

Also in the middle of May, General B. Kazanovich went to Moscow accompanied by A. A. Ladyshinskii, who was reputed to have contacts with financiers.[70] Although the Kazanovich mission did not accomplish its main purpose—getting financial support for the army—it was still important, for it reestablished the contact with Moscow political circles which had been broken at the time of the Ice March.

Kazanovich was very much disappointed by what he saw in Moscow. He arrived at the time when conservative political circles increasingly accepted the necessity for seeking German help. For example, the prominent tsarist politician and ex-minister of agriculture, Krivoshein, told him that in his opinion nothing could be done without German support, and that officers living in Moscow should not try to join the Volunteer Army but instead should attempt to overthrow Bolshevik rule with German help.[71]

Kazanovich was present at the meeting of the Right Center in which, after a passionate debate over approaching the Germans, the unity of the organization broke down. Soon after, the disaffected left formed the National Center. Ideologically, it was this newly formed organization which was closest to the Volunteer Army. In fact, M. M. Fedorov, a leading member of this group, even asked Kazanovich to join.[72] The General, however, felt that as representative of the Volunteer Army he had no right to support one group against another. But his relations deteriorated even with the National Center when he attempted to get in touch with the French mission directly. The National Center maintained that relations with foreign powers should be conducted entirely through this organization. (Kazanovich disregarded Fedorov's protest and received half a million rubles from the French consul in Moscow.)[73]

Kazanovich met a wide variety of people, representatives of all shades of the anti-Bolshevik spectrum. The impression of the General was that none of these groups possessed the decisiveness and courage to act, and that the Volunteer Army could expect no substantial help from them. At the end of June he decided to return to the South.[74]

As the political center of the anti-Bolshevik movement moved from Red Moscow to German-occupied Kiev, the Volunteer Army's contacts with political circles improved. Messengers and delegations frequently went from Mechetinskaia to the Ukrainian capital. At the same time, the army faced increasing pressure to change its attitude toward the Germans. Many of the same men who had advocated a monarchist platform now asked Denikin at least to moderate his hostility to the invaders. Krasnov, the chief supplier of munitions, also tried everything to make the army leaders see the situation in his way. However, the most important source of pressure must have been the army officers. Sensibly enough, they came to regard the Bolsheviks as their only enemies, and they did not want to keep up the costly pretense of hostility toward the Germans.

On the occasion when Denikin addressed the assembled officers in order to justify his position on the issue of monarchism, Alekseev argued against the danger of a German orientation. When Alekseev called the Germans "enemies as cruel and merciless as the Bolsheviks" one of the officers interrupted him: "Yes, they are enemies, but cultured ones."[75] Alekseev continued to argue that cooperation with the Germans was not only unacceptable from a moral point of view but also inexpedient, since the Germans would lose the war.

Why did Alekseev and Denikin not follow the example of Krasnov and dozens of other politicians and approach the Germans for help? No doubt, they sincerely believed in the ultimate victory of the Allies, but this belief must have been based purely on faith, since they had only unreliable and imprecise information about developments on the Western front. Any explanation of the Generals' attitude must take into account their notions of honor and their anti-German prejudices. They believed that Russia had committed herself to the cause of the Allies, and they applied the same standard of morality to nations as to individuals. (It was this characteristic of Denikin which made him so bitterly disappointed when he received only half-hearted aid from the Allies in 1919 and 1920.) They hated the Germans. Throughout his life Denikin never wavered in the belief that it was Germany which had forced the World War on Russia.

It is difficult to establish any connection between Denikin's political liberalism and his faithfulness to the Allies, as compared with Krasnov's conservatism and German orientation. Denikin never explicitly made that connection, but it is quite possible that his sympathy for England and France had something to do with his liking of their political and social systems.

Just as a year earlier Kerenskii's government had not been able to decide which was more important, "the deepening of the revolution," or the continuation of the war, so the generals leading the Volunteer Army could not make up their mind whether to suppress the Bolsheviks or continue the war. In the face of increasingly overwhelming evidence to the contrary, they rationalized their attitude by regarding the Bolsheviks as mere agents of Germany. This inflexibility is characteristic of men not experienced in politics and diplomacy. As it was unnecessary for Krasnov to commit himself completely to the Germans, it was hardly wise for the Volunteer Army to reject all approaches to them.

In the first months of their occupation of South Russia, the Germans were unquestionably eager to gain the good will of the Volunteer Army. It is difficult to establish to what extent this was a centrally planned policy, and to what extent it stemmed from the spontaneous sympathy of the German officers for their Russian counterparts. Individual Germans manifested their sympathy for anti-Bolshevik officers innumerable times, and showed their respect for the Russians. As long as the Volunteers did not threaten any vital German interests, they were willing to close their eyes even to the pro-Allied slogans of Alekseev and Denikin. For example, the Volunteer Army set up an enlistment bureau in Kiev under Colonel Riazianskii, who sent hundreds of officers to Mechetinskaia.[76] German authorities did not give the bureau permission to operate, but they did not disturb its work either and pretended not to notice it. No doubt, the Germans also knew that part of the munitions they gave to Krasnov regularly ended in the hands of an army which openly professed hostility to them. Denikin and Alekseev could not have expected better treatment from their "enemies."

The spontaneous good-will of the Germans greatly embarrassed Denikin and Alekseev. They benefited from German policy toward the White army in spite of themselves, and found it necessary to justify themselves in their own eyes. The army leaders rationalized their acceptance of weapons from Krasnov with the rather disingenuous explanation that those weapons were taken from the Bolsheviks and therefore they were Russian weapons. It is hardly necessary to add that in fact not all the weapons came from the Bolsheviks.

On one occasion in Novocherkassk, General Alekseev met a German representative in the presence of Ataman Krasnov. Alekseev was uncompromising almost to the point of insult. He avoided answering the German's question: "Would the Volunteer Army tacitly cooperate and keep quiet about its allied sympathy?" When he refused even to promise that his army would not help the insurgent Czechs, the German got up and said: "In this case you will meet German troops."[77]

The man who did more than anyone else for bringing the Germans and the Volunteer Army together was P. N. Miliukov, the Kadet leader, an old acquaintance of Alekseev. Miliukov, who had spent the months of Bolshevik rule in Rostov, was planning to go to Moscow after the German occupation of the town. However, the discipline of the German troops, and the setting up of the anti-Bolshevik governments of Skoropadskii and Krasnov, made a great impression on him. He came to believe that what the Germans had accomplished against the Bolsheviks in Kiev they might be willing to do in Moscow. Even if the Germans refused, Miliukov thought, the creation of independent governments on the peripheries of Russia under German protection would provide a base for the national anti-Bolshevik movement. He attributed great significance to the unity of the movement, and since the Germans occupied large parts of the former Empire, he understood that that unity could be created only under the German aegis.[78]

Miliukov, whose pro-German orientation was quite different from the subservience of a Skoropadskii or the unprincipled flattery of a Krasnov, still enjoyed great prestige among the anti-Bolshevik Russians, and therefore his change of orientation had great impact. He was able to win over a substantial number of his political friends, and he was not without influence even on General Alekseev.[79] He intended to go to Kiev, instead of Moscow, in order to establish contact with the German command. Before his departure he notified Alekseev about his intentions, and since Alekseev asked him to help the Kiev representative, Colonel Riazianskii, Miliukov felt that he would go to Kiev, at least to a limited extent, as a representative of the Volunteer Army.[80]

The Kadet politician tried to reconcile the Germans and the leaders of the Volunteer Army by underplaying the differences and interpreting one to the other. In Kiev he had several talks with the German diplomat Major Haase, on a wide variety of subjects, including the Volunteer Army. Haase expressed his doubts about the ability of the Volunteer Army to liberate Moscow, and recommended that if the army leaders persisted in their anti-German policies, the White Russians should remove them. To gain the good will of the Germans, Miliukov pretended to have information that the army was about to change its orientation.[81]

In his letters to Alekseev, Miliukov always depicted Germans in the most favorable light and professed to see signs that they would turn against the Bolsheviks. However, the change which came was not what Miliukov hoped for. In July, the Germans became increasingly worried about the successes of the Czechs, which raised the possibility that the Allies might succeed in reconstructing the Eastern front. In view of this development, the allied orientation of the Volunteer Army and the possibility of Denikin forming a united front with the Czechs became a danger to Berlin. On July 9, the Germans expressly forbade recruitment for the Volunteer Army and ordered the arrest of officers who belonged to that organization.[82] While few officers were actually arrested and many of those were soon freed through the intercession of the Hetman and other prominent pro-German Russians, the continuation of the work of the enlistment bureau of the Volunteer Army became impossible.

As the Germans realized that they could not win over the Volunteer Army leaders, they decided to organize separate White armies in order to channel the anti-Bolshevik feelings of the Russian officers. This development was a great blow to the Volunteer Army. The two German-sponsored armies, the Astrakhan and the Southern Army, started with monarchist slogans which proved to be a great attraction to hundreds of officers. Neither of the rightist armies ever became a serious force; the organizers of the Southern Army, Prince G. Leikhtenbergskii and M. E. Akatsatov, and the organizer of the Astrakhan army, Prince Tundutov, could not find well-known and talented generals to head their armies.[83] The two armies became the prey of adventurers; they had enormous staffs and few soldiers and were incapable of any independent undertaking. Nevertheless, the existence of these armies hurt the Volunteer Army because they siphoned off potential recruits.

Miliukov was the first to realize that his policy of bringing the Germans and the Volunteer Army together had failed. He wrote to Alekseev in early July that if the German army were to enter Moscow now, it would do so as an ally of the Bolsheviks, and that the Germans were bent on dismembering Russia, seeing this policy as the best guarantee of their security.[84]

The Germans became impatient with Miliukov's cautious pro-German orientation. Mumm, the German ambassador to the Ukraine, let Skoropadskii know that Miliukov was agitating for his removal. The infuriated Hetman wanted to arrest the Kadet leader, and did not do so only because of energetic protest from his cabinet. To avoid a threatening cabinet crisis over his fate, Miliukov decided to leave Kiev.

CHAPTER 6

Campaigns

As a result of a series of disagreements, fighting broke out on May 25, 1918, between the Czech corps, then being transported from European Russia to Vladivostok, and Soviet troops. The small Czech forces succeeded in overthrowing Bolshevik rule in some of the major cities along the Trans-Siberian railroad with amazing rapidity.

The clash between the Bolsheviks and the Czechs can be regarded as the beginning of the Russian Civil War. Because of lack of food, foreign enemies, and spreading anarchy, the Soviet regime had lived in a constant state of crisis from its very inception. The threat to its existence had not been chiefly military, however. Indeed, the Reds hardly had an army. After having helped destroy the Imperial army, they had tried to form a new one by voluntary enlistment, but with little success. The only reason they had survived this dangerous period was that their enemies were even weaker than they were.

L. D. Trotskii became Commissar of War on March 13, 1918, and as a result of his work the quality of the Red Army gradually began to improve. Almost immediately he introduced "military specialists," ex-tsarist officers who were cajoled and threatened into the service of the proletarian state. But the crucial turning point in the development of the Red Army occurred only after, and largely as a result of, the Czech revolt. Moscow decided to abandon the principle of voluntary enlistment and to introduce conscription, at first in selected areas and later throughout Soviet-held territory. On August 1, the Red Army had 331 thousand soldiers; a month later, on September 5, it had 550 thousand, and by the end of the year it had a million.[1]

The occasional battles which took place in the months following the November Revolution were fought by very small forces. The Bolsheviks frequently took advantage of their control of the railroads and pursued their numerically weaker but better disciplined enemies. This was the period of what was called "echelon" warfare. The beginning of the Civil War in the early summer of 1918 meant that conventional fronts came into being and battles were fought by increasingly large armies.

THE TSARITSYN DEBATE AND THE SECOND KUBAN CAMPAIGN

By coincidence, the meeting of Generals Krasnov and Denikin to coordinate strategies took place at the same time as the Czech revolt. At the Manychskaia meeting on May 28 two positions were considered: Krasnov wanted the Volunteer Army to march against Tsaritsyn, but Denikin announced that his army would liberate the Kuban rather than turn East after resting. To choose between Tsaritsyn and Ekaterinodar as the next objective was the most important strategic decision the Volunteer Army leaders had to make in 1918, and it is possible that the future course of the entire Civil War depended on this decision. Tsaritsyn's strategic importance was self-evident: the city was one of the most important railroad centers in Russia; it had valuable munitions factories, most of them built during the First World War, and it had a large working class population, which represented a potential source of recruits for the Red Army.[2] Indeed, in the second half of 1918 Tsaritsyn became the main theater of the Civil War. The Don army was besieging the city at the same time the anti-Bolsheviks in Siberia were achieving substantial success. Whether the eastern and southern fronts could be united depended on the battle for Tsaritsyn. It would have been extremely advantageous for the Whites to establish a common front, and the Bolsheviks did everything within their power to prevent it. In fact, in the course of the entire Civil War, the Whites never succeeded in uniting the two major fronts.

While not all these developments could be foreseen by the end of

May, Krasnov maintains in his memoirs that he argued as follows at Manychskaia:

> On the basis of the situation observed in Saratov district, an attack on Tsaritsyn promises full success to the volunteers. In Saratov district the uprising of the peasants has already begun. Tsaritsyn will give General Denikin a purely Russian base, with weapons and munitions factories and large stores of all kinds of military material —to say nothing of money. The Volunteer Army would cease to depend on the Cossacks. Besides, taking Tsaritsyn would bring the army closer to, and possibly would unite it with, the Czechoslovaks and Dutov [Ataman of the Ural Cossacks], and would create one menacing front. With the support of the Don *voisko*, the Army could begin its march to Samara, Penza, Tula, and then the Don soldiers would take Voronezh.[3]

To make the battle for Tsaritsyn more attractive, Krasnov promised to place Cossack troops under Denikin's command, and thereby take the first step toward realizing the principle of a united command of all White forces, a principle which had always been dear to Denikin's heart.

Krasnov could not have used exactly the arguments he remembered afterwards, because on May 28 it was impossible to realize the importance of the Czech revolt or to know about the offensive of the Ural Cossacks under Ataman Dutov, which was to take place two days later. But whatever arguments he used, there is no doubt that he had a genuine appreciation of Tsaritsyn's strategic importance. The Ataman, however, had another reason for trying to persuade the leaders of the Volunteer Army. As indicated on May 14, in his first speech to the *krug*, he believed that the Don must annex Tsaritsyn.[4] He feared that his Cossacks would be unwilling to go further than the boundaries of the *voisko*, and it therefore seemed to him that without Denikin's help he could never take that city.

Denikin was not only unwilling to agree with Krasnov; he became visibly angry that the Ataman dared to suggest a strategy to him. With great passion and little logic he argued that his army could not stage an offensive against Tsaritsyn because of the possibility of encountering Germans there. Krasnov tried to assure him that the Germans would not go farther east than Ust-Beloklitvenskaia (a few miles east of Kamenskaia), but Denikin remained unimpressed.[5] Denikin was attacked until the end of his life by emigre military historians for his decision at Manychskaia.[6] His defense always remained lame: he argued later that the Germans would not have allowed his army to unite with the Czechs, and that it would have been wrong to let the Germans occupy the Kuban, which was a rich area. He further maintained that it was necessary to occupy the Black Sea ports, for these became the main points of contact with the Allies.[7]

Denikin's arguments were so weak that it is impossible to take them seriously. First of all, he had no reason to think that the Germans would penetrate further east, and in fact the danger was much greater that they would take the Kuban in order to establish direct contact with the pro-German Georgian state. Surely the presence of a few thousand volunteers would not have frightened them away. Moving the army east would have been the best assurance of getting away from the German sphere of domination. Also, if the Allies won the war, they would have had little trouble in establishing contact with the White army, wherever it was.

One suspects that Denikin must have had reasons other than the ones stated for choosing the Kuban as his next objective. Whether he consciously understood it and was embarrassed to reveal it to Krasnov, or merely sensed it, the fact was that he could not have moved against Tsaritsyn because his army would not have followed him. He had promised the Kuban Cossacks that he would liberate their native district. He wanted to fulfill this promise, but aside from his good faith the Cossacks had the means to force him. Alekseev, unlike Denikin, flatly stated in the course of the discussions that the Kuban Cossacks would not march against Tsaritsyn, and without them the Volunteer Army would be no match for the Bolsheviks.[8] The other senior army generals must have agreed with him, because none of them believed that a campaign against Tsaritsyn could succeed.

Civil War strategy must not be judged on the basis of purely military considerations. Denikin made the correct decision because he understood that in May 1918 there was no effective anti-Bolshevik force in Russia aside from the Cossacks. From his actions, and from reading between the lines of his speeches, it appears that he had little faith in the Russian people. His army had come in contact with the *inogorodnye* on the Don and on the Kuban, and he had yet to find a settlement of Russian peasants where he was well received. He believed that the time for the decisive encounter with Bolshevism was still in the future, and he was correct. Had he ventured away from Cossack territories, even assuming that his small army would follow him, it is unlikely that he could have formed an army as large as he in fact succeeded in forming in the following months on the Kuban.

General Alekseev was even more pessimistic than Denikin. After he moved to Novocherkassk he began to wonder about the wisdom of the new Kuban campaign. This was not because he approved of trying to take Tsaritsyn, but because attacking Ekaterinodar seemed equally dangerous to him. He wrote about his fears to Miliukov and to Denikin, but by the time Denikin received his letter the army was on its way to Ekaterinodar.[9]

When the Volunteer Army began the second Kuban campaign on June 22, circumstances were quite different from those of a few months earlier, at the start of the Ice March. This time the army was not a small group of refugees in a hurry to escape capture, but a force sent to accomplish a specific strategic task on the basis of precise military plans.

The Red Army's superiority in numbers in the Northern Caucasus —the area Denikin wanted to conquer—was overwhelming. Against the eight or nine thousand volunteers, the Bolsheviks had more than seventy-five thousand men.[10] That the much larger army was soon defeated can be explained by the superior quality of the White troops, by the constant quarrels among the Red commanders, and by the unwitting help the Germans once again gave to the Whites.

The Reds mistakenly perceived the Germans as a greater threat to their possession of the Northern Caucasus than the Volunteer Army. When the Germans occupied the Ukraine, Taganrog, Rostov, and finally Bataisk, some of the Bolshevik forces retired to the Eisk district of the Kuban. On June 11, a small army of 6,400 men,

under the command of S. Klovno, executed a raid across the Azov
Sea on Taganrog. This was an insane venture; the small force was
quickly defeated, and this endangered the Red Army's position on
the Kuban by inviting German retaliation. Most important, it adversely affected relations between Moscow and Berlin, since the
Germans held Lenin's government responsible for the raid, which
they regarded as a violation of the Brest-Litovsk treaty. Chicherin,
the Bolshevik Foreign Commissar, immediately ordered the Eisk
army to put a stop to the engagement and start negotiation with the
enemy, but this was hardly helpful, for by the time the telegram
arrived the Soviet forces had been soundly defeated. As a result of
this hasty military action, the Reds had to concentrate their troops
against the Germans just at a time when the Volunteer Army was
starting its campaign.[11] A. I. Avtonomov, Commander-in-Chief of
the Red troops in the Northern Caucasus, was dismissed at the end
of May because of his inability to cooperate with the civilian leaders
of the district Soviet in Ekaterinodar.[12] Of the two men who were
competing for Avtonomov's job, I. L. Sorokin and K. I. Kalnin,
Kalnin was successful. In mid-June, Kalnin was stationed in the
area of Torgovaia and Tikhoretskaia with ten thousand men. It was
this group which was to bear the brunt of the fighting against the
Volunteer Army. The largest and best Soviet forces, under Sorokin,
faced the Germans near Rostov.[13] Sorokin took cruel revenge on
his successful rival when he disobeyed his commander at the time of
the crucial battle and did not send reinforcements. The heroism of
the volunteer troops and the leadership of their commanders deserve
admiration, but their victory against an enemy who was almost ten
times stronger can only be understood if one keeps in mind the Red
Army's disorder and lack of discipline.

During the Ice March the Whites had made great efforts to avoid
railroads, which then represented a great source of strength for the
Bolsheviks. This time Denikin chose a different strategy. After leaving one regiment behind to protect the rear of the army against
Sorokin, he led a surprise attack on *stanitsa* Torgovaia, which was
located on the Tsaritsyn-Ekaterinodar railroad line. The Volunteers
captured Torgovaia on June 25, but only at the price of losing General Markov, one of its most popular commanders.[14] In capturing the

stanitsa, the Volunteer Army succeeded in cutting the only railroad line between the Kuban and central Russia. In order to defend his conquest, Denikin ordered the construction of makeshift "armored cars" from trolley cars.

The next major battle was for Belaia Glina. In this battle, as so often in the course of the first campaign, the Whites found the entire population against them. When they succeeded in capturing the *stanitsa*, on July 6, for the first time the Volunteers drafted many of the five thousand prisoners they took. The Bolsheviks fell back in disorder to Tikhoretskaia.[15]

Commander-in-Chief Kalnin personally directed the defense of Tikhoretskaia, which was the railroad center of the entire Northern Caucasus. Aware of the danger, he requested Sorokin's help; however, the Red commander disobeyed him and instead attacked Pokrovskii's regiment, which Denikin had left behind to protect the rear of his army.[16] Since Pokrovskii was able to resist the enemy, Kalnin was left to his own resources at Tikhoretskaia.

Denikin prepared for the Tikhoretskaia operation with his usual thoroughness: after having eliminated Red units stationed in the neighboring *stanitsy*, Borovskii's division attacked Tikhoretskaia from the South with a large enveloping movement; Erdeli's division surrounded Tikhoretskaia from the North, cutting communications between Kalnin and Sorokin.[17]

When Tikhoretskaia fell on July 14, the consequences were enormous. The Whites defeated one of the largest concentrations of Bolshevik forces, and they acquired weapons, munitions, rolling stock, and control of the chief railroad center of the area. Sorokin's troops found themselves between two enemies, the Germans on the north and the Volunteer Army on the south. As the Cossacks confidence in liberating their native land revived, and they enlisted in the White army *en masse*, the Bolsheviks panicked. Kalnin appeared at the meeting of the Central Executive Committee of the North Caucasian Republic on July 15, and confessed that he had no plans for stopping Denikin's advance. He therefore recommended that the post of commander-in-chief be given to Sorokin.[18]

Before Denikin could attempt the capture of Ekaterinodar, he had to defeat substantial Bolshevik forces to the southeast and northwest of his army. Borovskii attacked Kavkazkaia with three thousand men and captured it. At the same time Denikin directed the main forces of the Volunteer Army—about ten thousand men under Erdeli, Pokrovskii, and Kutepov—against Sorokin's group. The Whites engaged Sorokin's army on a wide front and directed it to withdraw south, in the direction of Ekaterinodar. In this way Denikin compelled the Bolsheviks to abandon their inactive front against the Germans, and now it was his own army which faced the foreign enemy. Denikin ordered the railroad bridge at Kushchevka, on the Ekaterinodar Rostov line, to be blown up, which the Bolsheviks had neglected to do for some reason. Since this railroad was also a line of communication with the Don Cossacks, Krasnov was angered by Denikin's move and directed his representative, General Smagin, to ask the Volunteer Army to rebuild the bridge. Krasnov's request fell on deaf ears.[19]

Since the Ekaterinodar operation seemed to be succeeding in every detail, on July 27 Denikin concentrated his main forces in a move against the city. On this occasion, however, Sorokin took the initiative. He managed to reorganize his defeated army at Timashevskaia, and occupied Korenovskaia in a maneuver that took the Volunteer Army completely by surprise. This cut the White forces in two, since some of the advance guards under Drozdovskii were already on their way to Ekaterinodar. The fighting at Korenovskaia lasted for eleven days. The divided Volunteer Army was on the verge of destruction; some of the divisions lost 30 per cent of their men. The Bolsheviks imagined themselves victorious, and while the battle was still in progress they named Sorokin commander-in-chief of all Red forces in the Northern Caucasus. But the Whites ultimately won this battle, too, and on August 7 Sorokin gave up Korenovskaia and began to retreat toward Ekaterinodar.[20]

The Bolsheviks could not regroup their army again for the defense of the Kuban capital; some of Sorokin's orders were not carried out and some of the units withdrew without permission.[21] On August 16 the Whites entered Ekaterinodar. Denikin tactfully waited at the railroad station for the Kuban rada and government to enter the city before he made his presence known.[22] At the ceremonies, to celebrate the victory, army leaders and Kuban politicians affirmed that they would continue to fight together against Bolshevism.

BATTLES FOR TSARITSYN

The period from May to the end of July 1918 was one of uninterrupted successes for the Don army. As a result of their traditional military organization the Cossacks were able to mobilize quickly and by the end of July they had about forty thousand soldiers, which equalled the number of Red troops facing them.[23] The Cossacks, fighting for the liberation of their *voisko*, were excellent soldiers and in June and July they advanced successfully on all fronts. The crucial front followed the Likhaia-Tsaritsyn railroad line. The Cossacks were able to cut it at the time when the Volunteer Army occupied Torgovaia and Velikokniazheskaia on the Tsaritsyn Tikhoretskaia line, and consequently all the major railroad links between the Red troops at Tsaritsyn and the other Soviet armies were severed.[24]

The Bolshevik position was very difficult. The defeats on the Don coincided with the emergence of a new anti-Bolshevik front in the east created by the uprising of the Czechs and the offensive of the Ural Cossacks under Ataman Dutov. Thus in the second half of 1918 the Bolsheviks had to fight on two main fronts which they considered equally important, and to which they sent troops of equal strength.[25]

In the middle of July, S. K. Minin, J. V. Stalin, and K. E. Voroshilov formed the Soviet of the Northern Caucasus Military District, whose main task was to organize the defense of Tsaritsyn. It was also responsible for all Red armies in the Northern Caucasus, including those which faced the Volunteer Army.[26] Voroshilov, as Commander-in-Chief of the Southern front, gradually succeeded in building an army from the remnants of the Don and Ukrainian Soviet armies, and from the workers of Tsaritsyn.[27] By the end of July the Tsaritsyn front was stabilized.

In the second half of 1918, fortune changed several times on the crucial Tsaritsyn front. By the end of August the Bolsheviks felt strong enough to start for the first time a large scale counter-attack along the three major railroad lines. Initially the offensive was successful; but Krasnov withdrew some of his troops from the direction of Voronezh and used all his reserves, and by mid-September, Voroshilov had been stopped and the front pushed back to where it had been a month before. In early October Tsaritsyn was surrounded. Once again the Bolsheviks carried out a large scale reorganization. The ex-tsarist General Sytin was named commander on the Southern front, which was divided into six armies. Four of these fought the Cossacks of the Don: the Seventh and Eighth in the district of Voronezh, the Ninth in the district of Tambov, and the Tenth, under the personal command of Voroshilov, in Tsaritsyn.[28]

It was not the reorganization, however, but D. Zhloba's Steel Division which saved Tsaritsyn. The Division had belonged to Sorokin's Eleventh Army. Zhloba had left the North Caucasian front against the orders of his superior, and his departure caused great confusion there, enabling Denikin to seize Armavir. The fifteen thousand men made forced marches at night, covering the distance of 400 miles in such a short time that their arrival at Tsaritsyn took the enemy completely by surprise. Krasnov later blamed Denikin for not pursuing Zhloba, claiming that this was an act of treachery, but the Red commander was so skillful that the Whites knew nothing about his movements.[30] On October 15 Zhloba attacked the enemy's rear and forced it to withdraw. His Division was incorporated into the Tenth Army and this once again stabilized the Tsaritsyn front.

In November the heaviest fighting took place on the northern boundaries of the *voisko*. The fighting capacity of the Eighth and Ninth Red Armies improved more slowly than that of the Tenth Army, but by the end of November the numerical superiority of the Reds began to bring results.[31] The Cossacks again surrounded Tsaritsyn, once in December and for the last time in the middle of January. But the Cossacks' morale was declining, Bolshevik propaganda once again started to make inroads, and the Cossack army could not keep up with the growth of the Red Army.[32] While Krasnov had fifty thousand soldiers by the end of 1918, there were one hundred and thirty thousand of the enemy.[33] In January of 1919 the Red Army was pushing the Cossacks back on a wide front.[34]

The main cause for the Don army's failure—aside from the fact that the enemy could draw on incomparably larger resources—was that the Don Cossacks did not want to fight beyond the boundaries of their *voisko*. The period of uninterrupted successes coincided largely with the fighting on their own territory. As a Cossack delegate put it to the *krug* meeting at the beginning of September: "I want to touch on only one matter, gentlemen delegates. We stand on the basis of the principle that we do not give what is ours, and we do not need what belongs to others. . . . "[35] Krasnov succeeded in persuading the *krug* that cities bordering on the *voisko*—Tsaritsyn, Kamyshin, Balashov, Povorino, Novokhopersk, Kalach, and Boguchar—must be occupied; no formal decision of the *krug*, however, could do much about the Cossacks' lack of desire to fight.[36]

The Reds devised their strategy in the context of the entire Civil War, but the Cossacks thought only of their *voisko*. The Red Army leaders concentrated their best troops at Tsaritsyn, because they understood the vital strategic importance of that city; the Cossacks insisted on first liberating the northern part of their district, which was strategically much less important.

Don military and civilian leaders, with the exception of Krasnov, shared the narrow outlook of the soldiers. Poliakov and Denisov, Krasnov's closest military aides, had neither the experience nor the knowledge that would have enabled them to see their struggle within a larger framework. The army staff received daily reports from various Cossack commanders, but it had no information, and one suspects no interest, in the position of other anti-Bolshevik fronts. They knew even less about the final phase of the World War; the German collapse in October, which had great and immediate repercussions on the Don, took them completely by surprise.[37]

When it became clear to Krasnov that Denikin and Alekseev could not be persuaded of the necessity of capturing Tsaritsyn, the Ataman decided to build his own anti-Bolshevik, non-Cossack army. In this venture, as in so many other ways, he received decisive help from the Germans. It was the Germans, who, following the Czech uprising, decided to provide the anti-Bolshevik officers with an alternative to joining the pro-Allied Volunteer Army. They therefore financed the formation of three small independent armies. The largest of these was the "Nasha Rodina" group, formed in Kiev by Prince Leikhtenbergskii and Akatsatov; Colonel Manakin commanded a group of officers in Saratov; and Prince Tundutov headed a small army of Astrakhan Cossacks.[38] The Ataman's task was merely to develop German initiative by uniting the three small groups into an organization which he named the "Southern Army."

One of Krasnov's problems was to find a popular general to head this army. After Generals N. N. Golovin, Shcherbatov, and Dragomirov declined, one after another, the Ataman turned to N. I. Ivanov, who had been Commander-in-Chief of the Southwest front at the outbreak of the World War. Ivanov, an old and hesitant man, was totally unfit for his position and he became nothing but a tool in the hands of the Ataman.[39]

The Southern army never became a significant fighting force. It attracted adventurers, criminals, and men who had no desire to risk their lives. Krasnov described his first impressions of those who had just arrived from Kiev:

> The Ataman and Ivanov looked over those who had arrived and became convinced that "Nasha Rodina" worked not for military but for political purposes. In the "corps" there were hardly 2000 persons. Out of these not more than half were militarily able; the rest were priests, nurses, simply ladies and girls, counter-intelligence officers, policemen, old colonels signed up to command non-existent regiments, artillery divisions, squadrons, and finally people who were eager for the positions of governor and vice-governor, all of them with a more or less murky past.[40]

By October the army had twenty thousand mouths to feed, but, incredibly, only three thousand soldiers ready to fight.[41] It appears that those officers who were serious about fighting the Bolsheviks joined the Volunteer Army.

Krasnov named Semenov, one of the army officers, "governor" of Voronezh province (the part which had been liberated) and Colonel Manakin "governor" of Saratov province. Both of them were adventurers. Semenov pretended to be a general but never went to the front; he lived luxuriously and finally escaped with three-and-a-half million rubles.[42] Prince Tundutov, when the war ended, went to Ekaterinodar and attacked Krasnov for his pro-German policies, in spite of the fact that shortly before he had claimed to be a personal friend of the Kaiser.[43]

If anything, the Southern army harmed the anti-Bolshevik cause. The rabid reactionary views of the officers, and the forced requisitions they carried out, made the peasants receive the Bolsheviks as saviors in January of 1919. The Southern army had not one victory to its credit. At the end of December, when one defeat followed another, it was dissolved and about a thousand members later managed to join the Volunteer Army.[44]

DISSENSION IN THE VOLUNTEER ARMY

The occupation of Ekaterinodar, on August 16, was a most important turning point in the history of the Volunteer Army: it gave the Whites their first relatively secure base. As late as July 1918 they could still have been dispersed in one decisive battle, but the possession of a base allowed them to extend their military activities and conduct battles hundreds of miles from one another. The political importance of the Volunteer Army increased enormously from the middle of August. In the early summer of 1918, the center of anti-Bolshevik activities shifted from Moscow to Kiev, but by the end of the year Ekaterinodar became the political capital of White Russia.

Denikin, as de facto head of state, acquired difficult new responsibilities, such as organizing a local administration, maintaining ties with other anti-Bolshevik organizations, and taking a stand on land reform. But possessing an ever larger territory also provided him with an opportunity to increase his army. Even before the occupation of Ekaterinodar, the army had occasionally violated the voluntary principle by forcing prisoners-of-war to join; but the overwhelming majority of the soldiers had joined of their own accord. Learning that the other side had adopted conscription, Denikin considered drafting at the beginning of the second Kuban campaign, and again after the victories of Tikhoretskaia and Korenovskaia, but his division commanders dissuaded him, considering such a move premature.[45]

One of the first of Denikin's orders in Ekaterinodar was to draft two classes of *inogorodnye* and ten classes of Cossacks. As a result, the army had between 35 and 40 thousand soldiers by the middle of September.[46] Then the size of the army remained relatively static for several months because losses in the battles on the Kuban and the Northern Caucasus were so heavy that the new draftees could only replace them.[47] In fact the army ceased to be a volunteer army, and the name was retained only because of tradition. Those who had been bound only to four-month contracts now had the choice of accepting service without limitation or leave within seven days. In November Denikin went one step further and drafted all officers under the age of 40 who lived on the territory occupied by the Volunteer Army.[48]

An increasingly important source of recruits was the capture of prisoners-of-war. As both sides turned to conscription, the difference in social composition of the two armies, which had been pronounced in the first months following November 1917 was gradually diminishing. From the point of view of loyalty and reliability, there was not much difference between drafting and forcing prisoners-of-war to join the army. The Whites formed separate units from the captured soldiers and, remarkably, these units did not remain behind the others in performance. General Wrangel describes the forced enlistment:

> I ordered three hundred and seventy of the Bolsheviks to line up. They were all officers and non-commissioned officers, and I had them shot on the spot. Then I told the rest that they, too, deserved death, but I had let those who had misled them take responsibility for their treason, because I wanted to give them a chance to atone for their crime and prove their loyalty to their country. Weapons were distributed to them immediately, and two weeks later they were sent into the fighting line and behaved with great courage. Later this battalion became one of the best in the whole army, and covered itself with glory.[49]

In October Denikin made the mistake of publishing an order by which captured officers would be punished.[50] The order discouraged many ex-tsarist officers from defecting from the Bolsheviks, and it was all the less necessary because in fact officers were rarely punished, and were instead forgiven and accepted back in the army. By contrast, the Bolsheviks with skillful propaganda encouraged both officers and soldiers to defect from the enemy.

A chief consequence of drafting was that the army, which had

had a Cossack majority even before the Kuban campaign, now became an overwhelmingly Cossack force. Cossack separatist leaders,
seeing that the White army was made up largely of Cossacks, and
recalling that Krasnov had been able to free the Don without Denikin's help, believed that a Kuban army could liberate the *voisko*
and defend it against the Bolsheviks. They therefore demanded a
separate army with increasing passion. Unfortunately, the Novo-
Dmitrievskaia agreement was ambiguous on this point. While one
clause asserted that the two forces would merge, another mentioned
the "commander of the Kuban army." According to the interpretation of Cossack politicians, they had agreed in March merely to
recognize General Kornilov as temporary head of their army, not
as commander of the Volunteer Army, but as an individual. In their
view Kornilov's death annulled the March agreement.[51]

For the time being Denikin's strategy and the interests of the
Kuban politicians coincided, since they all wanted to complete the
liberation of the Kuban. But both sides questioned whether the
community of interest would last after the accomplishment of this
immediate task. Denikin and his advisers did not believe that an independent Kuban army would be willing to march on Moscow, and
Kuban politicians feared that the Volunteer Army, together with
its Cossack members, would some day leave the *voisko* to the mercy
of the Bolsheviks.[52]

Denikin saw the separatist demands as a deadly threat to the anti-
Bolshevik cause. He must have understood that a few thousand
Russian officers could have formed only an insignificant force, comparable to General Ivanov's Southern army. Also, he regarded an
independent Kuban army as a first step toward an independent
Kuban, and quite aside from all practical considerations, he could
never have been reconciled to it. He very much wanted to believe
that separatist demands were the work of a few dozen irresponsible
leaders. When Bych, the head of the Kuban government, declared
at a meeting that the time had come to form a separate army, and
voiced his dissatisfaction that Volunteer Army leaders purposely
distributed Cossacks among different regiments rather than allowing them to form their own, Denikin walked out of the meeting,
saying: "I do not allow agitation among the valiant Cossacks."[53]

If Cossack politicians had been united, they would have prevailed over the not too numerous Russian officers, and the army would have fallen apart, ending the White movement in South Russia. But fortunately for Denikin, Ataman Filimonov, a *lineets*, sought allies among the Russian officers against the Black Sea Cossacks, who dominated both the *rada* and the government. Filimonov saved the integrity of the army when he took Denikin's side against Premier Bych and speaker of the *rada* Riabovol, both of whom were convinced separatists. At the *rada* meeting on October 2, the Ataman defended the Volunteer Army and argued that if organic ties between the Kuban and the volunteers were broken, it would lead to the destruction of both.[54] When the Ataman could not prevent the *rada* from passing a resolution calling for a separate army in December 1918, he did everything within his power to sabotage this decision. Luckily for him, the *rada*-elected Field Ataman Naumenko as commander, and Naumenko, who was not a separatist, cooperated with the Ataman.[55]

Denikin did nothing to overcome his differences with the Kuban government. He might have made gestures of good will: he could have formed Cossack divisions, entrusting them entirely to Cossack officers; he could have given Cossack officers more responsible commanding posts; and above all, he could have paid lip service to the cause of Kuban autonomy. By doing none of these, he contributed to the aggravation of the problem, which became so serious by 1919 that he found it necessary to disperse the *rada* by force.

That the army was made up largely of Cossacks caused problems not only because of the separatist aspirations of some of the politicians, but also because of the differences in social background, style, ideology, and fighting methods between the ex-tsarist officers, who made up the commanding upper crust, and the Cossacks. These differences manifested themselves in the debate over the proper role of partisan warfare in the anti-Bolshevik struggle.

Interestingly, the same debate was being conducted on a much larger scale among the Bolsheviks, who were seriously weakened by the constant bitter quarrels among the advocates of "revolutionary warfare," and of regular military organization, and using "military specialists," (ex-tsarist officers). Among the Bolsheviks, indoctrinated with the principles of class war, Trotskii had to use his considerable power and ruthlessness to impose regular discipline, and the institution of military specialists, on an essentially partisan army.[56]

In contrast, on the White side, it was the ex-Imperial officers who had founded the army and set its tone, and they would have liked to fight the war according to principles in which they had believed all their lives. These principles, however, were not always relevant in a civil war. It is clear that both sides needed regular organizations and traditional discipline, but both also needed partisans. As a general of the old army must have felt strange in Bolshevik headquarters, so some of the Cossack partisans felt out of place among Denikin's advisers.

The most effective and famous of White partisan leaders was A. G. Shkuro.[57] Shkuro, a Kuban Cossack, was only 31 years old in 1918, but he had already become a colonel as a result of his unusually heroic performance in the World War, when he had organized and commanded a partisan detachment, harassing the German rear. When he returned from the front, the young colonel became aware of the growing anti-Bolshevik mood of the Cossacks, and therefore decided to form a partisan unit at the end of April 1918. He was soon arrested by the Bolsheviks, but at the time the Reds were much more afraid of the Germans than of local "counterrevolutionaries." Avtonomov, Commander-in-Chief of Bolshevik forces in the Northern Caucasus, therefore freed Shkuro in exchange for the promise of his help against the foreign invaders. Shkuro accepted the Bolsheviks' mandate to form a partisan detachment, but he betrayed them without hesitation by recruiting a unit against them and not against the Germans. He started his army with ten followers at the end of May in the mountains near Vladikavkaz. His force grew quickly, and by moving constantly he gave the impression to friend and foe that his group was much larger than in fact it was. The show of strength attracted more followers, and a month after starting his organization he felt strong enough to carry out a raid against the city of Kislovodsk. There could be no question of holding the city, and he withdrew after taking his booty. This and similar raids encouraged the growing Cossack rebellion. Soon other units were formed and Shkuro was able to absorb some of them. In a very short time an army of several thousand was under his command.

When Shkuro received the news that Denikin had occupied Tikhoretskaia, he decided to recognize the authority of the Volunteer Army. Some of his Cossacks disapproved and wanted to return to their native *stanitsy* rather than join a Russian army, but Shkuro ultimately succeeded in persuading the majority that they could not liberate the Kuban alone. When the partisan chief decided to visit Denikin's headquarters, he was very disappointed. He realized in talking with Denikin that the general had no clear concepts about the goals of his movement. However, the unfavorable impressions were mutual. The officers surrounding Denikin had no appreciation of Shkuro's achievements and methods, and were contemptuous of the partisan army, which could take but not hold a city. They also disapproved of Shkuro's methods of requisitioning, which appeared to them as close to banditry.

Denikin found himself in a difficult position. Shkuro was one of the few popular heroes of the White movement; there were legends about him and he could not easily be removed from his command post. On the other hand, generals of the imperial army intensely resented that this man, whom they considered unreliable with the money entrusted to him, in their eyes more a robber than a soldier, should receive a high command post.[58] When Shkuro occupied the important town of Stavropol and it seemed that his partisan army could not retain it, Denikin sent Colonel Ulagai to take command. Shkuro, obviously hurt, accepted a subordinate position in the army which he had founded.[59] Unlike the Headquarters of the Volunteer Army, the Kuban *rada* regarded him as a hero and it insisted in December 1918 that Denikin promote him to the rank of General. As time went on the mutual distrust between Cossack partisans and regular officers did not diminish.

General Pokrovskii was another uncouth upstart in the eyes of old-time officers. While not a Cossack, he had led their army in the Ice March and maintained close ties with the *rada* and the government. He was a talented commander, but also an intriguer and a sadist. Shkuro, who was by no means soft, was shocked by the unceremonious hangings ordered by his fellow general. In his memoirs he describes how Pokrovskii tried to convince him: "You brother, I hear, are a liberal and hang too few people. I asked my people to come here and help you in this matter." While eating breakfast, Pokrovskii suddenly opened a door which allowed Shkuro to see hanging prisoners, saying: "This is to improve the appetite."[60]

Above all, Pokrovskii wanted to be Ataman. Once he tried to persuade Shkuro to arrest those members of the *rada* who had opposed his ambition, pretending to Shkuro that it was Denikin who had ordered the arrests.[61] In spite of the distaste Denikin and his fellow leaders must have felt for the methods of people like Pokrovskii, they could not have removed them because of their popularity among the simple Cossacks.

The Volunteer Army, which had started as an organization of career officers, found it difficult to reestablish the principle of seniority, which was important to all career officers. The problem was that there were too many conflicting criteria. The highest posts were reserved for the ex-prisoners of Bykhov, those who had participated in the Kornilov mutiny.[62] Men who had taken part in the first campaigns also received responsible appointments. They had developed an *esprit de corps* which led them to look with suspicion upon the newcomers who had decided to join the struggle only when it promised success.[63] Denikin neither could nor wanted to remove officers who perhaps had held only low rank in the World War but had proved themselves at the most difficult time just to make room for some well-known general who had decided to join. Consequently famous soldiers like General E. N. Maslovskii, who had been Quartermaster General of the Caucasian front, General Irmanov, who had commanded an army corps against the Turks, and many others felt that they had not received the positions they deserved on the basis of their past achievements.[64] These men became the most determined enemies of the young Shkuros and Pokrovskiis. Everyone knew that the Don and Ukrainian governments, and especially the Southern army, bestowed high ranks remarkably freely. How were these ranks to be compared with ranks received in the old army? Denikin set up a commission to settle these problems and investigate the histories of senior commanders before they could receive their assignments, but no commission could satisfy everybody.[65]

Incidentally, while Denikin alienated Cossack partisans, many believed that he harbored anti-aristocratic prejudices, and for that reason had decided to abolish the special privileges of ex-officers of the Guard.[66] In this way Denikin acquired new enemies.

CAMPAIGNS IN THE NORTHERN CAUCASUS, AUTUMN 1918

Although the fall of Ekaterinodar was a great blow to the Soviet Republic of the Northern Caucasus, its army was not yet entirely defeated. That the Whites would ultimately succeed in eliminating that army can be explained not so much by the impressive heroism of the White soldiers as by the incredible confusion prevailing in the Red camp. The Red army prepared its own suicide; the Whites merely had to kick the chair from under the man who had already put the noose around his neck.

During the autumn of 1918, political conditions in the Northern Caucasus paralleled the anarchic conditions which had existed in the rest of Soviet Russia about six months earlier. The junior coalition partners of the Bolsheviks, the Left Social Revolutionaries, who had consistently opposed Lenin's peace policy with Germany, were forced out of the government after one of their followers assassinated the German Ambassador Count Mirbach in Moscow on July 6. In the Northern Caucasus, however, the coalition and the issue of war with Germany remained alive much longer. The Congress of Soviets which met in Ekaterinodar and founded the Republic of the Northern Caucasus on July 5, elected a presidium with five Bolshevik and four Social Revolutionary members.[67] As Denikin was leading his army against the Kuban capital, 131 delegates (out of 365) voted for renewing the war against Germany.[68] But the most important difference was, that while in Moscow and Petrograd the increasingly brutal policies of the Bolsheviks gradually bore fruit and some semblance of order was established, the Northern Caucasus, a Republic without a capital possessing an army without headquarters, remained utterly chaotic.

On October 3 the Northern Caucasus army became the Eleventh Red Army, but the new designation implied no change in substance, for Trotskii's reforms, which had done so much to improve the fighting capacity of the Red troops, were not introduced.[69] Moscow's authority remained nominal, partly because the only link of communication which went through Astrakhan and Tsaritsyn was tenuous, and partly because the Bolsheviks were much too occupied elsewhere to be able to pay much attention to what was happening on battlefields which they considered of secondary importance. The Eleventh Army was even more poorly equipped than other Red armies; and even when Moscow was finally able to send some supplies, Stalin diverted the shipments to Tsaritsyn.[70] The army had no "military specialists" and was cursed with the spirit of *partizanshchina;* so much so that when later Trotskii wanted to find terrifying examples of the baneful effects of lack of discipline, he usually mentioned the Eleventh Army.[71]

At the end of August the Reds had 70 to 80 thousand soldiers in the area, divided into several independent armies, according to White intelligence estimates: (1) Sorokin had about 15 thousand men, whom he had withdrawn from Ekaterinodar to between the rivers Laba and Kuban. (2) On the Taman peninsula, under Matveev, there were about the same number of soldiers. (3) Armavir had 6 to 8 thousand defenders. (4) There were about 8 to 10 thousand Red soldiers in Stavropol. The rest were distributed in Nevinomyskaia, the Mineral Waters district, and in Maikop.[72] It is interesting that after the defeats in July and August the size of all Red units increased, because many *inogorodnye* volunteered, fearing the victory of the Volunteer Army.[73] In October, when the Bolsheviks were finally able to count their soldiers, they had 124,427 men.[74] Under the circumstances, it was the Whites who turned to drafting first, and the Bolsheviks did not follow their example until November.

By far the best Red unit was the Taman army, though it, too, was infected with the disease of *partizanshchina.* It was hardly an army in the conventional sense, but a collection of insufficiently coordinated detachments. When Sorokin had to evacuate Ekaterinodar hastily, Soviet forces on the Taman peninsula found themselves isolated. At that time a Ukrainian infantry regiment under I. I. Matveev, a group under E. I. Kovtiukh, and a North Kuban cavalry regiment under Sofonov united to form the Taman army and elected

Matveev commander.[75] Matveev immediately embarked on a long and hazardous but ultimately successful march, which was immortalized by Serafimovich's novel *The Iron Flood*. Matveev's purpose was to unite his army with Sorokin's. As the army moved south along the Black Sea coast, 20 thousand *inogorodnye* refugees joined it, fearing Cossack terror. The large number of refugees attracted by an army on the run shows the great hostility the non-Cossack population must have felt toward the Whites.[76]

Denikin foresaw that Matveev would attempt to join forces with Sorokin. To prevent this he sent some regiments under Colonel Kolosovskii to pursue the Reds, and dispatched a division under Pokrovskii to the district of Maikop, to keep the two enemy units apart.[77] Matveev, however, was able to evade Kolosovskii and defeat Pokrovskii at Belorechenskaia on September 11.[78] By the time Denikin could send reinforcements, it was too late. Curiously, the last obstacle to unification came from Sorokin's own troops. Sorokin's staff had so little knowledge about the military situation, and its intelligence was so poor, that it was unaware that a friendly army was approaching—indeed, it did not know that such an army existed. There were rumors among Sorokin's men about a "Black army," which would defeat both Reds and Whites. Consequently, when Sorokin's men became aware of the approaching army, they burned the bridges on the Laba and fired on the Red soldiers.[79]

Shooting at their comrades was characteristic of the confusion which prevailed among Sorokin's forces. The Commander-in-Chief lost prestige because of continuous defeats, and his soldiers frequently did not carry out his orders. The Executive Committee of the Soviets, the highest organ of the Republic of the Northern Caucasus, which moved to Armavir after the fall of Ekaterinodar, did not enjoy more respect. On one occasion the Committee could not defend itself from marauding soldiers and lost its money.[80]

It seemed that the arrival of the Taman army might become a turning point. The new and better disciplined forces acted as a shield behind which Sorokin was able to reestablish some order among his forces. Now for the first time the Commander-in-Chief succeeded in establishing contact with all major Red army units in the Northern Caucasus, and they all recognized his authority at least in name.

The Central Executive Committee of the Soviets, which had moved from Armavir to Piatigorsk, decided to follow the example of other Red armies and form a Military Revolutionary Soviet. The MRS was headed by I. V. Poluian, and Sorokin was only one of five members; nevertheless, as Commander-in-Chief, he dominated the new organization.[81] Although the MRS accomplished much (it improved the supply situation, prepared the first census of the army, and introduced regular bookkeeping), it could not remedy the greatest ill of the army: dissension between commanders who advocated different strategies.[82]

Denikin who, unlike the Reds, always had a consistent strategy, never lost the initiative. His daring plan was to surround the main enemy forces from east, west, and north, and push them against the Caucasus. The plan required the dispersion of White forces and the covering of great distances, but it succeeded so well that after several important victories the Bolsheviks were almost completely surrounded by the end of September. However, to use Zaitsov's phrase, it was only a "theoretical encirclement," since the Red army was so much larger that it could easily have broken out in any direction.[83]

Matveev and Sorokin had different plans for breaking out of the encirclement. Although they agreed that the ultimate aim of the army should be unification with the Tenth Red Army, which was then fighting around Tsaritsyn, they differed on the methods for accomplishing unification. Matveev wanted to concentrate against Kavkazkaia and strike northwest. By taking Kavkazkaia the Reds could threaten Ekaterinodar or move along the Tikhoretskaia Tsaritsyn railroad toward the Tenth Army. Sorokin, on the other hand, planned the main blow in the northeast, and envisaged the decisive battle coming at Stavropol. From there he wanted to move to Vladikavkaz, then face the Terek Cossacks before moving to Tsaritsyn.[84]

It is difficult to determine which plan was better. Sorokin's was tried and failed, but that, of course, does not mean that the other would necessarily have brought victory. Matveev, however, deserves credit for predicting that if Sorokin's plan were followed the army would be destroyed on the Kalmyk steps. Because he foresaw this danger, he refused to carry out the Commander-in-Chief's order. Sorokin, who felt his authority threatened, decided to use draconian methods and persuaded the MRS to arrest and execute the leader of the Taman army on October 7.[85] This act set off a series of executions and acts of terrorism which ultimately destroyed the fighting capacity of the Reds. First of all, the execution had the worst possible effect on the Taman army, since Matveev had been a popular commander. Also, the MRS, which had been at least partially responsible for the execution, became afraid of the growing power of the Commander-in-Chief and therefore plotted his downfall. Sorokin, however, was quicker. When he heard rumors about the plans of the MRS to get rid of him, he arrested all four members and had them executed on October 21.[86] Then he started a reign of terror in Piatigorsk which was remarkable even by Civil War standards. Bolsheviks and anti-Bolsheviks suffered alike; innocent hostages, including Generals Radko-Dmitriev and Ruzskii, were executed and even the Bolshevik city organization had to go underground.[87] The Central Executive Committee of the Soviet escaped from Piatigorsk to Nevinomyskaia, and there the Bolshevik faction of the Soviet declared Sorokin a traitor and outside the law on October 27. The Commander-in-Chief went to Stavropol, where the most important battle was being fought at the time, and tried to get support from the army against the Executive Committee. However, on November 2 he was apprehended and killed by Matveev's men.[88]

The connection between changing military fortunes and disorders in the Bolshevik camp is evident. When a semblance of order was created among Sorokin's troops after the arrival of the Taman army and the creation of the MRS, the Reds won one victory after another, making it clear that "theoretical encirclement" had little significance. On September 26 the Taman army reoccupied Armavir, which had been lost when Zhloba left the front without permission.[89] Sorokin forced General Borovskii out of Nevinomyskaia on September 28, and even felt strong enough at this time to send a detachment of soldiers to Vladikavkaz to help the Terek Soviet Republic against the insurgent Cossacks.[90] The Bolshevik victories forced

Denikin to change strategy. Instead of narrowing the circle, he concentrated his main forces in the Stravropol-Armavir area. It was evident that the fate of the Northern Caucasus would be decided here.

On October 7, the day of Matveev's execution, Sorokin ordered the Taman army to begin operations aimed at occupying Stavropol. The actual attack on the city started on October 23, with 50 thousand men. In a daring night attack the Taman army defeated the defending Drozdovskii on October 29, and occupied the city the next day.[91]

The victory at Stavropol was a major success for the Reds, and for the first time Denikin worried about the stability of his entire front.[92] However, this was the time which is described by Soviet authors as the period of "Sorokin's adventure." The Bolsheviks were unable to proceed with their offensive, and Stavropol became the victim of anarchy. The soldiers in the city were waiting for instructions from the Commander-in-Chief, but none arrived.[93] These days, wasted by the Reds and well used by the Whites, marked the turning point of the battle for the Northern Caucasus. Denikin rushed reinforcements to Drozdovskii, who was able to surround the city by November 11. The Taman army succeeded in breaking out of its encirclement, but it had to give up Stavropol on November 14. The fighting continued until November 20, when the Bolshevik front finally collapsed.[94] The remnants of the Red army escaped to the Terek, where the Bolsheviks were putting down a Cossack rebellion.

By the end of November 1918 the Volunteer Army leaders considered the military situation very promising. News of the Allied victory on the Western front raised the hopes of anti-Bolsheviks all over Russia, but especially among Denikin's followers, who had always remained fiercely loyal. Although the army suffered extremely heavy losses in the twenty-eight day battle for Stavropol, casualties among the Bolsheviks were much higher.[95] Indeed, not only the Taman army but the entire Eleventh Red Army was never to recover. While the Whites suffered from epidemics at this time, these took a much more terrible toll among their enemies, who had lower standards of hygiene and lacked medical supplies.

The Volunteer Army still had not accomplished its task, the liberation of the Northern Caucasus, and the opponents' army still existed, but the Whites were close to complete victory. In early January the leaderless Red Army, with its best troops already destroyed, attempted an ill-considered offensive; the White counterattack finally destroyed the army of the Soviet Republic of the Northern Caucasus.

CHAPTER 7

The Politics of The Volunteer Army

THE CONSTITUTION OF THE VOLUNTEER ARMY

The occupation of Ekaterinodar on August 16 marked a turning point in the history of the political administration of the Volunteer Army. From its earliest days, finances, relations with foreign countries, and political questions in general were handled by General Alekseev with the aid of a few assistants. Following the Ice March, the General created a small Military-Political Department in Novocherkassk. But as the army grew, its budget had to be increased; after repeated victories, its reputation spread and it had to assume a leading role in the national anti-Bolshevik struggle, which required establishing contact with other anti-Bolshevik organizations; and as the army occupied more territory, it became responsible for the reorganization of local governments. In the changed circumstances, Alekseev's informal handling of political affairs became anachronistic.

In Ekaterinodar, politicians close to the Volunteer Army discussed several projects for the creation of an administrative apparatus and for a constitution, but it was a long time before any of these plans could materialize. One of the chief causes of the delay was that General Alekseev's health constantly deteriorated, and no one wanted to take the initiative in his absence since this would have meant infringing on his authority. Realization of the projects was also slowed down by the hostility of the Kuban politicians, who feared that the creation of an administration with national pretensions would somehow compromise the sovereignty of their *voisko*.

Among the projects discussed, the plans of V. V. Shulgin were the most influential. Shulgin, a prominent monarchist member of the last Duma, who had enjoyed the complete confidence of General Alekseev on the basis of their past association, came to Ekaterinodar in August. His influence was further enhanced when General A. M. Dragomirov joined the Volunteer Army. Dragomirov, the commander of an army in the World War and a friend of General Alekseev, immediately became the third most powerful man in the army, ranking only below Denikin and Alekseev. Before coming to the Kuban, General Dragomirov had been working with Shulgin in various anti-Bolshevik activities in Kiev.

Shulgin was amazed at how casually official business was handled. Later he wrote down his impressions: "I found that the situation there did not at all correspond to the role that the Volunteer Army should have played: there were only young adjutants around the late General Alekseev, and they were unable to write even the simplest official papers."[1] To correct the situation, Shulgin developed his plans in conversations with politicians and generals. His friend Dragomirov had an especially active role in these discussions and it was he who presented the draft for the formation of an administrative organ to General Alekseev on August 31. Alekseev approved it without change, but the plan was not publicized in order to avoid exacerbating relations with the Kuban government. Among other things, the project stated:

> The aims of Special Council are: (a) to work out questions connected with the problems of administration and local self-government in areas which are under the rule and influence of the Volunteer Army. (b) To discuss and prepare provisional legal projects in all areas of state organization, in projects of local significance as well as projects of wide national scale, aiming at the restoration of Russia as a great power within her former borders. (c) To establish contact with all parts of the previous Russian empire in order to find out the real situation in these areas and establish ties with governments and political parties which want the recreation of a great Russia. (d) To establish contact with Allied representatives and work out plans of common action against the Central

Powers. (e) To find the whereabouts of, and establish close ties with, the outstanding figures of all levels of government, and also with the most outstanding representatives of local self-government, commerce, industry, and finance, in order to prepare for the moment when the reorganization of the national state will be possible. (f) To attract the above-mentioned people to work on immediate problems.[2]

The draft envisaged eleven departments: state organization (*gosudarstvennoe ustroistvo*), internal affairs, diplomatic-agitation, finance, trade and industry, supply, agriculture, communication, justice, education (*narodnoe prosveshchenie*)[3] and control. There was to be no department of military affairs. In Shulgin's view, the purpose of the Special Council was not to lead the White movement, but merely to supplement the headquarters of the Volunteer Army by assuming some of the distasteful but necessary civilian tasks. Everything that the generals considered really important, that is, everything which directly concerned the army, remained under the exclusive authority of headquarters.

The chairman of the Special Council was to be General Alekseev and his deputies were to be Denikin, Dragomirov, and Lukomskii, in that order of importance.[4] The draft plan divided the Special Council into two assemblies: a large assembly under Alekseev, to discuss the most important political questions and complicated legislative projects, and a small assembly under Denikin, to make quick decisions in current matters. While the heads of all departments were to participate in the large assembly, only those department heads were to be invited to the meetings of the small assembly whose competence covered the matter under discussion.[5]

The formation of the Special Council progressed slowly. Fatally ill, Alekseev could not participate in the work of organization, and Denikin, who led the campaign against Sorokin personally, did not devote any attention to the Special Council either. The greatest problem was choosing the heads of departments, because there were not enough politicians in Ekaterinodar who were acceptable to the Volunteer Army.

In mid-september, General Dragomirov, who was increasingly assuming Alekseev's role, entrusted two Kadet lawyers, Professor

K. N. Sokolov and V. A. Stepanov, with the working out of a constitution for the Volunteer Army. The legal experts had a double task: they had to formulate the principles of authority within the Volunteer Army, and reconcile the rights of the Kuban government with the rights of the Volunteer Army command. As Sokolov noted in his memoirs, the second task was far more difficult.[6] Sokolov and Stepanov worked in the house of P. M. Kaplin, a Kuban Kadet lawyer who, interestingly enough, was working on the draft of the Kuban Constitution at this time.[7] The Constitution of the Volunteer Army was prepared in a relatively short time, and after some discussions with Dragomirov, Shulgin, and Lukomskii, Denikin accepted it on October 4.[8]

The generals as well as the politicians wanted a dictatorship; the central principle of the Constitution would be that the leader of the Army had supreme and unlimited authority. But Sokolov and Stepanov had a difficult task, because for a dictatorship they needed a dictator. In the past the situation had been conveniently ambiguous: Alekseev had no title whatever, and Denikin's title was simply Commander of the Army. While in effect all power belonged to Denikin, the Russian people regarded Alekseev as the chief of the movement. Since this did not disturb Denikin at all the situation was acceptable to everyone.

But a written constitution could not preserve a polite fiction; supreme power had to be vested either in Alekseev or in Denikin. The army leaders knew that Alekseev would not live long—his imminent death was freely discussed—but even if he had recovered, the old man would not have had the energy necessary to act as leader of the whole movement. Yet Denikin would have appeared a usurper had he declared himself dictator in Alekseev's lifetime. Although Sokolov and Stepanov could not decide this important and difficult question, they solved the problem in an ingenious fashion. The first article of the constitution stated: Supreme power in the regions occupied by the Volunteer Army is vested in the Supreme leader of the Volunteer Army.[9] This, presumably, meant General Alekseev. Then they added in brackets: "Commander of the Volunteer Army"; this, of course, meant Denikin.

Alekseev's death on October 8, four days after Denikin's acceptance of the constitution, resolved this dilemma. Denikin changed his
title from Commander of the Army to Supreme Commander of the
Army (*glavnokommandoiushchii DA*), and in the draft this title
was used throughout when referring to the "dictator."

The second paragraph of the Constitution affirmed: "In the regions occupied by the Volunteer Army the laws which were valid
in the territories of the Russian state prior to October 25 [O.S.]
shall remain in force, with such amendments as follow from the
present statute as well as from the laws to be enacted on the basis of
this statute."

This was perhaps the most important paragraph in the entire Constitution, for it explicitly accepted the democratic revolution of
1917. Among the many divisive issues within the White camp, none
was more fundamental than its attitude toward the reforms of the
Provisional Government. That Denikin recognized the legitimacy
of the reforms, at a time when Skoropadskii and Krasnov acted
otherwise, and when the majority of his followers were monarchists
and hated Kerenskii's government with a passion, showed not only
that he had courage but also that charges of reaction against him
were profoundly unfair.

The next paragraph contained a compromise: "All citizens of the
Russian state, irrespective of nationality, social status, and religion
have equal rights. The special rights and privileges enjoyed by the
Cossacks shall be held inviolable."

It is easy to see the dilemma of the framers of the Constitution. On
the one hand, they knew a modern state could not tolerate estates
and that it was dangerous to take the Cossack side against the *inogorodnye* in the local civil war; on the other, the army, which
depended entirely on Cossack support, could not stand for the
abolition of special privileges. Hence the solution: the second sentence of the paragraph partially negated the first.

The other paragraphs in Parts One and Two make up a bill of
rights promising freedom of religion, of press, of assembly, and freedom from arrest without due process of law. Paragraph ten, the last
one in Part Two, is concerned with property rights: "Property is

inviolable. Compulsory expropriation of immovable property, when necessary in the interests of the state and of society, will be carried out in accordance with law and for fair compensation."

The significance of this paragraph was that it foreshadowed the attitude the Volunteer Army was to take in the crucial issue of land reform. By emphasizing the inviolability of property, the Army held out little hope for the peasants to acquire land.

Part Three is an elaboration of paragraph one; it spells out the rights of the Commander-in-Chief of the Volunteer Army. The Commander-in-Chief was to be responsible for the armed forces, was to conduct foreign relations, issue laws and regulations, handle finances, and appoint high officials, and was to have the power to pardon criminals and declare martial law.

Part Four deals with the Special Council. This part was based largely on Shulgin's draft. A paragraph asserts that the Council is a purely consultative assembly and has no rights whatever, except to advise the Commander-in-Chief. The Commander-in-Chief was to select not only the Chairman of the Council, but also all heads of departments, who were to be responsible only to him. Sokolov and Stepanov did not retain the "small" and "large" assemblies of Shulgin's plan, and they made some changes in the planned departments by substituting a "military-naval department" for the department of "state organization." Part Five consists of only one paragraph, which states that judicial organs in the territory under Volunteer Army authority would be based on existing laws and decisions issued in "the name of the law."

Part Six concerned the limits of Kuban autonomy and was the most controversial part.

Paragraph 25: Subject to the jurisdiction of legislative and administrative authorities of the Kuban district government area are: (1) Local police. (2) Supervision of press, assemblies, and societies within limits of laws which are valid for the entire state. (3) Sanitation and medicine. (4) Local self-government. (5) prisons. (6) Establishment and collection of local taxes. (7) Means of communication of local significance. (8) Local trade and industry. (9) Supplies for the population. (10) Agriculture. (11) Education, taking into consideration the right of the state language (Russian).

(12) Control over local governmental and social organizations.

Paragraph 26: For dealing with the above-mentioned matters the Kuban district government, headed by the Ataman, may form these departments: (1) Internal affairs. (2) Finances. (3) Means of communications. (4) Trade and industry. (5) Kuban *voisko* affairs. (6) Supplies. (7) Agriculture and exploitation of the land. (8) Education. (9) Control.

Paragraph 27: The following matters are not subject to the jurisdiction of Kuban district authorities: (1) Foreign contacts. (2) Command of armed forces. (3) Penal and civil legislation, judicial systems, and legal procedures. (4) Post and telegraph. (5) Means of communication of state or strategic importance. (6) Monetary matters, state credit, tariff policy, and trade. (7) Direct and indirect taxation for national needs and state monopolies. (8) Merchant marine and ports. (9) Legislation concerning stockholding companies and trade regulations.

Denikin did not want to promulgate the Constitution without a previous agreement with the Kuban government. Under the circumstances, Part Six had no other significance than to outline precisely the limits of authority which the Volunteer Army leaders were willing to concede to the Kuban government. (Relations with the Kuban government will be discussed in the next chapter.)

The adoption of this document caused no changes in the life of the army. Not surprisingly, the "bill of rights" was largely ignored; at the time of a bitter civil war there could be no possibility of genuine freedom of press and assembly. "Illegal" arrests did not become less frequent. The constitution did not affect Denikin's authority; whatever powers he possessed he would have had without this document. The paragraphs concerning Kuban autonomy had no chance of being accepted by the local government and *rada*, and Denikin had neither the power nor the will to force the Constitution on them. To be sure, the Special Council did come into existence, but it remained largely an ineffectual organization.

Yet the Constitution is an interesting and valuable document because it reveals the ideals and thinking of the leaders of the White movement. Sokolov and Stepanov were leading Kadets and the document they produced represented the ideology of the party. What is more significant, this product of two Kadet lawyers was acceptable to Denikin and to other leading generals of the army; to a large extent, they shared the same ideology. Denikin, after all, was and always remained a liberal.

Perhaps the most interesting fact about the Constitution is that leaders of the Volunteer Army and those who drafted the document felt the need to compose it. Instead of writing appeals to the Russian people, instead of inventing concise and effective slogans, they cared about the legal basis on which authority of the commander of the army was founded. To be sure, some attention to legality is necessary for the functioning of any "state," but this document exhibits an excessive concern with questions of form—perhaps in order to avoid facing questions of substance.

The White movement did not spell out its aims and its leaders refused to speculate about the future of Russia. However, it is implicit in their proclamations that they cared most about the creation of a *Rechtsstaat*. Progressive as this aim was in the context of nineteenth- and early twentieth-century Russian politics, at the time of the Civil War it was simply irrelevant. Perhaps the best way to judge the political acumen of the leaders of the opposing sides in the Civil War is to contrast this major document of the White movement, composed after almost a year of fighting, with the simple Bolshevik proclamation promising land and peace immediately after they assumed power. The Reds, unlike the Whites, knew how to capitalize on the mood of the Russian people.

THE SPECIAL COUNCIL

After General Alekseev's death, Denikin became supreme leader of the Volunteer Army, in name as well as in fact. Since Denikin had to choose the members of the Special Council, and since they were responsible to him alone, the performance of the Council largely depended on his leadership. Unfortunately, he had neither the temperament nor the background for the role he had to assume; Denikin failed as a political leader. He did not understand that exceptional circumstances required exceptional methods; as N. I. Astrov, a sympathetic observer and a member of the Special Council writes: "The failure was all the more tragic because the supreme leader was and remained utterly devoted to the Russian national idea, selfless, self-sacrificing, a most honest and noble man, but . . . not at home in the revolutionary atmosphere. The same was true of the men surrounding him."[10] One of Denikin's major shortcomings was his provincialism; a Soviet historian has written: "The stamp of provincialism was on all of Denikin's acts and views. He was never a central Russian figure. He came to the foreground of counter-revolution only because he was one of the most important figures of the Kornilov conspiracy. After the deaths of Kornilov and Alekseev the headquarters of counter-revolution were given to Denikin. . . ."[11]

The Commander-in-Chief simply did not know enough about politicians to choose the best men as his aides. Modest man that he was, he readily admitted his ignorance: "Because of the circumstances of my life and military service mostly on the peripheries [of Russia] I had very little contact before with the political world and with public figures, and therefore experienced great difficulties in selecting people for the highest posts in administration. In the beginning I used this method in enlisting: when the candidacy of a 'rightist' was suggested I asked the 'leftists' questions and vice versa."[12]

Denikin frequently complained that he had not enough qualified men to take responsible positions in the administration.[13] These complaints are partially justified. Indeed, many politicians and intellectuals shirked their duty and did not help the Volunteer Army to recreate the Russia they believed in. Some chose exile prematurely, and others did not want to soil their reputations by collaborating with the White army and taking responsibility for errors and unpopular actions.

But the command of the army was far from blameless. To a large extent, the senior generals shared the bias of most military men against politicians and the intelligentsia in general. Because of this bias the army never contemplated giving responsible positions to civilians. The Special Council was an emasculated organization; it had no rights whatever and it rarely discussed genuinely important business. Nevertheless, even in this institution military men dominated. It is revealing that the Journals of the Special Council, when enumerating the members present, always gave the names of officers first, no matter who they were.[14]

First-rate men had no desire to take unimportant jobs and were insulted by the treatment they received in Ekaterinodar. Shulgin, a man with great energy and imagination who had much influence on the leaders of the Army, did not find a seat in the Special Council attractive. He was nominally a member "without portfolio" but he did not attend the meetings. He traveled first to Jassy, later to Odessa, and found little to do in Ekaterinodar when he was there.[15] A man like Miliukov would not have found it worthwhile to spend time at the Special Council meetings. It was a vicious circle: distrusting politicians, the officers offered them no responsible posts, and only second-rate men accepted subordinate positions. With very few exceptions, the civilians participating in the work of the Special Council were incapable of initiative.

The chairman of the Special Council was General Dragomirov. Its first members were: Lukomskii, head of the military-naval department; V. A. Lebedev, trade and industry; E. P. Shuberskii, communications; I. A. Geiman, finance; Lieut. Gen. A. A. Makarenko, justice; A. A. Neratov (until the arrival of S. D. Sazonov), diplomacy; V. A. Stepanov, department of control.[16] The department of interior was offered to Astrov, but he refused to accept. He participated in the meetings but took no official position, and therefore the post of head of the department of the interior remained vacant for four months. Lieut. General A. S. Sannikov, who had returned from a mission at the end of October, took charge of the department of supplies.[17] Lukomskii rarely came to the meetings and his place was taken by his deputy, General Viazmitinov.

N. I. Astrov, a liberal Kadet statesman with a national reputation and a broader vision than anyone in the Council, describes his impressions of the meetings in his memoirs:

> The leaders of the departments hurriedly reported on "their" business, many times matters without significance, answered Dragomirov's questions, and fell silent. Other department heads did not interfere and kept silent, as if the matters under discussion were no concern of theirs. It seemed that decisions were taken not by the Special Council but by its president. Only very rarely did one of the members ask a question or express an opinion. A. A. Neratov, head of the department of diplomacy, did not participate in the

discussions at all. Geiman, head of the department of finance, and an ex-official of the ministry of finance, made a comic impression. The presence of General Makarenko as head of the department of justice, simply did not make sense. But the one who deserved most disapproval, and created most confusion, was a certain V. A. Lebedev. I remember this gentleman from the first Duma. [He was then] a slight, dexterous youth. No one knew where he was from, who appointed him, and what task he had in the chancellery of the Duma. But he always appeared when needed, when it was necessary to send someone somewhere, to look for something. . . .[18]

Reading the Journals of the Special Council, it is impossible not to agree with Astrov's characterizations. It is remarkable that this body of advisers almost never discussed questions of high policy. In November and December of 1918, relations between the Volunteer Army and Ataman Krasnov were a central concern for the entire White movement, but there is no mention of this issue in the minutes. The Council did not discuss land reform, had no plans for arrracting workers, and almost entirely neglected foreign policy. Most frequently the participants discussed problems of finances, supplies, and trade. They wasted much time on trivial matters: they discussed whether the Stavropol school district should use old or new orthography (characteristically, they chose the old), problems of postal service, or where to buy a special type of machinery.[19]

As Astrov indicates, it is striking to what a great extent the department heads restricted their interest to their own specialties. One must add, however, that Astrov did not differ from his colleagues. He too gave reports and almost always made remarks only about local self-government. The first meeting of the Special Council took place on October 11. From that date to the end of the year the Council held 21 meetings, but on only two or three occasions were differences of opinion significant enough to warrant filing minority reports. Denikin participated in only two sessions out of the first thirty-eight. He read only the journals of the meetings and made remarks on the margin. If he disapproved, it was the end of the matter; there could be no appeal, no further discussions.

The Council met on Tuesdays and Fridays at 6:30 P.M. Petrograd time. (All institutions of the Volunteer Army observed Petrograd time!)[20] Aside from the "official" meetings, members of the Council gathered in the apartment of the Commander-in-Chief every Wednesday evening. The main purpose of these Wednesday meetings was to inform the guests about military and political developments in an informal manner, and no minutes were kept. In the first weeks only the heads of departments participated, but later their deputies were also invited, and according to Sokolov, this meant a loss of the earlier intimacy.[21]

The Constitution relegated all power to the Commander-in-Chief of the Army, and the Special Council was a largely impotent organization, but from these facts it would be wrong to conclude that Denikin alone directed the movement. A modest, jovial, moderately talented, and moderately intelligent man, Denikin was not cut out to be a dictator. He lacked that intense concern for power which makes some leaders take an interest in every question of detail. Under the circumstances, Denikin's closest military advisers, Generals Dragomirov, Lukomskii, and Romanovskii acquired extraordinary influence.

When Denikin left Ekaterinodar to visit the troops, which happened frequently, Dragomirov and Lukomskii negotiated in his name, received visitors, and made decisions. Since both had better contacts with politicians and knew politics better than Denikin, they had a great influence in appointing people to important positions. It is difficult to establish to what extent they followed an independent policy. According to Astrov, the respect they showed for Denikin was a sham, and they frequently acted contrary to his wishes. Both Astrov and Vinaver, the liberal Kadet politician, considered Lukomskii unreliable and cunning.[22] Judging from Denikin's anger at Lukomskii when the latter took Wrangel's side against him in the dispute of 1920, it is likely that the Commander-in-Chief felt betrayed.

Dragomirov and Lukomskii stood considerably further to the right than Denikin and the civilian members of the Special Council. Both of them were monarchists, but they did not publicly reveal this because they did not consider it expedient.[23] Lukomskii more than once advised Denikin to come to terms with the monarchists.[24] Whatever their exact role was, there can be no doubt that Lukomskii and Dragomirov made the army pursue a more rightist policy.

It is much more difficult to assess the character and influence of General I. P. Romanovskii, who was one of the most mysterious figures of the White movement. Almost everyone seemed to have disliked him, though for different reasons. According to one observer, liberals regarded him as a member of the ultra-reactionary and anti-Semitic Black Hundreds, and rightists considered him a mason.[25] It was the rightists who conceived such a violent hatred for him that they ultimately forced Denikin to dismiss him, though Romanovskii was his best friend. He died in 1920, not as a victim of the Bolsheviks, but by the bullet of a White Russian officer in Constantinople.

There are remarkable contradictions in opinions about his character and politics. Denikin looked on him as the most liberal military member of the Special Council; Sokolov did not think that he stood further to the left than the other generals, but that he was simply more intelligent; the socialist Vendziagolskii believed him to be a monarchist who understood the need for cooperation among all anti-Bolshevik forces; Miliukov described him as simply "weak."[26]

It would appear that Romanovskii was somewhat more liberal than his fellow generals, and therefore his political views stood closest to those of Denikin. Perhaps the venom of the attacks against him can be explained by the officers' dislike of some of Denikin's more liberal policies. They found it easier to blame the adviser, and to them Romanovskii became the scapegoat. Aside from his political views, he was well suited for the role of scapegoat for his real failings; he practiced nepotism, which infuriated the rank-conscious officers, and almost all contemporaries agree that he was arrogant.[27]

He exercised power through his influence on Denikin. As chief of staff, he was present at Denikin's most important receptions and negotiations, and he freely gave his views on all debated issues. His superior had extraordinary affection for him. Sokolov noted that there was unusual warmth and tenderness in Denikin's voice when he talked about his closest aide and friend.[28] He frequently interspersed his conversations with the remark, "as a result of my discussion with Ivan Pavlovich" and "Ivan Pavlovich and I decided." Denikin must have enjoyed finding someone in the military who shared his political views; he appreciated his friend's loyalty, and above all admired his legendary courage. A memoirist quotes him: "I am not a coward and I have been frequently under fire, but I have never seen as much calm as Ivan Pavlovich has. If a grenade were to cut off his feet, he would not blink his eyes, he would not interrupt the sentence he began. Let bullets fly around him and he is as calm as in his office."[29]

When Denikin took the title Supreme Commander of the Armed Forces of South Russia in December 1918, after the unification with the Don Cossack army, he wanted to entrust the original Volunteer Army to the Command of General Romanovskii. The Chief of Staff considered it for a day, but preferred to remain in his present position. Denikin named Wrangel instead.[30]

LOCAL GOVERNMENT, FINANCES, AND PROPAGANDA

The leaders of the army had no taste for tackling political issues and postponed facing them as long as possible. Some of the tasks, however, could not be avoided. One of these was to reorganize local government in the territories under their control. As long as the army fought on the Don and on the Kuban, the problem was relatively simple: the Cossack *voisko* governments assumed responsibility both for conquered *inogorodnye* villages and liberated Cossack *stanitsy*. Denikin's abdication of responsibility implied that Cossack supremacy over the *inogorodnye* was reestablished, but one must admit that Denikin was not in a position to endanger his alliance with the Cossacks.

But when the volunteers liberated large areas of the Stavropol and Black Sea districts, the army became directly responsible for the organization and working of local administration. Denikin would have preferred to rid himself of the responsibility by joining these districts temporarily to the Kuban; however, he realized that this arrangement would not work because of the passionate opposition of the population to Cossack rule.[31] When Denikin was forced to send governors, he chose military men instead of civilians: Colonel Glazenap went to Stavropol and Colonel Kutepov to Novorossisk. Under Civil War conditions, when the governmental apparatus in Ekaterinograd was hardly functioning and the communication system was unreliable, these men acquired extraordinary powers.

Kutepov's administration was not liberal, but Glazenap and his deputy, General Uvarov, established an openly reactionary regime in Stavropol. They disregarded the existing organs of self-government and turned to ex-tsarist officials for help instead. Contrary to the Constitution of the Volunteer Army, they annulled all laws of the Provisional Government, took land away from the peasants and returned it to the landlords, and ordered criminals to be killed without trial at the place of capture.[32]

Stavropol had been a radical province before the Civil War; non-socialist candidates there received less than one-thirtieth of the vote for the Constituent Assembly, and the populace received the Volunteer Army with great hostility.[33] In such a province the political effects of the reactionary administration were disastrous. When Denikin learned what was happening in Stavropol, he removed General Uvarov, but the damage had already been done to the Volunteer Army and it could not easily be repaired.[34]

The situation was even worse at the district (*uezd*) level. Denikin was far more liberal than the average officer in his army, and his moderating influence prevailed in Ekaterinodar. But in distant districts and towns, where a militantly anti-revolutionary officer was usually in charge, the Volunteer Army pursued much more reactionary policies than Denikin or the Volunteer Army would have approved. Over-zealous officers punished officials who had collaborated with the Bolsheviks, even for such trivial acts as registering marriages.

Perhaps the greatest failure of the army command in the provinces was its inability to defend the population from marauding soldiers. N. I. Astrov, a leading Kadet and a man of experience in problems of local government (*zemstvo*), spoke to Denikin about the behavior of soldiers in villages and towns who supplied themselves at the expense of the population and treated the people with great brutality. Denikin, who was aware of the problem, entrusted Astrov with the reform of local government. At the same time, he complained that to stop the marauding, he would first have to hang commanding officers—in this instance General Pokrovskii—but he wrote "right now Pokrovskii is accomplishing miracles."[36]

On November 19, the Special Council ordered Astrov and General Lukomskii to prepare a project for dealing with the problems of local administration.[37] Astrov formed a committee and invited experts to testify, but as he observed himself, projects alone could not help. The ills were directly related to the ills of the White movement, and he was not in a position to introduce basic changes. He recommended the separation of military and civilian powers—by which he meant giving authority to civilian leaders—putting an end to forced requisitions, and restraining marauding troops. The Whites never successfully solved these problems.

Soon after the occupation of Ekaterinodar in August, members of the "Zemstvo-City Union" came to that city hoping to work there for the anti-Bolshevik cause. The Zemstvo-City Union was an organization of local governments with a long history and strong tradition of liberalism. Many of the newcomers to Ekaterinodar were members of the Social Revolutionary Party, and obviously would have preferred to work for the Siberian anti-Bolshevik government, which at that time was led by the largely socialist Union for Regeneration. However, they needed financial support from the Volunteer Army, and the Army needed expert help in local administration, and thus a short period of cooperation began on the basis of this mutual need.[38]

The break came as soon as the generals discovered that the politicians, while receiving financial help, intended to pursue their own political line. Lukomskii reported to the Special Council on October 18 that the army could not continue to cooperate with the South-East Committee, an organization formed by members of the Zemstvo-City Union.[39] The Council then invited four members of the Committee to its next session to clear up disagreements, but efforts at compromise failed.[40]

The Special Council demanded that the City-Zemstvo organization not occupy itself with politics, that the money which they had received from the army be spent only in the interest of the Army, and that the South-East Committee accept a representative of the Volunteer Army as a full member of their body. The socialists found these conditions unacceptable and all cooperation ceased.

The financial and supply situation of the Army greatly improved as a result of the conquest of the Kuban and the larger part of the entire Northern Caucasus. The Kuban was one of the richest agricultural areas of Russia, and the population—sometimes willingly, sometimes under the threat of force—could easily feed the army.

The Army had several sources of revenue: contributions from the Rostov state bank, the Kuban government, tribute levied on communities which had fought the White army, sale of war booty, and newly printed money. In the second half of 1918 the most important source remained the Rostov state bank, which regularly sent money to Ekaterinodar.[41] Next in importance was the Kuban government, which contributed a percentage of its tax revenue.

The sale of property taken from the enemy and tribute imposed on the defeated caused more harm to the Army than the gain was worth. The army command demanded enormous tribute from some of the defeated communities. For example, a single town, Belaia Glina, had to pay two-and-a-half million rubles as punishment.[42] This was not the way to win over an already hostile population. Frequently the population was simply unable to pay the large sums demanded from them, so that the army, after suffering the ill effects of this politically unfortunate demand, did not even receive the money.

The issue of war booty gave rise to another serious disagreement between the Volunteer Army and the Kuban government. Under the conditions of the Civil War, when both sides lacked proper equipment, captured weapons and munitions had great value. The Kuban, which had no army, conceded this materiel to the volunteers as a matter of course. However, aside from military hardware, the army captured much else and the Kuban government claimed everything which had been taken from the enemy on *voisko* territory. Alekseev rejected the demand and argued that most of the Bolshevik materiel was seized from the stores of the ex-Caucasian front, so that everything taken from the Bolsheviks was Russian national property. He was, however, willing to hand over the booty to the Kuban government on the condition that the Kuban assume responsibility for the supply of the entire army. This condition, understandably, was not acceptable to the Kuban politicians and the debate was not resolved.[43]

The Cossacks traditionally interpreted the concept of legitimate booty rather broadly: they plundered not only enemy storehouses but *inogorodnye* villages which had resisted them. Against orders from headquarters, soldiers under Shkuro and Pokrovskii gave property taken from the "enemy" to their own units, and sometimes even to the Cossack populations of nearby *stanitsy*. But in order to retain perspective, one must remember that the behavior of the Kuban Cossacks still compared favorably to the actions of the Don Cossacks. Krasnov made no effort to restrain his men and in fact encouraged them; for example, hc promised that the capture of Tsartisyn would bring a "rich reward."

Even before taking Ekaterinodar, Alekseev and Denikin set up a committee to control the sale of captured enemy property.[44] They named N. Paramonov chairman, and he chose Rostov and Novo-cherkassk for his headquarters. On August 17 Paramonov was arrested for "anti-Krasnov" activities, and the committee never functioned properly. According to Denikin, the value of the goods the committee sold was several million rubles but the army received only one million.[45]

The founding of the Special Council and the department of finances under I. A. Geiman greatly helped maintain orderly financial administration, and the introduction of planning brought better utilization of resources. At its meeting on October 11 the Council decided that the departments should prepare budgets for the next three months.[46] A month later the Council decided to form a state bank. (Incidentally, this was one of the few decisions taken against the opinion of the chairman of the Council, General Dragomirov.)[47] The bank was empowered to issue 500 million rubles, which the Council wanted to look as much as possible like tsarist money. However, for various technical difficulties, the printing began only in the second half of 1919.[48]

The severe inflation complicated financial planning. The cost of living increased enormously and the army constantly had to raise salaries. Prices doubled in the course of a few months at the end of 1918, and the salaries of soldiers and officers did not keep up with the rise in prices. Both the Don and Kuban governments paid much higher salaries to employees and soldiers than the Volunteer Army, and this adversely affected the morale of some.[49]

The preservation of the pretense of an indivisible Russia was an objective of the financial and trade policies of the Special Council. For united monetary, tariff, banking, and trade policies the Army initiated negotiations with the governments of the Crimea, the Don, and the Kuban, but the negotiations remained largely fruitless.[50] The new governments wanted to pursue independent policies, and this led to increasing chaos. A bewildering variety of currencies were in circulation in 1919 in South Russia: tsarist, Soviet, Provisional Government, Ukrainian, Crimean, Don, and Volunteer Army. The failure to coordinate independent financial systems was one measure of the failure of the Volunteer Army's leadership to unite competing factions in the common anti-Bolshevik struggle.

Insufficient propaganda work was another of the major weaknesses of the White movement. Although the propaganda apparatus was constantly reorganized, it achieved very little. In September 1918 General Alekseev organized an information and agitation section (osvag) whose task was to inform army headquarters of political and military developments in Russia and abroad and to agitate for the ideals of the Volunteer Army.[51] Under S. S. Chakhotin, a man totally inexperienced in matters of propaganda, osvag had hardly begun to function when, at the time of the formation of the Special Council, it was attached to the department of diplomacy.[52] This curious arrangement reveals the thinking of the leaders in Ekaterinodar, according to which the chief goal of propaganda was not to influence domestic public opinion but to attract foreign aid.

The absurdity of combining foreign affairs and domestic propaganda soon became evident and the Special Council ended this combination, but only in order to create another unpromising one. The new bureau of information, which was directly under the supervision of General Dragomirov, was also entrusted with maintaining ties with parts of the former Russian empire.[53] The Council reasoned that if the department of diplomacy were put in charge of relations with the new governments, it might be construed as recognition of the independence of these governments.[54]

That this arrangement was also unsatisfactory is shown by the fact that the Special Council soon ordered M. M. Fedorov to study ways in which propaganda work could be improved.[55] Finally the Council decided to form a department of propaganda, which was first headed by the Don Kadet N. E. Paramonov. Since he believed in the necessity of uniting all the enemies of Bolshevism, he hired socialists and Jews, which caused great consternation in Ekaterinodar. He soon found that he could not cooperate with the Army and resigned after two weeks in office.[56]

Not until February 1919 did the department acquire a permanent and reasonably competent leader in the person of K. N. Sokolov.[57] He opened local offices in several cities, subsidized many newspapers, and hired agents. One of the most effective operations of the department was the setting up of a Commission to investigate Bolshevik atrocities; it was headed by Meingard, an ex-justice of the peace in Moscow. The Commission included jurists, politicians, military men, churchmen, and representatives of Allied missions. The inclusion of Allied representatives indicates that the revelations were primarily aimed at a foreign audience.[58]

In spite of Sokolov's diligent work, White propaganda never became very effective; this was due in part to the lack of imaginative, experienced personnel and insufficient funds, but much more to the fundamental weakness of the White movement—the lack of a coherent ideology.

THE VOLUNTEER ARMY IN THE RUSSIAN POLITICAL SPECTRUM

One of the most frequently repeated of Denikin's statements was that the Army stood above politics. As he put it in one of his speeches:

> The Volunteer Army, proceeding on its thorny path, wishes to count on the support of all nationally–minded groups of the population. It cannot be the tool of any one political party or organization. Were that to happen it would cease to be the Russian National Army, causing dissatisfaction, impatience, and political strife within the Army. But if it is to live up to its traditions, the Army cannot take upon itself the suppression of the ideas of others. It says directly and openly: be Right or Left, but love our harassed fatherland and help us save it.[59]

The principle of depending on everyone can easily lead to the point of depending on no one. The army repudiated support from the left, in order not to alienate the right, and vice versa. Right and left were interpreted very broadly. All socialists without exception were too "leftist" for the army, and all open advocates of the monarchy—among politicians not among soldiers—Denikin considered too far on the right. This left a very small residue, and not everyone within this small circle was welcome in Ekaterinodar.

Miliukov's case is interesting, because one is not sure whether the rightists, the leftists, or both objected to his appointment. The famous Kadet leader believed in constitutional monarchy at the time, but agreed with Denikin that the question of what form the state should take be postponed.[60] It is possible that the rightists found him objectionable because of his participation in the Provisional Government, and the leftists objected to his monarchism and past cooperation with the Germans. Any well-known politician was likely to have opponents, and consequently to be unacceptable. This was one of the reasons that the Special Council had to consist of nonentities. Denikin, who had frequently complained about the selfishness of politicians who had not come to his aid, rejected so many offers of help from so many different quarters that one cannot have much sympathy for his plight.

For Denikin, being "above politics" meant not only that he accepted no party label or close cooperation with any one party; it also meant the avoidance of all controversial national issues. In the months immediately following the Bolshevik revolution, there was much to be said for not developing a political program. Then the leaders could still hope that anti-Bolshevik slogans and faithfulness to the Allies would appeal to a wide segment of the Russian people. Under the circumstances, precisely defining the goals of the army might have limited the appeal of the movement.

But by the time Denikin assumed command, he should have realized that in fact there was no national unity; the Volunteer Army, willingly or unwillingly, came to stand for a definite political philosophy in the public mind. The issue was merely whether to articulate that philosophy. In not doing so, the Whites allowed their enemies, the Bolsheviks, to spell out their program for them, and of course, in their definition, it did not sound appealing.

Denikin's political philosophy was closest to that of the Kadets, and to a large extent he succeeded in putting his personal stamp on the entire army. The peasants, interestingly enough, clearly understood the ideological kinship between the Kadet party and Denikin's soldiers, and called both of them "kadets," playing on the similarity of the words for students in military schools and members of the Constitutional Democratic Party. It was a bitter irony that the party which advocated democracy and constitutionalism came to be identified with a marauding army in a civil war. The soldiers also disliked the identification, for it meant that the peasants saw through the army's pretense of being above parties.

In the fall of 1918, the political situation in anti-Bolshevik Russia was exceedingly complex. In Siberia, in the Crimea, in Kiev, and in Ekaterinodar dozens of old and new political organizations, many of them with hazy and contradictory programs, quarrelled with one another about genuine and ephemeral issues. Denikin was correct in his evaluation that none of the groups had significant influence outside the narrow circle of the intelligentsia, and that the debates had little bearing on the actual course of events. (What Denikin failed to understand was that the very same politicians could have performed a most useful service to the Volunteer Army as administrators and agitators, had he only known how to attract and use them.)

Most people in Russia appreciated that the end of the war in Europe would start a new phase of the Civil War. In order to adjust to new circumstances, to overcome their differences, to discuss how the victorious countries could best help the anti-Bolshevik cause, a conference of representatives of White groups was called in the small Romanian town of Jassy on November 16.[61] The conference accomplished little and had no importance in the history of the Volunteer Army. But since it provided a forum for the broad spectrum of anti-Bolshevik public opinion, it is worthwhile to follow its discussions briefly, because they reflect the attitude of politically–minded society to the Volunteer Army at this time.

The two men who could be regarded as representatives of the Army had only small roles in the debates. One of the organizers of the conference was V. V. Shulgin, who, however, became ill.

General Grishin-Almazov, the other delegate, only arrived at the conference on November 30, when it had already moved from Jassy to Odessa, and he had only recently come to the Volunteer Army from Siberia and had insufficient knowledge of the aims and principles of the Army.[62] Although the role of the Volunteer Army in the anti-Bolshevik war was one of the central issues, under the circumstances, the Army had to be defended by outsiders.

The delegates who came to Jassy made up an inevitably haphazard group, in which many represented only themselves. The three most powerful organizations represented were the rightist State Unity Council of Russia, the centrist National Center, and the leftist Union for Regeneration.

The precursor of the State Unity Council (*sovet gosudarstvennogo ob'edineniia*) was the Council of Members of Legislative Bodies (*soveshchanie chlenov zakonodatel'nykh palat*), which had been formed by conservative politicians in Kiev in the early fall of 1918. This had been a monarchist organization, which had many members tainted by their German orientation.[63] The organization took upon itself the task of forming a "broad national front," the result of which was the State Unity Council. However, since only rightist groups participated, it was far from being a broad coalition. The Council of Members of Legislative Bodies succeeded in attracting five groups: (1) representatives of the Orthodox Church; (2) members of the Senate of tsarist times; (3) some *zemstvo* (local self-government) and city administration figures with pre-revolutionary fame; (4) representatives of industrial, commercial and financial circles; and (5) representatives of landowners' organizations.[64]

The State Unity Council sent V. I. Gurko and N. N. Shebeko, the former Imperial Ambassador to Vienna, to Ekaterinodar at the beginning of November to establish contact with the Volunteer Army. The encounter was disappointing. Gurko and Shebeko believed that the aim of the anti-Bolshevik movement should be the reconstruction of pre-revolutionary Russia, but the philosophy which they discerned behind the apolitical façade in Ekaterinodar seemed to them merely a watered-down version of Bolshevism. They deplored the influence of Kadet politicians, because in their

eyes these people had compromised themselves by their participation in the Provisional Government.[65]

From Ekaterinodar Gurko and Shebeko went to Jassy. At the
conference the State Unity Council supported the candidacy of
Nikolai Nikolaevich Romanov, a former Commander-in-Chief of
the Russian armies, as the leader of the anti-Bolshevik movement.[66]
N. V. Savich, a member of the Octobrist Party, argued that the
Grand Duke was popular among the peasants as well as among
other segments of the population, whereas Denikin was an unknown outside the circle of officers. The position taken by the
State Unity Council was that bringing in a man who "stood above
politics" would be the only way to resolve the existing disagreements among anti-Bolshevik leaders (such as Denikin, Krasnov,
and Skoropadskii). The Council was willing to compromise and
accept the actual leadership of Denikin if the supremacy of Nikolai
Nikolaevich were recognized and the monarchist principle thereby affirmed.

Among conference participants, representatives of the National
Center were closest to the position of the Volunteer Army. The
backbone of the National Center was made up of members of the
Party of People's Freedom (narodnaia svoboda), that is, of
Kadets.[67] On October 28 the Kadets held a meeting in Ekaterinodar, which they called a district meeting but which in fact
embraced the entire "district" of anti-Bolshevik Russia with the
exception of Siberia.[68] Aside from issues of foreign policy and
monarchism, the meeting discussed the relation of the Party to
the Volunteer Army. With the partial exception of Vinaver and
Panina, who were worried about the army's rightist orientation
and feared that identification with it might mean the isolation
of the Party from the majority of the Russian people, conference
members gave overwhelming approval to Denikin's policies.

Denikin followed the work of the conference closely. To
Astrov, who visited him on November 2, he jokingly expressed
disappointment that the Kadets had plagiarized his program.[69]
Indeed, Denikin's criticism was perfectly justified. The Party
could have served a more useful purpose by offering friendly
criticism rather than blanket approval.

Two old friends of the Volunteer Army, P. N. Miliukov and M. M. Federov, argued at Jassy that the White movement should recognize Denikin's dictatorship. In their view, the opposition of Krasnov and Skoropadskii did not matter because the Allied victory would make the Hetman change his mind about the Volunteer Army, while Krasnov should simply be removed. According to the Kadets in the Volunteer Army, a base for leadership already existed and the Allies would look more favorably on Denikin than on the Grand Duke, whose choice would mean a commitment to monarchism. They also doubted that Nikolai Nikolaevich had the qualities to become leader of the national struggle.[70]

At the Jassy conference it was the Union for Regeneration which was the most critical of the Volunteer Army. The Union, a predominantly socialist organization, focused its activities in Kiev, where it worked underground against the government of Hetman Skoropadskii.

Although many socialist leaders lived in Ekaterinodar, they had no role in the institutions of the Volunteer Army. Officers and soldiers who regarded all leftists as Bolsheviks treated them with mistrust.[71] When politicians, mostly Kadets, planned to form a political center in Ekaterinodar in cooperation with the Volunteer Army, the majority of the Kadets, fearing reaction among the officers, decided not to ask for socialist cooperation.[72] No socialist was ever a member of the Special Council.

At the time of the Kadet meeting in Ekaterinodar, some Kadet representatives had an exchange of views with socialist politicians in the city. The debate centered on the role of the Volunteer Army in the anti-Bolshevik struggle. Against Kadet arguments defending the Army, of course, the socialists maintained that the reactionary Volunteer Army would never be able to win over the population and would always remain no more than an isolated military force. Therefore, they argued, the anti-Bolshevik movement should be organized anew with the participation of the political parties.[73]

At the beginning of November, as a consequence of the Shreider incident, relations between the socialists and the Volunteer Army deteriorated sharply. Shreider, a former mayor of Petrograd in the era of the Provisional Government and a member of the moderate Popular Socialist Party *(narodnyi sotsialist)*, edited *Syn Otechestva*, a socialist paper in Ekaterinodar. The paper was closed down and Shreider was arrested. Vinaver describes the incident:

> I remember how late at night a woman, whom I did not know, ran to me with a little boy. They were G. I. Shreider's wife and son. Agitated, tears in her eyes, she told me that Shreider had just been arrested by order of the Volunteer Army. No one gave reasons and no one could guess them. The newspaper had contained nothing exceptional lately and Shreider took no active part in political life. We Petersburgians well remembered that Shreider, while mayor, had fought the Bolsheviks fearlessly, that he had been arrested by them and had participated in anti-Bolshevik organizations after his liberation. After quarrels and determined efforts to free him, we succeeded in finding out what was the matter. Shreider's guilt, as it turned out, was that in August 1917, when the Provisional Government was fighting Kornilov, the Petersburg city council had adopted a resolution against Kornilov and this had been published over his signature.[74]

Two Kadet politicians, Astrov and Vinaver, interceded for Shreider and he was freed, but he was forced to leave Ekaterinodar and his paper had to shut down.[75]

The affair had wide repercussions. Understandably, it made the socialists even less anxious to cooperate with the Volunteer Army. After all, not only Shreider but all socialists had opposed Kornilov in 1917. The arrest of an obviously innocent man as a result of political vendetta even repelled some of the Kadets. Astrov, who had been thinking of accepting Denikin's offer to head the department of the interior in the Special Council, decided not to have any formal connections with the Army.[76] The incident also adversely affected the relations of the Army with the Kuban government, which felt that it alone had the right to close down a newspaper in the capital of the province.[77]

It was predictable and understandable, considering the background, that the socialist representatives in Jassy did not endorse Denikin's dictatorship. I. I. Bunakov-Fundaminskii, a member of the Union for Regeneration, argued that while Denikin ought to be recognized as the military leader of the anti-Bolshevik movement in the South, the national leadership ought to consist of a military man, a Kadet, and a socialist politician. In his view only such a triumvirate could attract the support of the majority of the population.[78] Miliukov defended Denikin's position against the socialists as he had defended it against attacks from the right. He argued that the experience of the Provisional Government had shown that a coalition government could not be a strong one. Denikin's dictatorship already existed, he said, and all anti-Bolshevik parties should accept it.[79]

The Jassy conference arrived at no agreement. Its failure mirrored the disagreements between the political parties about the organization of the anti-Bolshevik war. Monarchists, and those who wanted to postpone the adoption of a type of government, found it easier to reconcile their differences than the socialists and non-socialists. The Volunteer Army and the Kadets, who represented the Army's point of view at Jassy, promised nothing to the socialists in exchange for their help. In their scheme for organizing the anti-Bolshevik war, the socialists had no place.

Denikin was not disturbed by the narrowness of his support. He made no effort to attract politicians to his cause and he would make no compromises. After Gurko's visit to Ekaterinodar, Lukomskii was inclined to accept the terms of the State Unity Council because he was afraid that the Volunteer Army would find itself alone. Denikin wrote Lukomskii: "The Volunteer Army should not become the weapon of a political party—especially not of one with an unsteady orientation . . . What they are suggesting now has already been suggested by Rodzianko in Mechetinskaia. It is not expedient to counter this combination against others. An armed force 'never finds itself alone.' It will always be considered desirable!"[80]

The last two sentences best show Denikin's lack of appreciation of politicians. He did not understand that just as the politicians needed soldiers, the soldiers also needed politicians. They needed them, above all, to help attract the sympathy of the majority of the Russian people. But Denikin never considered this his task. He expected the support of the people simply because he was convinced that his cause was a just one. To make deals and compromises, to attract support by promises, to try to find out what the people wanted and incorporate their wishes into one's own program —this, in Denikin's view, would be less than absolutely honest. He fought for what he believed in, and he believed it was the duty of the Russian people to follow him.

CHAPTER 8

"A Russia Great, United, and Indivisible"

Of the many political failures of the White movement none was more serious and none had more disastrous consequences than the inability of the anti-Bolshevik governments and organizations to work together. The Volunteer Army fought for a "united and indivisible Russia," but the newly formed "states"—the Ukraine, Georgia, the Don, and the Kuban—desired different degrees of autonomy. The conflict between the federalists and the centralists was never resolved; after the Civil War they blamed each other for the victory of communism, and undoubtedly both were right. Denikin writes, for example, that had the Georgians accepted his program, they would not have suffered occupation by the Red Army in 1921.[1] Denikin may have been correct, but it is interesting that it did not even occur to him that the statement could be turned around: had he compromised with the autonomists, federalists, or separatists, the Volunteer Army would have gained a great deal of strength.

The attitude toward the separatist aspirations of border nationalities was a crucial problem for the Volunteer Army from its very inception. It was more than a practical problem of day-to-day relations; it had important ideological implications. The White movement always suffered from a lack of positive goals. The volunteers could not define the purpose of their movement more precisely than by saying they were fighting for "Russia." Nationalism did not appeal to the peasants, who cared little about the future boundaries of Russia, but it helped those fighting in Denikin's army to think of themselves as fighting for the resurrection and glory of their fatherland rather than for class interests.

It was particularly unfortunate for the anti-Bolshevik movement that a resurgence of nationalism among Russian officers coincided with a new sense of identity on the part of the nationalities, a natural result of the collapse of strong central authority. They, too, needed their nationalisms as a force for cohesion in fighting against the Russian Bolsheviks. It is not surprising that the newly found aspirations could assert themselves only at each other's expense.

Denikin was no blinder than other anti-Bolshevik leaders, but neither was he more clearsighted. He shared the prejudices and misconceptions of those around him. Only an extraordinary leader, who could rise above his prejudices, stood a chance of defeating the Bolsheviks; Denikin was not such a man.

THE KUBAN

The Army had bad relations with all the new governments which had sprung up on the peripheries of the old Russian empire, but relations with the Kuban caused the most bitterness. There were two governments in Ekaterinodar: the headquarters of the Volunteer Army and the government of the Kuban *voisko*. Since each interpreted its authority more broadly than the other was willing to recognize, constant disagreements and quarrels poisoned the atmosphere of the Kuban capital. Because of the proximity and interdependence of the two groups, fighting between them was extremely harmful to the White cause.

The Kuban regime, as it evolved after the liberation of the *voisko*, bore striking similarities to the anti-Bolshevik Don. Cossack nationalism, which had been the guiding force in the Don struggle against the Bolsheviks, played the same role in the Kuban. In both areas the victims of the nationalist revival were the *inogorodnye*; discrimination against them in the Kuban was only a shade less blatant.

The Kuban government called for an election to the legislative *rada* on August 20, only a few days after the liberation of the capital.[2] The election law gave the right to vote to Cossacks, members of mountain tribes (*gortsy*), and members of communes formed by the "original inhabitants" (*korennoe naselenie*). The last group belonged to the *inogorodnye*, but they were atypical, being richer and therefore more comfortable with the status quo. This election law disenfranchised the majority of the population: the *inogorodnye*, who made up 52 per cent of the population of the district, had only 10 per cent of the representatives.[3]

As far as the Kuban population was concerned, the Civil War meant a struggle between Cossacks and *inogorodnye*. Since the simple Cossacks regarded all Russian peasants as Bolsheviks, even those *inogorodnye* who at first had little sympathy for the Soviet regime had to join the Reds, if only in self-defense. It is ironic that the fate of Russia was decided in a struggle between two segments of the population of an outlying province, where neither side cared much for the issues which were ultimately at stake.

The *rada*, which met in October, seriously discussed the possibility of expelling all *inogorodnye* from the *voisko*. One representative, Tolkunov, went so far as to recommend killing them all.[4] This was too much even for prime minister L. L. Bych; he drew the line at expulsion.[5] Neither the *rada*, nor the government hid the fact that they governed in the interest of a minority: when, for example, the *rada* decided to found a polytechnical institute in Ekaterinodar, it explicitly excluded *inogorodnye* students.[6]

The authorities in Ekaterinodar pursued a selfish and narrow policy, but the situation in the *stanitsy* was even worse, for there *atamans* treated Russian peasants as defeated enemies. Sushkov, the Kuban minister of education, the man who had created the polytechnical institute and therefore could by no means be characterized as pro-*inogorodnye*, said in the *rada*:

> The burning hatred of the Kuban Cossack population was vented above all on the *inogorodnye*. Even innocent children suffered. While fighting the fathers, who are contaminated by Bolshevism, the Cossacks did not spare the children either: in a large number of *stanitsa*, *inogorodnye* children were expelled from school even when there was room. . . . The innocent *inogorodnye* teachers also suffered, simply because they were *inogorodnye*.[7]

The Volunteer Army and the Kuban government quarreled on innumerable issues, many of them of little substance, but there is no record that the Army leaders objected to the treatment of *inogorodnye*, their fellow Russians. The Army and the Cossacks concluded their alliance at the expense of the non-Cossack population of the *voisko*. The Army could not afford to alienate the Cossacks, and therefore in the *inogorodnye*-Cossack controversy it was bound to the Cossack side. But the White generals could at least have used their substantial influence to restrain their allies from the most odious excesses. Instead of doing this, they tacitly accepted the notion that the sympathies of the *inogorodnye* inevitably lay with the Reds. The Army made no gesture toward them, and it never disassociated itself from the Kuban government in the matter of their treatment.

The Cossacks' behavior, deplorable as it was from a moral point of view, made sense in terms of their conception of the Civil War, according to which the peasants, coveting their land and estate privileges, were the enemies. They wanted to defeat them by all available means. The Volunteer Army, however, had national pretensions and to write off the support of peasants was bad politics indeed. In November and December of 1919, when the White front collapsed, the final calamity was brought on by the instability of the rear. The peasants often gave support to the Red partisans, which was the price the Whites had to pay for their previous policies. If Denikin had chosen the handling of the *inogorodnye* as a ground for conflict with the Kuban government, instead of many other spurious issues, the collapse of his movement would not have been as sudden and as irremediable.

The Kuban Cossacks had a long tradition of limited self-government and a simple form of democracy. Their political views were more "leftist" than those of the White Russian officers: monarchism had little appeal to the Kuban and during the Civil War socialists continued to play important roles in the *rada* and the government. This "leftism" was perhaps the most important source of quarrels with the Volunteer Army. Why would the generals trust socialists in the Kuban government when they did not trust them elsewhere? The Cossacks, on the other hand, distrusted the "reactionaries" in the leadership of the Army. Not surprisingly, their *bêtes noires* were Generals Lukomskii and Dragomirov, whom they rightly recognized as monarchists.

Among the two groups of Cossacks, the Black Sea Cossacks, who consistently sent socialists to the *rada*, stood further to the left than the *lineitsy*. Being ethnically related to the Ukrainians, they wanted to establish friendly ties with the socialist and nationalist anti-Bolshevik groups of the Ukrainians under Petliura. This caused great anxiety and consternation among the White generals, who objected to Petliura almost as strongly as if he were a Bolshevik, and the Ukrainian issue became a chief source of discord. It is difficult to determine the extent of separatist feelings among the simple Black Sea Cossacks at the time, but it is clear that their leaders wanted either to join the Ukraine in some form of federation or to establish an independent Kuban. Since the Black Sea Cossacks were more numerous than the *lineitsy*, they dominated the political life of the district by controlling both the *rada* and the government.

The *lineets* politicians were liberals, not socialists; they wanted to preserve ties with Russia and desired only autonomy. (As Denikin notes, there were no conservative Cossack politicians.)[8] In the person of Ataman Filimonov, they held the highest office in the *voisko*.

The Volunteer Army took full advantage of the division within the Cossack ranks. Denikin and his advisers found the position of the *lineitsy* more congenial—or less offensive—than that of their opponents, and they consistently supported the Ataman against the *rada* and the government. Filimonov in turn helped the Army against the separatists. However, he had to be circumspect in his pro-Army policies, because too close an identification with headquarters would have led to political suicide. When the Army took a step particularly unpopular among the Black Sea Cossacks, he usually remained silent instead of actively supporting the Army. This was a very difficult position to maintain and frequently both the separatists and the White generals were dissatisfied with Filimonov.

The leaders of the Volunteer Army frequently used *lineitsy* to mediate between themselves and the separatists. When working on the Constitution of the Army, Sokolov and Stepanov maintained contact with *lineitsy*, many of them Kadets. In the house of P. M. Kaplin, the drafters of the Constitution discussed the limits of the autonomy of the Kuban with the *lineets* politicians F. S. Sushkov, D. E. Skobtsov, A. I. Litovnik, and Ataman Filimonov.[9] The Cossacks refused to accept the principle of dictatorship.[10] They argued that the White movement could best present an alternative to the Bolsheviks by following the wishes of the majority of the population.

The failure of discussions between the *lineitsy* and the civilian representatives of the Army, who were more diplomatic and moderate, should have warned Denikin that it would be difficult to find a compromise satisfactory to both the Cossacks and the Army officers. The Cossacks promised to work out counter-proposals to the Constitution, but they never presented their project.

On Denikin's initiative, the Special Council formed a committee on October 29 to review relations with the Kuban. M. S. Voronkov, F. F. Zeeler, and V. A. Kharlamov were members of this committee.[11] The report they prepared contained nothing new.[12] It made the following points: (1) The Army must insist on the principle of unified command. (2) There should be one government with the authority to negotiate with the Allies. (3) The Volunteer Army should not proclaim a dictatorship without a previous agreement with the Kuban government. (4) The leaders of the Army must have unlimited power in military and diplomatic matters. (5) It was necessary first to arrive at an agreement with the Kuban; then this model could be used in negotiating with Terek, the Don, the Crimea, the Ukraine, and Georgia. (6) The question of a future federal organization of Russia should not be discussed with Kuban representatives. Voronkov, Zeeler, and Kharlamov started talks with the Kuban government on the basis of principles they had introduced in their report to the Special Council. These negotiations, as others before them, remained inconclusive and fruitless.[13]

This was the status of relations between the Kuban government and the Volunteer Army when the extraordinary *rada* met on November 10. The composition of this assembly was similar to that of the *krug* for the Saving of the Don: the majority of the 500 delegates were simple Cossacks with little political experience.[14] Perhaps for this reason the *rada* accepted a series of high-sounding but contradictory resolutions.

At the time, Denikin was leading operations against Stavropol and therefore asked that the opening of the *rada* be postponed until his return.[15] The *rada* arrived at a compromise: it began its work on schedule but delayed the formal opening until Denikin could participate. On November 14, the Supreme Commander gave an address to the assembly which all observers agreed was one of his most effective speeches. Returning from a victorious battle, he spoke earnestly of the sacrifices and privations of the volunteers.[16] He pleaded for a united army, formed from all anti-Bolshevik forces: "There should not be Volunteer, Don, Kuban, and Siberian Armies. There should be one united Russian Army, with a united front and a united command, possessing all powers and responsible only to the Russian people. . . . " He made no concessions to Kuban separatists: "The Volunteer Army gathers around itself both armed forces and experienced politicians, and it invites them from all parts of the Russian state—all those who want a united, indivisible Russia, a new organization of the state, a common struggle against the enemies of Russia, and a united government for the defense of Russian interests at the future peace conference."[17]

In spite of this apparently provocative speech, the audience applauded enthusiastically. The speaker concluded from the reception that his original idea had been correct: the simple Cossacks cared little for separatism, which was entirely the work of scheming politicians. But events soon bitterly disappointed him. A representative of the Ukrainian National Union, a socialist-nationalist organization, addressed the *rada* in a spirit diametrically opposed to his, and received the same ovation.[18]

Worse was to follow. On November 23 and 24, L. L. Bych, the prime minister, gave a defense of the policies of his government in two long speeches, after which he submitted his fundamental theses to a vote. His theses were:

> (1) Independent governments are being formed on the territory of what was the old Russian state, and are assuming supreme power. This is an inevitable act, for it is an act of self-defense.
> (2) The chief aim of these governments is to fight Bolshevism, which is far from being defeated in Central and Northern Russia.
> (3) For a successful struggle it is necessary to form a united front with a united command within the shortest possible time.

(4) It is necessary to form a united government, from the South Russian governmental organizations, for the forthcoming peace conference. For the purposes of international representation, this government ought to be formed without waiting for the organization of a federal structure in territories which have been freed from anarchy.

(5) For the achievement of the aims mentioned in points 3 and 4, it is necessary to form a South Russian Union on a federal basis.

(6) The reconstruction of Russia is possible only in the form of an All-Russian Federation.

(7) The Kuban district would join the Russian federation as a member.

(8) The Kuban *rada*, fighting against Bolshevism, is fighting for the introduction of the principle of sovereignty of the people.

(9) The choice of the future form of state for Russia, according to the population of the Kuban district, should be made by the All-Russian Constituent Assembly, after new elections.[19]

These proposals contain some contradictions, some imprecisions, and some peculiar expressions. Russian nationalists did not like contrasting the interests of South Russia with those of the North and Center by referring to the North and Center as areas "where Bolshevism was still far from being defeated"—as if it was in the South! It is not clear from Bych's position what powers should be relegated to the Kuban government, to the non-existent South Russian federation, and to the future All-Russian Constituent Assembly, which was to decide on the form of the state.

Yet Bych's policies did not endanger the fundamental interests of the Volunteer Army. In the most important and immediate question Bych appeared to compromise: he recognized explicitly the principle of united command and made no mention of a separate Kuban army. Because of the contradictions, which allowed different interpretations, the Army would have been in a good position to negotiate with the Kuban government. Mention of federal Russia concerned only the distant future and this question could have been easily disregarded. The possibility of a South Russian delegation to the Peace Conference was disturbing to the immediate policy of the Army; but the problem was vaguely phrased, and could have been circumvented by the participation and probable domination of the Army representatives in this delegation.

There could be no question that Bych's proposals represented the views of the great majority of the Cossacks of the *voisko*. The *rada* accepted them without a single negative vote, and out of the 500 delegates only 17 abstained.[20] In the face of such overwhelming approval for Bych's policy statement, prudence dictated that the Army should accept the bitter pill silently. But Denikin and his colleagues decided differently. They could accept the suppression of Russian peasants, the *inogorodnye*, but talk about a federal Russia was too obnoxious. Lukomskii, the head of the Army delegation to the *rada*, walked out of the meeting after the vote, and with Denikin's approval.[21] This act had an enormous effect not only on the assembly but on public opinion in Ekaterinodar. The Cossacks construed it as a break between the two anti-Bolshevik organizations, and became frightened of the consequences. Pokrovskii and Shkuro heightened this fear by announcing to the *rada* that in their opinion the *voisko* could not be defended if the Volunteer Army left the Kuban.[22]

Rumors of plots and counterplots spread in Ekaterinodar, and they had some substance. Pokrovskii considered dispersing the *rada* by force and tried to persuade Shkuro to help him.[23] Denikin, on hearing of Pokrovskii's intentions, objected to an attempted *coup,* and this saved the *rada* and the government. While Denikin decided to oppose Pokrovskii's move, he apparently made up his mind only after some hesitation. He said to Generals Dragomirov and Lukomskii:

> The issue is not a matter of decisiveness, but of cool calculation of factors such as the military-political situation and the composition of the Army. [Presumably he had in mind the large percentage of Cossacks.] It is possible, however, that I am mistaken. If you tell me now that forcible measures would lead to desirable results, then tomorrow I will disperse the Kuban government with the Kornilov regiment.[24]

Both Generals advised against forcible measures, and therefore nothing happened, but the fact that Denikin posed this question at all shows the seriousness of the crisis.

Bych did not expect such strong objections to his policies from the leaders of the Volunteer Army, and the crisis which developed took him by surprise. He looked for ways of reconciliation. In the company of Ataman Filimonov and the Speaker of the *rada*, Riabovol, he visited the Army headquarters and asked for protection against possible *coup* attempts. Denikin, and especially Dragomirov, used the occasion to lecture the Cossack statesmen about the errors of their past policies, and made help conditional on the promise that the government would change its attitude. Bych's position was weak even within his own government: the *lineitsy* blamed him for the crisis because he had not revealed his proposals to the ministers before giving his speech in the *rada*.[25] Under the circumstances Bych had to back down.

In a conversation with Romanovskii on November 29 he agreed that his first two theses should be regarded merely as statements of fact rather than as a basis for policy, and that the other seven points should be construed as an expression of desire on the part of the *rada*.[26] Romanovskii and Bych also agreed that the Army and the Kuban government should start negotiations on improving relations. For these talks both sides formed a committee of sixteen members.

The *rada* elected the Kuban representatives: I. L. Makarenko was chairman of the delegation, which consisted of both Black Sea Cossacks (a majority) and *lineitsy*. Denikin chose Lukomskii as the leader of the Army's delegation. This was a characteristically undiplomatic choice in view of the fact that the Cossacks disliked Lukomskii very much, and blamed him for starting the crisis by walking out of the meeting of the *rada*. The Army delegation had eleven military members, and only Astrov, V. F. Zeeler, A. A. Neratov, Sokolov, and Kovalevskii were civilians. The preponderance of conservative generals excluded the possibility of compromise.

Negotiations went on for ten days, but neither side modified its rigid point of view. The Army representatives claimed absolute power for the Commander-in-Chief and recognized Kuban autonomy only as something granted voluntarily by the Army. The Cossacks, on the other hand, argued that after the victory of the

Bolshevik revolution no central authority existed, and that under the circumstances the new governmental organizations which had grown up on the peripheries of Russia had to fend for themselves. According to this view the Russian state could be reconstructed only by agreement between the already existing organizations.[27] The disagreements between the two sides all resulted from this fundamental difference of attitude toward the organization of the anti-Bolshevik movement. The debates remained fruitless: the Volunteer Army continued to reject the *rada* demand for a separate army, and the Kuban politicians refused to recognize the limitation on their authority as envisaged in the Constitution of the Volunteer Army.

There was much that was plainly childish in this conference. The Kuban politicians, men of provincial background and views, insisted on observing the protocols of international conferences. The two delegations sat at separate tables facing each other, and a table was reserved for the "presidium" consisting of the chairmen of the two delegations and secretaries.[28] There was a long debate on the method of voting and who should be the secretaries. An incident described by Sokolov is characteristic of the tone of the discussions:

> One of our speakers mentioned that the Volunteer Army took on the functions of a state. A voice from the Kuban table said: "state without territory!" From our table they answered him: "How about the Black Sea province?" To which S. F. Munzhul retorted: "Yes, won by Kuban Cossacks!" This caused a great commotion. General Lukomskii declared angrily that he could not stay at a meeting where the Volunteer Army was abused, and left.[29]

To be sure, Lukomskii soon returned and the negotiations continued, but neither side was willing to give an inch. It was the issue of the separate Kuban army which convinced the conference that further discussions were useless. Not only did the generals refuse to allow the formation of a separate army; they did not even concede the right of the Kuban Cossacks, always recognized by the tsarist government, to fight in separate units.[30] The conference ended without any agreement. The Army representatives did not even go to the last meeting, and instead merely summarized their position in writing and sent it to the Kuban delegation. After the bitter exchanges at the fruitless conference relations between the Kuban government and headquarters became, if possible, even worse.

On December 18 the district *rada* accepted a constitution, which in essence was based on Bych's proposals: it called for the creation of a federal Russia and envisaged the Kuban as a part of this future federation. At that time, Bych and Filimonov campaigned for the post of Ataman, and the *rada* re-elected Filimonov; presumably the delegates feared the reaction of the Volunteer Army to the election of Bych.

Sushkov, a *lineets*, formed a new government in which many friends of the Volunteer Army participated.[31] The change of government, however, did not resolve the differences between the Cossacks and the volunteers. The strength of the Volunteer Army Command encouraged the separatists in the *rada* to be more discreet, but it did not change their views. In 1919, relations deteriorated further, leading to the destruction of the *rada* and the execution of some Kuban politicians by the Volunteer Army.

THE DON

Ataman Krasnov's popularity reached its peak at the time of the Large *krug* meeting at the end of August: his armies were advancing victoriously and the Germans were giving him moral and material support. He was the hero of most of the delegates who had gathered in Novocherkassk on August 29 for the opening of the *krug*.[32] He gave an optimistic speech and his listeners shared his optimism. The *krug*, in recognition of his services, raised him to the rank of General of the Cavalry.

But signs of future disaster had already begun to appear. To be sure, the Don army had succeeded in clearing the district of the Bolsheviks, but this had been accomplished only with a maximum expenditure of effort. While the Red Army was rapidly growing, the Don army could not find new recruits. As the Cossacks reached the boundaries of their *voisko*, their morale declined and Krasnov complained to the *krug* of insubordination and a lack of fighting spirit among his troops.[33]

The united front of Cossack politicians, which had accomplished much during the *krug* for the Saving of the Don, was gradually disintegrating. At first Krasnov's enemies agitated against him only privately. They circulated his "secret" letter to Kaiser Wilhelm, which aroused indignation and hurt his popularity. Then the opponents became increasingly vocal. They attacked Krasnov for his ill-concealed monarchism and conservatism, for his close alliance with Germany, and blamed him for the unsatisfactory relations of the Don with the Volunteer Army.

Krasnov had even less patience with political opponents than an average army officer turned politician. He used the terms politician and intellectual interchangeably, and he had nothing but contempt for both. Almost all military leaders of the anti-Bolshevik movement disliked politics, and tended to equate intellectuals, politicians, and socialists, but Krasnov's denunciations of intellectuals were notable for their shrillness. When he enumerated his four "enemies" he gave first place to the intelligentsia, which in his opinion placed party interests higher than the interests of the Fatherland. (The other "enemies" were General Denikin, foreigners, and the Bolsheviks. "The last I fear the least because I fight against them openly and they do not mask themselves as my friends.")[34] He compared the August meeting of the Large *krug* unfavorably with the *krug* for the Saving of the Don in May, because the Large *krug* included more intellectuals.[35] It was not easy to please him: in the Large *krug* only 11 per cent of the delegates had a higher education and 18 per cent a secondary education.[36] Evidently, even this was too much erudition for the Ataman.

Krasnov dealt with politicians in a high-handed manner. After bitter exchanges he expelled M. V. Rodzianko, the ex-President of the Imperial Duma, from the territory of the Don.[37] When the Germans arrested N. E. Paramonov, a leading Don Kadet politician, the Ataman made no attempt to intercede for him. He dealt unceremoniously with the military opposition too: General Popov, the leader of the Steppe March, General Semiletov, the best-known partisan leader, General Sidorin, and Colonel Gushin were removed from their posts. Most of these soldiers and politicians went to Ekaterinodar and continued their anti-Krasnov activities in the sanctuary provided by the Volunteer Army.

Krasnov's intemperate attacks on politicians and intellectuals failed to break the opposition and actually increased sympathy for it. By refusing cooperation from politicians, Krasnov forced them into opposition. This opposition came almost exclusively from the left. Interestingly enough, while Don Cossack leftists turned to the leaders of the Volunteer Army for help, the situation in the Kuban was the reverse; there leftist Cossacks bitterly attacked the policies of the Army. But compared with Krasnov, in most respects the Army was progressive.

While the *krug* was in session, opposition constantly gained strength. The election of the President of the Krug was the opposition's first victory. V. A. Kharlamov, a Kadet and ex-Professor of history at the Moscow theological academy—and an intellectual by any definition—received the largest number of votes.

The *krug* had two important tasks: to draft a constitution for the *voisko* and to elect an ataman. The constitution which the Krug accepted on September 28 and published on October 17 declared the Don to be an independent republic.[38] The *krug* proclaimed the principle of the sovereignty of the people and gave supreme power to elected representatives. The question of the limits of the Ataman's authority caused the most heated debate: Krasnov would have liked to increase his powers, but his opponents called for a larger degree of "collective authority."[39] Krasnov sharply protested the original draft and the *krug* made concessions, but at the end the Ataman received less than he wanted.

The election of the Ataman aroused interest even outside the boundaries of the *voisko*. The *krug* became the battlefield of the opponents and partisans of General Krasnov. The opposition tried to postpone elections as long as possible, hoping to gain further strength.[40]

The Germans considered opposition to Krasnov dangerous to themselves and therefore decided to aid Krasnov against his political enemies. German interference went further than support for the re-election of the Ataman; Major von Kochenhausen also helped him to retain those powers which the *krug* wanted to limit. The methods of German interference ranged from subtle propaganda to crude threats. Shortly before the session of the *krug* German troops were withdrawn from Taganrog, which raised the prestige of the Ataman, for it seemed to prove the correctness of his pro-German policies. At the same time, the Germans began repatriating Don Cossack prisoners of war.[41] Other methods were not as subtle. Major von Kochenhausen wrote to General Denisov:

I have the honor to inform you in the name of the German Supreme Command: Events of the last days in the *krug* show that there are efforts to limit the authority of the Ataman. In view of this, one can foresee the danger that a government would be formed with weak authority, a government which would not be able sufficiently to combat the large number of internal and external enemies of the Don. The Supreme Command can maintain good relations only with those states which are constructed in such a fashion as to be able to have a strong government and defend their own freedom. The German High Command considers itself bound to halt all supplies of weapons and munitions as long as the situation [on the Don] appears doubtful. This will continue until an Ataman has been chosen whom the German Command can trust to pursue a policy of friendship toward Germany and who has been entrusted by the *krug* with the full powers necessary for the present difficult moment.

I ask you to inform His Excellency, the Don Ataman, in whom the German High Command has full confidence, about this, and also to inform the President of the Council of Ministers, Lieutenant General Bogaevskii.[42]

In other words, von Kochenhausen warned that unless the Ataman was allowed to continue his pro-German policies, support would be interrupted. Since the Don army depended on German weapons, this letter must have played an important role in convincing the delegates that they had to make concessions to the Ataman.

Aside from Krasnov, the only serious candidate for the post of Ataman was Lieutenant General A. P. Bogaevskii. He had the reputation of being pro-Allies and had the full confidence of the leaders of the Volunteer Army. Von Kochenhausen indicated to Krasnov that the Germans would not tolerate the election of Bogaevskii:

The German High Command does not want to interfere in the internal matters of the Don, but it cannot keep silent when the weakening of the power of the Ataman would mean less friendly relations between the Don and the Germans. . . .

Furthermore, we received news that Lieutenant General Bogaevskii criticized your activities and claimed credit for the great creative activities of the Don exclusively for himself in one of the sessions of the *krug* in which your Excellency did not participate. In another session he attempted to contradict the speech of Cheriachukin, in which Cheriachukin dispassionately described the situation on the Western front. General Bogaevskii expressed doubt about the ultimate German victory, and mentioned the creation in the near future of an Eastern front by the Allies. He described the withdrawal of our troops from Taganrog as a consequence of our misfortunes on the Western front, when in fact this was done on our part as a proof of our friendly and neighborly intentions.[43]

The German interference achieved its purpose: General Bogaevskii retired from the race and the *krug* reelected Krasnov. However, the strength and bitterness of the opposition is shown by the fact that out of the 338 delegates only 234 voted for Krasnov. In spite of Bogaevskii's withdrawal, 70 voted for him.[44] (Ianov received one vote and the rest abstained.)

Krasnov blamed the Volunteer Army for his troubles with the *krug*.[45] This was unfair. Denikin sent General Lukomskii to Novocherkassk as his representative, and since the Volunteer Army enjoyed respect among the Don Cossacks, its representative was well received and presumably possessed some influence.[46] But the Volunteer Army did not want to limit the Ataman's powers, and it did not oppose Krasnov's reelection. Interestingly, von Kochenhausen and Lukomskii worked for the same end. Denikin gave the following instructions to Lukomskii:

(1) It is essential to have a single, firm, non-collective authority.
(2) The *krug* should obligate the future Ataman to straight, honest, and completely friendly relations with the Volunteer Army.
(3) Splits among the political parties on the Don, new disorders, and constriction of the Ataman's power are not at all desirable. Therefore, if the opposition does not have firm ground under its feet and strong candidates, and considers it necessary to support the candidacy of General Krasnov, the Volunteer Army will not ob-

ject, provided the second point is observed. (4) Since the personal policy of Ataman Krasnov is entirely inconsistent with the position of the Volunteer Army, *active* support (for example a public appearance with the appropriate speech, an official agreement, etc.) would not be fitting. The content of point three should be communicated confidentially to important individual leaders of the opposition.[47]

Denikin and his colleagues disliked Krasnov and his policies, and had the best relations with General Bogaevskii, who had participated in the Ice March as one of the respected leaders. They disapproved of Krasnov's German orientation and agreed with Bogaevskii's pro-Allied views, but they considered it inadmissable to participate in politics by secretly encouraging the opposition. This was contrary to their code of ethics; in their opinion, only despicable politicians intrigued.

In the months between the re-election of the Ataman and the defeat of the Germans on the Western front, one can observe a subtle change in the tone of communications between the Volunteer Army and the Don government. Military success and the growth of the army had enhanced the prestige of Denikin; and at the same time, Krasnov's military fortunes had declined. As Bogaevskii's statement to the *krug* about the motives of German evacuation of Taganrog shows, the Don leaders may have had some premonition of the coming German defeat in the European war. They understood well that this would greatly increase the standing of the Volunteer Army. Because of these developments the tone of the letters of the Ataman became less demanding and more imploring. He wrote to Lukomskii on November 3:

> Tell me, then, according to your conscience, do I have the right under these circumstances to turn down weapons and supplies, not taking the little bird into my hands but waiting for the crane to fly from the sky?
> Believe me, the politicians and journalists who gathered like crows in Ekaterinodar will not save Russia. What is happening now in Ekaterinodar is similar to January and February of this year in Novocherkassk. Talk of the future Russia—entire Russia is still too early. One must not divide the skin of the bear before the bear is

killed. It is very difficult for any of us alone to kill this bear—almost
impossible. We must unite.

We have to talk to each other and understand each other. *Tout
comprendre c'est tout pardonner*.[48]

The balance in the struggle between Denikin and Krasnov, which
was slowly shifting in favor of Denikin, completely tipped as a result of the defeat of the German army in Europe.

THE UKRAINE

The Volunteer Army in Rostov published a small pamphlet in
1919 entitled "A Short History of the Relations of the Volunteer
Army with the Ukraine."[49] After emphasizing that the Volunteer
Army aimed at restoring a unified Russia, the pamphlet continued:

> Therefore all efforts of some people and parties to create divisions
> among the Russian people, or to take away this or that district, is
> regarded as treachery. Because of this basic position, the Volunteer
> Army did not recognize as legal authority in Little Russia the
> authority of Hetman Skoropadskii, who had used forces which
> were hostile to Russia for the purpose of creating an independent
> Ukrainian state.

Denikin found much that was disagreeable in the regime of Hetman Skoropadskii: the Hetman surrounded himself with politicians
whom Denikin rightly regarded as reactionary, and he based his
power on German arms.[50] But what Denikin found most obnoxious
was the desire of the Ukrainian government to establish an independent state. He failed to see that it was not Skoropadskii who had
aroused the desire for independence in the Ukrainians, but that the
Hetman had only responded to this desire. The Volunteer Army's
pamphlet expressed the quite unjustified hope that "after the past
experiences, the idea of Ukrainian independence *(ukrainstvo)* which
is alien to the people, will lose ground forever in Little Russia."[51] It
is likely that Russian nationalists could not hope for anyone better
in the Ukraine than the ex-tsarist general Skoropadskii.

As events were to show, any alternative to Skoropadskii would
have been worse from the point of view of the Volunteer Army.
Ukrainian nationalists bitterly attacked the Hetman because they

questioned his devotion to the idea of an independent Ukraine and considered the speed of "Ukrainization" carried out by his government too slow. When the Hetman's regime collapsed, the new government took a far more extreme nationalist position. Denikin knew Skoropadskii's political difficulties well, but to accept the Hetman as a lesser evil would have been contrary to his political style. Denikin recognized only friends and enemies, and Skoropadskii was in the second category.

Aside from the blanket condemnation of Skoropadskii's regime, the Volunteer Army had no policy toward the Ukraine. With one exception, neither Denikin nor Alekseev made any attempt to establish direct contact with the government in Kiev; this exception was a letter Denikin wrote to Skoropadskii asking his help in freeing an agent of the Volunteer Army, Colonel Riazianskii, who had been arrested by the Germans. Denikin did not address Skoropadskii as a head of state, but "turned to him as one Russian general to another."[52] Perhaps this insulted the Hetman; in any case he did not answer.

Neither the Ukrainian government nor the Volunteer Army could simply forget the other's existence, however; they had too many mutual concerns. For the Army, Kiev was important as a chief recruiting center and as a station on the line of communications with Moscow. The success or failure of the Volunteer Army's recruiting center depended on the good will, or at the least tolerance, of the Kiev government. The Ukrainian government did not take energetic measures against recruiting activity (in spite of German pressure, which increased in the late summer of 1918), because many Russians who lived in Kiev regarded Alekseev and Denikin as leaders of the anti-Bolshevik war and the Ukrainian government wanted to gain the support of these Russians. Also, while Skoropadskii disapproved of Denikin's specific policies, he could not help but be sympathetic to the cause of the Volunteer Army.

The other issue of mutual concern was the future of the Kuban. Skoropadskii wanted to annex the Kuban to the Ukraine. A large minority, perhaps even a majority, of Kuban Cossacks also envisaged the future of their *voisko* as a federal state within an independent Ukraine. Riabovol, one of the most determined separatists and Speaker of the *rada*, led a delegation to Kiev in June.[53] Negotiations remained fruitless because socialist Cossack delegates disliked Skoropadskii's conservative policies and disapproved of his German orientation. The government in Kiev would have given aid only on condition that the Kuban become an autonomous, not a federal, part of the Ukraine.[54] Alekseev and Denikin were extremely suspicious of these negotiations, and Alekseev bitterly attacked the *rada* for carrying out these talks and pursuing an independent foreign policy.[55] In June 1918, the first serious quarrel took place between the Army command and Kuban politicians, who protested that the elected representatives of the people should not be ordered around by Russian generals.[56] The relations of the Army with the Kuban and with the Ukraine remained tangled.

Alekseev and his fellow leaders had reason to be suspicious of Skoropadskii's intentions concerning the Kuban. The Ukrainians wanted to prevent the Volunteer Army from gaining control over the district. The Kiev government wanted to transport fifteen thousand troops across the Azov Sea, under the command of General Natiev, to capture Ekaterinodar before the arrival of the Volunteer Army. A Russian official in the Ukrainian war ministry mislaid the plans long enough to allow Denikin to take the Kuban capital.[57] It appears that Denikin never found out anything about Skoropadskii's intentions because in his memoirs, where he enumerates the "sins" of the Hetman, he makes no mention of this one.

The conservative nationalist government of the Ukraine could not survive a German defeat. Skoropadskii faced a dilemma: he could either bid for the support of extreme Ukrainian nationalists, most of them socialists, or ask for the backing of conservative Russians living in the Ukraine. The Hetman's background and world view impelled him to choose the second solution, even though it compromised his nationalist program. This policy, predicated on German defeat, called for improved relations with Denikin. Skoropadskii understood that the Allies would regard Denikin as leader of the anti-Bolshevik movement, and furthermore, that the Russian officers who lived in Kiev, and whose support he needed, would not fight for him against Denikin's advice. Having given up the idea of an independent Ukraine for federation with Russia,[58] Skoropadskii asked Ataman Krasnov to mediate between himself and Denikin. Krasnov met Skoropadskii on November 2 at Skorokhodovo *stanitsa*, between Poltava and Kharkov, in the presence of German representatives.[59] The main concern of the meeting was relations with the Volunteer Army. The Hetman asked Krasnov to convene a conference of the representatives of the Volunteer Army, the Don, the Kuban, the Ukraine, Georgia, and the Crimea for the organization of a common anti-Bolshevik struggle.[60] To bribe Denikin Skoropadskii offered material and financial help.

The leaders of the Volunteer Army were not interested in holding such a conference; it made no sense in their opinion to compromise their post-war standing by cooperating with the pro-German Skoropadskii, nor did they want to negotiate with the Crimea and Georgia, lest this be construed as recognition of their independence. Answering Krasnov's letter on November 10, Lukomskii wrote that the conference could take place only on the basis of a recognition of General Denikin's united command—a clearly unacceptable condition—and that the Volunteer Army would not participate in a conference at which Georgian representatives were present.[61]

Skoropadskii also tried to establish direct contact with Ekaterinodar. In the middle of October he sent Shidlovskii, an ex-member of the Imperial State Council, to Army headquarters with offers of financial and material aid on the condition that the Volunteer Army declare itself neutral in relation to Germany.[62] Denikin turned down the offer without giving it serious consideration.

Denikin found the growing strength of the National Union under Petliura and Vinnichenko disturbing. (The situation in the Ukraine, at the end of 1918, will be discussed in some detail in the next chapter.) Skoropadskii's moderate nationalist, conservative regime was repugnant to him, but he regarded Petliura as a semi-Bolshevik. The civil strife in the Ukraine further poisoned the relations of the Army with the Kuban Cossacks. Petliura's brand of socialism had many adherents among the Black Sea Cossacks. Cossacks and volunteers blamed each other for interfering in the Ukrainian civil war.

In late November, at the request of Ataman Krasnov, Denikin sent a division under Mai-Maevskii to the Donets in order to strengthen the left flank of the Don front against the Bolsheviks;

Bych immediately protested: "The Volunteer Army is sending troops against the Ukraine. And if they support the hetmanite government, this will be awkward for us Cossacks. *I cannot support this bourgeois* [Skoropadskii's] government."[63]

The Volunteer Army arrested Polivan, secretary of the Ukrainian delegation in the Kuban, and two weeks later, in November, it arrested Baron Borzhinskii, the Ambassador himself, on charges of collaboration with Petliura's forces. The arrests deeply insulted the Kuban politicians, because they showed that Kuban sovereignty was a fiction.[64] The arrests took place shortly after the crises which had developed between the Army and the *rada* over Bych's proposals. Under the circumstances, the Cossack politicians did not dare to challenge the authority of the Army in the matter.[65]

As a result of the Allied Victory in the West and increased confusion in the Ukraine, the Volunteer Army's involvement in Ukrainian matters greatly increased at the end of the year. The Army command assumed increasing authority over those Russian officers who lived in the Ukraine and who came to play an important role in the Ukrainian Civil War.

GEORGIA

The vicissitudes of the relations between the Volunteer Army and the Menshevik government of Georgia make up only a tiny fraction of the enormously complicated history of the Civil War. Nevertheless, these relations deserve our attention for they show the nature and extent of the differences between the enemies of Lenin's regime. In the microcosm of the Georgian-Volunteer quarrel one sees why anti-Bolsheviks found it so difficult to cooperate. The two groups of leaders could not have been further from each other on the political spectrum: the Georgian government enjoyed German support, espoused socialist principles, and declared independence; the Volunteers stood for an "indivisible Russia," abhorred socialism, and remained faithful to the Allies. With statesmanship, a self-destructive struggle could have been avoided in spite of these differences; but as happened all too often in the White camp, it was precisely statesmanship which was lacking.

The people of Transcaucasia did not welcome the Bolshevik

revolution. The collapse of the Turkish front, which resulted directly from the fall of the Provisional Government, meant a great danger to this area: Georgians and Armenians, traditional enemies of the Turks, remained defenseless. Politicians formed a federal government, the Transcaucasian commissariat, with the participation of Georgians, Armenians, Azerbaijanis, and Russians in order to cope with the immediate problems of the area and to organize some sort of defense.[66] This government condemned the Bolshevik revolution. In view of later developments, it should be mentioned that strong separatist feelings at the time did not exist, and that the only cause of the de facto independence of the government was the demise of central Russian authority.

The Brest-Litovsk treaty made necessary the formal declaration of independence. The government did this only after much soul-searching, for Transcaucasian political leaders had traditionally taken a strong position against separatism; but it had to be done in order to escape the diplomatic commitments of Lenin's government, which had given the Turks large territories with Georgian and Armenian populations at Brest-Litovsk.[67] Because of the divergent interests of its members, the Transcaucasian Federation soon fell apart, and Azerbaijan, Armenia, and Georgia declared their independence.

The Mensheviks completely dominated Georgian politics. Their government introduced an ambitious program of social reform: it divided large estates and nationalized large-scale industries. The Republic of Georgia soon found an ally against the great external threat, Turkey. This ally, surprisingly, was Germany. In his memoirs General Ludendorff explains German policy toward Georgia as follows:

> During the negotiations at Batum [discussions between Turkey and the Transcaucasian Federal Republic], representatives of the Georgian Republic had approached General von Lossow with a request for the protection of the German Empire. In 1915 and 1916 we had employed Georgian volunteers in Armenia, though without success. In so doing we had come in contact with influential Georgians. I could only welcome this connection, and also Georgia's request for the protection of the German Empire. We

had acquired a means of securing the raw materials of the Caucasus, independently of Turkey, and of getting a hold on the working of the Tiflis railway. The latter was of decisive importance in any fighting in North Persia, and would give better results under a management influenced by us than under one in which the Turks shared. Finally, we must endeavor to reinforce ourselves by raising Georgian troops who might be used against England. Besides, we could never tell what difficulties we might have to meet from the Volunteer Army commanded by General Alexeieff on the North of the Caucasus.[68]

From the point of view of relations between the Volunteer Army and Georgia, the last sentence of this quotation is the most important, for it shows that the Germans considered using the Georgians against the Whites if the necessity arose—though it never did. In the voluminous materials of the German Foreign Office Archives, there is no evidence that the Germans ever tried to influence the Georgian government not to maintain cordial relations with Alekseev and Denikin.[69]

Whatever the Georgian Mensheviks felt about the Germans, the Republic desperately needed their help; they were the only force with the means to restrain the Turks. Indeed, the German Command pressured the Turks into accepting a reasonable treaty with Georgia. German troops soon arrived and took possession of the most important roads and railways. The Germans behaved better in this country than in other occupied areas and fulfilled a genuinely popular service—giving protection against the hated Turks; the population therefore regarded them more as saviors than as occupying troops.

The Georgian state wished to maintain neutrality in the Russian Civil War. The Menshevik ministers could not sympathize with the aims of the White Movement, as expressed by Denikin and Alekseev, or with Lenin and Trotskii. Trotskii, however, was undoubtedly right in his bitter accusation that the "neutrality" of Georgia was neutrality in favor of the Whites.[70] One should not search for the reason for Georgia's partiality in ideology; it was simply that the Reds presented a far greater threat to Georgia than did the Tsarist generals, with their few tens of thousands of soldiers. The leaders in

Tiflis understood this perfectly well; they mercilessly suppressed the local Bolsheviks and started to fight the Red Army immediately after coming into contact with it in the beginning of May 1918.[71]

After the capture of the Kuban, the Red Army moved South along the Black Sea coast. This alarmed the Georgians, who signed a treaty with Turkey and hurriedly sent their troops to fight the Bolsheviks. The Georgians also armed the Kuban Cossacks and together they fought successfully: by the middle of July they had occupied Tuapse.[72]

In these months the Georgian government did not yet have a policy toward the Volunteer Army. Because of the difficulties in wartime communications in Tiflis, there were only vague rumors about the existence of an anti-Bolshevik army under Alekseev and Kornilov. A large number of Russian officers had remained in Tiflis after the collapse of the Caucasian front. The Menshevik government gave asylum to these men and even paid their salaries.[73] As the officers learned about the struggles of the Volunteer Army, many of them wanted to join; the government had no objections, but the German Command in Tiflis, under General Kress von Kressenstein, was hostile to the officers and prevented them from leaving. Kress von Kressenstein's reports to the Foreign Office frequently included complaints against the Russian officers in Georgia, who in his opinion agitated against the government's pro-German policy.[74] In view of the circumstances, one wonders why Kressenstein did not encourage the officers to leave Georgia. Those few who cared enough to join the anti-Bolsheviks had to escape from Georgia first.[75]

The Georgians learned about the Volunteer Army's successful Second Kuban campaign only after the fall of Ekaterinodar, in August.[76] In order to establish contact, Denikin sent E. V. Maslovskii, the ex-Quartermaster General of the Caucasian front, who knew many Georgians through his war service in Tuapse. It is clear from Maslovskii's memoirs that the Volunteer Army approached the Georgians with the greatest prejudice and mistrust. Denikin simply did not understand political realities well enough to appreciate that the Georgians' alternative to German orientation was Turkish occupation. Nor did he understand the complex motives underlying the Georgians' belated separatism. (In his eyes the Georgians were separatists, even though they had declared their independence.) Denikin was disturbed that the Georgians held Tuapse in spite of the fact that they had come into possession of the city by the defeat of the Bolsheviks. Tuapse was the terminal of the oil pipeline from the Caspian oil fields as well as the terminal of the Maikop railway, and Denikin wanted it to be under the authority of the Volunteer Army.[77]

The desire of the Army to hold territory was larger than its capacity to do so; Denikin would have liked to dominate the entire Black Sea coast to the Georgian border, but he could spare only 25 to 30 Cossacks to accompany Maslovskii.[78] At this time the Whites were fighting crucial battles against the Bolsheviks in the foothills of the Caucasus, and Denikin could spare no more soldiers. The realistic Maslovskii was dubious about his mission; he believed that the Volunteer Army, instead of trying to occupy as much territory as possible, should cooperate with the Georgians. He therefore thought it would be wiser to negotiate with the government in Tiflis rather than with the local commander in Tuapse. Denikin disagreed; he did not want to send a delegation to a city that was under German occupation.

Maslovskii arrived in Tuapse on August 31 and was given an excellent reception. General Mazniev, the commander of the Georgian garrison, had held a series of important command posts in the European front in the World War and considered himself a Russian patriot. He continued to wear decorations which he had received in the service of the Tsar. Mazniev was willing to cooperate with the Volunteer Army, even if it meant subordinating himself temporarily to a representative of the Russian army.[79]

At this time, a group of Bolsheviks under Matveev was threatening Tuapse. With the aid of the Georgians who provided the weapons, Maslovskii mobilized the officers who lived in the city and formed a unit of 120 men.[80] As the Bolsheviks approached, the Georgians fled in panic all the way to Sochi. Maslovskii's tiny detachment, however, remained to put up resistance. With clever tactics, its officers led the enemy to believe that it faced a substantial force. The Bolsheviks thus prepared for a long battle and lost valuable time. After hard fighting the Whites evacuated the city.

Matveev had no interest in pursuing them or in fighting the Georgians; his aim was unification with the major Bolshevik forces under Sorokin, which were around Maikop at the time. Consequently, after the Bolsheviks left for Maikop, Maslovskii succeeded in reoccupying Tuapse with barely a hundred officers. In this way he accomplished his very difficult mission with the unwitting aid of the Bolsheviks, and the important Black Sea port came under the authority of the Volunteer Army.[81] The Georgian army remained in Sochi and Mazniev came alone to Tuapse, where he was greeted as a guest.

The Tuapse episode did not spoil the good relations between Mazniev and Maslovskii, for both men understood the importance of amicable cooperation. They discussed several possibilities: Georgia needed grain, which the territory under the rule of the Volunteer Army could supply, and the volunteers needed munitions which had remained in Georgian territory after the end of the war against Turkey. Maslovskii persuaded General Romanovskii by telegraph to send a wagon of grain to Georgia on credit as a gesture of good will. According to Mazniev, this made a very favorable impression on his government which, to reciprocate, gave the Volunteer Army its only armored train in the Black Sea district.[82] Maslovskii immediately sent the train on to Maikop, where the volunteers were fighting the Red Army.

The first month in the history of the relations between the Volunteer Army and Georgia was the best. Immediate contact was entrusted to two men who, fortunately for both sides, knew how to get along. When contact was established on the highest level the picture changed radically. In September, a Georgian delegation consisting of E. P. Gegechkori, the foreign minister, and General G. I. Mazniev came to Ekaterinodar to negotiate.[83] This conference was to be of crucial importance, for it determined the entire course of future relations between the two anti-Bolshevik powers. It is worthwhile to investigate the protocols of the meeting in detail, for they clearly show the participants' lack of statesmanship. Statements made in the heat of debate betray the thinking and quality of mind of the men to whom the anti-Bolshevik cause was entrusted.

The Georgians' visit to White territory started badly: when they arrived at the Black Sea port of Novorossisk, the military governor,

Colonel Kutepov, did not come to meet the delegation. Nor was there any important person waiting for them at the Ekaterinodar railroad station. Worse yet, the foreign minister of Georgia was kept waiting for two days before being received by the leaders of the army. Undoubtedly this discourteous reception alienated the representatives of the newly independent state, who were, precisely because of their newly acquired independence, exceptionally sensitive about protocol. Maslovskii, apparently anticipating trouble, had asked his superiors to give a good reception to the guests, but his appeal was in vain.[84]

The Conference took place on September 25 and 26. Generals Alekseev, Denikin, Dragomirov, Lukomskii, and Romanovskii and civilians Shulgin and Stepanov represented the Volunteer Army; Bych and Vorob'ev, who were hardly more than observers, represented the Kuban government. On the second day the Kuban Ataman, General Filimonov, also participated in the discussions.[85]

General Alekseev's behavior at this conference must have been influenced by the illness which was to take his life within two weeks: he was rude and unbending. While one may find extenuating circumstances for Alekseev, there is no excuse for the other Army representatives, all of whom followed the old general's bad example. The hosts constantly insulted their negotiating partners, and introduced irrelevant subjects which only poisoned the atmosphere. Reading the protocols of the meeting one wonders why Alekseev and Denikin decided to negotiate if they felt so much hostility.

Only the first two or three sentences of Alekseev's opening remarks contained any friendly words: Alekseev unconditionally recognized the independence of Georgia. (Incidentally, this "concession," too, was withdrawn after the failure of the conference.) Then he began a long tirade, attacking the Georgians for a variety of "sins." He made two specific accusations: The Georgians mistreated Russians in general and Russian officers in particular, and they collaborated with the Germans. Gegechkori indignantly protested:

Concerning the accusation against the Georgian government for persecuting Russian officers, I, as official representative of the

Georgian Republic, consider it my duty to declare categorically
that this accusation is completely false. . . . I can say with pride that
at a time when almost all Russia was ruled by nightmarish anarchy,
only in our country, in Georgia, thanks to the consciousness of the
masses and the work of political leaders, there was not one instance
of violence, or of the lynching of Russian officers.[86]

This declaration did not satisfy the Russians and they kept returning
to the matter. Obviously Gegechkori was not in a position to disown
his German allies; however, he accepted without debate Alekseev's
reasonable condition that if a trade agreement were to be concluded
and the Army sent grain to Georgia, it might not be re-exported to
Germany. In February 1919, when the leaders of the Volunteer
Army wanted to gain the help of the English against the Georgians,
they prepared a memorandum for the English which distorted the
truth; they claimed that one of the causes of the failure of the
Ekaterinodar conference had been the unwillingness of the Georgians to guarantee that Russian grain would not be re-exported.[87]

Most of the time was taken up not with negotiation but in bitter
exchanges on irrelevant subjects. The tone of the White Army generals was more fitting for criminal prosecutors than for diplomats
seeking an alliance. Alekseev blamed the Georgians for things which
they could not possibly have helped:

It is difficult to imagine how much money they [the Russians]
spent on the Caucasus. During the war much Russian property was
accumulated in the Caucasus, and it is still Russian property [i eto
vse russkaia kopeika]. And the railroads which were built, are they
not ours, Russia's? And should everything which was collected in
the Caucasus from the center of Russia and found its way there,
accidentally, go to the Georgians, Armenians, and Tatars, in spite
of the fact that everything was brought from the center and created by the work of the Great Russian muzhik?[88]

What did Alekseev want the Georgians to do—tear up the rails and
send them back to Russia?

Shulgin introduced the red herring of Gegechkori's subversive
role in the defunct Russian Empire, whereas a good diplomat would
have done everything to avoid the subject of past disagreements and
mistakes. Shulgin came closest to betraying what really made co-

operation between White Russians and Menshevik Georgians difficult; the representatives of the anti-Bolshevik Russians were not able to forget that two years before they all had had leading positions in Tsarist Russia, while the socialists had been outcasts. Shulgin continued his attack by asking Gegechkori to state whether Georgia was part of the encirclement of the Volunteer Army.[89] This hostile question was entirely uncalled for, since the Georgian army had been collaborating with the Kuban Cossacks and even with the Volunteers in fighting the Bolsheviks, and had sent the armored train as a present.

Alekseev reached the low point of the conference when he criticized the gift of the train: "General Maslovskii was given an armored train, but everything was destroyed on the train which could have been destroyed. This attitude of the Georgian officers is far from loyal."[90] Mazniev answered that General Maslovskii had put his signature on a document confirming that the train was in good condition at the time the Army took possession of it. Whether the machine-guns on the train were in working condition or not, it was worse than tactless of Alekseev to blame the Georgian government.

The issue over which the conference broke down was the possession of the district of Sochi. The Georgian army had occupied Sochi in the spring of 1918 as a defensive move against the Bolsheviks. The question of whether Sochi should be under the authority of the Volunteer Army or under Georgia first arose in the middle of September. Social Revolutionaries and Mensheviks, who dominated Sochi city politics, regarded the Volunteer Army as a military dictatorship and a monarchist organization, and they had no desire to come under its rule. They passed resolutions in which they asked Georgia to annex the district temporarily.[91]

There was only a small Georgian minority in the district of Sochi (11 per cent), which Gegechkori claimed was 22 per cent.[92] In all 50 villages there was only one with a Georgian majority.[93] There is no doubt that Georgia had no legitimate claim to Sochi. Gegechkori's argument that Georgia had to retain the city because of its strategic significance hardly makes sense; surely the Volunteer Army was better able to defend Sochi than Georgia was.

Gegechkori and Mazniev came to Ekaterinodar with instructions to insist on retaining Sochi. The Georgian position was that the Republic had annexed the district only temporarily, and would hand it back to Russia when a united state was recreated. Georgia did not recognize the Volunteer Army as capable of speaking for all Russia, and therefore it refused to negotiate border issues. In the heat of the argument Gegechkori called the Volunteer Army a private organization, which deeply insulted the generals.[94] (It is hard to see why: the Volunteer Army never claimed to be an all-Russian national organization.)

One has the feeling that both sides used the divisive Sochi issue as an excuse for breaking off negotiations. Subconsciously the generals and socialists did not want an agreement, but they could not admit failure just because the machine-guns on the gift train were not in working order.

If the chief aim of the Volunteer Army leaders was to get the Georgians out of Sochi, they could not have chosen worse tactics. Their violent attacks on the Georgian representatives, which at times degenerated into arguments *ad hominem*, made it practically impossible for the Georgians to compromise honorably. Avalishvili, a Georgian diplomat, maintained that the young republic did not want to withdraw under pressure because it considered this behavior inimical to its prestige.[95] No one asked Alekseev to renounce Sochi in the name of the Russian nation; the issue concerned temporary administration, something which had no bearing whatever on the chief and only legitimate aim of the White movement: fighting the Bolsheviks. From the point of view of the real interests of the Volunteer Army, it was an advantage to have the Georgians in Sochi: the small White Army did not have to use troops to keep the Bolsheviks out.

The entire second day of negotiations was devoted to the Sochi issue. After fruitless wrangling, in the course of which it became evident that neither side would give an inch, Alekseev closed the meeting with these words:

> We will keep on living and will continue our work, but you will remain dependent on those areas of Russia which can supply you

with bread and much else. The Germans can give you little, and that is your only constant source. However sad it is for me, I declare that in view of the absence of agreement on the main issue, the meeting is closed.[96]

The Ekaterinodar meeting set the pattern for future relations. The history of these relations is a dreary series of bitter exchanges, border skirmishes, and at times even large-scale fighting. Immediately after the conference, relations sharply deteriorated. The Georgian government removed General Mazniev from his post because his pro-Russian policies were discredited, and gave his post to General Vashakidze, a man of limited intelligence, according to Maslovskii.[97] Tiflis ordered Vashakidze to have no dealings with the White Russian representatives. The Georgians soon replaced him with General Koniev, an outspoken opponent of Mazniev's conciliatory policy.[98]

Denikin ordered Maslovskii to attack Sochi. Maslovskii considered his commander's position profoundly mistaken; he did not carry out the order, and tried to persuade Denikin to change his mind. The order was rescinded, but a week later headquarters decided to follow the original plan and Maslovskii was replaced by Colonel Kolossovskii, who attacked the Georgians with his small detachment, but was repulsed. Denikin frequently made the error of entrusting a task to an insufficient force.[99]

At the time, Denikin suspected that the Germans encouraged the Georgians to take an inflexible position against the Whites. This suspicion is not borne out by evidence. Kress von Kressenstein notified Berlin about the conference only on October 17, almost a month after the event.[100] Through Ambassador Joffe in Berlin, the Soviets tried to put pressure on the Germans to stop Georgian-White collaboration. In fact, the German foreign office first learned about the negotiations from Joffe's note.[101] From the German answer to Joffe it is clear that Berlin was not interested. It was the Georgian Minister of the Interior, Ramishvili, who turned to Kress von Kressenstein asking for German aid in case of an all-out war against the Volunteer Army.[102] By this time the front of the Central Powers in the Balkans had crumbled and Germany had lost the war. Nevertheless, the effects of the Allied victory were not yet clear in Tiflis, and the German representative promised help to Ramishvili in case of war.

The defeat of Germany affected the course of the Russian Civil War in general, and of Georgian-Volunteer Army relations in particular. Denikin and his fellow generals had assumed that the English, who were to take the place of the Germans in Transcaucasia, would punish the Georgians for their disloyalty. The Georgians, on the other hand, remembering Wilson's principle of self-determination of peoples, believed that Allied policy would lend support to their cause. Both sides were bound to be disappointed.

The English were much more ambitious than the Germans had been: the former occupying forces wanted nothing more than to advance their own immediate interests. The English, in contrast, hoped to reconcile the differences between the anti-Bolsheviks, because they understood that this was essential for toppling the Soviet regime. Ultimately they failed: in 1919 Georgian-Volunteer relations were worse than they had been in the previous year. This was not the fault of the foreigners; no outside power could have brought the antagonists together. The English can, however, be blamed for inconsistency. Their representatives in Ekaterinodar—first General Poole, then General Briggs, and later General Holman—came to understand the Volunteer position and became partisans of the White Russians, while representatives in Tiflis frequently supported Georgian claims. Contradictory policies were caused by faulty communications and by a lack of central direction. These policies, understandably, alienated both sides.[103]

After Kolossovskii's impetuous attack on the Georgians, a "neither war nor peace" situation existed along the dividing line for a short time.[104] The relative quiet ended with the withdrawal of the Central Powers. Georgians and Armenians came to fight one another for territories cleared by the Turks.[105] This war forced the Georgians to withdraw their troops a few miles on the Black Sea Coast, and Volunteer troops occupied a few villages there without firing a shot.

In the course of 1919, fighting was frequently renewed on the Georgian border, and sometimes, as in February and April, on a relatively large scale. The Volunteer Army could never be entirely certain about the security of its rear. The Georgians hindered the Whites most by fomenting rebellion in the rear of the Volunteer Army. They also allowed Red Army units, pursued by the Whites, to take refuge in their country.

There is no doubt that the policy of the Volunteer Army toward Georgia contributed to the ultimate defeat of the Whites in the Civil War.

CHAPTER 9

The Volunteer Army and the End of the World War

Everyone in Russia understood that the end of the World War in Europe would affect the course of the Civil War. Strangely enough, the news of the German defeat filled Reds and Whites with about equal optimism.

Communism was still a profoundly internationalist movement. The Bolshevik leaders, who had always regarded Germany as the center of world socialism, saw the first stirrings of the German revolution as signs of the dawn of a new era. To be sure, the Russians neither respected nor liked the socialists who came to power in Berlin on November 9, but the communist mind, trained to seek historical parallels, chose to look at Ebert as a German Kerenskii. Men who had talked about world revolution for most of their lives and who were now leaders of an embattled, impoverished country naturally clung to the reassuring hope that a Red Germany would soon join communist Russia in forming an invincible bloc in Europe. A tangible proof of internationalist enthusiasm was the offer of two carloads of grain for the starving German proletariat from the even more cruelly starving Russians.[1]

It is not that Lenin and his colleagues were unaware of the danger of vastly increased Allied intervention. They believed in the internationalism of the "exploiting classes" quite as firmly as in the proletarian variety, and they expected that they would soon be challenged by the combined might of the French and British empires. Nonetheless, they remained optimistic.[2]

Aside from their grandiose schemes for world revolution, the Bolsheviks expected to benefit immediately from the withdrawal of German troops by expanding their rule into the previously occupied parts of Russia. On November 13 the Soviet government annulled the Brest-Litovsk treaty and in the following months the Red army easily advanced into the Ukraine, White Russia, and even into the Baltic states.

The Whites also had reason to be optimistic. The Allies had been involved in the Civil War from its inception and now it seemed that this involvement would greatly increase. The needs of the European war had dictated the first moves of intervention: the anti-German coalition had been convinced, as it turned out incorrectly, that it was necessary to recreate the second front in order to win the war.[3] Following the Brest-Litovsk treaty, which was signed on March 3 and revealed that the Bolsheviks could not be induced to enter the war, the Allies became increasingly active supporters of the White cause. They landed in Archangel to safeguard the military materiel which they had sent in the course of the World War and hoped that the Czechs in Siberia, perhaps supported by the Japanese and the Americans, would act as a nucleus around which a new anti-German Russian army could be formed.

However, for reasons of logistics and because of enormous commitments elsewhere, their contribution had to be limited. The Volunteer Army especially received little help. Since the Germans controlled the Ukraine, the Black Sea, and the Caucasus, it was impossible to supply Denikin's army from outside Russia. Although the rich Cossack areas had great strategic significance in the Civil War, the Allies had been far more interested in the North and in Siberia, fearing that materiel which the Russians had received from the Allies in the course of the World War might fall into the hands of the enemy.

In November 1918 Denikin fully expected that the armies which had defeated the Germans would soon come to his aid. He did not ask for intervention as a favor, for he profoundly believed that it was the duty of the English and the French to punish the Bolsheviks.

He assumed that the Allies would see as clearly as he did that the Bolsheviks were merely German agents, and that to allow Lenin to remain in the Kremlin meant ending the World War without victory.[4] The Volunteer Army had been formed in order to continue Russia's participation in the World War, and the overthrow of Bolshevism had been envisaged at the time only as a means to that end. Now Denikin expected that the Allies would pursue the anti-Bolshevik war with the same determination as he had pursued the anti-German one. In 1918 the Volunteer Army could not cooperate with the Germans, and in 1919 Denikin made such unreasonable demands upon the Allies, and understood so poorly their motivations and the constraints under which they operated, that relations with them were bound to be poisoned soon.

But the disappointment was still in the future. In the period following the end of the war the Whites everywhere benefited from Allied help and an important part of the help was a boost in morale. Denikin especially gained much. The fact that the Allies recognized him as the most important White leader in South Russia helped him to bring a semblance of unity into the anti-Bolshevik camp. The sudden collapse of pro-German governments created a power vacuum in Kiev, Odessa, and the Crimea, and the Volunteer Army was able to extend its influence practically overnight.

Shortly after the end of the World War in Europe, an important political development took place in Siberia. By September 1918 the Czechs had succeeded in conquering most of Siberia, and were finding it far more difficult to provide the territory with an effective government than it had been to overthrow the weak Bolshevik government there. Independently of the Czechs, two rival governments emerged from the political chaos: a leftist one in Samara, formed by some members of the dispersed Constituent Assembly and claiming authority over entire Russia, and a more rightist one in Omsk, which called itself the Siberian Regional Government. In mid-September, after some prompting by the Czechs, the two governments decided to compromise and established a Directorate of five members, consisting of two Social Revolutionaries from Samara, two representatives from Omsk, and General Boldryev, a soldier distinguished by his liberal political views.

The Directorate was founded on an uneasy compromise: it was not to be responsible to the Constituent Assembly, yet it was committed to reconvening it if 250 members could be gathered by January 1, 1919, or 170 by February 1, 1919.[5] The new government had little power for it possessed no administrative apparatus. As the mood of the officers in Siberia became increasingly conservative, the Directorate became isolated from the only active anti-Bolshevik force. When a group of officers staged a coup on November 18 and imprisoned the Social Revolutionary politicians, no one was surprised.

The military named Admiral A. V. Kolchak Supreme Ruler. Kolchak, a man totally lacking in political experience, was an even more hopeless amateur than the leaders in Southern Russia. His administration was more scandal-ridden, his military and political strategies more short-sighted, his successes more ephemeral, and his ultimate failure sooner in coming than Denikin's. The national significance of the November coup was that it revealed that officers and socialists could nowhere work together and that the center of the Russian political spectrum was certain to be ineffective in the bitter Civil War.

The leaders of the Volunteer Army had little reliable information about the complex political developments in the East.[6] They were so distressed to learn that the Directorate included socialists and intended to reconvene the dispersed Constituent Assembly that they promptly refused to recognize its claim to be the government of all Russia.[7] In early October General Boldryev suggested that the Volunteer Army take Tsaritsyn and thus bring closer the unification of the two fronts. The Volunteer Army at this time was fighting at Stavropol, and Denikin was no more willing to follow Boldryev's advice than he had been to accede to the wishes of Ataman Krasnov, who had proposed the same strategy in May.

The news of Kolchak's coup was greeted in Ekaterinodar with the greatest satisfaction, and it contributed to the general feeling of optimism which prevailed in the closing months of 1918.

FIRST CONTACT WITH THE ALLIES

General A. S. Sannikov, who had just returned from Jassy, reported to the Special Council on October 25 about his contacts with

Allied envoys in the temporary Romanian capital.[8] He received assurances precisely on those points which concerned the Volunteer leaders the most: the foreign envoys indicated that they regarded Denikin as the man around whom the White movement should unite, they promised material support, and they recognized that the military hardware left by the Russian armies on the Romanian front was Russian national property and therefore belonged to the legitimate heir of the Imperial Army, the Volunteer Army. Sannikov, while in Jassy, also had satisfactory conversations with the Romanian Prime Minister Ion Bratianu, who proposed an exchange of munitions for grain which Romania needed badly.

The English and French ambassadors in October could give support only in general terms. A short time later another Volunteer representative, General D. G. Shcherbachev, was able to relay more specific and even more far-reaching promises.[9] He had been the Commander of the Russian armies on the Romanian front, and through his war service had excellent contacts with English and French generals. He had always been an enthusiastic advocate of an Allied orientation and had chosen to remain in Romania after the Russian front collapsed. Even before the end of the war, General Alekseev had entrusted Shcherbachev with representing the Volunteer Army before the Allies. Shcherbachev had planned to go to Paris and take up his duties there, but his interviews with General Berthelot, chosen by the French to prepare their intervention, were so promising that he decided to stay in Jassy.

On November 15 Shcherbachev could write Denikin that Berthelot's ideas corresponded to the wishes of the White generals down to the smallest details and that Berthelot possessed the full confidence of Premier Clemenceau. He made these specific points in his letter:

(1) Twelve divisions will be sent for the occupation of South Russia as soon as possible. One of these will go to Odessa in the immediate future.

(2) The divisions will be French and Greek.

(3) On the recommendation of the Allies and General Berthelot I will participate in making all decisions.

(4) The Allied base will be at Odessa; Sevastopol will be occupied also.

(5) General d'Anselme, who will have his headquarters in Odes-

sa, will command the Allied forces at the beginning. I will also stay in Odessa and will be helped by people whom you know.

(6) General Berthelot will stay in Bucharest with his main head-quarters for the time being.

(7) Apart from the occupation of Odessa and Sevastopol—which will undoubtedly take place by the time of the arrival of this letter—the Allies will quickly occupy Kiev and Kharkov, together with Krivoi Rog, the Donets basin, the Don, and the Kuban, which will give an opportunity to the Volunteer and Don armies to organize and will free them for further large-scale active operations.

(8) Under the cover of Allied occupation, the immediate or-ganization of Russian armies in South Russia is necessary in the name of recreating a Great and United Russia. . . .

(9) Enormous quantities of all kinds of weapons, military sup-plies, tanks, railroad and road equipment, and airplanes will arrive at Odessa, the main base of the Allies.

(10) The military supplies of the ex-Romanian front and of the Ukraine and Don from now on can be regarded as completely ours. Only some slight diplomatic efforts will have to be made, and suc-cess is assured, since we have the support of the overwhelming power of the Allies.

(11) Special plans will be worked out about Allied financial support.[10]

In his letter of November 20, reporting further conversations with Berthelot, Shcherbachev was again exuberantly optimistic.[11] He assumed that the nature of the collaboration between the Russians and the Allies would be the same as it had been during the World War: complete equality in command, with the Allies to undertake no action in Russia without consulting representatives of the Volun-teer Army.[12]

English and French naval squadrons entered the Black Sea as soon as they could. On November 23 Allied representatives disembarked at Novorossisk and proceeded to Ekaterinodar, where they arrived on December 3. General F. C. Poole, the English representative, and Lieutenant Erlich, a Frenchman, assured their hosts that their coun-tries had the same goals as the Volunteer Army, the recreation of a united and indivisible Russia. To achieve this aim the Allies would support the forming of a united South Russian anti-Bolshevik front under General Denikin.[13] The army and the population of Ekaterinodar gave a joyous and enthusiastic welcome to the visitors. Everyone believed that the Civil War could not last long now because the countries which had defeated the magnificent German armies would have no trouble at all in dispersing Bolshevik bands.

Encouraged by the promises coming from so many sources, Denikin decided on December 3 to write General Franchet d'Esperey, the French commander in the Eastern theater of operations and Berthelot's immediate superior. The chief of the Volunteer Army was writing not as a supplicant, but as a man consulting his equal about strategy. He envisaged that the next areas of struggle would be the territories freed from the Germans. He wanted to transform these areas, primarily the Ukraine, into bases from which the main blow could be struck against Moscow. He proposed that the Allies send 18 infantry and four cavalry divisions and added: " These forces will be used exclusively for covering our deployment and protecting our communications. They would not have to participate in any action. . . . We do not need force so much as the encouragement of friendly help."[14] Denikin attached to his letter a list of the military materiel which he needed most and hoped to get from the French.

It was at this point, around the middle of December, that high hopes for the success of the intervention began to fade in Ekaterinodar. Reports of a quick German evacuation caused nervousness. Allied troops were not arriving to take the place of the Germans, and Denikin rightly feared that the Bolsheviks would seize the opportunity. It was ironic—though very likely the irony was not understood by the Whites—that those Russians who had always regarded the Bolsheviks as German agents now wanted the German troops to remain as occupation forces in order to prevent the expansion of Bolshevik power. Denikin telegraphed Franchet d'Esperey on December 7 asking him to speed up the dispatch of troops to the Ukraine.[15] He received no answer either to his telegram or to his previous letter. A week later the Volunteer Army asked the Allies at least to stop the Germans from evacuating the district of Kharkov, for the Germans were needed there "for maintaining order."[16]

Time passed, and aside from the occupation of Odessa and Sevastopol by the French on December 18, the Allies did nothing to activate the plans for intervention. Denikin did not yet know that Clemenceau had vetoed the Berthelot-Shcherbachev project. Berthelot, perhaps out of embarrassment or because he still hoped to change Clemenceau's mind, did not inform Shcherbachev of this development until two weeks after the event, and even then he gave the impression that the project was not canceled but merely postponed.[17] No material help arrived until February 1919, and then it came from the British and not from the French.

One disappointment followed another. It became increasingly clear that the Allies would not be satisfied merely with supporting the Volunteer Army, but that they would pursue an independent policy in Russia. The French supported the Ukrainian separatists, whom Denikin regarded as mortal enemies, and the British gave aid to the new Caucasian states. When the Allies captured the Russian Black Sea fleet from the Germans, they did not hand it over to the Volunteer Army as Denikin had demanded. In Odessa the French took over civil administration from the volunteer representatives and Denikin's wishes were simply disregarded.

But the greatest disappointment of all was that the Allies never intervened in force. They had neither the means—their people were war-weary, their public opinion hesitant—nor the will to carry out intervention on a scale sufficiently large to defeat the Bolsheviks. Denikin felt himself betrayed.

THE FORMING OF A DELEGATION TO THE PARIS PEACE CONFERENCE

Even before the armistice was signed at Compiégne on November 8, anti-Bolshevik politicians had begun negotiations on the issue of how Russia should be represented at the coming peace conference. It was generally understood that the country's interests would be harmed by sending several independent anti-Bolshevik delegations, and this understanding gave a unique opportunity to the leaders of the Volunteer Army. No other organization could have a comparable claim to take upon itself the forming of a united delegation: the Volunteer Army was untainted by any collaboration with Germany, and the only other anti-Bolshevik movement with national pretensions, the Siberian one, was beset with internal problems at the time. The leaders of the Volunteer Army did not seize the opportunity to assert leadership within the White movement, and the delegation which ultimately went to Paris was not widely accepted among anti-Bolshevik Russians and it commanded little respect abroad.

The first preparations for forming a delegation were made in October 1918. Krasnov, who perceived that the Germans had lost the war, realized that he had to turn to the Volunteer Army in matters of foreign relations and instructed his foreign minister, General A. P. Bogaevskii, to discuss the issue at Ekaterinodar. In his letter to Denikin Bogaevskii asserted that the Don should be represented at the coming peace conference.[18] Denikin, in his answer, evaded the issue by emphasizing the necessity of sending men who were well-known in Europe. He considered the time right to bring up the question of a united command, which was in fact a euphemism for the Don Army's subjection to his own authority.[19]

The Special Council first discussed representation at the Conference on October 25. That Denikin attributed great importance to this matter is shown by the fact that he participated in the meeting. The Council discussed not only the problems of forming a delegation, but also the policies which the delegation should pursue in Paris. It made the following decisions: (1) Russia should have a single delegation. (2) The delegation should be formed from organizations which: (a) repudiated the Treaty of Brest-Litovsk; and (b) fought for a united Russia. (3) All treaties with Germany should be abrogated, and Russian property taken by the Germans should be returned. (4) The Germans should free the territories they occupied (including Finland); Polish efforts to free their territory from the Germans should be supported. (5) Important strategic areas which were occupied by the Germans should be occupied by Russians, or temporarily by the Allies. (6) Germans should immediately free prisoners of war. (7) The Germans should recognize in principle the united Russian state, and therefore should be forbidden to support any Bolshevik, or covertly Bolshevik, organizations.[20]

Thus the Special Council in principle recognized that the participation of other anti-Bolshevik organizations in the formation of the delegation was necessary. Indeed, this conclusion was inevitable. It was simply not within the power of the leaders in Ekaterinodar to prevent the Kuban and the Don, to say nothing of Georgia and the Ukraine and a variety of other new governments, from sending diplomats to Paris. The only way to avoid that was to arrive at a compromise satisfactory to everyone.

M. M. Vinaver, a liberal Kadet leader who was in Ekaterinodar at the time in connection with the Kadet conference, presented his plan to the Special Council for forming a committee to devise a foreign policy and organize Russia's representation in Paris. Vinaver, a federalist, wanted the composition of the committee to mirror the existing relation of forces within the anti-Bolshevik camp. According to his plan, the Volunteer Army would have four, the Ufa Directorate three, the Ukraine two, and the Don, the Kuban, and the Crimea one representative each in the committee, which would work under Denikin's chairmanship.[21] The Special Council accepted the plan, but Denikin wanted substantial modifications: he wanted six votes for his army, and instead of assuming the chairmanship himself, he proposed to give this position to ex-Imperial foreign minister S. D. Sazonov, who at the time was the head of the department of foreign affairs of the Special Council. Most important, Denikin claimed the right to veto decisions of the committee.[22] This last change in Vinaver's plan destroyed its entire *raison d'être;* if the decisions of the majority could be vetoed by Denikin, then in fact the new governments would have no say in the formulation of foreign policy.

The plan was never realized. It seems that the leaders of the Volunteer Army lost the patience necessary for handling such a delicate matter. They made no attempt to establish contact with Ufa or with the Ukraine. The Don and the Kuban governments were dissatisfied with having only one representative against six from the Volunteer Army and therefore declined to participate.[23] Vinaver, who had left Ekaterinodar with the understanding that he would be recalled when the committee convened, had no further communication from the Volunteer Army.[24]

Reversing their previous decisions, the Commander-in-Chief and the Special Council named S. D. Sazonov as Russian representative in Paris at the end of December without making further efforts to create a united delegation. This had disastrous results: as could have been foreseen, the Crimea, the Don, and the Kuban sent independent delegations, which at times worked at cross purposes. The disunity of the anti-Bolshevik camp was demonstrated to the outside world and the Volunteer Army missed an opportunity to assume leadership.

The choice of Sazonov was particularly unfortunate. He was closely connected in the public mind with the policies of tsarism, and in fact he remained an unrepentant monarchist who could imagine Russia's future only in terms of her past. Nor did he have any sympathy for the aspirations of border nationalities. The ex-foreign minister of Imperial Russia was a centralist who saw in federalism only an attempt to weaken the state, and he was unwilling to make any concessions.[25] Clemenceau, a man aware of the importance of public opinion, not only refused to have any personal dealings with him but even warned the Council of Ten against hearing him, "lest it be alleged that the Conference was conspiring with tsarism."[26] By sending Sazonov to Paris, the Volunteer Army needlessly projected the image of a monarchist organization.

THE FOUNDING OF THE ARMED FORCES OF SOUTH RUSSIA: AGREEMENT WITH THE DON

The defeat of Germany was a blow to the Don Cossacks and in particular to the political standing of Ataman Krasnov. The withdrawal of German troops from the Ukraine meant that the Don's left flank was no longer protected, and the front line became extended at a time when the Cossacks were hardly able to contain the Red Army on their northern and eastern boundaries. Those Don politicians who had objected to Krasnov's pro-German policies now wanted him to resign.

But Krasnov was not a man to accept defeat easily. It was the debacle of German armies in the Balkans which made him understand that he had to change "orientation." With characteristic "flexibility," he tried to save the situation. On November 19 he sent G. P. Ianov and a certain General Sazonov to Jassy in order to establish contact with General d'Esperey. Instead of d'Esperey, the Don delegates found General Berthelot, to whom they handed the Ataman's letter. The letter was a typical product of Krasnov's literary imagination, written in a style remarkably similar to the earlier one he had sent to the German Emperor. He declared that only the Allies could save Russia from Bolshevism and reminded the Allies of past glorious battles. He wisely changed the examples of glorious battles, however; instead of talking about past cooperation against Napoleon, or the English-Boer war, at this time he chose to remember the fighting between 1914 and 1916, when the Russian and above all, the Cossack armies "saved France."[27]

He understood that the Allies would support General Denikin against him, and the main purpose of his letter was to save himself from subordination to his hated adversary. He made the completely unrealistic suggestion of giving the command of the South Russian armies either to General D. G. Shcherbachev or to N. I. Ivanov. Of course, even if the Allies had wanted to remove General Denikin, a man who had remained scrupulously faithful to England and France, for the sake of the pro-German Krasnov, they simply were not in a position to do so. Most important, neither Ivanov nor Shcherbachev was willing to assume the post Krasnov was so anxious to give away.[28] A measure of Krasnov's blind hatred for Denikin was his willingness to entrust the united anti-Bolshevik armies to Ivanov, a man for whose abilities he had a low regard, and who had just proven himself incapable of commanding the small and ill-fated Southern army.[29]

The Cossack delegates got a cool reception. Allied soldiers in Jassy had already established ties with the leaders of the Volunteer Army and they understood and accepted Denikin's point of view on the issue of united command. Ianov's and Sazonov's attacks on Denikin made such a bad impression on Berthelot that he even refused to send a representative to Novocherkassk.[30]

While Krasnov did everything to avoid being subjected to Denikin's authority, he desperately needed help from the Volunteer Army. The Germans were evacuating the Ukraine and no Allied troops had yet appeared. The Cossack armies had to occupy the strategic cities of Lugansk and Mariupol before the Bolsheviks' arrival in order to preserve the stability of the front. Krasnov sent detachments from the Tsaritsyn sector for this purpose, giving up any hope of capturing that city in the foreseeable future. Late in November, however, he turned to Ekaterinodar for aid. At first, he asked for armored trains and heavy guns, but later he also requested soldiers.[31]

The changed relation of forces between the Volunteer Army and the Don encouraged Denikin to strive harder for the creation of a united command. He had always insisted on it in principle, and now he felt the time had come to realize it in fact. He gave some war materiel to the Ataman and a division under Mai-Maevskii, which went to fight in the Donets basin, but Krasnov had the probably correct impression that substantial help from the Volunteer Army would come only at the price of recognizing Denikin's command. Krasnov procrastinated. He sent a delegation to Ekaterinodar to discuss common problems on November 26, but he instructed his representatives, Generals Poliakov, Svechin, and Grekov, not to accept subordination of the Don Army to the Volunteer Army.[32] Under the circumstances discussions were fruitless and the two sides merely repeated old arguments. Aside from recognition of the necessity of Russia's having a united delegation at the Peace Conference, there was no agreement.

It was the Allied intervention which broke the long stalemate between Krasnov and Denikin. Allied representatives in Ekaterinodar made clear that they supported Denikin's position. General Poole was especially emphatic. On one occasion he went so far as to ask Denikin whether he wanted the Allies to remove Krasnov from the Don by force, "for the good of the cause." Denikin wisely advised against it.[33] As a sign of their displeasure with Krasnov's policies, for a time the English and the French did not even make an attempt to establish direct contact with Novocherkassk. Only on December 8 did some low-ranking English and French officers go to the capital of the Don.[34] Krasnov, a man with a flair for the theatrical, organized a reception which made a good impression on the foreigners, who presumably reported favorably on their experiences to their superiors in Ekaterinodar. This report, however, made no change in the position of English and French officers who were attached to the headquarters of the Volunteer Army.

As the military situation of the Don armies further deteriorated and as Krasnov's opponents among the Don politicians blamed him for the misfortunes of the *voisko*, he decided to turn to General

Poole. He sent the Englishman a letter asking him to inspect the achievements of the Don personally. He could not restrain himself from making an attack on the "intriguers in Ekaterinodar," who spread falsehoods about him. As in his previous letter to General Franchet d'Esperey, on this occasion again he wrote that the command of the united armies should be entrusted to anyone except General Denikin.[35]

As the complaints of one Russian general against another made a bad impression on General Berthelot, they also further alienated General Poole. Behind the diplomatically polite phrases of Poole's answer, one can discern the contempt he felt for the Ataman.

> If I have to return and report to my government that mutual hatred and distrust exist among the Russian generals, this would create the most negative impression and unquestionably diminish the chances that the Allies would give any kind of help. I would prefer to report that Your Excellency showed himself such a great patriot that he even agreed to subordinate his own wishes to the general good of Russia and agreed to serve under the command of General Denikin.[36]

Elsewhere in his letter, Poole indicated that his government had entrusted him with establishing contact with General Denikin, who, in the opinion of the English government, was the leader of the Russian national army fighting the Bolsheviks. Consequently, Poole wrote, he could not recognize the independent authority of any other army in South Russia. However, Poole was willing to meet Krasnov in an unofficial capacity. As another blow to the Ataman, Poole wrote that General Dragomirov, the representative of General Denikin, would be present at the meeting.

The meeting took place at *stanitsa* Kushchevka on December 26. It had an unpleasant beginning. At the Kushchevka railroad station, Poole's train from Ekaterinodar and Krasnov's from Novocherkassk arrived at about the same time. Poole, to avoid the impression that this was an official visit which might be construed as some form of recognition of the independence of the Don, wanted Krasnov to come to his railroad carriage. Krasnov absolutely refused. He said to one of General Poole's aides:

Tell General Poole that I am the elected head of a free people of five million, which has no need for anything. Listen: Nothing! It does not need your weapons, guns, and ammunition. It has everything of its own and it has cleared its territory of the Bolsheviks. Tomorrow it could conclude peace with the Bolsheviks, and could live excellently. But we have to save Russia and for this we need the help of the Allies. The head of a strong and powerful nation will talk to General Poole and he demands for himself a certain respect. General Poole is obliged to appear in front of me. I will not delay my return visit.[37]

The two trains stood side by side. Time passed and neither Krasnov nor Poole left his carriage. The situation became tense; aides ran from one train to another, hoping that the other side would give in. Krasnov gave an order to the machinist to prepare the train for departure when Poole, to his credit, decided to visit Krasnov in his compartment.[38]

This was, however, Krasnov's only satisfaction. In the three-hour conversation Dragomirov, in the name of Denikin, demanded complete subordination of the Don armies. Poole supported Dragomirov. Krasnov, realizing that he was fighting a losing battle, wanted to save as much as could be saved: he conceded the subordination of his army to the Commander-in-Chief of the Volunteer Army, but hoped to preserve it as a unit. He wanted relations between Cossack troops and Volunteer Army headquarters to take place entirely through the person of the Ataman. This suggestion was unacceptable to the leaders of the Volunteer Army, who wanted to integrate the Don troops into the united Army on the same basis as they had integrated the Kuban Cossacks.[39]

The significance of the Kushchevka meeting was that it convinced the Ataman that he could expect no aid from abroad unless he accepted Denikin's conditions. General Shcherbachev, who had come from Rumania to Ekaterinodar and had the confidence of both Generals Denikin and Krasnov, took upon himself the role of bringing the leaders of the two armies together.

Shcherbachev arranged a meeting on January 8, 1919, at the Torgovaia railroad station. Ataman Krasnov, Generals S. V. Denisov, I. A. Poliakov, A. A. Smagin, and A. V. Ponomarev represented

the Don; Denikin, Dragomirov, Romanovskii, and Engel'ke represented the Volunteer Army. Shcherbachev was also in the Volunteer
Army delegation but in fact he was a neutral mediator.[40] Significantly, no Kuban Cossack participated in the talks; perhaps the
Russian generals were afraid that the Kuban Cossacks might support
Krasnov's position. The exclusion of the Kuban representatives from
this obviously important conference warned Ataman Krasnov that
he could not expect good treatment once he accepted subordination.

But the Cossacks were not in a position to resist: while the issue
of united command had gone unresolved, the Bolsheviks had won
several victories, and in January 1919 they threatened to overrun
the entire *voisko*. The longer the Ataman waited, the less his Cossacks were able to resist the Bolsheviks and the weaker his bargaining
position became.

On a number of issues there was immediate agreement. Krasnov
accepted common finances, foreign affairs, railroad administration,
postal services, and administration of justice. He mentioned that the
Don would be the greatest financial supporter of the united armies
and therefore it should have a say in financial administration, but this
was not a divisive issue.[41] As could be anticipated, the debate centered almost entirely on the position of the Don Cossack troops
within the United Army. The Cossacks wanted to retain a degree
of autonomy and Denikin demanded complete subordination. Two
questions of detail caused sharp debate: Krasnov insisted on retaining
the right to name officers in the Don Army, while the Russian generals regarded this as a violation of the principle of united command;
and the leaders of the Volunteer Army wanted the right to dispose
of the military property and supplies which had accumulated on the
Don front, while the Cossacks wanted to reserve this material for
the Don.

A great deal of time was wasted on mutual recriminations. The
Don delegates, conscious of defeat in their long rivalry with the
Volunteer Army, constantly brought up past injuries. Repeatedly
they blamed the leaders of the Volunteer Army for sheltering their
political opponents and encouraging dissent in the Don. The most
implacable among the Cossack generals was General Denisov. Once
he burst out:

United Command under the Volunteer Army! Show the Cossack well-organized, strong Volunteer units on the Don front, show your superiority over him, and he will accept command from a Russian general. But as long as he knows that there is a strong Don Army of a hundred thousand and a strong Kuban army of thirty thousand and only ten thousand Volunteer officers, he will never understand why it is necessary to subordinate himself to the Volunteers, since he has made all the sacrifices for the fatherland. You do not appreciate the Cossacks to such an extent that you invited not a single Kuban Cossack to this meeting.

The conference was on the verge of breaking up several times, and only the persuasion of Shcherbachev and Smagin made the disputants continue negotiations. The meeting did not resolve all the controversial issues, and it ended with an order by General Denikin and another by Ataman Krasnov, which were to a certain extent contradictory. Denikin's order was short:

"The order of the Commander-in-Chief of the Armed Forces of South Russia: By agreement with the Atamans of the All-Great Don Voisko and Kuban I take command today of all land and sea forces acting in South Russia. [Signed] Lieutenant General Denikin."

(Of course, Filimonov, who was not present at the meeting, could not give his consent.) The Ataman added his own order:

Proclaiming this order [Denikin's] to the Russian Armies on the lands of the All-Great Don *voisko*, I announce that by agreement with the Commander-in-Chief of the Armed Forces in South Russia, Lieutenant General Denikin, the Constitution of the All-Great Don *voisko*, as it was accepted by the Great *voisko krug* on September 15th [28th] will not be demolished. The position of Don Cossacks, their land, property, conditions of life, and service in the Don Army will not be changed. United command is a necessary and timely measure for the achievement of complete and quick victory in the struggle against the Bolsheviks.

Ataman of the Don, General of the Cavalry,
Krasnov.

This way neither side gave in. Denikin did not explicitly recognize the Constitution of the Don or the autonomy of the Don Army. What would happen with the war materiel on the Don front, and who had the right to name officers in the Don army remained open questions. It was hoped that these problems would be solved in time. The diehards on both sides objected to this ambiguous arrangement: Dragomirov feared that Krasnov's order nullified the significance of Denikin's, and Denisov exclaimed that Krasnov had signed the death warrant of the Don *voisko*.[42]

Even in its ambiguous form, the Torgovaia agreement had enormous significance. The Don Army came under the command of men who had national objectives, men who were not satisfied with merely defending the boundaries of the *voisko* but wanted to liberate Moscow, Petrograd, and the entire country from the Bolsheviks. The area under Denikin's control greatly expanded; the unification made possible a more effective use of the resources and troops of the hitherto separate armies. The Volunteer Army gained by the acquisition of Cossack cavalry units and the Don front was strengthened by the addition of Volunteer infantry. The unification of the two armies made possible the development of large-scale strategy which greatly benefited the White cause.

The forming of the Armed Forces of South Russia necessitated large-scale reorganization. The bulk of the Volunteer Army, which was fighting in the Northern Caucasus, became the Caucasian Volunteer Army under the command of General Wrangel.[43] Aside from the Caucasian Volunteer Army and the Don army, Denikin's command also included the Crimean army and a volunteer unit in Odessa. The unification of the Don and Volunteer armies started a new chapter in the history of the White movement in South Russia; the movement gained greatly in strength and became far more complex.

Krasnov's capitulation to Denikin did not save his political life, nor did it solve the immediate problems of the Don. The main motive for Krasnov's acceptance of the unified command was the promise of quick Allied help, but the Allies disappointed him. The situation on the front continued to deteriorate; discipline loosened to such an extent that the orders of the Ataman frequently were not carried out and troops left the battlefield. The Ataman's submission to Denikin's command did not placate his political opponents in the *krug*. They maintained that as long as "Germanophile" Krasnov retained his post, the Allies would send no aid.[44] The argument was in fact incorrect—all contacts with the Allies were handled by the Ekaterinodar headquarters—but it sounded convincing to the Cossacks.

Too many sharp words had passed between Denikin and Krasnov for them ever to work together successfully. Krasnov was bitterly conscious of his defeat and he was surrounded by people such as Denisov and Poliakov, who were even more fanatic enemies of General Denikin than he was. Denikin, on the other hand, could not forgive Krasnov for turning against him in representations to Franchet d'Esperey and to Poole. When Krasnov asked Denikin's support against the opposition in the *krug*, Denikin was not eager to help. He declared that disputes in the *krug* were internal matters of the *voisko*, in which he did not want to interfere.[45]

The problem was finally resolved by Krasnov's resignation. The *krug*, which assembled on February 14, demanded the resignations of Denisov and Poliakov. Krasnov rightly interpreted this demand as a sign of the *krug's* lack of confidence in his leadership. He told the *krug* that if it insisted on the removal of his closest associates, he too would step down. The Assembly voted against him.

EXPANSION OF THE VOLUNTEER ARMY'S INFLUENCE: KIEV, ODESSA, AND THE CRIMEA

In its first year the Volunteer Army was an organization of only regional significance in spite of its national pretensions. Suddenly, after the armistice, its influence greatly expanded as a result of a series of victories, Allied moral support, German evacuation, and unification with the Don Army.

In the course of 1918, thousands of Russian officers had escaped from Soviet rule to German-controlled areas, above all to the Ukraine and the Crimea. The Volunteer Army regarded these men as potential recruits and sent trusted agents to organize them and persuade them to go to the Kuban. This created small detachments of officers who were nominally members of the Volunteer Army but who were almost completely cut off from the main forces because of poor communications. In the power vacuum created by the

German withdrawal, these isolated bands acquired great significance and involved the name and prestige of the Volunteer Army in the extremely complicated civil war of the Ukraine and the Crimea.

As soon as the defeat of Germany in the World War became obvious, Hetman Skoropadskii of the Ukraine, like Ataman Krasnov, tried to save his regime by a change of policies. He hoped to gain the good will of the Allies by dismissing those ministers in his cabinet who had compromised themselves most by cooperating with the Germans. However, discontent with Skoropadskii's regime had been great, and his enemies started to organize as quickly as they could. The Germans in April 1918 had destroyed the *rada* for being too radical. Now, the leading figures of the dispersed *rada* formed a socialist and nationalist Ukrainian National Union headed by a five-man Directorate. The Directorate set up its headquarters at Belaia Tserkov', only 50 miles from Kiev. Its army under Semen Petliura was growing rapidly and presented an immediate danger to Skoropadskii.[46]

The Hetman, in his desperate situation, placed all his hopes on the Russian officers living in the Ukraine. For their sake he jettisoned Ukrainian nationalism and stressed only the restorationist elements in his program. On November 19 he named as commander of his armies General Count Keller, a man who was such a determined monarchist that he had refused service under both the Provisional Government and General Denikin. Keller, apparently incorrectly, understood his appointment to mean that he had become a dictator and immediately introduced far-reaching political changes: he surrounded himself with reactionary politicians and declared the Ukraine to be a part of indivisible and monarchist Russia.[47]

Since almost the entire small Ukrainian army had defected to Petliura, Keller's army consisted mostly of Russian officers. Under the circumstances it was vitally important for him to gain the co-operation of General Lomnovskii, Denikin's representative in Kiev. Denikin, who had been alarmed by the growth of the Ukrainian nationalist army, reluctantly gave his permission for officer units, formed under the aegis of the Volunteer Army, to fight against Petliura. But since communications between Ekaterinodar and Kiev were unsatisfactory, the responsibility for giving leadership to the officers fell on Lomnovskii. His dilemma was that by supporting Keller he associated the Volunteer Army with a reactionary and monarchist regime. On the other hand he understood that any alternative to the Skoropadskii-Keller regime had to be worse.[48] Lomnovskii resolved the dilemma by subordinating officer units to Count Keller, without declaring these units to be part of the Volunteer Army and without providing them with a flag of the Army. Lomnovskii, a weak and vacillating man with little personal authority among the officers, was not very successful, and many officers left their units rather than fight for Skoropadskii.[49]

Keller's term in office was short. On November 26 Skoropadskii removed him from office for "overstepping the bounds of his authority" and replaced him with General Prince Dolgorukov. But it was a change from bad to worse. Dolgorukov shared Keller's political views and was a most undiplomatic person.[50] Immediately after he took command of the Ukrainian forces, relations with the Volunteer Army sharply deteriorated. He did not recognize the authority of the representative of the Volunteer Army and instead of using persuasion he simply drafted all officers into his army. The Kievan Kadets contributed to the embitterment of relations by their agitation on behalf of Lomnovskii's appointment as commander in place of Dolgorukov. Dolgorukov was understandably disturbed by this agitation, and in order to guard his authority he arrested Lomnovskii on December 6. As an Azbuka agent realized at the time, this arrest actually served the interests of the Volunteer Army by enabling Russian officers to defend Kiev against Petliura and at the same time dissociate themselves from the reactionary policies of Dolgorukov and Sokoropadskii.[51] Because of the energetic protest of conservative politicians, Dolgorukov soon freed Lomnovskii, who agreed to continued cooperation.

But the days of Skoropadskii's rule were numbered. The few thousand Russian officers who remained to fight for him were hardly strong enough to maintain order in Kiev. In the rest of the country his rule simply vanished. Because of their hatred of Skoropadskii, thousands of peasants joined the forces of the Directorate. No matter how disorganized and ill-disciplined these troops were, their numerical superiority was such that they could not be stopped. On

December 14, after the Directorate arrived at an agreement with the Germans, who were anxious to complete their evacuation and therefore promised neutrality, the Army of the Directorate under General Konovalets entered the Ukrainian capital and met only sporadic resistance. Fifteen hundred Russian officers were sequestered in the Pedagogical Museum; their weapons were taken away and they were regarded as prisoners of war.[52] The Ukrainian nationalists, who did not want to alienate the Allies, treated the captured officers well. Strangely, it was the Germans who extended the most effective support to the captured Russians by offering to take with them on their trains anyone who wanted to go to Germany. Many officers from the Pedagogical Museum used this opportunity; others went to Odessa and joined volunteer formations there, and some managed to get through the Don to the Kuban to join the main Army.[53]

The defeat at the hands of the troops of the Directorate ended the influence of the Volunteer Army in Kiev. The next struggle for the Ukraine took place between the Directorate and the Bolsheviks. In this struggle the Volunteer Army took no sides.

*　　*　　*

While Odessa was still occupied by the Central Powers, a volunteer unit about 1500 strong was formed there by Denikin's representative, Admiral Neniukov.[54] Neniukov faced the same dilemma as Lomnovskii had and resolved it in a similar fashion: when Petliura's forces threatened the city, he temporarily subordinated his troops to General Biskupskii, Skoropadskii's military governor. But the Russian officers alone were obviously not strong enough to defend Odessa, and the Ukrainians did not want to fight against the Directorate. On December 8 the volunteers telegrammed Denikin for help, but the Volunteer Army, which was engaged in fighting in the Northern Caucasus, had just sent a division to Krasnov and was unable to spare any more soldiers.[55] Under the circumstances, Biskupskii capitulated and Petliura's soldiers entered the city without fighting on December 11.[56]

Some regiments of the Polish legion, which happened to be stationed in Odessa, saved the Russians from the fate of the Kiev volunteers. The Poles cordoned off a part of the city as a "neutral zone," and here the Russians regrouped their forces. V. V. Shulgin and General Grishin-Almazov, who represented the Volunteer Army at the Jassy-Odessa conference, took an active part in the reorganization. Shulgin later persuaded Neniukov to hand over command to Grishin-Almazov, whom he regarded as an energetic young man and more suitable for the task.

On December 17, the long-promised French occupation forces arrived at Odessa harbor. After consulting with their leaders, the volunteers, with the aid of French naval guns, cleared the city of the numerically much stronger Ukrainian troops. On December 18 the foreign troops disembarked, and their commander, General Borius, entrusted Grishin-Almazov with the handling of civilian affairs in the city and made him military governor.[57]

Thus French occupation began most propitiously for the volunteers: the foreigners on the day of their arrival made common cause with them against the Ukrainians. For a relatively small sacrifice, Denikin's authority was extended to one of the major cities of South Russia, which promised to become a center of recruiting and point of contact with the outside world.[58]

The gradual dissipation of hope and optimism belongs to a different period in the history of the Volunteer Army, beyond the subject of this study. The causes of the disappointment, however, may be briefly noted. The French had only an elementary understanding of the complex Russian affairs and no consistent policy. They did not comprehend the bitterness of the divisions within the anti-Bolshevik camp. Their commanders arrived in Russia with vague instructions to support all "patriotic" Russians, and they had no idea that there existed so many varieties of "patriotism."[59] Borius sided with the Volunteer Army, but he was replaced in January by General d'Anselme, who interpreted his instructions differently and intended to establish contact with the Directorate. He made futile efforts to bring together the followers of Denikin and the followers of the Directorate and supported first one group and then the other. General d'Anselme removed Grishin-Almazov from the military governorship and entrusted to his own Chief of Staff, Colonel Friedenberg, the duties but not the title of that office. The fact that the French did not look on the Volunteer Army as the only legitimate heir to Imperial Russia, but only as one of the quarreling factions within the anti-Bolshevik movement, caused bitter disappointment in Ekaterinodar.

But the most important source of disappointment for the White Russians was that the French did not want to fight. The morale of their troops was extremely low, and they never had enough men to undertake a major operation or to extend their area of occupation. Because of the lack of will to fight, the French adventure in South Russia was to end in total and rather ignominious disaster.

*   *   *

General S. Sulkevich was the Skoropadskii of the Crimea: he supported the landowners in their efforts to retrieve the land they had lost in 1917 and 1918 and he cooperated with the occupation troops in sending food to Germany.[60] Having been warned by the Germans that evacuation was imminent, and realizing that he lacked indigenous support, on November 17 Sulkevich turned to Denikin for help. Denikin was neither willing nor able to help the pro-German General.[61]

From the point of view of the Volunteer Army, the political situation in the Crimea was far more promising than in the Ukraine. Here the alternative to the pro-German, conservative regime was not a socialist and separatist one, but a liberal Kadet government with which the army should have been able to cooperate. As the Germans withdrew, Sulkevich, finding his own position hopeless, peacefully handed over the government to S. S. Krym, a Kadet elected by the organization of Crimean *zemstva*. [62] Krym named as his foreign minister M. M. Vinaver, who was in Ekaterinodar at the time. Vinaver used the opportunity to persuade Denikin to send a small detachment to the Crimea, as a token of his support for the new government. (Originally only 600 soldiers went, but later the force was expanded to about four and a half thousand.) On Vinaver's request, Denikin published a telegram to the population of the Crimea in which he promised that the volunteers would not interfere with local affairs and that they would not pursue reactionary goals.[63]

When French troops landed in Odessa, they also landed at the Crimean port of Sevastopol. Denikin expected the French to defend the peninsula and was sending his own soldiers there largely to encourage recruitment. Since the Crimea was the most popular place of refuge for the thousands of officers who had escaped from Bolshevik Russia, Denikin's hopes were high. However the Crimea, like Kiev and Odessa, was to disappoint him.

The recruitment drive attracted few volunteers. General Korvin-Krukovskii, Denikin's representative, then issued an order of general mobilization of officers. The Kadet government regarded the order as a violation of the Army's promise not to interfere in local matters and protested. Denikin yielded and removed Korvin-Krukovskii, but he felt bitter toward the government and believed that its attitude made successful recruitment impossible.[64] Relations between the Kadets and the volunteers constantly deteriorated. The Kadets in the Crimea, the only place where they were able to form a government during the Civil War, wanted to put into practice the liberal and democratic principles of their party.[65] They believed that the greatest service they could perform for Russia was to show that their principles could work in practice. They allowed socialist organizations to operate freely—in fact some socialists even joined the government—and used insufficient force to combat Bolshevik subversion. It was a difficult period in which to institute a liberal regime. The soldiers of the Volunteer Army, who came in increasing numbers to the Crimea, were incensed by what they regarded as the "weakness" of the government and repeatedly disregarded its wishes. The ill-concealed reactionary views of the officers, and their looting, inevitably discredited the Kadets, who ultimately—in view of the inactivity of the French—depended on the support of the Volunteer Army.

When the French withdrew in April 1919, the volunteer troops were too weak to defend the Crimea and the government had little prestige and indigenous support. The Bolsheviks captured the peninsula with relative ease.

CHAPTER 10

Conclusion

The end of the war in Europe marked the beginning of a new period in the Russian Civil War, a period characterized by increased popular involvement. The collapse of the German-supported governments and enlarged foreign intervention carried the fighting into areas which until then had been relatively uninvolved. But intervention merely accelerated a process which was already occurring.

In the months following the Bolshevik take-over, only small armies fought on both sides. The Bolsheviks could not have had more than 50,000 armed men in the entire country at the time of their victory, and even as late as the middle of 1918, only 50,000 Czechs and Slovaks controlled Siberia. The overwhelming majority of the Russian people wanted nothing more than to escape involvement. Between January and April of 1918, in Petrograd, the great working-class center, there were only 18,000 volunteers to defend the new regime against foreign and domestic enemies, despite Lenin's warning, "The Socialist Fatherland is in danger!"[1] In the same period of time only about one in a hundred of the ex-tsarist officers enrolled in White armies. Meanwhile, the scope of the conflict which would inevitably involve them was expanding. As the Bolsheviks attempted to establish their rule everywhere in the country, the fighting directly touched an ever-increasing part of the population; as both sides introduced conscription in the second half of 1918 more and more people realized to their dismay that it was impossible to keep out of the struggle.

The end of 1918 was a turning point for the Volunteer Army in particular. The Army was completing the significant military task of clearing the Northern Caucasus of Bolsheviks, thereby creating a secure rear which allowed it to move against the North in 1919. On January 8, 1919, it incorporated the army of the Don Cossacks, who were to play a great role in the march on Moscow in the fall of the same year. It became directly involved in the Ukrainian and Crimean civil wars. It was in the process of creating the rudiments of local administration and political institutions.

The number of soldiers in the Volunteer Army increased more than tenfold during 1918, and only this remarkable growth made possible the victories. But the negative aspect of gaining so many new soldiers was that the original homogeneous composition of the army disappeared. The Cossacks who enlisted in the First and Second Kuban campaigns had different goals from the volunteers who came to Novocherkassk at the end of 1917; and the conscripted peasants shared neither the aims of the Cossacks nor those of the officers.

The year 1918 was one of successes and substantial achievements for the Volunteer Army. As the army grew, the territory under its control expanded and it acquired national and even international significance. The seeds sown in 1918 brought a fruitful harvest in the following year, for the march on Moscow would have been impossible without that preparation. However, investigating the policies of the army in 1918, it is possible to discern some of the causes of its ultimate failure. Militarily, the volunteers accomplished miracles, but the leaders of the army failed politically. While the achievements of victorious campaigns were immediate and readily visible, the price of the political failures was to be paid only later.

Perhaps the greatest success of the army was its survival during the extremely difficult months of the Ice March. Few armies of comparable size in world history accomplished as much, and suffered privations as severe, as the Volunteer Army between February and May of 1918. In these months—and many times afterwards—the Whites defeated Bolshevik units several times larger. The army won victories because its leaders were able and its soldiers exceptionally determined and willing to accept risks and sacrifices. However, one must not overlook another reason for its success: Bolshevik forces in the Northern Caucasus were disorganized, lacked leadership, and were badly equipped. In the following year the Whites were to encounter much better armies.

But the outcome of a civil war is not decided by military factors alone. If war is the continuation of diplomacy by others means, then a civil war is the continuation of politics by others means. The leaders of the Volunteer Army were such poor politicians that they did not understand the nature of the war they were fighting. They misunderstood politics to such an extent that they believed it could simply be avoided. Such ostrich-like behavior invited disaster.

A good politician knows and can articulate his goals, he knows how and when to compromise, he can realistically evaluate the balance of forces and separate the attainable from the unattainable. According to these criteria the leaders of the Volunteer Army failed miserably.

Their inability to develop positive goals was perhaps their most important failure. In the first stages of the civil war, a good case could be made against presenting a political program. The generals believed that defining the goal of the army more precisely than saying that it was to fight the Germans, and their Bolshevik agents, would hinder the development of a broad national front. But as time went on the argument made less and less sense. National unity obviously did not materialize, and the army, contrary to the wishes of its leaders, acquired an identification in the public mind with reaction and restoration. By refusing to take a stand on controversial issues, the generals played into the hands of their enemies. The army made no effort to win the support of the majority of the Russian people, the peasantry. In the struggle between the *inogorodnye* and the Cossacks, the volunteers invariably took the side of the Cossacks. In 1918 the army had no policy on land reform. Lenin, by contrast, published his decree on land on the first day of Soviet rule. To be sure, Lenin could easily permit the peasants to seize land, whereas it would have been difficult for Denikin to follow the same policy since he drew his active support from conservatives, among them landlords. Even considering Denikin's difficult position, it still seems that he did far too little to counteract the negative image of his army and to win the support of the uncommitted.

No failure was more glaring than Denikin's inability to unify the anti-Bolshevik camp. Because the generals frequently allowed themselves to be influenced by personal antipathies, even the army's leadership was not always united. Kornilov and Alekseev disliked each other and could not work together. One suspects that the chief reason for insufficient cooperation between the Don and the Volunteer armies was the incompatibility of the personalities of Denikin and Krasnov. (Lenin and Trotskii, whose relations before 1917 were no better than those between Kornilov and Alekseev, managed to find a *modus vivendi*: Trotskii unquestioningly accepted Lenin's leadership, and Lenin, in turn, overlooked Trotskii's past "mistakes." Surely Trotskii and Stalin did not like each other more than Denikin and Krasnov; however, the Bolsheviks possessed an ideology which bound them together and a leader, Lenin, whose authority was recognized by all.)

The generals made no concession either to the left or to the right: the monarchist Gurko and the socialist Savinkov left the headquarters equally disappointed. Denikin, following his narrow political line, making compromises with no one and receiving support from few, believed that this behavior was the same as standing above political parties. (By contrast, the peasant anarchist Nestor Makhno's visit to Lenin comes to mind. The differences in background, goals, and temperament between Lenin and Makhno were greater than those between Denikin and Gurko or Alekseev and Savinkov, yet Makhno left Moscow with the desire to work with the new regime and in the civil war anarchist bands caused far more damage to the Whites than to the Reds.)[2]

The study of the White movement in South Russia is a study in disunity. Of course, not all blame for lack of unity should fall on the leaders of the Volunteer Army. After the collapse of the Russian empire, national minorities living on the peripheries gained de facto independence. These peoples developed a nationalism which gave a *raison d'être* to their newly independent states and provided a cohesion which was necessary for fighting Bolshevism. However, the new governments were deluded by their own slogans and forgot that only in cooperation could they defend their independence. Nationalist passion caused the ludicrous debate between the Don and the Ukraine over the possession of Taganrog, and the unfortunate wars among the Caucasian republics, and it inspired Georgia's unjustified desire to annex Sochi.

But the fault of the generals in Ekaterinodar was greater than that of the governments of the new states. It was the Volunteer Army's responsibility to bring unity into the anti-Bolshevik camp in South Russia, since it was the only organization which had national goals, but Denikin and his friends were even more blinded by narrow nationalism than the governments in Novocherkassk, Tiflis, and Kiev. Since the army developed no positive program, its announced goal could not be more precise than fighting for "Russia, united, great, and undivided." Russian nationalism, the mainstay of the White movement, and the newly found self-awareness of Cossacks, Ukrainians, and Georgians could be asserted only at each other's expense. However, pettiness in those men who wanted to occupy Moscow and Petrograd was more incongruous and unfortunate than in leaders who avowedly cared only for local interests. Considering only the immediate interests of the Georgian government, the war for the possession of Sochi was a senseless adventure; in the perspective of the all-Russian struggle, it was simply insane. An inability to separate the important from the superficial, a lack of understanding of the positions of others, and the refusal to compromise disqualified the headquarters in Ekaterinodar from assuming leadership among the diverse and competing forces.

The generals showed no more wisdom in their relations with foreigners. They never moderated their hostility toward Germany; this kept them from taking advantage of possible German help, and it dissuaded potential recruits, who took seriously the announced intention of fighting Germany and who lacked the desire to do so. As it turned out, Germany lost the war and probably the Volunteer Army profited somewhat by its previous uncompromising attitude. But it is likely that even if German victory had been apparent to all, these men of lofty ideals, who lacked the most elementary political sense, would not have followed a different course. The other side of the coin was the self-righteous, demanding attitude Ekaterinodar assumed toward the Allies. Unduly high expectations led to disappointment and unsatisfactory relations with the representatives of England and France. The men who understood little about Russian realities knew even less about the nature of international affairs.

The military men failed as politicians because their background and education did not prepare them for the tasks they were forced to undertake. Their schooling in the last decades of the nineteenth century made them suspicious of the intelligentsia, which had been enamoured of radical and revolutionary politics. Then, as students in military schools, they rejected not only radicalism but also politics in general. The gulf between intellectuals and politicians on the one hand and officers on the other further widened as a result of their experiences during the era of the Provisional Government: the officers and politicians blamed each other for the failures. The prejudice of the leaders of the Volunteer Army against politicians was so deeply rooted that they gave none of the responsible positions in its administration to civilians. The White movement in South Russia remained an exclusively military affair.

It has been frequently said that most of the ills of the White movement followed from one basic weakness, a lack of ideology. But how could one expect officers brought up with disdain for politics, and with an unquestioned acceptance of the existing political and social system, to compete on equal terms with the Bolshevik intellectuals, who had spent years in prison or in exile contemplating revolution? For the officers, revolutions and civil war were traumatic experiences, not only because they destroyed a Russia which they had basically liked, but because for the first time in their lives they were forced to confront social and political issues. It should not be a surprise that in the enormously complex situation they could come up with no more precise goals for the struggle than "Russia" and have no better understanding of their opponents than to regard them as German agents. Frustration must have been one of the chief sources of their great hatred for those whom they held responsible for destroying their secure and comfortable world, socialists and communists alike.

Perhaps the Whites were destined to be defeated in the Civil War in any case. Perhaps it was impossible even for the most far-sighted leader to win over the peasants for an active struggle. Perhaps it was impossible to combine all the anti-Bolshevik forces in the country because their differences in aims and backgrounds were too great. It is certain, however, that the White cause, entrusted to mediocre leaders who were incapable of rising above the prejudices of their military way of life, never had a fair chance.

Notes

$\mathcal{N}otes$

INTRODUCTION

1. William H. Chamberlin, *The Russian Revolution*, 2 vols. (New York, 1935).

2. K. N. Sokolov, *Pravlenie generala Denikina* (Sofia, 1921), p. 84.

CHAPTER 1

1. Leonard Schapiro, *The Communist Party of the Soviet Union* (New York, 1960), p. 151. Schapiro regards even ten thousand as too high an estimate.

2. Adam B. Ulam, *The Bolsheviks* (New York, 1965), p. 325.

3. The issue of German financial support for the Bolsheviks had long been controversial. Lenin had always denied it and Soviet historians have never contradicted Lenin. Today, after the opening of the German Foreign Ministry Archives (Auswaertiges Amt), it is clear beyond reasonable doubt that the Bolsheviks were in fact supported by the enemies of their country.

4. About the pre-revolutionary Russian Army see: A. I. Denikin, *Staraia armiia*, 2 vols. (Paris, 1929-1931); N. N. Golovine, *The Russian Army in the World War* (New Haven, 1931); Sir Alfred Knox, *With the Russian Army*, 2 vols. (London, 1921); Hans-Peter Stein "Der Offizier des russichen Heeres im Zeitabschnitt zwischen Reform und Revolution (1861-1905)," *Forschungen Zur osteuropäischen Geschichte* (Berlin, 1967), XIII, 346-507; and P. A. Zaionchkovskii, *Voennye reformy 1860-1870 godov v Rossii* (*Moscow 1952*).

5. A. I. Denikin, *Put' russkogo ofitsera* (New York, 1953), p. 63.

6. Sir Alfred Knox, *With the Russian Army*, p. 26.

7. N. N. Golovine, *The Russian Army in the World War*, p. 29.

8. Kornilov made some attempts. In his proclamation to the Russian people on August 27 (O.S.) he wrote "I, General Kornilov, son of a Cossack peasant, declare to all and sundry that I want nothing for myself, except the preservation of great Russia. . . ." E. I. Martynov, *Kornilov* (Leningrad, 1927), p. 111.

See also R. P. Browder and A. F. Kerensky, eds., *The Russian Provisional Government 1917; Documents* (Stanford, 1961), III, 1573.

9. A. Shliapnikov, *Semnadtsatyi god,* 3 vols. (Moscow-Leningrad, 1923-1927), II, 102, and Gerhard Wettig, "Die Rolle der russischen Armee im revolutionaeren Machtkampf, 1917," *Forschungen zur osteuropäischen Geschichte* (Berlin, 1967), XII, 67-68.

10. Gen. A. A. Brussilov, *A Soldier's Notebook 1914-1918* (London, 1930), p. 21.

11. A. I. Denikin, *Staraia armiia,* II, 10.

12. A. I. Denikin, *Put' russkogo ofitsera,* p. 98.

13. Brussilov, *A Soldier's Notebook,* pp. 21-25.

14. Knox, *With the Russian Army,* p. 27.

15. A. I. Denikin, *Put',* p. 64.

16. A. I. Denikin, *Staraia armiia,* II, 89-90.

17. *Rossiia v mirovoi voine 1914-1918 (v tsifrakh)* (Moscow, 1925), p. 23.

18. *Ibid.,* p. 24.

19. Golovine, *The Russian Army in the World War,* p. 99.

20. *Ibid.,* p. 100.

21. *Ibid.,* p. 25.

22. Knox, *With the Russian Army,* p. 85.

23. A. Lukomskii, *Vospominaniia,* 2 vols. (Berlin, 1922), I, 136-138, and G. Katkov, *Russia 1917: The February Revolution* (New York, 1967), pp. 330-335.

24. E. Martynov, *Tsarskaia armiia v fevralskom perevorote* (n.p. 1927), p. 195.

25. *Ibid.,* p. 192.

26. Lukomskii, *Vospominaniia,* I, 144.

27. Browder and Kerensky, eds., *The Russian Provisional Government* II, 848. See also the conflicting interpretations of the origin of Order No. 1 in John R. Boyd, "The Origins of Order No. 1," *Soviet Studies,* XIX (January 1968), pp. 359-372; and Katkov, *Russia 1917,* pp. 367-374.

28. L. D. Trotsky, *History of the Russian Revolution,* 3 vols. (New York, 1932), I, 276.

29. Browder and Kerensky, eds., *The Russian Provisional Government,* I. 883.

30. On the work of the Polivanov commission, see A. I. Denikin, *Ocherki russkoi smuty,* 5 vols. (Berlin and Paris, 1921-1925), I, Part II, chap. XIX, pp. 14-20.

31. Denikin, *Ocherki,* I, Part I, p. 78.

32. *Ibid.,* I, Part I, p. 77.

33. *Ibid.,* I, Part II, p. 9.

34. *Ibid.,* I, Part II, p. 9.

35. Robert S. Feldman, "The Russian General Staff and the June 1917 Offensive," *Soviet Studies,* XIX, (April 1968), pp. 526-543.

36. Rex A. Wade, "Why October? The Search for Peace in 1917," *Soviet Studies*, XX (July 1968), pp. 36-45.

37. Brussilov, *A Soldier's Notebook*, p. 291.

38. R. H. Bruce Lockhart, *British Agent* (New York and London, 1933), p. 288.

39. Denikin, *Ocherki*, I, Part II, chap. XXVI, pp. 106-116.

40. *Ibid.*, I, Part II, p. 188.

41. *Ibid.*, I, Part II, p. 186.

42. *Ibid.*, I, Part II, pp. 193-194.

43. *Ibid.*, I, Part II, p. 195.

44. P. N. Miliukov, *Istoriia vtoroi russkoi revoliutsii*, 3 vols. (Sofia, 1921-1924), I, Book II, p. 60.

45. Lukomskii, *Vospominaniia*, I, p. 227.

46. *Ibid.*, I, 228-229. English translation in Browder and Kerensky, eds., *The Russian Provisional Government*, III, 1548.

47. From the memoirs of V. N. Lvov published in *Poslednie Novosti*, No. 186 (November 30, 1920), p. 2; No. 190 (December 4, 1920), p. 2; No. 192 (December 7, 1920), p. 2, and No. 194 (December 9, 1920), p. 2. Lvov wrote: "Kornilov is guaranteeing Kerensky's life." I said, "Ah, how can the Supreme Commander guarantee life to Kerensky!" exclaimed Zavoiko.

"He did say so, however."

"He may have said a lot of things! How can Kornilov vouch for every step Kerensky takes? So he leaves the house and is killed."

"But who would kill him?"

"Even the selfsame Savinkov—how should I know who!"

"But this is terrible!"

"There is nothing terrible. His death is necessary as an outlet for pent-up feeling of the officers."

. . .

Then looking at me fixedly in the eyes, Zavoiko pronounced with deep significance: "Bring Kerensky!"

(Translated into English in Browder and Kerensky, ed., *The Russian Provisional Government*, III, 1566-1567.) Lvov was an admirer of Kornilov. There is no reason to doubt his veracity.

48. Browder and Kerensky, *The Russian Provisional Government*, III, 1558-1568.

49. *Ibid.*, p. 1557.

50. N. Ia. Ivanov, *Kornilovshchina i ee razgrom* (Leningrad, 1965), pp. 124-209.

51. For example, Boris Elkin, "The Kerensky Government and its Fate," in *Slavic Review*, XXIII, No. 4 (December 1964), pp. 717-736; and Leonid I. Strakhovsky, "Was There a Kornilov Rebellion? A Re-appraisal of the Evidence," *The Slavonic and East European Review*, XXIII, No. 81 (June 1955), pp. 372-395.

52. The attitude of political groups and social organizations to the Kornilov affair can be seen by reading the documents presented in Browder and Kerensky, eds., *The Russian Provisional Government*, III, 1527-1613.

53. *Ibid.*, pp. 1604-1606.

54. Lukomskii, *Vospominaniia*, I. 259.

55. The best study of the origins of the Cossacks is G. Stoekl, *Die Entstehung des Kosakentums* (Munich, 1953). See also G. Vernadsky, *Russia at the Dawn of the Modern Age* (New Haven, 1959).

56. During the World War two additional *voiska* were formed. In 1917 the following *voiska* were in existence: Don, Kuban, Terek, Orenburg, Ural, Astrakhan, Transbaikal, Amur, Semirechensk, Ussuriisk, Siberia, Enisei, Krasnoiarsk.

57. I. Borisenko, *Sovetskie respubliki na severnom Kavkaze*, 2 vols., (Rostov, 1930), I, 23 and 108.

58. *Ibid.*

59. *Ibid.*, and G. Pokrovskii, *Denikinshchina, God politiki i ekonomiki na Kubani (1918-1919 gg.)*, p. 12.

60. Borisenko, *Sovetskie respubliki*, I, 23 and 108.

61. O. N. Znamenskii, *Iiul'skii krizis* (Moscow-Leningrad, 1964), p. 92.

62. See the articles of G. P. Ianov, "Revoliutsiia i donskie kazaki" in *Donskaia Letopis'*, II, 5-39, and "Donskoe nastroenie ko vremeni revoliutsii" in *Donskaia Letopis'*, I, 61-68; and K. P. Kakliugin, "Organizatsiia vlasti na donu v nachale revoliutsii," in *Donskaia Letopis'*, II, 63-107.

63. A. Zaitsov, *1918 god: ocherki po istorii russkoi grazhdanskoi voiny* (Paris, 1934), p. 34.

64. A. A. Smagin, "Vospominaniia," p. 15, Columbia University Russian Archives. MS.

65. Browder and Kerensky, eds., *The Russian Provisional Government*, III, 1478-1480.

66. K. P. Kakliugin, "Voiskovoi ataman A. M. Kaledin i ego vremia," in *Donskaia Letopis'*, II, 138-139.

67. Borisenko, *Sovetskie respubliki*, I, 48.

68. On the history of the Kuban *voisko* see D. E. Skobtsov, *Tri goda revoliutsii i grazhdanskoi voiny na Kubani* (Paris, n.d.), pp. 5-16; and G. Pokrovskii, *Denikinshchina*, p. 10.

69. A recent Soviet study, A. P. Aleksashchenko, *Krakh Denikinshchiny* (Moscow, 1966), p. 48, maintains that the Black Sea Cossacks stood for Kulak interests and the *lineitsy* for the bourgeoisie, a ridiculous assertion.

70. Skobtsov, *Tri goda revoliutsii*, p. 25.

71. A. P. Filimonov, "Kubantsy," in *Beloe Delo*, II, 75.

CHAPTER 2

1. See A. I. Denikin, *Ocherki russkoi smuty*, 5 vols. (Paris and Berlin, 1921-1925), II, 147-148.

2. This point is made by S. Melgunov, in *Kak bol'sheviki zakhvatili vlast'* (Paris, 1963), p. 244.

3. On the views of the Social Revolutionaries following the Bolshevik uprising see Oliver S. Radkey, *The Sickle Under the Hammer* (New York, 1963), especially chapters one and two.

4. Trotskii mentions the case of a Colonel Walden who led the sailors against Krasnov: "apparently he hated Kerensky so strongly that this inspired him with temporary sympathy for us." W. H. Chamberlin, *The Russian Revolution* (New York, 1935), I, 331.

5. For example, it was widely assumed that German officers led the sailors against Krasnov. P. N. Miliukov, *Istoriia vtoroi russkoi revoliutsii*, 3 vols. (Sofia, 1921-1924) I, part III, 254.

6. Izvestiia reported rumors that aside from the Social Revolutionary politicians, Miliukov and Geneeral Alekseev also came to Mogilev. M. S. Lazarev "Likvidatsiia stavki staroi armii kak ochaga kontrrevoliutsii," *Voprosy Istorii* 1968, No. 3, Mar., p. 45.

7. The activlilcs of Social Revolutionaries in Mogilev are described in great detail in Radkey, *The Sickle Under the Hammer*, pp. 76-91.

8. Description of the last days of the Stavka can be found in V. V. Shapkin, "Poslednie dni stavki verkhovnogo" (MS Columbia Univ. Russian Archives) and V. B. Stankevich, *Vospominaniia, 1914-1918* (Berlin, 1920) and also in M. S. Lazarev, "Likvidatsiia stavki staroi armii."

9. On conditions of imprisonment see A. S. Lukomskii, *Vospominaniia*, 2 vols. (Berlin, 1922), I, 260-267; and Denikin, *Ocherki russkoi smuty*, II, 85-103 and 136-151.

10. Shapkin, "Poslednie dni stavki verkhovnogo," p. 4.

11. The letter is printed in Denikin, *Ocherki*, II, 137-139.

12. Lukomskii, *Vospominaniia*, I, 266.

13. Shapkin, "Poslednie dni stavki verkhovnogo," p. 4.

14. Lazarev, "Likvidatsiia stavki staroi armii," p. 50.

15. *Ibid.*

16. Shapkin, "Poslednie dni stavki verkhovnogo," p. 5.

17. Denikin, *Ocherki*, II, 144.

18. Report of Krylenko published in *Izvestiia* Dec. 4, 1917, p. 1.

19. Denikin, *Ocherki*, II, 143.

20. The march of the regiment is described in Denikin, *Ocherki*, II, 151-155.

21. Lukomskii, *Vospominaniia*, I, 269.

22. *Donskaia Volna* No. 3, June 24, 1918.

23. Denikin, *Ocherki*, II, 147-148.

24. M. Volkonsky, *The Volunteer Army of Alexeiev and Denikin* (London, 1918), p. 5.

25. R. P. Browder and A. F. Kerensky, eds., *The Russian Provisional Government 1917, Documents* (Stanford, California, 1961). Alekseev's letter to Miliukov in III, p. 1606.

26. V. E. Pavlov, ed., *Markovtsy v boiakh i pokhodakh za Rossiiu v osvo-

boditelnoi voine (Paris, 1962), p. 21. Mss. in Columbia Univ. Russian Archives.

27. *Ibid.*, p. 22.

28. *Ibid.*, p. 25.

29. *Boris Savinkov pered voennoi kollegiei verkhovnogo suda SSSR: Polnyi otchet po stenogramme suda* (Moscow, 1924), p. 30.

30. Pavlov, *Markovtsy*, p. 45.

31. M. A. Nesterovich-Berg, *V bor'be s bol'shevikami* (Paris, 1931), p. 45.

32. The letter is printed in N. N. Golovin, *Rossiiskaia kontr–revoliutsiia*, V, 1917-1918 gg, 5 Vols. (Paris, 1937), 48-56. Golovin does not indicate his source.

33. A. N. Grekov, "Soiuz Kazachikh Voisk v Petrograde v 1917 godu" in *Donskaia Letopis'*, II, 274.

34. I. N. Liubimov, ed., *Revoliutsiia 1917 goda; Khronika sobytii* (Moscow, 1930), VI, 12.

35. A. Suvorin, *Pokhod Kornilova* (Rostov, 1918), p. 6. Suvorin believed that Kerenskii had been in Novocherkassk. *Donskaia Volna* (June 24, 1918), p. 3, reported on the rumors which had been current in December 1917 about Kerenskii's presence in the capital of the Don. For Kerenskii's whereabouts following the November Revolution, see A. F. Kerensky, *Russia and History's Turning Point* (New York, 1965).

36. I. Borisenko, *Sovetskie respubliki na severnom Kavkaze v 1918 godu* (Rostov, 1930), 2 vols., I, 51.

37. The voting pattern of the elections for the Constituent Assembly is the evidence of Bolshevik strength among the non-Cossack regiments in the Don. The majority of the soldiers voted for the Bolsheviks. See K. P. Kakliugin, "Voiskovoi Ataman A. M. Kaledin i ego vremia," *Donskaia Letopis'*, II, 115.

38. G. Ianov, "Paritet," in *Donskaia Letopis'*, II, 173.

39. I. Borisenko, *Sovetskie respubliki*, I, 52.

40. *Ibid.* See also O. H. Radkey, *The Election to the Russian Assembly of 1917* (Cambridge, Mass., 1950).

41. *Ibid.*

42. K. P. Kakliugin, *op. cit.* in *Donskaia Letopis'*, II, 148.

43. *Donskaia Volna*, No. 18, October 18, 1918.

44. *Ibid.*, and Pavlov, *Markovtsy*, p. 47.

45. Pavlov, *Markovtsy*, p. 46.

46. *Ibid.*, p. 48.

47. *Ibid.*, p. 50.

48. Nesterovich-Berg, *V bor'be s bol'shevikami*, p. 67.

49. According to Denikin *(Ocherki*, II, p. 156), Alekseev received only 400 rubles from financial circles during the first month of the existence of the army. This figure was accepted by other writers, e.g., Golovin, *Rossiiskaia kontr-revoliutsiia*, book 5, p. 22, and Pavlov, *Markovtsy*, p. 50. This is, beyond doubt, a gross understatement. Nesterovich-Berg mentions several donors who gave thousands of rubles in this period. Since she delivered the money

and Denikin was not even present at the time, her word is more trustworthy in this matter.

50. Nesterovich-Berg, *V bor'be s bol'shevikami*, p. 72.

51. Pavlov, *Markovtsy*, p. 49.

52. *Ibid.*, p. 52.

53. V. Dobrynin, *Bor'ba s bol'shevizmom na iuge Rossii, Uchastie v bor' be Donskogo Kazachestva* (Prague, 1921), p. 40. The Don District gave two-thirds of the coal production of prewar Russia. L. Kliuev, *Bor' ba za Tsaritsyn* (Moscow, 1928), p. 10.

54. K. P. Kakliugin, "Ataman Kaledin i ego vremia," in *Donskaia Letopis'*, II, 149, and *Pavlov, Markovtsy*, I, 53.

55. Dobrynin *Bor'ba s bol'shevizmom*, p. 41, and Borisenko, *Sovetskie respubliki*, I, 54.

56. Anonymous, *General Kornilov*, p. 59, Columbia Univ. Russian Archives.

57. Boriseno, *Sovetskie respubliki*, I, 53.

58. Lukurynin, p. 39. Misdated. Dobrynin confused new and old style.

59. K. P. Kakliugin, *op. cit.*, in *Donskaia Letopis'*, II, 149.

60. Borisenko, *Sovetskie respubliki*, I, 55-56.

61. Anonymous, *General Kornilov*, p. 59.

62. *Ibid.*, p. 60.

63. A. I. Denikin, *Ocherki*, II, 173. Denikin describes this scene: "the distressed Ataman went to General Alekseev and said: 'Mikhail Vasilievich. I came to you for help. Let us be like brothers and help each other. All misunderstandings between us are finished. Let us save what still can be saved.' Alekseev brightened up, warmly embraced Kaledin and answered, 'Dear Aleksei Maksimovich. Everything I have I gladly give for the common cause.'"

64. Anonymous, *General Kornilov*, p. 64.

65. K. P. Kakliugin, *op. cit.* in *Donskaia Letopis'*, II, 150.

66. *Ibid.*

67. Lanov, "Paritet," in *Donskaia Letopis'*, II, 175.

68. K. P. Kakliugin, *op. cit.* in *Donskaia Letopis'*, II, 151, and Borisenko, *Sovetskie respubliki*, I, 26.

69. K. P. Kakliugin, *op. cit.* in *Donskaia Letopis'*, II, 152.

CHAPTER 3

1. A. S. Lukomskii, *Vospominaniia*, (Berlin, 1922), p. 287.

2. Most of the officers were in Petrograd and Moscow but a large number of them lived in the provincial cities. According to data from the summer of 1918, some 40,000 lived in Kiev, 8,000 in Ekaterinoslav, 5,000 in Poltava, 10,000 in Simferpol, 15,000 in Kherson, 12,000 in Kharkov, 2,600 in Elizavet-

grad, 10,000 in Minsk, 5,000 in Zhitomir. A Suvorin, *Pokhod Kornilova* (Rostov, 1918), p. 3.

3. A. I. Denikin, *Ocherki russkoi smuty*, (Paris and Berlin, 1921-1925); A. S. Lukomskii, *Vospominaniia*.

4. Description of the Rostov enlistment bureau is taken from V. E. Pavlov (ed.), *Markovtsy v boiakh i pokhodakh za Rossiu v osvoboditel'noi voine, 1917-1920* (Paris, 1962), I, pp. 63-65.

5. *Ibid.*, p. 72.

6. Denikin, *Ocherki*, II, p. 197.

7. *Proletarskaia Revoliutsiia na Donu*, IV, p. 273.

8. V. Volin, *Don i Dobrovol'cheskaia Armiia* (Novocherkassk, 1919), p. 30.

9. Pavlov, *Markovtsy*, I, 64.

10. *Ibid.*, p. 65.

11. B. A. Suvorin, *Za rodinoi* (Paris, 1922), p. 80.

12. Pavlov, *Markovtsy*, I, 64.

13. M. V. Alekseev, "Account Book of the Volunteer Army," MS. Hoover Archives.

14. This organization was the Deviatka, an anti-Bolshevik group formed in Moscow after the November Revolution. N. I. Astrov, "Moskovskaia Organizatsiia," MS. Russian Archives, Columbia University.

15. One hundred thousand rubles is a rough estimate. It is based on the fact that Nesterovich collected half of this money alone. One would assume that there were other agents of the Army doing similar work, though perhaps less successfully than Nurse Nesterovich.

16. Denikin, *Ocherki*, II, p. 192.

17. In November 1917 officers and soldiers alike received only food. In December officers got 100 rubles a month and the soldiers, 30. In January 1918 officers got 270 rubles and the soldiers 150. In February for the first time allowances were given to the families. Denikin, *Ocherki*, II, p. 201.

18. R. H. Ullman, *Anglo-Soviet Relations*, 1917-1920 Vol. 1: *Intervention and the War* (Princeton, 1961), p. 52.

19. J. F. N. Bradley, "The Allies and Russia in the Light of the French Archives," *Soviet Studies*, XIV, October 1964, p. 178. Captain Bordes, with four million francs, was searching unsuccessfully for the Whites in South Russia. Hucher took three million with him to Moscow.

20. Denikin, *Ocherki*, II, p. 188, and K. N. Sokolov, *Pravlenie generala Denikina* (Sofia, 1921), p. 3.

21. Denikin, *Ocherki*, II, p. 187.

22. *Ibid.*, p. 188.

23. Lukomskii, *Vospominaniia*, I, p. 280.

24. Denikin, *Ocherki*, II, p. 189. Miliukov, disagreeing with Denikin and Lukomskii, who wrote that the politicians were instrumental in keeping Alekseev and Kornilov together, maintains that the politicians were, in fact, trying to separate the two generals and wanted Kornilov to start his own

organization in Tsaritsyn. Miliukov, *Rossiia na perelome* (Paris, 1927), II, p. 56. Lukomskii's and Denikin's independent versions are much more convincing and consistent with everything we know about the soldiers and the politicians. Miliukov's memory must have been faulty in this instance.

25. Denikin, *Ocherki*, II, p. 189.

26. *Ibid.*, p. 190.

27. Victor Chernov, *The Great Russian Revolution* (New Haven, 1936), p. 325.

28. Lukomskii, *Vospominaniia*, I, p. 291.

29. Denikin, *Ocherki*, II, p. 193.

30. Lukomskii, *Vospominaniia*, I, p. 292.

31. *Belyi Arkhiv*, II, p. 173: Paramonov was a prominent Kadet and a rich industrialist.

32. Roman Gul', *Ledianoi pokhod* (Berlin, n.d.), pp. 16-17.

33. Miliukov, *Russia na perelome*, II, p. 57.

34. Nesterovich-Berg, *V bor' be s bol'shevikami* (Paris, 1931), pp. 96-97.

35. A. Suvorin, *Pokhod Kornilova*, p. 8.

36. General E. V. Maslovskii, "Nekotroye stranitsy moei zhizni," Columbia University Russian Archives, p. 1285. K. Vendziagolskii, "Savinkov," *Novyi Zhurnal*, LXX, 1962, p. 164.

37. Denikin, *Ocherki*, II, p. 199. The English version is taken from Bunyan and Fisher, *Russian Civil War*, p. 415.

38. The debate between socialists and Kadets over the Constituent Assembly is discussed in the unpublished Memoirs of N. I. Astrov, Columbia University Russian Archives, Panina file No. 5, Appendix No. 1.

39. An original copy of Kornilov's program can be found in Miliukov's Archives 8161 13 in Columbia University Russian Archives. It is printed in *Belyi Arkhiv*, II, pp. 173-182.

40. *Ibid.*, p. 175.

41. Miliukov Archives 8161 13, Columbia University Russian Archives.

42. *Ibid.* It is worthwhile to note that while all other letters of Miliukov to Alekseev were published in *Poslednie Novosti*, this one was not.

43. A. N. Grekov, "Soiuz Kazachikh Voisk v Petrograde v 1917 godu," in *Donskaia Letopis'*, II, p. 276.

44. Vendziagolskii, "Savinkov," p. 161.

45. Lukomskii, *Vospominaniia*, p. 283. Vendziagolskii, "Savinkov," p. 161.

46. Vendziagolskii, "Savinkov," p. 162.

47. Lukomskii, *Vospominaniia*, p. 284.

48. Vendziagolskii, "Savinkov," p. 177.

49. Lukomskii, *Vospominaniia*, p. 285.

50. Denikin, *Ocherki*, II, p. 191.

51. Vendziagolskii, "Savinkov," p. 166. Vendziagolskii describes an incident which shows Savinkov's courage and presence of mind. Vendziagolskii and Savinkov were warned that an attempt on Savinkov's life would take

place at a certain hour. Savinkov did not want to turn to the generals of the Volunteer Army for protection. He wanted proof. He decided to disarm the assailant himself. In this he succeeded. The young would-be assassin was so impressed by the courage of the ex-terrorist that he gave his revolver to him as a memento of the occasion. Later Vendziagolskii found out that the assassination was planned by Zavoiko.

52. *Ibid.*, p. 165.

53. Denikin, *Ocherki*, II, p. 192.

54. Lukomskii, *Vospominaniia*, I, p. 275.

55. *Ibid.*, pp. 56-59.

56. Denikin, *Ocherki*, II, p. 187.

57. The protocol of the meeting is in *Donskaia Letopis'*, II, pp. 209-304.

58. *Donskaia Letopis'*, II, p. 301.

59. A. Suvorin, *Pokhod Kornilova*, p. 8.

60. A. Lokerman, *74 dnia sovetskoi vlasti* (Rostov, 1918), p. 79.

61. A. P. Bogaevskii, *Vospominaniia 1918 god* (New York, 1963), p. 32. On another occasion junkers were sent to a railroad workers' meeting to maintain order. When a shot was fired and a worker died, the officers were attacked and defended themselves. In the melee, four workers were killed. A. Suvorin, *Pokhod Kornilova*, p. 10.

62. *Ibid.*, p. 9.

63. *Ibid.*, p. 11.

64. N. Kakurin, *Kak srazhalas' revoliutsiia* (Moscow, 1925), I, p. 177.

65. K. P. Kakliugin, "Ataman Kaledin," *Donskaia Letopis'*, II, p. 162; G. P. Ianov, "Paritet" in *Donskaia Letopis'*, II, p. 180.

66. K. Gubarev, ed., *Bor'ba s Kaledinshchinoi (po dokumentam belykh)*, (Taganrog, 1929), p. 5.

67. Ianov, in *Donskaia Letopis'*, II, p. 182.

68. *Ibid.*, p. 184.

69. V. Volin, *Don i Dobrovol'cheskaia Armiia* (Novocherkassk, 1919), p. 36.

70. Anonymous, "General Kornilov," p. 67.

71. Kaledin's last appeal. Bunyan and Fisher, p. 419.

72. V. V. Dobrynin, "Vooruzhennaia bor'ba Dona s bol'shevikami," *Donskaia Letopis'*, I, p. 96. Esaul is a Cossack captain.

73. *Donskaia Volna*, January 20, 1919.

74. L. Kliuev, *Bor'ba za Tsaritsyn* (Moscow, 1928), p. 8. Kakurin, *Kak srazhalas' revoliutsiia*, p. 176.

75. V. A. Antonov-Ovseenko, *Zapiski o grazhdanskoi voine*, 4 vols. (Moscow, 1924) I, p. 201.

76. The entire protocol is reprinted in *Donskaia Volna*, No. 27, December 16, 1918, and *Donskaia Letopis'*, II, pp. 306-318.

77. Delert, *Don v ogne*, p. 23.

78. Antonov-Ovseenko, *Zapiski*, I, p. 59; and Kakurin, *Kak srazhalas' revoliutsiia*, I, p. 174.

79. Kakurin, p. 175.

80. Pavlov, *Markovtsy*, I, pp. 86, 88.

81. Denikin, "Navet na beloe dvizhenie," Denikin Archives, Columbia University Russian Archives, p. 25; Anonymous, "General Kornilov," Columbia University Russian Archives, p. 77.

82. Kakurin, *Kak srazhalas' revoliutsiia*, p. 182. Kornilov entrusted the organization of defense to Denikin, who chose Markov as his chief of staff.

83. I. Borisenko, *Sovetskie respubliki*, I, 70.

84. *Ibid.*

85. Pavlov, *Markovtsy*, I, p. 96.

86. Kakurin, *Kak srazhalas' revoliutsiia*, p. 12.

87. *Belyi Arkhiv*, I, p. 99. In a meeting on January 28 Alekseev said that if it became impossible to continue the fight in Rostov and Novocherkassk, the army would go to the Volga, perhaps to Saratov, and continue resisting the Bolsheviks. Kaledin was bitterly disappointed and angrily reproached Alekseev.

88. Lukomskii, *Vospominaniia*, p. 293.

89. Kakllugin, "Voiskovoi Ataman A. M. Nazarov i ego vremia," *Donskaia Letopis'*, II, p. 205.

90. *Ibid.*, p. 206.

91. N. Duvakin, "Voisko Ataman A. M. Nazarov," *Donskaia Letopis'*, II, p. 266.

92. Lukomskii, *Vospominaniia*, p. 295. Lukomskii had been Kornilov's chief of staff. This post was given after the departure of Lukomskii to General Romanovskii.

93. A. Lokerman, *74 dnia sovetskoi vlasti*, p. 5. Lukomskii, *Vospominaniia*, p. 297.

94. N. A. Svechin, "Vospominaniia," Columbia Russian Archives, p. 23.

CHAPTER 4

1. For example, the Russian Fascists, who claimed descent from the Whites, put the Ice March into the center of their political mythology. Erwin Oberlaender, "The All-Russian Fascist Party," in Walter Laqueur and George L. Mosse, eds., *International Fascism, 1920 to 1945* (New York, 1966), p. 163.

2. V. A. Antonov-Ovseenko, *Zapiski o grazhdanskoi voine* (Moscow, 1933), II, p. 268.

3. Anonymous, "General Kornilov," MS. Columbia University Russian Archives, p. 103.

4. V. T. Sukhorukov, *XI Armiia v boiakh na severnom Kavkaze i nizhnei Volge* (Moscow, 1961), p. 12.

5. Antonov-Ovseenko, *Zapiski*, II, p. 269.

6. A. I. Denikin, *Ocherki*, II, p. 266.

7. V. E. Pavlov, ed., *Markovtsy*, I, p. 121. (MS. in Columbia University Russian Archives)

8. A. P. Bogaevskii, *Vospominaniia 1918 god*, (New York, 1963), p. 55.

9. *Ibid.*, p. 56.

10. *Ibid.*, pp. 57-58.

11. Pavlov, *Markovtsy*, p. 123.

12. The description of the composition of the Army is based on Denikin, *Ocherki*, II, p. 228; Pavlov, *Markovtsy*, p. 123, and Bogaevskii, *Vospominaniia*, p. 55.

13. A. Zaitsov, *1918 god: ocherki po istorii grazhdanskoi voiny* (Paris, 1934). Zaitsov's figure is disputed by P. L. Makarenko in a review of Zaitsov's book in *Volnoe Kazachestvo* (25 April, 1935), pp. 14-18. Makarenko maintained that the Volunteer Army at the beginning of the campaign could not have had more than 2,500 soldiers. Makarenko is contradicted by a number of participants in the march.

14. Denikin, *Ocherki*, II, pp. 232-233.

15. A. Suvorin, *Pokhod Kornilova* (Rostov, 1918), p. 12.

16. Denikin, *Ocherki*, II, p. 227; B. Suvorin, *Za rodinoi: geroicheskaia epokha Dobrovol'cheskoi Armii 1917-1918* (Paris, 1922), p. 132.

17. K. N. Nikolaev, "Vospominaniia," MS. Columbia University Russian Archives.

18. B. Suvorin, *Za rodinoi: geroicheskaia epokha Dobrovol'cheskoi Armii. 1917-1918 gg* (Paris, 1922), p. 46.

19. "Spisok uchastnikov pervogo Kubanskogo pokhoda," MS. Columbia University Russian Archives. Data from the end of the campaign.

20. Pavlov, *Markovtsy*, p. 125.

21. Denikin, *Ocherki*, II, p. 228.

22. V. I. Birkin, "Kornilovskii pokhod," MS. Columbia Universiy Russian Archives, p. 8.

23. Lukomskii, *Vospominaniia*, I, p. 10, and Denikin, *Ocherki*, II, pp. 229-231. The first important strategic decision of the Volunteer Army has been scrutinized by historians of the White movement. Colonel A. Zaitsov, a military historian, considered the choice of the Kuban a serious error. He believed that Alekseev had not ceased to think in terms of large armies in an international war, and that was the reason he was so afraid of being surrounded and risked the army in a desperate attempt to break out of encirclement. (A. Zaitsov, *1918 god*, p. 72.) General N. N. Golovin, another military historian, believed that Alekseev, by this quixotic gesture, wanted to show the Russian people that the White movement was still alive. (N. N. Golovin, *Rossiiskaia kontr-revoliutsiia v 1917-1918*, Paris, 1937, Book 5, pp. 76-77.) Denikin angrily rejected Golovin's charges and reiterated that the

decision was well taken. A. I. Denikin, "Navet na beloe dvizhenie," p. 27. MS. Columbia University Russian Archives.

24. For evidence on Alekseev's deep pessimism at this time see his correspondence with P. N. Miliukov, Personal Archives, MS. Columbia University Russian Archives.

25. Denikin, *Ocherki*, II, p. 231.

26. B. Suvorin, *Za rodinoi*, p. 46. The privations of the march were well described by the writers and journalists who had participated: R. Gul', *Ledianoi pokhod* (Berlin, n.d.); A. Suvorin, *Pokhod Kornilova* (Rostov, 1918); V. I. Birkin, *Kornilovskii pokhod*, MS. Columbia University Russian Archives.

27. Sukhorukov, *XI Armiia*, p. 10.

28. Pavlov, *Markovtsy*, I, p. 136.

29. Bogaevskii, *Vospominaniia*, p. 68.

30. Denikin, *Ocherki*, II, p. 238.

31. P. L. Makarenko in *Volnoe Kozachestvo*, April 10, 1935.

32. Bogaevskii, *Vospominaniia*, p. 74.

33. *Ibid.*, p. 76.

34. K. N. Nikolaev, "Pervyi Kubanskii pokhod," MS. Columbia University Russian Archives.

35. Denikin, *Ocherki*, II, p. 247.

36. Sukhorukov, *XI Armiia*, p. 16.

37. A. P. Filimonov, "Kubantsy," in *Beloe Delo*, II, p. 62.

38. The points of the agreement are printed in G. Pokrovskii, *Denikinshchina: god politiki i ekonomiki na Kubani (1918-1919 gg.)* (Berlin, 1923), p. 19.

39. *Ibid.*, p. 22.

40. The anti-Bolshevik Cossacks counted on forming a Southeast Union, a Federation of Don Kuban and Terek Cossacks. The Federation never came into being. See V. A. Kharlamov, "Iugo-Vostochnyi Soiuz v 1917 godu," *Donskaia Letopis'*, 3 vols. (Vienna, 1923), II, pp. 284-292.

41. V. Naumenko, "Iz nedavnogo proshlogo Kubani," (n.d., n.p.), Hoover Institution, Stanford University, p. 2.

42. I. Borisenko, *Sovetskie respubliki*, I, p. 118.

43. K. N. Nikolaev, "Smutnye dni na Kubani," A. P. Filimonov, "Kubantsy," p. 76.

44. K. N. Nikolaev, "Smutnye dni na Kubani," MS. Columbia University Russian Archives.

45. Sukhorukov, *XI Armiia*, p. 7.

46. A. P. Filimonov, "Kubantsy," p. 83. Filimonov first entrusted the young and popular Colonel Ulagai to enlist volunteers among the Cossacks. But Ulagai, discouraged by the inadequate response, soon resigned.

47. Naumenko, "Iz nedavnogo," I, p. 2.

48. *Ibid.*, I, p. 4. Out of 1,500 they possessed they sent 700, and out of 3,700,-000 bullets they gave 1,800,000 to Kaledin.

49. K. N. Nikolaev, "Smutnye dni na Kubani."

50. V. Leontovich, *Pervye boi na Kubani; Vospominaniia* (Munich, 1923), p. 31.

51. The Whites thought that the Bolsheviks had only 4,000 soldiers. In fact they had 6,000. Leontovich, *Pervye boi*, p. 33.

52. *Ibid.*, p. 42. Galaev died in this battle.

53. The White source is Naumenko, "Iz nedavnogo," I, p. 5. The Bolshevik source is Sukhorukov, *XI Armiia*, p. 15.

54. Naumenko, "Iz nedavnogo," I, p. 6.

55. The first one, General Chernyi, resigned on January 22. His successor, General Bukretov, lasted only eight days. He resigned because of "ill health." When Filimonov pressed him, Bukretov confessed that he resigned because he had no faith in success.

56. Naumenko, "Iz nedavnogo," I, p. 5.

57. *Ibid.*, I, p. 7.

58. *Volnoe Kazachestvo* (August 1936), p. 203.

59. Naumenko, "Iz nedavnogo," II, p. 2.

60. *Ibid.*, II, p. 3.

61. The phrase is D. E. Skobtsov's. D. E. Skobtsov, *Tri goda revoliutsii i grazhdanskoi voiny na Kubani* (Paris, n.d.), p. 74.

62. *Ibid.*

63. Naumenko, "Iz nedavnogo," II, pp. 5-6.

64. *Ibid.*, II, p. 6.

65. *Ibid.*

66. Denikin, *Ocherki*, II, p. 274.

67. "N. S. Riabovol," in *Volnoe Kazachestvo* (August 1936), CCIII-CCIV, pp. 11-13. The separatists had no confidence in the judgment of Pokrovskii, who was a non-Cossack officer. The *rada* decided that it could not leave the army, since it had called the soldiers to arms and felt responsible for them.

68. The agreement is printed in Denikin, *Ocherki*, II, p. 279.

69. Pavlov, *Markovtsy*, I, p. 129.

70. Denikin, *Ocherki*, II, p. 273.

71. Zaitsov (*1918 god.*, pp. 85-96) suggested that temporary unification would have been better and that after the march the two armies could have regained their freedom of action. Cossack separatists in emigration professed to believe that the Cossack army could have liberated the Kuban alone. The separatists strongly implied thet the Kuban should have been liberated from all Russians, who were almost all Bolsheviks anyway. "N. S. Riabovol" in *Volnoe Kazachestvo* (August 1936), pp. 11-16.

72. Denikin, *Ocherki*, II, pp. 275-277. It was General Markov who called the First Kuban Campaign the "Ice March" in a lecture he gave in Novocherkassk (Gul', *Ledianoi pokhod*, p. 133). This name surpassed in popu-

larity others given to the campaign—as for example, the First Kuban Campaign or the Kornilov March.

73. Kazanovich, "Ataka Ekaterinodara i smert' Kornilova," MS. Columbia University Russian Archives, p. 2.

74. *Ibid.*

75. Denikin, *Ocherki,* II, p. 293.

76. Borisenko, *Sovetskie respubliki,* I, p. 138.

77. Kazanovich, *"Ataka Ekaterinodara,"* p. 2.

78. Denikin, *Ocherki,* II, p. 294.

79. Filimonov, "Kubantsy," p. 103.

80. The conference is described in Denikin, *Ocherki,* II, pp. 294-295; Filimonov, "Kubantsy," p. 103; Bogaevski, *Vospominaniia,* pp. 133-134.

81. Kazanovich, "Ataka Ekaterinodara," p. 7.

82. Denikin, *Ocherki,* II, p. 295.

83. Pavlov, *Markovtsy,* I, p. 203.

84. Birkin, "Kornilovskii pokhod," p. 26.

85. The order is printed in Denikin, *Ocherki,* II, p. 304. Alekseev first did not know how to sign the order; he had no official title. Under what authority could he name a new commander? Accepting Romanovskii's advice, he simply signed the order "Alekseev, General of the Infantry."

86. B. Suvorin, *Za rodinoi,* p. 98. People in Alekseev's entourage resented the fact that Kornilov treated the older general without due respect.

87. Denikin, *Ocherki,* II, p. 304.

88. Sukhorukov, *XI Armiia,* p. 25. Bolshevik soldiers found the bodies of Nezhintsev and Kornilov.

89. A. Suvorin, *Pokhod Kornilova,* p. 180.

90. Denikin, *Ocherki,* II, p. 343.

91. V. I. Lenin, *Sochinenia,* 4th ed., XXXVI, p. 649 and p. 224.

92. Borisenko, *Sovetskie respubliki,* I, p. 76. The Bolsheviks, at least from their own point of view, had some achievements. The delivery of food to Central Russia began immediately and the mines of the Donets started producing for Petrograd and Moscow. The miners were on the side of the Soviet regime, and they resumed production, which they had interrupted in the last months of the Kaledin regime. L. I. Berz and K. A. Khmelevskii, *Geroicheskie gody; Oktiabrskaia Revoliutsiia i grazhdanskaia voina na Donu* (Rostov, 1954), p. 125.

93. Lenin, *Sochineniia,* XXXVI, p. 649 notes and p. 442.

94. Berz and Khmelevskii, *Geroicheskie gody,* p. 148.

95. A. Lokerman, *74 dnia sovetskoi vlasti* (Rostov, 1918), p. 34; and Berz and Khmelevskii, *Geroicheskie gody,* p. 121.

96. *Ibid.,* p. 152.

97. "Rabochie kazaki o Brest-Litovske," *Krasnyi Arkhiv,* LXXV, 1936, p. 188.

98. Borisenko, *Sovetskie respubliki,* I, p. 89.

99. It appears that the soldiers of the Red Army did not expect support from the population. They entered Rostov nervously, shooting at random. Lokerman, 74 *dnia*, pp. 7-8.

100. Wrangel Military Archives, Hoover Institution, Stanford University, file 116. Documents of the Commission of Investigation of Bolshevik Atrocities, 1919, May 20.

101. Lokerman, 74 *dnia*, p. 80.

102. Berz and Khmelevskii, *Geroicheskie gody*, p. 127.

103. Lokerman, 74 *dnia*, p. 80.

104. Borisenko, *Sovetskie respubliki*, I, p. 95.

105. *Ibid.*, I, p. 81. The complete lack of discipline among the Red soldiers is admitted even by the Bolshevik author Borisenko.

106. Wrangel Archives, file 116, May 20, 1919.

107. *Ibid.*, May 11, 1919.

108. *Ibid.*, file 116, May 18, 1919.

109. Borisenko, *Sovetskie respubliki*, I, p. 82.

110. Lokerman, 74 *dnia*, p. 47.

111. K. P. Kakliugin, "Stepnoi pokhod v Zadon'e 1918 goda i ego znachenie," *Donskaia Letopis'*, III, p. 7.

112. For Golubov's biography see Anonymous, "General Kornilov," Columbia University Russian Archives, pp. 94–103; S. V. Denisov, *Zapiski. Grazhdanskaia voina na iuge Rossii*, vol. 1, (Constantinople, 1921). As a student during the tsarist regime, Golubov was known for his rightist monarchist views. Yet it was he who arrested the last appointed Ataman, Grabbe, in March 1917. He supported the election of Kaledin, but in September 1917 he was in favor of giving up Kaledin to the Provisional Government. The Kaledin regime jailed him, but he was freed at Christmas 1917, when he promised he would not fight against the government. He violated his word in less than a month when he joined Podtelkov. It was Golubov who captured Chernetsov, Ataman Kaledin's best soldier, who was in many ways a remarkably similar character.

113. Anonymous, "General Kornilov," p. 105. Bogaevskii was captured by the Reds, who executed him on April 14.

114. G. P. Ianov, "Don pod bol'shevikami vesnoi 1918 g.i vostanie stanits na Donu," *Donskaia Letopis'*, III, pp. 23-24; Anonymous, p. 107; N. A. Svechin, "Vospominaniia," Columbia University Russian Archives, p. 29.

115. I. A. Poliakov, *Donskie kazaki v bor'be s bol'shevikami*, (Munich, 1962), p. 164; Denisov, *Zapiski*, p. 48.

116. V. Volin, *Don i Dobrovol'cheskaia Armia*, p. 53; and Anonymous, "General Kornilov," p. 110; Svechin, "Vospominaniia," p. 29.

117. G. P. Ianov, "Osvobozhdenie Novocherkasska i 'Krug Spaseniia Dona," *Donskaia Letopis'*, III, p. 34.

118. *Ibid.*, p. 34. A difficult problem for the Council was the lack of funds; it had only 25,000 rubles, which it took from a Novocherkassk bank.

119. Poliakov, *Donskie kazaki*, p. 181.

120. Anonymous, "General Kornilov," p. 113.

121. Poliakov, *"Donskie kazaki,"* p. 180.

122. Ianov, "Osvobozhdenie Novocherkasska," pp. 39-40.

123. *Ibid.*, p. 42.

124. Anonymous, "General Kornilov," p. 172.

125. Ianov, "Osvobozhdenie Novocherkasska," p. 33.

126. Denisov, *Zapiski*, p. 55.

127. Ianov, "Don pod bol'shevikami," p. 25.

128. Ministerstvo inostrannykh del SSSR, *Dokumenty vneshnei politiki SSSR* (Moscow, 1957), I (November 7, 1917-December 31, 1918), pp. 269-271.

129. Berz and Khmelevskii, *Geroicheskie gody*, p. 171.

130. Borisenko, *Sovetskie respubliki*, I, pp. 98-101.

131. *Ibid.*, p. 101. The episode is well described in M. Sholokhov, *And Quiet Flows the Don*.

132. Berz and Khmelevskii, *Geroicheskie gody*, p. 171.

133. E. Ludendorff, *My War Memories* (London, 1919), II, p. 622. Ludendorff gives a frank picture of German war aims in South Russia.

134. Denikin, *Ocherki*, II, p. 332.

135. F. G. Val, *K istorii belogo dvizheniia: Deiatel'nost' gen.-adjutanta Shcherbacheva* (Tallin, 1935), p. 32.

136. Denikin, *Ocherki*, II, p. 328.

137. A. V. Turkul, *Drozdovtsy v ogne* (Munich, 1948), p. 15.

138. Denikin, *Ocherki*, II, p. 333.

139. *Ibid.*

140. Turkul, *Drozdovtsy v ogne*, pp. 21-22.

141. M. Drozdovskii, *Dnevnik* (Berlin, 1923), pp. 108-109. English version in Bunyan and Fisher, eds., *The Bolshevik Revolution* (Stanford, 1934), pp. 431-432.

142. Drozdovskii, *Dnevnik*, p. 134.

143. Ianov, "Osvobozhdenie Novocherkasska," p. 43.

144. *Ibid.*

145. Poliakov, *Donskie kazaki*, p. 196.

146. Lokerman, *74 dnia*, p. 98.

CHAPTER 5

1. V. I. Lenin, *State and Revolution* (New York, 1932), p. 83.

2. There is no satisfactory literature on German policies in Russia in 1918. The best primary source on the subject is the voluminous collection of Russian files of *Auswaertiges Amt*.

3. On developments in the Ukraine, see John S. Reshetar, *The Ukrainian Revolution* (Princeton, 1952).

4. See R. H. Ullman, *Anglo-Soviet Relations, 1917-1921,* 2 vols. (Princeton, 1961), and George F. Kennan, *Soviet-American Relations, 1917-1920,* 2 vols. (Princeton, 1956-1958).

5. S. L. Fraiman, *Revoliutsionnaia zashchita Petrograda* (Moscow and Leningrad, 1964), p. 165.

6. There is no monograph dealing with underground political life in Moscow in the spring of 1918. The most valuable reminiscences are: V. A. Miakotin, "Iz nedalekogo proshlogo," *Na chuzhoi storone* II, 179; N. I. Astrov, "Moskovskaia organizatsiia 1917-1918," MS. Russian Archives, Columbia Univ.; Gen. B. Kazanovich, "Poezdka iz Dobrovol'cheskoi Armii v krasnuiu Moskvu," *Arkhiv Russkoi Revoliutsii,* VII, pp. 189-200.

7. G. P. Ianov, "Osvobozhdenie Novocherkasska i 'Krug Spaseniia Dona'," *Donskaia Letopis',* III, 51-52.

8. *Ibid.,* p. 50.

9. *Donskoi krai,* May 18, 1918.

10. K. P. Kakliugin, "Donskoi ataman P. N. Krasnov i ego vremia," *Donskaia Letopis',* III, 70.

11. G. P. Ianov, "Osvobozhdenie Novocherkasska i Krug Spaseniia Dona," *Donskaia Letopis',* III, 59.

12. *Ibid.,* p. 60.

13. The basic laws of the Don *voisko* were published in *Donskaia Letopis',* III, 323-326.

14. P. N. Krasnov, "Vsevelikoe Voisko Donskoe," *Arkhiv Russkoi Revoliutsii,* V. 197. The Ataman in his article refers to himself in the third person.

15. Some novels of his were even translated into English. The best known is P. N. Krassnoff, *From Double Eagle to Red Flag* (New York, 1926). This is a novel, incidentally, without any literary merit.

16. V. Dobrynin, *Bor'ba s Bol'shevizmom na iuge Rossii: Uchastie v bor'be Donskogo Kazachestva* (Prague, 1921), p. 111.

17. *Ibid.*

18. See Krasnov's first letter to Wilhelm in Denikin, *Ocherki,* III, 66-67.

19. An abbreviated version of the second Krasnov letter in Bunyan, ed., *Intervention, Civil War, and Communism in Russia, April-December 1918* (Baltimore, 1936). I have used some sentences from Bunyan's translation. The full version is in A. V. Cheriachukin, "Donskaia delegatsiia na Ukrainu i Berlin," 1918-1919, *Donskaia Letopis',* III, pp. 163-231.

20. Max Hoffman, *War Diaries and Other Papers* (London, 1929), I, 216, 219.

21. For German policy toward the Don, see *Auswaertiges Amt* Documents, St. Antony Reels 143-144. Russland file 107.

22. V. A. Kharlamov, "Iugo-Vostochnyi Soiuz v 1917 godu," *Donskaia Letopis',* II, 284-292.

23. Krasnov, "Vsevelikoe Voisko Donskoe," p. 209. The ratio of exchange was one *pud* of grain for a rifle and 30 cartridges.

24. Some of the correspondence between Krasnov and the German Command can be found in *Auswaertiges Amt*, Russland file 107. St. Antony Reels 143-144.

25. Major Stefani's letter to Krasnov is printed in "Germanskaia interventsiia i Donskoe pravitel'stvo v 1918 g," *Krasnyi Arkhiv*, LXVII, 111.

26. *Ibid.*, LXVII, 107.

27. The Don had established ties with the Ukraine even before the election of Krasnov. Two independent delegations were sent to Kiev *(Krasnyi Arkhiv,* LXVII, 107, and Bogaevskii's report to the *krug*, Wrangel Military Archives, Hoover Institution, file 133.) After his election Krasnov sent General Cheriachukin to Skoropadskii with the following instructions: (1) Insist that the Ukraine would recognize the Don as an independent and neutral state. (2) Get a declaration from the Hetman that he is not interested in any part of Don territory. (3) Insist on the recognition of Tsaritsyn as part of the Don. (4) Get aid from the Ukrainians and the Germans to make the Soviets recognize the independence of the Don and withdraw their soldiers. (5) Get military aid. (Bogaevskii's report to the *krug*, Wrangel Military Archives, Hoover Institution, file 133.)

28. Kakliugin, *Donskaia Letopis'*, III, 82.

29. The letters are printed in *Krasnyi Arkhiv*, LXVII, pp. 97-100.

30. *Ibid.*, p. 99.

31. *Ibid.*, pp. 99-100.

32. *Ibid.*, p. 101.

33. A. V. Cheriachukin, "Donskaia delegatsiia na Ukrainu i Berlin v 1918-1919 gg," *Donskaia Letopis'*, III, 167.

34. N. A. Svechin, "Vospominaniia," Russian Archives, Columbia University, part 3, p. 10.

35. Denikin, *Ocherki*, III, 130.

36. M. Drozdovskii, *Dnevnik* (Berlin, 1923), 139.

37. *Ibid.*, p. 139.

38. A. V. Turkul, *Drozdovtsy v ogne* (Munich, 1958), p. 33.

39. V. E. Pavlov, *Markovtsy v boiakh i pokhodakh za Rossiiu v osvoboditel'noi voine 1917-1920* (Paris 1962), 2 vols. MS. Russian Archives, Columbia Univ., I, 246-247.

40. Denikin, *Ocherki*, III, 154-156; See Alekseev and Miliukov's correspondence in *Poslednie Novosti*, No. 1214, 6 Apr. 1924. Original letters in Miliukov files, Russian Archives, Columbia Univ.

41. *Belyi Arkhiv*, I, p. 145

42. *Denikin, Ocherki*, III, 129.

43. *Ibid.*, p. 130; and Drozdovskii, *Dnevik*, p. 72.

44. Denikin, *Ocherki*, III, 130.

45. Of course it is impossible to establish conclusively whether the peasants were monarchists during the Civil War. This question of the attitude of the

peasants was frequently discussed among anti-Bolshevik politicians; by and large, those with monarchist sympathies tended to attribute monarchist beliefs to the Russian peasant. (See for example General A. S. Sannikov's report to the Special Council, Journals of the Special Council, No. 5, October 25, 1918.) Denikin and many others believed that the majority of the peasants did not want the restoration of the monarchy at that particular time. *(Ocherki,* III, 132) To this author the arguments of those who questioned the monarchist view of the peasants appear convincing.

46. A. I. Denikin, *Put' russkogo ofitsera* (New York, 1953), p. 96.

47. Denikin *Ocherki,* III, 131.

48. *Ibid.,* 132.

49. The lower figure is taken from A. I. Denikin, "Navet na beloe dvizhenie," Russian Archives, Columbia Univ., p. 42. Denikin wrote this rather long pamphlet to dispute the views presented in N. N. Golovin's book *Rossiiskaia kontr-revoliutsiia v 1917-1918* (Paris, 1937). The higher figure is given by G. Pokrovskii, *Denikinshchina: god politiki i ekonomiki na Kubani* (Berlin, 1923), p. 35.

50. D. E. Skobtsov, *Tri goda revoliutsii i grazhdanskoi voiny na Kubani* (Paris, n.d.), pp. 97-98.

51. Article on Riabovol, in *Volnoe Kazachestvo,* July 1936, pp. 11-13.

52. Denikin, *Ocherki,* III, 139; and Skobtsov, *Tri goda revoliutsii,* p. 115.

53. G. P. Ianov, "Osvobozhdenie Novocherkasska i 'Krug Spaseniia Dona'," *Donskaia Letopis',* III, 52; and Denikin, *Ocherki,* II, 339-340.

54. Denikin, *Ocherki,* III, 64.

55. Krasnov, 'Vsevelikoe Voisko Donskoe," p. 200.

56. *Ibid.,* p. 201.

57. *Ibid.,* p. 202.

58. *Ibid.,* p. 201.

59. Poliakov, *Donskie kazaki,* p. 237.

60. P. N. Miliukov, "Dnevnik," MS. Russian Archives, Columbia Univ., p. 15.

61. Krasnov could complain with justice that the headquarters of the Volunteer Army became a center of intrigues against him. At times the Army gave refuge even to common criminals and Krasnov asked extradition in vain. See Alekseev's letter to Denikin dated June 1918, *Belyi Arkhiv,* I. 140.

62. Krasnov, "Vsevelikoe Voisko Donskoe," p. 205.

63. *Ibid.*

64. *Ibid.,* p. 206. Alekseev, who was in Novocherkassk, at times tried to mediate between Krasnov and Denikin. To overcome their disagreements, Krasnov and Denikin agreed to send permanent envoys to one another. General Elsner went to Novocherkassk and General Smagin to the headquarters of the Volunteer Army. Smagin, a good diplomat, arranged for all correspondence to go through his hands, and at times he managed to tone

down some undiplomatic expressions. (A. A. Smagin, "Vospominaniia," MS. Russian Archives, Columbia Univ., p. 23.)

65. Gen. B. Kazanovich, "Poezdka iz Dobrovol'cheskoi Armii v Krasnuiu Moskvu," *Arkhiv Russkoi Revoliutsii*, VII, 185.

66. Alekseev's letter to Miliukov, in Miliukov files, Russian Archives, Columbia Univ.

67. For example, in Taganrog, where the army had one of the most important and successful recruiting offices, Gen. M. I. Shtengel, the head of the bureau, had to start working with only five thousand rubles. Shtengel received no more money from Alekseev and his bureau had to be financed from inadequate private contributions. (See the report of Gen. Shtengel, Aug. 16, 1919, in *Belyi Arkhiv*, II, 133-135.)

68. See the letter of Miliukov to Alekseev, May 21, 1918 (O.S.), in Miliukov files, Russian Archives, Columbia Univ.

69. Denikin, *Ocherki*, III, 140.

70. Kazanovich, in *Arkhiv Russkoi Revoliutsii*, VII, 184.

71. *Ibid.*, 197.

72. *Ibid.*, 194.

73. *Ibid.*, 200.

74. When Kazanovich decided to return to the Volunteer Army, he chose Gen. Khrostitskii as the permanent representative of the army in Moscow. Khrostitskii, however, never sent a single report. *Ibid*

75. Denikin, *Ocherki*, III, 132. It is interesting that Alekseev wanted to convince Miliukov that it was the officeres of the army who would not have tolerated a German orientation. He wrote to Miliukov on June 7: "It is difficult to dispute your conclusions logically (that the army should adopt a pro-German stance), however to force our officer corps to agree with them is hardly possible without a shock which would endanger the very existence of the Army." (Miliukov files, Russian Archives, Columbia Univ.) It seems that Alekseev misled Miliukov about the anti-German feelings of the officers in order to free himself from the burden of disagreeing with the Kadet politician.

76. Denikin, *Ocherki*, III, 39.

77. P. N. Miliukov, "Dnevnik," MS. Russian Archives, Columbia Univ., p. 142. Miliukov's source was Gen. Danilov, the ex-Quartermaster General of the Imperial Army, who traveled from Novocherkassk to Kiev, where he met Miliukov.

78. Denikin, *Ocherki*, III, 92. See also Miliukov, "Dnevnik," and an article of Miliukov in *Poslednie Novosti*, Apr. 3, 1924.

79. Denikin, *Ocherki*, III, 133.

80. *Poslednie Novosti*, Apr. 3, 1924.

81. See Miliukov, "Dnevnik." This part of the diary is published in *Novyi Zhurnal*, LXVI, 173-203, and LXVII, 180-218.

82. Miliukov, "Dnevnik," MS., p. 68.

83. Prince G. Leikhtenbergskii, "Kak nachalas' Iuzhnaia Armiia," *Arkhiv Russkoi Revoliutsii*, VIII, 178.

84. Miliukov, "Dnevnik," MS., p. 64.

CHAPTER 6

1. W. H. Chamberlin, *The Russian Revolution*, 2 vols. (New York, 1935), II, p. 29.

2. L. Kliuev, *Bor'ba za Tsaritsyn* (Moscow, 1928), p. 14.

3. P. N. Krasnov, "Vsevelikoe Voisko Donskoe," *Arkhiv Russkoi Revoliutsii*, V. 202.

4. G. P. Ianov, "Osvobozhdenie Novocherkasska i 'Krug Spaseniia Dona' *Donskaia Letopis'*, III, 59.

5. Krasnov, "Vsevelikoe Voisko Donskoe," p. 202.

6. Denikin's decision to return to the Kuban has been frequently discussed —and generally condemned—by Russian emigré military historians. The most articulate and persuasive among them, Colonel A. Zaitsov, in his book *1918 god: ocherki po istorii russkoi grazhdanskoi voiny* (Paris, 1934), p. 198, argued that the Northern Caucasus could have been liberated easily by taking Tsaritsyn. The entire region would have been cut off from Central Russia, and because the Bolsheviks could not have sent munitions the local White forces would have been sufficient for ending Red rule. It is interesting to note that Soviet strategy in the Second World War was exactly what Zaitsov had suggested: the Red Army, victorious at Stalingrad, forced the Germans to evacuate the Northern Caucasus and the Kuban. Colonel N. V. Piatnitskii, in his article "Problema Tsaritsyna," *Signal*, June 15, 1939, also blamed Denikin for not appearing at the crucial time and place and maintained that the capture of Tsaritsyn would have been the decisive battle of the Civil War. General N. N. Golovin, the best known authority on military affairs among the Russian exiles, in his book *Rossiiskaia kontr-revoliutsiia*, 5 vols. (Paris, 1937), also attacked Denikin for his decision. To defend himself from Golovin's attack Denikin composed "Navet na beloe dvizhenie," MS., Columbia University Russian Archives.

7. A. I. Denikin, "Navet na beloe dvizhenie," p. 43.

8. Krasnov, "Vsevelikoe Voisko Donskoe," p. 201.

9. Alekseev's letter to Miliukov, July 1, 1918, Miliukov files, Russian Archives, Columbia University; Denikin, *Ocherki*, III, 155.

10. V. T. Sukhorukov, *XI Armiia v boiakh na severnom Kavkaze i nizhnei Volge* (Moscow, 1961), p. 42. According to Denikin, the Red Army had between 80 and 100 thousand soldiers. *Ocherki*, III, 156.

11. Sukhorukov, *XI Armiia*, pp. 34-36.

12. *Ibid.*, p. 30.

13. *Ibid.*, pp. 41-43.

14. V. E. Pavlov, ed., *Markovtsy v boiakh i pokhodakh za Rossiiu v osvobo-ditel'noi voine, 1917-1920*, 2 vols. (Paris, 1962), I, 267-275.

15. Denikin, *Ocherki*, III, 166.

16. Sukhorukov, *XI Armiia*, p. 58.

17. Denikin, *Ocherki*, III, 169-176.

18. Sukhorukov, *XI Armiia*, p. 64.

19. A. A. Smagin, "Vospominaniia," MS., Russian Archives, Columbia University, p. 23.

20. Denikin, *Ocherki*, III, 194.

21. Sukhorukov, *XI Armiia*, p. 72.

22. D. E. Skobtsov, *Tri goda revoliutsii i grazhdanskoi voiny na Kubani* (Paris, n.d.), p. 139. In spite of Denikin's efforts to avoid hurting the pride of the Cossacks, some of them thought he had entered the capital too soon.

23. V. V. Dobrynin, *Bor'ba s bol'shevizmom na iuge Rossii. Uchastie v bor'be Donskogo Kazachestva* (Prague, 1921), p. 111.

24. Dobrynin, "Vooruzhennaia bor'ba Dona s bol'shevikami," *Donskaia Letopis'*, I, 103.

25. N. Kakurin, *Kak srazhalas' revoliutsiia* (Moscow and Leningrad, 1925), 2 vols. I, 261.

26. I. I. Berz and K. A. Khmelevskii, *Geroicheskie gody; Oktiabr'skaia Revoliutsiia i grazhdanskaia voina na Donu* (Rostov, 1964), p. 198.

27. *Ibid.*, p. 100.

28. *Iuzhnyi front: Sbornik dokumentov* (Mai 1918-Mart 1919) (Rostov, 1962), pp. 150-151.

29. Sukhorukov, *XI Armiia*, p. 94. On Zhloba, see D. P. Saenko, *Dmitrii Zhloba* (Krasnodar, 1964).

30. Sukorukov, *XI Armiia*, p. 95.

31. Kakurin, *Kak srazhalas' revoliutsiia*, I, 240.

32. Dobrynin, "Vooruzhennaia bor'ba Dona s bol'shevikami," *Donskaia Letopis'*, I, p. 113.

33. Dobrynin, *Bor'ba s bol'shevizmom*, p. 111.

34. Berz and Khmelevskii, *Geroicheskie gody*, pp. 231-232.

35. Dobrynin, "Vooruzhennaia bor'ba Dona s bol'shevikami," *Donskaia Letopis'*, I, p. 117.

36. Krasnov, "Vsevelikoe Voisko Donskoe," p. 253.

37. Dobrynin in *Donskaia Letopis'*, I, p. 105.

38. Krasnov, "Vsevelikoe Voisko Donskoe," p. 243.

39. P. I. Zalesskii, "Iuzhnaia Armiia," *Donskaia Letopis'*, III, 240. Before accepting Krasnov's offer Ivanov turned to Denikin for advice. While Denikin did not encourage him, he did not object.

40. Krasnov, "Vsevelikoe Voisko Donskoe," p. 244.

41. Zalesskii in *Donskaia Letopis'*, III, p. 244.

42. *Ibid.*, p. 238.

43. Krasnov, "Vsevelikoe Voisko Donskoe," p. 245.

44. Zalesskii in *Donskaia Letopis'*, III, p. 256.

45. Denikin, *Ocherki*, III, 178.

46. *Ibid.*, III, 210.

47. *Ibid.*, IV, 80.

48. *Ibid.*, IV, 83.

49. P. N. Wrangel, *Memoirs* (London, 1929), p. 59.

50. Denikin, *Ocherki*, IV, 92.

51. Pokrovskii, *Denikinshchina: god politiki i ekonomiki na Kubani (1918–1919 gg)* (Berlin, 1923), p. 164.

52. Lukomskii, *Vospominaniia*, 2 vols. (Berlin, 1922), II, 89.

53. Skobtsov, *Tri goda revoliutsii*, p. 143.

54. Pokrovskii, *Denikinshchina*, pp. 105-106.

55. *Volnoe Kozachestvo*, January 10, 1935, p. 6.

56. John Erickson, *The Soviet High Command* (London, 1962), chapters 2 and 3.

57. For the biography of A. G. Shkuro, see A. Avramov, *General A. G. Shkuro* (Rostov, 1919), and A. G. Shkuro, *Zapiski belogo partizana* (Buenos Aires, 1961).

58. E. V. Maslovskii, "Nekotorye stranitsy moei zhizni," MS., Russian Archives, Columbia University, p. 1278.

59. Denikin, *Ocherki*, III, 188.

60. Shkuro, *Zapiski*, p. 170.

61. *Ibid.*, p. 173.

62. Maslovskii, "Nekotorye stranitsy," p. 1273.

63. I. V. Kalinin, *Russkaia Vandeia* (Moscow, 1926), p. 30.

64. Maslovskii, "Nekotorye stranitsy," pp. 1271-1278.

65. Denikin, *Ocherki*, IV, 91.

66. *Ibid.*, III, 211; Wrangel, *Memoirs*, p. 71.

67. I. Borisenko, *Sovetskie respubliki na severnom Kavkaze* (Rostov, 1930), 2 vols., II, 125.

68. *Ibid.*, II, 126.

69. *Iuzhnyi front*, pp. 150-151.

70. Sukhorukov, *XI Armiia*, p. 76.

71. Chamberlin, *The Russian Revolution*, II, 146.

72. Denikin, *Ocherki*, III, 212.

73. Sukhorukov, *XI Armiia*, p. 72.

74. *Ibid.*, p. 122.

75. *Ibid.*, p. 96; Borisenko, *Sovetskie respubliki*, II, 165.

76. Sukhorukov, *XI Armiia*, p. 96; Denikin, *Ocherki*, III, 214.

77. Maslovskii, "Nekotorye stranitsy," p. 1286.

78. Sukhorukov, *XI Armiia*, p. 98.

79. Borisenko, *Sovetskie respubliki*, II, 171.

80. *Ibid.*, II, 168.

81. *Ibid.*, II, 172-173.

82. M. Svechnikov, *Bor'ba Krasnoi Armii na severnom Kavkaze* (Moscow, 1926), p. 25.

83. Zaitsov, *1918 god*, p. 239.

84. Borisenko, *Sovetskie respubliki*, II, 175-176.

85. Sukhorukov, *XI Armiia*, p. 120.

86. *Ibid.*, pp. 130-132.

87. Documents of the Commission for the Investigation of Bolshevik Atrocities, Wrangel Military Archives, File 116, Hoover Institution, Stanford, California; Borisenko, *Sovetskie respubliki*, II, 181.

88. Svechnikov, p. 32.

89. Denikin, *Ocherki*, III, 222.

90. *Ibid.*, III, 223; and Zaitsov, *1918 god*, p. 240.

91. Zaitsov, *1918 god*, p. 244.

92. Sukhorukov, *XI Armiia*, p. 124.

93. E. Kovtiukh, *Ot Kubani do Volgi i obratno* (Moscow, 1926), p. 64.

94. Zaitsov, *1918 god*, p. 247.

95. Denikin, *Ocherki*, III, 237; and Kovtiukh, *Ot Kubani*, p. 64.

CHAPTER 7

1. Letter from V. V. Shulgin to unknown addressee February 9, 1919. Azbuka reports from Odessa. Wrangel Archives, File 132, Hoover Institution, Stanford, California.

2. K. N. Sokolov, *Pravlenie generala Denikina* (Sofia, 1921), pp. 30-31; and Denikin, *Ocherki*, III, 264.

3. Sokolov, *Pravlenie generala Denikina*, p. 31.

4. *Ibid.*

5. *Ibid.*, p. 32.

6. *Ibid.*, p. 34.

7. *Ibid.*, pp. 32-33.

8. Denikin, *Ocherki*, III, 271.

9. The quotations from the Constitution are taken from Denikin, *Ocherki*, III, 267-269. For an abbreviated English version see J. Bunyan, ed., *Intervention, Civil War, and Communism in Russia, April-December, 1918* (Baltimore, 1936), pp. 48-49.

10. N. I. Astrov, "*Vospominaniia*," MS., Panina Files No. 5, Russian Archives, Columbia Univ.

11. D. Kin, *Denikinshchina* (Leningrad, n.d.), p. 51.

12. Denikin, *Ocherki*, IV, 206.

13. Astrov, "Vospominaniia," p. 511.

14. Journals of the Special Council (hereafter referred to as *Journals*), Wrangel Archives, Hoover Institution, Stanford, California.

15. Letter from V. V. Shulgin to unknown addressee, February 9, 1919. Azbuka reports from Odessa, Wrangel Archives, File 132, Hoover Institution, Stanford, California.

16. *Journals*, No. 1, October 11, 1918; Sokolov, *Pravlenie generala Denikina*, pp. 43-44; Denikin, *Ocherki*, III, 265.

17. *Journals*, No. 5, October 27, 1918; A. S. Sannikov, "Vospominaniia," MS., Russian Archives, Columbia University, p. 4.

18. Astrov, "Vospominaniia," pp. 509-510.

19. *Journals*, No. 22, January 3, 1919.

20. Sokolov, *Pravlenie generala Denikina*, p. 80.

21. *Ibid.*, p. 84.

22. Astrov, "Vospominaniia," p. 509; M. M. Vinaver, *Nashe pravitel'stvo* (Paris, 1929), p. 31.

23. Vinaver, *Nashe pravitel'stvo*, p. 31. According to Vinaver, the Special Council discussed the issue of asking Grand Duke Nikolai Nikolaevich to become Commander-in-Chief. Only Stepanov and Astrov objected in principle. The only reason the Council decided not to ask the Grand Duke was that some members thought open monarchism would make a bad impression on President Wilson. The discovery of covert monarchism made a painful impression on Vinaver. Interestingly, the Journals of the Special Council contain nothing about this discussion.

24. Denikin, *Ocherki*, IV, 185. A representative of Azbuka, the White intelligence service, reported from Kiev that the officers disliked Lukomskii because of his past association with the ex-minister of war, Sukhomlinov. Azbuka reports from the Ukraine. Report of "Buki," January 1919, Wrangel Archives, File 131, Hoover Institution, Stanford, California.

25. I. V. Kalinin, *Russkaia Vandeia* (Moscow, 1926), p. 35.

26. Denikin, *Ocherki*, IV, 206; Sokolov, *Pravlenie generala Denikina*, p. 82; K. Vendziagolskii, "Savinkov," *Novyi Zhurnal*, No. LXX, p. 164; Astrov, p. 6.

27. E. V. Maslovskii, "Nekotorye stranitsy moei zhizni," MS., Russian Archives, Columbia University, p. 1337.

28. Sokolov, *Pravlenie generala Denikina*, p. 42.

29. A. A. Smagin, "Vospominaniia," MS., Russian Archives, Columbia University, p. 34.

30. Denikin, *Ocherki*, IV, 82.

31. *Ibid.*, III, 179.

32. Astrov, "Vospominaniia," p. 512.

33. O. H. Radkey, *The Election to the Russian Constituent Assembly of 1917* (Cambridge, Massachusetts, 1950), p. 79.

34. Denikin, *Ocherki*, III, 262.

35. Kalinin, *Russkaia Vandeia*, p. 38.

36. Astrov, "Vospominaniia," p. 569.

37. *Journals*, No. 12, November 19, 1918.

38. Denikin, *Ocherki*, III, 261.

39. *Journals*, No. 3, October 18, 1918.

40. *Journals*, No. 4, October 22, 1918. The four representatives were Elachich, Rizeman, Makaev, and Kirilov.

41. *Journals*, No. 14, December 4, 1918.

42. Denikin, *Ocherki*, III, 179.

43. *Ibid.*

44. *Journals*, No. 1, October 11, 1918.

45. Denikin, *Ocherki*, III, 180.

46. *Journals*, No. 1, October 11, 1918.

47. *Journals*, No. 10, November 12, 1918.

48. *Journals*, No. 18, December 20, 1918. Lebedev, the head of the department of trade reported to the Council about his conversations with the English representative, General Poole, who suggested that the money might be printed in England, or that England might provide machines for the purpose.

49. Denikin, *Ocherki*, IV, 89-90.

50. *Journals*, No. 12, November, 19, 1918 and No. 13, November 27, 1918.

51. Denikin, *Ocherki*, IV, 232.

52. Sokolov, *Pravlenie generala Denikina*, p. 95.

53. *Journals*, No. 1, October 11, 1918; Sokolov, p. 95.

54. *Journals*, No. 1, October 11, 1918.

55. *Journals*, No. 21, December 31, 1918.

56. Sokolov, *Pravlenie generala Denikina*, pp. 96-97; Denikin, *Ocherki* IV, 232-233. Paramonov set up his headquarters in Rostov rather than in Ekaterinodar because the larger city afforded technical advantages. Paramonov was the leader of the opposition to Krasnov and could never devote his entire attention to propaganda matters.

57. Sokolov, *Pravlenie generala Denikina*, p. 103.

58. *Journals*, No. 21, December 31, 1918. It is worth noting that the idea of setting up a Commission came from the British. Sokolov, *Pravlenie generala Denikina*, p. 85.

59. Denikin, *Ocherki*, III, 262, as translated in Bunyan, *Intervention, Civil War, and Communism*, p. 48.

60. P. N. Miliukov, "Dnevnik," *Novyi Zhurnal*, LXVII, 182.

61. For the description of the Jassy conference, see M. R. H. McNeal, "The Conference of Jassy: An Early Fiasco of the Anti-Bolshevik Movement," *Essays in Russian and Soviet History in Honor of Geroid Tanquary Robinson* (New York, 1963), pp. 221-236; N. I. Astrov, "Iasskoe soveshchanie," *Golos minuvshego na chuzhoi storone*, III, 39-76; and V. I. Gurko, "Iz Petrograda cherez Moskvu, Parizh i London v Odessu 1917-1918 gg," *Arkhiv Russkoi Revoliutsii*, XV, 45-47.

62. McNeal, "The Conference of Jassy," p. 224.

63. Denikin, *Ocherki*, IV, 184.

64. Astrov, "Iasskoe soveshchanie," p. 42.

65. Gurko, "Iz Petrograda cherez Moskvu," pp. 38-42.

66. Astrov, "Iasskoe soveshchanie," p. 54.

67. *Ibid.*, p. 42.

68. The conference has been described by many of the participants, such as Astrov, "Vospominaniia," Vinaver, *Nashe pravitel'stvo*, Sokolov, *Pravlenie generala Denikina*, and Miliukov, "Dnevnik."

69. Astrov, "Vospominaniia," p. 501.

70. Astrov, "Iasskoe soveshchanie," p. 55.

71. Vinaver, *Nashe pravitel'stvo*, p. 48.

72. Denikin, *Ocherki*, IV, 185.

73. Astrov, "Vospominaniia," p. 500.

74. Vinaver, *Nashe pravitel'stvo*, p. 49.

75. Astrov, "Vospominaniia," p. 507.

76. *Ibid.*

77. *Ibid.*, p. 526; Vinaver, *Nashe pravitel'stvo*, p. 49.

78. Astrov, "Iasskoe soveshchanie," pp. 56-59.

79. *Ibid.*, pp. 60-61.

80. Denikin, *Ocherki*, IV, 185.

CHAPTER 8

1. Denikin, *Ocherki*, III, 244.

2. G. Pokrovskii, *Denikinshchina: god politiki i ekonomiki na Kubani (1918-1919 gg)* (Berlin, 1923), p. 42.

3. *Ibid.*

4. *Ibid.*, p. 43; Denikin, *Ocherki*, III, 206.

5. Pokrovskii, *Denikinshchina*, p. 43. Pokrovskii was quoting from the stenographic record of the meeting of the *rada*.

6. *Ibid.*

7. *Ibid.*, p. 47.

8. Denikin, *Ocherki*, III, 203.

9. K. N. Sokolov, *Pravlenie generala Denikina* (Sofia, 1921), pp. 37-38.

10. D. E. Skobtsov, *Tri goda revoliutsii i grazhdanskoi voiny na Kubani* (Paris, n.d.), p. 163.

11. Journals of the Special Council. Wrangel Archives, Hoover Institution, Stanford, California (hereafter referred to as *Journals*), No. 6, October 29, 1918.

12. *Journals*, No. 7, November 1, 1918.

13. Sokolov, *Pravlenie generala Denikina*, p. 45.

14. Pokrovskii, *Denikinshchina*, p. 63.

15. Skobtsov, *Tri goda revoliutsii*, p. 175.

16. M. M. Vinaver, *Nashe pravitel'stvo*, (Paris, 1929), p. 41.

17. Denikin's speech to the *rada* is printed in Denikin's *Ocherki*, IV, 45-48.

18. *Ibid.*, IV, 49.

19. Skobstov, *Tri goda revoliutsii*, pp. 192-193.

20. Pokrovskii, *Denikinshchina*, p. 63.

21. A. Lukomskii, *Vospominaniia*, 2 vols. (Berlin, 1922), II, 121.

22. A. G. Shkuro, *Zapiski belogo partizana* (Buenos Aires, 1961), p. 170; Denikin, *Ocherki*, IV, 50.

23. Shkuro, *Zapiski*, p. 173; Denikin, *Ocherki*, IV, 50.

24. Denikin, *Ocherki*, IV, 52.

25. Skobtsov, *Tri goda revoliutsii*, p. 197.

26. N. I. Astrov, "Vospominaniia," MS. Russian Archives, Columbia University, p. 531.

27. *Ibid.*, pp. 533-534.

28. Skobtsov, *Tri goda revoliutsii*, p. 199; Sokolov, *Pravlenie generala Denikina*, pp. 55-56.

29. Sokolov, *Pravlenie generala Denikina*, p. 59.

30. Skobtsov, *Tri goda revoliutsii*, p. 201.

31. Denikin, *Ocherki*, IV, 53.

32. K. P. Kakliugin, "Donskoi Ataman P. N. Krasnov i ego vremia," *Donskaia Letopis'*, III, 102.

33. *Ibid.*

34. P. N. Krasnov, "Vsevelikoe Voisko Donskoe," *Arkhiv Russkoi Revoliutsii*, V, 200.

35. *Ibid.*, p. 214

36. Kakliugin, "Donskoi Ataman," p. 100.

37. Azbuka reports on Cossack territories. Wrangel Archives, File 133, Hoover Institution, Stanford, California.

38. Kakliugin, "Donskoi Ataman," p. 105.

39. I. A. Poliakov, *Donskie kazaki v bor'be s bol'shevikami*, (Munich, 1962), p. 284.

40. According to Lukomskii, *Vospominaniia*, II, 97, it was Krasnov who wanted the elections postponed. This would have made little sense from Krasnov's point of view, and this interpretation is contradicted by a confidant of Krasnov, Poliakov, *Donskie kazaki*, p. 290; by Denikin, *Ocherki*, III, 250; and by Kakliugin, "Donskoi Ataman," p. 118.

41. Lukomskii, *Vospominaniia*, II, 98-99.

42. *Ibid.*, II, 99-100.

43. Kakliugin, "Donskoi Ataman," pp. 120-121.

44. Poliakov, *Donskie kazaki*, p. 293.

45. Krasnov, "Vsevelikoe Voisko Donskoe," p. 234.

46. Lukomskii's speech is printed in Lukomskii, *Vospominaniia*, II, pp. 92-95.

47. Denikin, *Ocherki*, III, 251.

48. Krasnov, "Vsevelikoe Voisko Donskoe," p. 239.

49. *Kratkaia zapiska istorii vzaimootnoshenii D.A. s Ukrainei*, (Rostov, 1919); Denikin files, Russian Archives, Columbia University, p. 3.

50. John S. Reshetar, *The Ukrainian Revolution: A Study in Nationalism* (Princeton, 1952), pp. 145-207.

51. *Kratkaia zapiska istorii vzaimootnoshenii D.A. s Ukrainei*, p. 15.

52. P. N. Miliukov, "Dnevnik," *Novyi Zhurnal*, LXVI, 182.

53. See Chapter 5.

54. P. N. Miliukov, "Dnevnik," 176.

55. "Nikolai Stepanovich Riabovol," *Volnoe Kazachestvo*, August 1936.

56. *Ibid.*

57. Reshetar, *The Ukranian Revolution*, p. 187. Unfortunately Reshetar does not indicate the source of this story.

58. Reshetar, *The Ukranian Revolution*, pp. 197-198.

59. Krasnov, "Vsevelikoe Voisko Donskoe," p. 236.

60. *Ibid.*, p. 238.

61. *Ibid.*, p. 240.

62. Denikin, *Ocherki*, IV, 92.

63. *Ibid.*, IV, 56. Italics in the original.

64. Pokrovskii, *Denikinshchina*, pp. 68-70.

65. *Ibid.*

66. Firuz Kazemzadeh, *The Struggle for Transcaucasia* (New York and Oxford, 1951), p. 57.

67. Richard E. Pipes, *The Formation of the Soviet Union* (Cambridge, Massachusetts, 1957), p. 106.

68. E. Ludendorff, *My War Memoirs, 1914-1918*, 2 vols. (London, 1919), II, 620-621.

69. See German Foreign Office Archives, St. Antony's Reels 97 and 98, Matters relating to Georgia, 1918-1919.

70. See Trotskii's pamphlet on the Georgian Mensheviks. L. Trotsky, *Between Red and White* (London, 1922).

71. Denikin, *Ocherki*, III, 48-49.

72. E. Gegechkori's letter to the editor, *Poslednie Novosti*, January 13, 1933.

73. Georgia, Ministerstvo Vneshnikh Del., *Dokumenty i materialy po vneshnei politike Zakavkaz'ia Gruzii* (Tiflis, 1919), hereafter referred to as *Documents*, pp. 395-396.

74. Telegram from Kress von Kressenstein to the Foreign Office, July 5, 1918. German Foreign Office Archives, St. Antony's Reel 97.

75. E. V. Maslovskii, "Nekotorye stranitsy moei zhizni," MS., Russian Archives, Columbia University, p. 644.

76. E. Gegechkori's letter to the editor, *Poslednie Novosti*, January 13, 1933.

77. Maslovskii, "Nekotorye stranitsy," p. 1282.

78. *Ibid.*, p. 1286.

79. *Ibid.*, p. 1289.

80. *Ibid.*, p. 1293.

81. *Ibid.*, p. 1309.

82. *Ibid.*, p. 1311.

83. It is a debated point who initiated the negotiations. Denikin maintains that the idea came from the Army's headquarters (*Ocherki*, III, 240 and "Answer to Gegechkori," in *Poslednie Novosti*, January 25, 1933). Gegechkori claims that his government called for negotiations (*Poslednie Novosti*, January 13, 1933). Maslovskii presents a third version, according to which the idea came from him ("Nekotorye stranity," p. 1313). The Wrangel Military Archives (File 133 Reports from Transcaucasia, p. 20) contains a telegram from Maslovskii to General Romanovskii on August 30 (O.S.) according to which Georgian General Vashakidze suggested talks at Tuapse between the Volunteer Army and the Georgian Government.

84. Maslovskii, "Nekotorye stranitsy," p. 1323.

85. The protocols of the conference are printed in *Documents*, pp. 391-414.

86. *Ibid.*, pp. 395-396. There is contradictory evidence about the Georgian treatment of Russian officers. General P. Shatilov, who was in Georgia during the summer of 1918, complains about the Georgian authorities ("Zapiski," MS., Columbia University, Russian Archives, p. 636). While Maslovskii, who was in Georgia at the same time as Shatilov, believes that restrictions were imposed on Russian officers because of German demands ("Nekotorye stranitsy," p. 1263). There is no doubt that as time went on and Georgian nationalism increased the position of Russian officers became increasingly difficult. At the time of the fighting against the Volunteer Army, members of the officers' organization in Tiflis were arrested. Denikin, *Ocherki*, IV, 156-157.

87. "Kratkaia zapiska istorii vzaimootnoshenii D.A. s Gruziei," a report prepared by the headquarters of the Volunteer Army for General Briggs in February 1919. Wrangel Military Archives, File 153 (Matters relating to Transcaucasia), Hoover Institution, Stanford, California.

88. *Documents*, p. 393.

89. *Ibid.*, p. 399.

90. *Ibid.*, p. 393.

91. These resolutions are full of praise of Georgian democracy and condemnation of Denikin's dictatorship. Socialist support for Georgian occupation was the main moral justification for Georgia's retaining the district. See these resolutions in *Documents*, pp. 414-416. The socialist resolutions should be balanced against requests of the Abhazian minority and of some Russians in the district to Denikin to free them from Georgian rule. Denikin, *Ocherki*, IV, p. 154.

92. Denikin, *Ocherki*, III, 49. Gegechkori in *Poslednie Novosti*, January 13, 1933.

93. Denikin, *Ocherki*, III, p. 242.

94. *Documents*, p. 410.

95. Z. Avalishvili, *The Independence of Georgia in International Politics 1918-1921* (London, 1940), p. 177.

96. *Documents*, p. 414.

97. Denikin and Maslovskii disagree about the timing and reasons for re-calling Mazniev. According to Denikin (*Ocherki*, III, 240) Mazniev was re-called because the Georgian government disapproved of the Volunteer Army taking Tuapse. According to Maslovskii ("Nekotorye stranitsy," p. 1326) the change in the attitude of the Georgian government toward the Volunteer Army was entirely the result of the unsuccessful conference. In view of the fact that Mazniev was one of the delegates to Ekaterinodar conference after the Tuapse episode, Maslovskii's version sounds more convincing.

98. Maslovskii, "Nekotoryne stranitsy," p. 1325.

99. Denikin and Maslovskii give different versions of this event also. Deni-kin writes in his memoirs that the Army closed the borders with Georgia for grain trade, but it took no hostile action (*Ocherki*, III, 242). Maslovskii contradicts this; he maintains that Denikin ordered him to attack Sochi ("Ne-kotorye stranitsy," p. 1326). Again, Maslovskii's account of the events is more convincing. The Commander-in-Chief might have forgotten about Kolossovskii's venture, but Maslovskii, who was on the scene and whose career was significantly influenced by this decision, is likely to have remem-bered correctly.

100. Telegram from Kress von Kressenstein to Foreign Office, No. A 402086, October 17, 1918. Foreign Office Archives, St. Antony's Reel 98.

101. Verbal note from Ambassador Joffe to Foreign Office, October 8, 1918. German Foreign Office Archives, St. Antony's Reel 98.

102. Kress von Kressenstein's report to Foreign Office, October 3, 1918. German Foreign Office Archives, St. Antony's Reel 98.

103. English mediation in the Georgian-Volunteer controversy is de-scribed in G. Brinkley, *The Volunteer Army and Allied Intervention in South Russia, 1917-1921* (Notre Dame, Indiana, 1966), chapter 5.

104. Denikin, probably deliberately, uses Trotskii's term often. *Ocherki*, IV, chapter 17.

105. The Turks played a malicious trick: before they withdrew they promised the disputed territory to both the Armenians and the Georgians.

CHAPTER 9

1. The Germans, afraid to compromise themselves in the eyes of the Allies, turned down the offer. E. H. Carr, *The Bolshevik Revolution*, 3 vols. (New York, 1953), III, 106.

2. *Ibid.*, pp. 100-116.

3. The complicated subject of Allied policy toward Russia cannot be dis-cussed here. This has been done excellently and in great detail by George A. Brinkley, *The Volunteer Army and Allied Intervention in South Russia, 1917-1921* (Notre Dame, Indiana, 1966). I merely would like to describe how Allied policies seemed to the leaders of the Volunteer Army.

4. See, for example, A. I. Denikin, *World Events and the Russian Problem*

(Paris, 1939), or his autobiography, *Put' russkogo ofitsera* (New York, 1953).

5. William H. Chamberlin, *The Russian Revolution*, 2 vols. (New York, 1935), II, 21.

6. In January 1918, Kornilov, who had been very much interested in Siberia, sent General Flug and Colonel Lebedev east to establish volunteer units to fight the Bolsheviks and conduct negotiations with local political organizations in the name of the Volunteer Army. Neither of them returned. Only one letter from Flug arrived in the South and this only after a delay of two and a half months. In the course of the Ice March almost all contact between the Army and the outside world stopped. When the volunteers returned to the Don they learned about the existence of the anti-Bolshevik movement in the Urals and in Siberia from newspapers and occasional travelers.

7. Denikin, *Ocherki*, III, 259; Journals of the Special Council, Wrangel Military Archives, Hoover Institution, Stanford, California, No. 5, October 25, 1918, hereafter cited as *Journals*.

8. *Journals*, No. 5, October 25, 1918.

9. On Shcherbachev's activities, see E. G. Val' *K istorii belogo dvizheniia: Deiatel'nost' Gen. ad' 'iutanta Shcherbacheva* (Tallin, 1935).

10. Shcherbachev's letter is printed in· Val', *K istorii*, pp. 34-37; Denikin, *Ocherki*, IV, p. 38; A. S. Lukomskii, *Vospominaniia*, 2 vols. (Berlin, 1922), II, 259 261; and "Organzhevaia kniga" in *Arhkiv Russhoi Revoliutsii*, XVI, 234 235.

11. Val', *K istorii*, pp. 37-41.

12. Shcherbachev attended the Jassy conference. Had he revealed there the nature of Berthelot's promises the standing of the Volunteer Army would have been greatly enhanced. Robert H. McNeal, "The Conference of Jassy: An Early Fiasco of the Anti-Bolshevik Movement," J. S. Curtis, ed., *Essays in Russian and Soviet History in Honor of Geroid Tanquary Robinson* (New York, 1963), p. 236. It seems, however, that whatever the momentary advantages, abusing Berthelot's confidence would have been harmful to the White cause.

13. Lukomskii, *Vospominaniia*, II, 259; Denikin, *Ocherki*, IV, 36-37. At the time when the Allies had planned to reconstruct the Eastern front, it was rumored that General Poole would be named commander of that front.

14. "Oranzhevaia kniga," pp. 235-236; Denikin, *Ocherki*, IV, 38-39.

15. Lukomskii, *Vospominaniia*, II, 263.

16. *Ibid*.

17. Val', *K istorii*, p. 42.

18. Letter from Bogaevskii to Denikin, October 25, 1918. *Belyi Arkhiv*, II, 187.

19. Letter from Denikin to Bogaevskii, November 7, 1918. *Belyi Arkhiv*, II, 188-189.

20. *Journals*, No. 5, October 25, 1918.

21. M. M. Vinaver, *Nashe pravitel'stvo* (Paris, 1929), p. 30.

22. *Ibid.*, p. 32.

23. Denikin, *Ocherki*, IV, 237.

24. Vinaver, *Nashe provitel'stvo*, p. 33.

25. *Ibid.*, pp. 27-29.

26. United States, Department of State, *Papers Relating to the Foreign Relations of the United States: The Paris Peace Conference, 1919*, 13 vols. (Washington, 1942-1947), IV, 53-54, as quoted in Brinkley, p. 106.

27. P. N. Krasnov, "Vsevelikoe Voisko Donskoe," *Arkhiv Russkoi Revoliutsii*, V. 253.

28. Val', *K istorii*, p. 33.

29. For Krasnov's views on Ivanov, see Krasnov, "Vsevelikoe Voisko Donskoe," pp. 242–246.

30. *Ibid.*, pp. 253-254.

31. *Ibid.*, pp. 262-264.

32. I. A. Poliakov, *Donskie kazaki v bor'be s bol'shevikami* (Munich, 1962), pp. 315-322.

33. Denikin, *Ocherki*, IV, 71.

34. Krasnov, "Vsevelikoe Voisko Donskoe," p. 275; K. P. Kakliugin, "Donskoi Ataman P. N. Krasnov i ego vremia," *Donskaia Letopis'*, III, 124-126.

35. Kakliugin, "Donskoi Ataman," p. 126; Krasnov, "Vsevelikoe Voisko Donskoe," p. 278; Poliakov, *Donskie kazaki*, p. 331.

36. Kakliugin "Donskoi Ataman," p. 127.

37. Krasnov, "Vsevelikoe Voisko Donskoe," p. 281.

38. A. A. Smagin, "Vospominaniia," MS., Russian Archives, Columbia University, p. 29.

39. Krasnov, "Vsevelikoe Voisko Donskoe," p. 281.

40. The protocol of the meeting is printed in Poliakov, *Donskie kazaki*, pp. 339-354. For other descriptions see Krasnov, "Vsevelikoe Voisko Donskoe," p. 284 ff.; Denikin, *Ocherki*, IV, 72-73; Smagin, "Vospominaniia," pp. 31-32.

41. Poliakov, *Donskie kazaki*, p. 341.

42. *Ibid.*, p. 354.

43. Denikin, *Ocherki*, IV, 82. The staff of the Volunteer Army became the staff of the AFSR and Wrangel formed a new staff for himself.

44. Kakliugin, "Donskoi Ataman," p. 134.

45. Denikin, *Ocherki*, IV, 77.

46. On developments in the Ukraine, see John S. Reshetar, *The Ukrainian Revolution* (Princeton, 1952).

47. Report of "Az," November 22, 1918, Azbuka reports. Wrangel Military Archives, File 151, Hoover Institution, Stanford, California.

48. Denikin, *Ocherki*, IV, 197.

49. Report of "Az," December 21, 1918, Azbuka reports. Wrangel Military Archives, File 131, Hoover Institution, Stanford, California.

50. *Ibid.*

51. Report of "Buki," December 30, 1918, Azbuka reports. Wrangel Military Archives, File 131, Hoover Institution, Stanford, California.

52. *Ibid.*

53. Report of "Oko," January 3, 1919, and report of "Az," January 2, 1919, Azbuka reports. Wrangel Military Archives, File 131, Hoover Institution, Stanford, California.

54. A. I. Gukovskii, *Frantsuzkaia interventsiia na iuge Rossii. 1918-1919* (Moscow-Leningrad, 1928), pp. 52-53.

55. Denikin, *Ocherki*, V, 8-9.

56. *Ibid.*, p. 10.

57. For the situation in Odessa, see Azbuka reports from Odessa, Wrangel Military Archives, File 132, and A. S. Sannikov, "Vospominaniia," MS., Russian Archives, Columbia University.

58. Sannikov, "Vospominaniia," p. 3. Odessa had great military stores left from the World War, which the volunteers expected would be given to them.

59. Jean Xydias, *L'Intervention francaise en Russie, 1918-1919: souvenirs d'un temoin*, (Paris, 1927), p. 163.

60. Richard E. Pipes, *The Formation of the Soviet Union* (Cambridge, Massachusetts, 1957), p. 187.

61. Denikin, *Ocherki*, III, 13; Vinaver, *Nashe pravitel'stvo*, p. 40.

62. Pipes, *The Formation of the Soviet Union*, p. 187. Krym was supported by local landowners and officials and refugees from the center of the country.

63. Vinaver, *Nashe pravitel'stvo*, pp. 51-52; Denikin, *Ocherki*, V, 55.

64. General Baron de Bode, who had been the head of the Crimean recruitment center, took Korvin-Krukovskii's place. Denikin, *Ocherki*, V. 58.

65. An important source of disagreement between the Crimean Kadets and the leaders of the Volunteer Army was the issue of federalism. The leading Crimean Kadets had all played important roles in national politics before the Civil War and had no intention whatever of creating a permanently independent Crimea. Nevertheless, as ministers of a de facto independent state, they came to associate themselves with the interests of the Crimea. In their view the most effective organization of the anti-Bolshevik movement was an alliance between existing governments. These federalist plans met with great hostility at the headquarters of the Volunteer Army. The best description of Kadet policies in the Crimea can be found in the unpublished doctoral dissertation of William G. Rosenberg, "Constitutional Democracy and the Russian Civil War" (Harvard, 1967).

CHAPTER 10

1. A. L. Fraiman, *Revoliutsionnaia zashchita Petrograda v fevrale-marte 1918 g* (Moscow-Leningrad, 1964), p. 247.

2. David Footman, *Civil War in Russia* (London, 1961), pp. 252-256.

Bibliography

PRIMARY SOURCES

UNPUBLISHED MATERIALS AND ARCHIVES

Collection of the Russian and Eastern European Archives
of Butler Library, Columbia University

Aprelev, In. P. "Zametki o sobytiiakh v Rossii, 1917 1918 1919." MS. (MSS are typed unless otherwise indicated.)

Birkin, V. N. "Povesti minuvshykh let," vol. 7, "Kornilovskii pokhod." MS.

Bogaevskii, A. P. Papers, 10 dossiers. MSS.

Denikin, A. I. Papers. 26 dossiers. MSS. The papers contain MSS. of his published writings, correspondence, speeches, press reports about him, and some unpublished writings, among them "Navet na beloe dvizhenie."

Istoriia Markovskoi artilleriiskoi brigady. MS. 2 vols.

Kefeli, Ia. I. "S Generalom A. V. Shvartsem v Odesse, osen' 1918-vesna 1919 gg. Vospominaniia." MS.

Kazanovich, B. Gen. "Ataka Ekaterinodara i smert' Kornilova." MS.

Kisiev, N. "Pervyi Kubanskii pokhod." MS.

Makhrov, P. S. "General Vrangel i B. Savinkov." MS. (handwritten)

———. "V Beloi armii generala Denikina." MS. (handwritten)

Mandrajy (Mandrachi) Constantin. "Begin at the Beginning." Memoirs translated by Vera Mandrajy. MS.

Maslovskii, Gen. E. V. "Nekotorye stranitsy moei zhizni." 6 parts. MS.

Miliukov, P. N. "Dnevnik." MS.

Miliukov, P. N. Personal archives. MSS.

Nikolaev, K. N. "Pervyi Kubanskii pokhod." MS.

———. "Smutnye dni na Kubani." MS.

———. "Vospominaniia." MS.

Melnikov, N. M. "Pochemu belye na iuge ne pobedili krasnykh. Grazhdanskaia voina na iuge Rossii." MS.

Panina. Papers. 9 dossiers. MSS. (typed and handwritten). Especially valuable was dossier No. 3, which contains material about the Partiia Narodnoi Svobody in 1917-1918 and an extensive study of the Civil War by N. I. Astrov; dossier No. 5 includes N. I. Astrov's memoirs; dossier No. 8 consists of material concerning P. N. Miliukov.

Poliakov, I. A. "General Kornilov." MS.
Sannikov, A. S. "Vospominaniia, 1918-1919." MS.
Shapkin, V. V. "Poslednye dni stavki Verkhovnogo." MS.
Shatilov, P. N. "Zapiski." MS.
Smagin, A. A. "Vospominaniia." MS.
Svechin, M. A. "Dopolninie k vospominaniiam." MS.
Tikhobrazov, D. "Vospominaniia." MS. (handwritten)
Anonymous. "General Kornilov." MS.

Collection of the Hoover Institution, Stanford, California

Alekseev, M. V. Account Book of the Volunteer Army. MS. TS Russia A366.
Akaemov, N. "Kaledinskie miatezhi." MS. V.W. Russia A313.
Cheriachukin, A. V. Papers. MSS. 4 dossiers (typed and handwritten). V. W. C521.
Documents of the Crimean Government. MSS. 19 dossiers. V.W. Crimea D. 636.
Documents of the Terek Cossack Government. MSS.
Delegatsiia Donskoi Respubliki na konferentsii mira. Papers. V.W. Russia 346.
Don Cossack Republic. Papers. T.S. Russia D. 674.
Ergushev, P. "Kazaki i gortsy." MS. V.W. Russia G. 628 p(2).
Economic Conditions of the Kuban Black Sea Region. MS. V.W. Russia K. 95.
Fedorov, G. "Iz vospominanii zalozhnika v Piatigorskom kontsentratsionnom lagere." MS. D.K. 265.7 F. 294.
Gessen, G. V. Archives. MSS. V.W. Russia G. 392.
Golovine, N. N. Minutes of the session of the Russian Academy in Paris devoted to the discussion of S. P. Melgunov's criticism of General Golovine's book. T. S. Russia G. 628 m.
———. Russian Counterrevolution, 1917-1918. MS. T.S. Russia G. 628c.
Kornilov, G. L. Speech to the Moscow State Conference. MS. V.W. Russia K. 75.
Krasnov. P. N. Discours du General Krasnov, Ataman du Don le 13 Dec. 1918 lors de sa rencontre avec le General Pool. MS.
Lukomskii, A. S. Letter to General Golovin. V.W. Russia L. 954.
Maklakov, V. A. Arkhiv russkogo posol'stva v Parizhe, 1918-1923. MS. 4 boxes.
Melgunov, S. P. Civil War collection. 11 boxes. MSS. and newspaper articles. T.S. Russia M. 521.
Prikazy i rasporiazheniia po Dobrovol'cheskoi i Donskoi armiiam, otnosiash-

chiesia k periodu grazhdanskoi voiny na iuge Rossii, 1918-1919 gg. MSS. V.W. Russia P. 951.

Prikazy, mandaty, tsirkuliary i t.d. otnosiashchiesia k periodu grazhdanskoi voiny na iuge Rossii 1918-1920 gg (Bolshevik materials). MSS. V.W. Russia P. 952.

Relations between the South Russian Volunteer Army and the Georgia Mensheviks 1919-1920. Compiled by D. P. Dratsenko. MSS. 3 folders. Vault, Annex II.

Rodzianko, M. V. Documents. MSS. V.W. Russia R. 697.

Shcherbachev, D. G. Papers. MSS. 64 files. Vault, Annex II.

Vatatsi, M. P. "The White Movement, 1917-1920 Memoirs." MS. T. S. Russia V. 342.

Vinaver, R. G. "Vospominaniia." MS.

Wrangel, P. N. Archives. 222 files. MSS. Parts of the Archives, including the minutes of the meetings of the Special Council, are restricted until 1979. Vault, Annex II.

Documents of the German Foreign Office. St. Antony's College, Oxford Microfilm reels 143-144. (Documents concerning the Ukraine, the Don, and the Crimea, 1918.)

PRINTED DOCUMENTS

Bor'ba za pobedu sovetskoi vlasti v Gruzii: dokumenty i materialy, 1917-1921 gg. Tbilisi, Gosizdat G.S.S.R., 1958.

Bor'ba za sovetkuiu vlast' na Kubani v 1917-1920 (Documenty). Krasnodar, Krasnodarskoe knizhnoe izdatel'stvo, 1957.

Browder, R. P., and A. F. Kerensky (eds.). The Russian Provisional Government 1917: Documents. 3 vols. Stanford, Stanford University Press 1961.

Bunyan, J., and H. H. Fisher (eds.). The Bolshevik Revolution, 1917-1918. Stanford, Stanford University Press, 1934.

Bunyan, J. (ed.). Intervention, Civil War, and Communism in Russia, April-December 1918: Documents and Materials. Baltimore, Johns Hopkins Press, 1936.

Cumming, C. K., and W. W. Pettit (eds.). Russian-American Relations, March 1917-March 1920: Documents and Papers. New York, Harcourt, Brace and Howe, 1920.

Degras, Jane (ed.). Soviet Documents on Foreign Policy. Vol. 1. London, Oxford University Press, 1951.

"Demokraticheskoe'pravitel'stvo Gruzii i angliiskoe komandovanie," Krasnyi Arkhiv, vol. 21, pp. 122-173, and vol. 22, pp. 96-110. Moscow, Gosizdat, 1927.

"Denezhnye dokumenty Generala Alekseeva," Arkhiv Russkoi Revoliutsii, vol. 5, pp. 345-357. Berlin, Izdatel'stvo "Slovo," 1922.

Die deutsche Okkupation der Ukraine: Geheimdokumente. Strasbourg, 1937.

Dokumenty o geroicheskoi oborone Tsaritsyna v 1918 godu. Moscow, Gospolitizdat, 1942.

"Dokumenty po istorii chernomorskogo flota v marte-iiune 1918 g.," *Arkhiv Russkoi Revoliutsii,* vol. 14, pp. 151-224. Berlin. Izdatel'stvo "Slovo," 1924.

"Dokumenty," *Donskaia Letopis',* vol. 1, pp. 301-341; vol. 2, pp. 293-371; and vol. 3, pp. 320-371.

Don Cossack Army, Upravleniia General-kvartirmeistera Donskoi Armii. *Ocherk politicheskoi istorii Vsevelikago Voiska Donskogo.* Novocherkassk, Obl. V. Voiska Donskogo Tip., 1919 (Hoover Library).

"Germanskaia interventsiia i Donskoe pravitel'stvo v 1918 g," *Krasnyi Arkhiv,* vol. 67, pp. 93-130. Moscow, Gosizdat, 1934.

Georgia, Ministerstvo Vneshnikh Del. *Dokumenty i materialy po vneshnei politike Zakavkazia i Gruzii* Tiflis. Tip. Pravitel'stva Gruzinskoi Respubliki, 1919.

Golder, F. A. (ed.). *Documents of Russian History, 1914-1917.* New York, Century, 1927.

Gubarev, K. (ed.). *Bor'ba s Kaledinshchinoi (po dokumentam belykh) Dekabr' 1917-Ianvar' 1918.* Taganrog, Izdatel'stvo Istparta Donkoma, 1929.

Ispoved' Savinkova: protsess Borisa Savinkova. Berlin, Izdanie zhurnala "Russkoe Ekho," 1924.

Iuzhnyi Front: Sbornik Dokumentov (mai 1918-mart 1919). Rostov on the Don, Rostovskoe knizhnoe izdatel'stvo, 1962.

Ivangorodskii, P. Ia. (ed.). *Kak my osvobozhdali Rostov.* Rostov on the Don, Azcherizdat, 1935.

Iz istorii grazhdanskoi voiny v SSSR: sbornik dokumentov i materialov. 3 vols. Moscow, Institut Marksizma-Leninizma pri TsK KPSS, Izdatel'stvo "Sovetskaia Rossiia," 1960-1961.

Krug Spasenia Dona. Novocherkassk, 1918 (Hoover Library).

"Krym v 1918-1919 gg," *Krasnyi Arkhiv,* vol. 28, pp. 55-85; and vol. 29, pp. 142-181. Moscow, Gosizdat, 1928.

"Krymskoe kraevoe pravitel'stvo v 1918-19 g.," *Krasnyi Arkhiv,* vol. 22, pp. 92-152. Moscow, Gosizdat, 1927.

Ministerstvo inostrannykh del SSSR, *Dokumenty vneshnei politiki SSSR,* vol. 1. Moscow, Gosizdat, 1957.

Mints, I. I., and E. N. Gorodetskii (eds.). *Dokumenty o razgrome germanskikh okkupantov na Ukraine v 1918 godu.* Moscow, Gosizdat, 1942.

Lenin, V. I. *Polnoe sobranie sochinenii.* 5th edition. 55 vols. Moscow, Institut Marksizma-Leninisma pri TsK KPSS, Gospolitizdat, 1960.

"Ocherk vzaimootnoshenii vooruzhenykh sil iuga Rossii i predstavitelei frantsuzkogo komanodovaniia" (Oranzhevaia kniga"), *Arkhiv Russkoi Revoliutsii,* vol. 16, pp. 233-262. Berlin, Izdatel'stvo "Slovo," 1925.

"Organizatsiia vlasti na iuge Rossii v period grazhdanskoi voiny, 1918-1920 gg: dokumenty," *Arkhiv Russkoi Revoliutsii,* vol. 4, pp. 241-251. Berlin, Izdatel'stvo "Slovo," 1922.

"Oktiabr'skii perevorot i Stavka," *Krasnyi Arkhiv*, vol. 8, pp. 153-175; and vol. 9, pp. 156-170. Moscow, Gosizdat, 1925.

Piontkovskii, S. A. (ed.). *Grazhdanskaia voina v Rossii 1918-1921 gg: khrestomatiia*. Moscow, Izdaniia kommunisticheskogo universiteta im. Ia. M. Sverdlova, 1925.

"Pismo Shcherbacheva Denikinu," *Krasnyi Arkhiv*, vol. 21, pp. 220-223. Moscow, Gosizdat, 1927.

"Revoliutsionnoe kazachestvo Dona v bor'be s kontrrevoliutsiei," *Krasnyi Arkhiv*, vol. 76, pp. 24-30. Moscow, Gosizdat, 1936.

Shafir, I. M. (ed.). *Secrets of Menshevik Georgia; The Plot Against Soviet Russia Unmasked: Documents*. London, Communist Party of Great Britain, 1922.

Sidorov, N. I. "Novye materialy po delu Gen. Kornilova," *Bor'ba Klassov*, No. 1 - 2, pp. 273-287. Moscow, 1924.

"Trudovoe kazachestvo Donskoi oblasti o Brestskom mire i o zashchite Sovetskoi strany," *Krasnyi Arkhiv*, vol. 75, pp. 185-188. Moscow, Gosizdat, 1936.

Vneshniaia politika kontr-revoliutsionnykh 'pravitelstv' v nachale 1919 g." *Krasnyi Arkhiv*, vol. 37, pp. 69-101. Moscow, Gosizdat, 1929.

Zeman, Z. A. B. (ed.). *Germany and the Revolution in Russia, 1915-1918: Documents from the Archives of the German Foreign Ministry*. London, Oxford University Press, 1958.

Contemporary Newspapers and Pamphlets

The most useful contemporary journal used by the author was *Donskaia Volna*. Editor: Victor Sevskii, Rostov on the Don. Published between June 1918 and November 1919, altogether 61 issues. The New York Public Library has 20 issues.

Arefor, S. *Na rodine*. Rostov on the Don, Narodnaia biblioteka, 1919. (Columbia University).

Avramov, P. *Gen. A. G. Shkuro*. Rostov on the Don, Narodnaia biblioteka, 1919 (Harvard University).

Chirikov, E. N. *Narod i revoliutsiia*. Rostov on the Don, 1919 (Harvard University).

———. *Za synom*. Rostov on the Don, 1919 (Hoover Institution).

Denikin, A. I. *Za chto my boremsia?* No date, no publisher (Columbia University).

Dobrovol'skii, N. G. *Gen. Shkuro*. Rostov on the Don, 1919 (Harvard University).

Dolgorukov, P. D. *Natsional'naia politika i partiia narodnoi svobody*. Rostov on the Don, Svobodnaia rech, 1919 (Hoover Institution).

Lebedeff, Col. V. I. *The Russian Democracy in its Struggle Against the Bol-*

shevik Tyranny. New York, Russian Information Bureau, 1919 (Hoover Institution).

Lokerman, A. *74 dnia sovetskoi vlasti.* Rostov on the Don, 1918 (Hoover Institution).

Makoshin, Roman. *Chto sdelala Dobrovol'cheskaia Armiia?* Rostov on the Don, 1919 (Hoover Institution).

Nizhegorodtsev, A. *Pochemu Dobrovo'cheskaia Armiia voiuet protiv kommunistov Lenina i Trotskogo.* Kharkov, 1919 (Hoover Institution).

Ocherk politicheskoi istorii Vsevelikogo Voiska Donskogo. Novocherkassk, Obl. V. Voiska Donskogo Tipografiia, 1919 (Hoover Institution).

Prezhde i teper'. Rostov on the Don, 1919 (Columbia University).

Rostov, B. *Pochemu i kak sozdalas Dobrovoi'cheskaia Armiia i za chto ona boretsia.* Biblioteka Dobrovol'cheskoi Armii, 1919 (Hoover Inistitution).

Shchepkin, G. *General-leitenant A. I. Denikin.* Novocherkassk, 1919 (Columbia University).

Suvorin, A. (Aleksei Poroshin). *Pokhod Kornilova.* Rostov on the Don, Knigoizdatel'stvo "Novyi chelovek," 1918 (Harvard University).

Volin, V. *Don i Dobrovol'cheskaia Armiia.* Izdanie A. Ia Vasileva, Novocherkassk, 1919 (Harvard University).

Volkonskii, P. M. *The Volunteer Army of Alexeiev and Deniken.* London, Russian Liberation Committee (Harvard University).

Volunteer Army. *Kratkaia zapiska istorii vzaimootnoshenii Dobrovol'cheskoi Armii s Ukrainei.* Rostov on the Don, 1919.

Volunteer Army. *Sobranie uzakonenii i rasporiazhenii pravitel'stva.* 2 vols. Rostov on the Don, Osobym Soveshchaniem pri Glavnokomanduiushchem Vooruzhenymi Silami na Iuge Rossii, 1918-1919 (Hoover Institution).

Volunteer Army. *The Volunteer Army as a National Factor in the Renaissance of Great Russia, One and Indivisible.* Ekaterinodar, Volunteer Army, 1919 (Hoover Institution).

SECONDARY SOURCES

BOOKS

Adams, A. E. *Bolsheviks in the Ukraine; the Second Campaign.* New Haven, Yale University Press, 1963.

Alekseev, S. A. (ed.). *Denikin, Iudenich, Vrangel.* Moscow, Gosizdat, 1927

——. (ed.). *Nachalo grazhdanskoi voiny.* Moscow, *Gosizdat,* 1926.

——. (ed.). *Revoliutsiia na Ukraine po memuaram belykh.* Moscow, Gosizdat, 1930.

Aleksashchenko, A. P. *Krakh Denikinshchiny.* Moscow, Izdatel'stvo Moskovskogo Universiteta, 1966.

Allen, W. E. D., and P. Muratoff. *Caucasian Battlefields: A History of the Wars on the Turco-Caucasian Border, 1828-1921.* Cambridge, Cambridge University Press, 1953.

Allen, W. E. D. *The Ukraine.* Cambridge, Cambridge University Press, 1940.

Antonov, A. E. *Boevoi vosemnadtsatyi god; Voenye deistviia krasnoi armii v 1918 nachale 1919 g.* Moscow, Voenizdat, 1961.

Antonov-Ovseenko, V. A. *Zapiski o grazhdanskoi voine.* 4 vols. Moscow, Gosvoenizdat, 1924-1933.

Aten, Marion, and Arthur Orrmont. *Last Train Over Rostov Bridge.* New York, Messner, 1961.

Avalishvili, Zourab. *The Independence of Georgia in International Politics, 1918-1921.* London, Headley Brothers, 1940. (Avalov, Z. D. *Nezavisimost' Gruzii v mezhdunarodnoi politike 1918-1921.* Paris, 1924).

Azan, P. J. L. *Franchet d'Esperey.* Paris, Flammarion, 1949.

Bechhofer-Roberts, C. E. *In Denikin's Russia and the Caucasus, 1919-1920.* London, W. Collin's Sons and Co., Ltd., 1921.

Belaia Rossiia Al'bom No. 1. New York, Izdanie glavnogo pravleniia zarubezhnogo soiuza Russkikh voennykh invalidov, 1937.

Beliaevskii, V. A. *Kto vinovat?* No place, no publisher, no date.

——. *Pravda o gen. Denikine; Prichiny prekrashcheniia belogo dvizheniia na iuge Rossii v 1920 g.* San Francisco, no publisher, 1958.

Berz, L. I., and K. A. Khmelevskii. *Geroicheskie gody; Oktiabr'skaia Revoliutsiia i grazhdanskaia voina na Donu,* Rostov on the Don, Rostovskoe knizhnoe izdatel'stvo, 1964.

Bever, Hans. *Die Mittelmaechte und die Ukraine, 1918.* Munich, Isar, 1956.

Blair, Dorian, and C. H. Dand. *Russian Hazard: The Adventures of a British Secret Agent in Russia.* London, Robert Hale, 1937.

Bogaevskii, A. P. *Vospominaniia, 1918 god.* New York, Izdanie "Muzeia belogo dvizheniia," 1963.

Borisenko, I. *Sovetskie respubliki na Severnom Kavkaze v 1918 godu.* 2 vols. Rostov on the Don, Severnyi Kavkaz, 1930.

Bromberg, L. M. *Bol'sheviki—organizatory razgroma Kornilovshchiny.* Moscow, Gospolitizdat, 1957.

Brussilov, Gen. A. A. *A Soldier's Note-book, 1914-1918.* London, Macmillan & Co., 1930.

Bubnov, A. *V tsarskoi stavke.* New York, Izdatel'stvo imeni Chekhova, 1955.

Bubnov, A. S., S. S. Kamenev, and R. P. Eideman (eds.). *Grazhdanskaia voina 1918-1921.* 3 vols. Moscow, Gosizdat, "Voennyi vestnik," 1928-1930.

Carr, E. H. *The Bolshevik Revolution.* 3 vols. London, Macmillan and Co., 1953.

Chamberlin, W. H. *The Russian Revolution.* 2 vols. New York, Macmillan and Co., 1935.

Chemodanov, G. *Poslednye dni staroi armii.* Moscow, Gosizdat, 1926.

Chernov, Victor. *The Great Russian Revolution.* Translated and abridged by P. E. Mosely. New Haven, Yale University Press, 1936.

Coates, W. P., and K. Zelda. *Armed Intervention in Russia, 1918-1922.* London, W. Gollancz, Ltd., 1935.

Danilov, G. N. *Rossiia v mirovoi voine*. Berlin, 1924.

De-Lazari, A. *Grazhdanskaia voina v Rossii v skhemakh*. Moscow, Gosizdat, 1926.

Delert, Dan. *Don v ogne*. Rostov on the Don, Sevkavkniga, 1927.

Denikin, A. I. *Brest-Litovsk*. No place, no publisher, no date.

——. *Kto spas' sovetskuiu vlast' ot gibeli*. Paris, Izdanie Soiuz Dobrovol'tsev, 1937.

——. *Ocherki russkoi smuty*. 5 vols. Berlin, Russkoe Natsional'noe Knigoizdatel'stvo, and Paris, J. Povolozky et Cie., 1921-1925.

——. *Ofitsery*. Paris, 1928.

——. *Pokhod i smert' generala Kornilova* (pod. red. Shchegoleva). Moscow, Gosizdat, 1928.

——. *Put' russkogo ofitsera*. New York, Izdatel'stvo im. Chekhova, 1953.

——. *Staraia armiia*. 2 vols. Paris, Izdanie knizhnogo dela Rodnik, 1929-1931.

——. *The Russian Turmoil*. London, Hutchison and Co., 1932.

——. *The White Army*. Translated by Catherine Zvegintsov. London, J. Cape and Co., 1930.

——. *World Events and the Russian Problem*. Paris, Imprimerie Rapide C. T., 1939.

Denisov, S. V. *Zapiski: grazhdanskaia voina na iuge Rossii 1918-1919 gg*. Constantinople, izdanie avtora, 1921.

Deutscher, I. *The Prophet Armed: Trotsky, 1879-1921*. New York, Oxford University Press, 1954.

Dobrynin, Col. V. *Bor'ba s bol'shevizmom na iuge Rossii: uchastie v bor'be donskogo kazachestva*. Prague, Slavianskoe Izdatel'stvo, 1921 (*La lutte contre le bolchevisme*, Prague, Imprimerie, "Melatrich", 1920).

——. *Don v bor'be s kommunoi na Dontse i Manyche Febr.-Mai 1919*. Prague, 1922.

Drabkina, E. *Gruzinskaia kontr-revoliutsiia*. Leningrad, Priboi, 1928.

Dreier, V. Von. *Krestnyi put' vo imia rodiny: dvukhletniaia voina krasnogo severa s belym iugom 1918-1920 gg*. Berlin, no publisher, 1921.

Drozdovskii, M. G. *Dnevnik*. Berlin, Knigoizdatel'stvo Otto Kirchner, 1923.

Dunsterville, L. C. *The Adventures of Dunsterforce*. London, Edward Arnold, 1920.

Egorov, A. I. *Razgrom Denikina*. Moscow, Gosvoenizdat, 1931.

Eliseev, F. I. *Labintsy i poslednye dni na Kubani*. New York, published by the author, 1962.

——. *Na beregakh Kubani i partizan Shkuro*. New York, published by the author, 1955.

——. *S Kornilovskim polkom na beregakh Kubani v Stavropole i Astrakhanskikh stepiakh, 1918-1919*. New York, published by the author, 1959.

Ellis, C. H. *The British "Intervention" in Transcaspia, 1918-1919*. Berkeley, University of California Press, 1963.

Eremenko, V. *Bol'sheviki v bor'be za rabochii kontrol' Mart- iiul' 1917 goda* (*po materialam Donbassa*). Moscow, izdatel'stvo Moskovskogo Universiteta, 1962.

Erickson, John. *The Soviet High Command: A Military-Political History, 1918-1941*. London, Macmillan and Co., 1962.

Fischer, Louis. *The Soviets in World Affairs: A History of Relations Between the Soviet Union and the Rest of the World, 1917-1929*. London, Jonathan Cape, 1930.

Footman, David. *Civil War in Russia*. London, Faber and Faber Ltd., 1961.

———. (ed.). *Soviet Affairs Number Two, St. Antony's Papers. No. 6*. New York, Praeger, 1959.

Freund, Gerald. *Unholy Alliance*. New York, Harcourt Brace and Co. 1957.

Goigova, Z. A. G. *Narody Checheno-Ingushetii v bor'be protiv Denikina*. Groznyi, Checheno-Ingushetii nauchno-issledovatel'skii institut, 1963.

Goleevskii, M. M. *Materilaly po istorii gvardeiskoi pekhoty i artillerii v grazhdanskoi voiny s 1917 po 1922 god*. No place, no publisher, no date.

Golovin, Gen. N. N. *Rossiiskaia kontr-revoliutsiia v 1917-1918 gg. 5 vols*. Paris, Biblioteka "Illiustrirovannoi Rossii," 1937.

Golovine, N. N. *The Russian Army in the World War*. New Haven, Yale University Press, 1931.

Golubintsev, Gen. *Russkaia Vandeia (Ocherki grazhdanskoi voiny na Donu 1917-1920 gg.)*. Munich, no publisher, 1959.

Gordon, A. G. *Russian Civil War*. London, Cassel and Co., 1937.

Gourko, Gen. Basil. *War and Revolution in Russia, 1914-1917*. New York, Macmillan Co., 1919.

Gukovskii, A. I. *Antanta i Oktiabr'skaia Revoliutsiia*. Moscow, Gosudarstvennoe sotsialno-ekonomicheskoe izdatel'stvo, 1931.

———. *Frantsuzkaia interventsiia na iuga Rossii, 1918-1919*. Moscow, Gosudarstvennoe sotsialno-ekonomicheskoe izdatel'stvo, 1928.

Gul, Roman. *Ledianoi pokhod*. Berlin, Izdatel'stvo S. Efron, 1921.

Hill, G. A. *Go Spy the Land: Being the Adventures of I. K. 8 of the British Secret Service*. London, Cassel, 1932.

Hodgson, J. *With Denikin's Armies*. London, Lincoln Williams Co. Ltd., 1932.

Hoffmann, Max. *War Diaries and Other Papers*. 2 vols., London, Martin Secker, 1929.

Hurwicz, Elias. *Geschichte des russischen Burgerkriegs*. Berlin, E. Laubsche Verlagsbuchhandlung G.m.b.h., 1927.

———. *Staatsmaenner und Abenteuer*. Leipzig, 1925.

Ianchevskii, N. L. *Grazhdanskaia bor'ba na Severnom Kavkaze*. Rostov on the Don, Gosizdat, 1927.

Ivanov, N. Ia. *Kornilovshchina i ee razgrom: Iz istorii bor'by s kontrrevoliutsiei v 1917 g*. Leningrad, Izdatel'stvo Leningradskogo Universiteta, 1965.

Kadishev, A. B. *Interventsiia i grazhdanskaia voina v Zakavkaze*. Moscow, Voenizdat, 1960.

Kakurin, N. *Kak srazhalas' revoliutsiia.* 2 vols. Moscow and Leningrad, Gosizdat, 1925.

Kalinin, I. V. *Russkaia Vandeia.* Moscow, Gosizdat, 1926.

Kantorovich, V. P. *Frantsuzy v Odesse.* Petrograd, Izdatel'stvo "Byloe," 1922.

Katkov, George. *Russia, 1917: The February Revolution.* New York, Harper, 1966.

Kautsky, Karl. *Georgia, a Social-Democratic Peasant Republic.* Translated by H. J. Stenning. London, International Bookshops Ltd., 1921.

Kazemzadeh, Firuz. *The Struggle for Transcaucasia, 1917-1921.* New York, Philosophical Library, 1951.

Kennan, G. F. *Russia and the West Under Lenin and Stalin.* Boston, Atlantic-Little Brown and Co., 1960.

——. *Soviet-American Relations, 1917-1920.* 2 vols. Vol. 1: *Russia Leaves the War,* Princeton, Princeton University Press 1956. Vol. 2: *The Decision to Intervene,* Princeton, Princeton University Press, 1958.

Kerensky, A. F. *The Catastrophe: Kerensky's Own Story of the Russian Revolution.* New York, D. Appleton, 1927.

——. *The Crucifixion of Liberty.* New York, John Day, 1934.

——. *The Prelude to Bolshevism: The Kornilov Rebellion.* New York, Dodd, Mead and Co., 1919.

——. *Russia and History's Turning Point.* New York, Duell, Sloan and Pearce, 1965.

Khachapuridze, G. V. *Bor'ba gruzinskogo naroda za ustanovlenie Sovetskoi vlasti.* Moscow, Gospolitizdat, 1956.

Kin, D. *Denikinshchina.* Leningrad, "Priboi," 1927.

Kluev, L. *Bor'ba za Tsaritsyn.* Gosizdat, Moscow, 1928.

Knox, Major General A. W. F. *With the Russian Army, 1914-1917.* 2 vols. London, Hutchinson and Co., 1921.

Kovtiukh, E. *Ot Kubani do Volgi i Obratno.* Moscow, Gosudarstvennoe voennoe izdatel'stvo, 1926.

Kritskii, M. A. *Kornilovskii udarnyi polk.* Paris, Imprimerie "Val," 1936.

Lampe, A. A. von (ed.). *Beloe Delo: letopis' beloi bor'by.* 7 vols. Berlin, Russkoe natsional'noe knigoizdatel'stvo "Mednyi Vsadnik," 1926-1928.

Lampe, A. A. von (ed.). *Glavnokomanduiushchii russkoi armiei general baron P. N. Vrangel; sbornik statei.* Berlin, knigoizdatel'stvo "Mednyi Vsadnik," 1938.

——. *Prichiny neudachi vooruzhenogo vystupleniia belykh.* Berlin, 1929.

——. *Puti vernykh: sbornik statei.* Paris, 1960.

Lang, D. M. *A Modern History of Georgia,* London, Weidenfeld and Nicolson, 1962.

Lelevich, L. G. *Oktiabr' v stavke.* Gomel, Kooperativnye izdatel'stvo, 1922.

Leonidov, O. L. *Po tylam Krasnova.* Moscow, Gosudarstvennoe voennoe izdatel'stvo, 1939.

Leontovich, V. *Pervye boi na Kubani; vospominaniia.* Munich, Izdatel'stvo "Molodaia Rossiia," 1923.

Liubimov, I. N. (ed.). *Revoliutsiia 1917 goda: Khronika sobytii.* vol. 6. Oktiabr'-Dekabr' Moscow and Leningrad, Gosizdat, 1930.

Lisovoi, Ia. M. *Belyi Arkhiv: sborniki materialov po istorii i literature voiny, revoliutsii, bol'shevizma, belogo dvizheniia i t.d.* 3 vols. Paris, no publisher, 1926-1928.

Lockhart, R. H. Bruce. *Memoirs of a British Agent.* London, Putnam, 1932.

Ludendorff, Erich von. *My War Memoirs, 1914-1918.* London, Hutchinson and Co. 1919.

Lukomskii, A. S. *Vospominaniia.* 2 vols. Berlin, Otto Kirchner, 1922. (Memoirs of the Russian Revolution translated and abridged by Olga Vitali, London, T. F. Unwin, Ltd., 1922).

Makarov, P. V. *Adiutant generala Mai-Maevskogo; iz vospominanii nachal'nika otriada krasnykh partizan v Krymu.* Leningrad, Rabochee izdatel'stvo "Priboi," 1929.

Makharadze, F. *Sovety i bor'ba za sovetskuiu vlast' v Gruzii, 1917-1921.* Tiflis, Gosizdat, SSRG., 1928.

Makhrov, P. *Kto i pochemu mog' pokhitet' gen. Kutepova i gen. Millera?* Paris, no publisher, 1937.

Margolin, A. D. *From a Political Diary: Russia, the Ukraine, and America, 1905-1945.* New York, Columbia University Press, 1946.

————. *Ukraina i politika antanty.* Berlin, Izdatel'stvo S. Efron, 1921.

Margulies, M. S. *God interventsii.* 3 vols. Berlin, Izdatel'stvo Z. I. Grzhebina, 1923.

Marty, Andre P. *The Epic of the Black Sea Revolt.* New York, Workers' Library Publishers, 1941.

Martynov, E. I. *Kornilov: Popytka voennogo perevorota.* Moscow, Voennoe Idatel'stvo, 1927.

————. *Tsarskaia armiia v fevral'skom perevorote.* Moscow, Izdatel'stvo Narkomvoenmor, 1927.

Masaryk, Thomas G. *The Making of a State: Memoirs and Observations, 1914-1918.* London, G. Allen and Unwin, Ltd., 1927.

Melgunov, S. P. *N. V. Chaikovskii v gody grazhdanskoi voiny: materialy dlia istorii Russkoi obshchestvennosti, 1917-1925 gg.* Paris, Librarie "La Source," 1929.

————. *Grazhdanskaia voina v osveshchenii P. N. Miliukova.* Paris, Rapid Imprimerie, 1929.

————. *Kak bol'sheviki zakhvatili vlast.* Paris, "La Renaissance," 1963.

————. *The Red Terror in Russia.* London, I. M. Dent and Sons, Ltd., 1926.

Melnikov, N. M. (ed.). *M. P. Bogaevskii.* Izd. "Rodimogo kraia," 1964.

————. *Kak izvrashchaetsia istoriia.* Paris, Izdatel'stvo Rodimogo Kraia, 1963.

Melnikov, N. M. *Pochemu belye na iuge ne pobedili khasnykh: Grazhdanskaia voina na igue Rossii.* No place, no publisher, no date.

Miliukov, P. N. *Beloe dvizhenie.* Paris, Izdanie Respublikansko-demokrati-cheskogo obdedineniia, 1929.

——. *Istoriia vtoroi russkoi revoliutsii.* 3 vols. Sofia, Rossiiski-Bolgarskoe Knigoizdatel'stvo, 1921-1924.

——. *Russia Today and Tomorrow.* New York, Macmillan and Co., 1922.

——. *Russlands Zusammenbruch.* 2 vols. Obelisk Verlag, Berlin, 1926 (*Rossiia na perelome,* 2 vols. Paris, 1927).

Mints, I. I. (ed.). *Sovetskaia Rossiia i kapitalisticheskii mir v 1917-1923 gg.* Moscow, Akademiia nauk SSSR, Institut istorii, Gospolitizdat, 1957.

Nabokoff, C. *The Ordeal of a Diplomat.* London, Duckworth and Co., 1921.

Naida, S. F. et al. (eds.). *Istoriia grazhdanskoi voiny v SSSR, 1917-1922.* 3 vols. Moscow, Institut Marksizma-Leninizma pri TsK. KPSS, Gospolitiz-dat, 1959.

Naumenko, V. G. *Iz nedavnogo proshlogo Kubani.* Belgrad, 193? No publisher.

Nesterovich-Berg, M. A. *V bor'be s bol'shevikami: vospominaniia.* Paris, Imp. de Navarre, 1931.

Nikulikhin, Ia. *Na fronte grazhdanskoi voiny (1918-1921).* Izdanie Priboi, Petrograd, 1923.

Pamiati pogibshchikh. Paris, Imprimerie de la Societe nouvelle d' editions franco-slaves, 1929.

Pares, Sir Bernard. *The Fall of the Russian Monarchy.* New York, Alfred A. Knopf, 1939.

Pavlov, V. E. (ed.). *Markovtsy v boiakh i pokhodakh za Rossiiu v osvobo-ditel'noi voine 1917-1920.* Paris, 1962.

Pipes, R. E. *The Formation of the Soviet Union: Communism and National-ism, 1917-1923.* Cambridge, Harvard University Press, 1957.

Pokrovskii, G. *Denikinshchina: God politiki i ekonomiki na Kubani (1918-1919 gg).* Izdatel'stvo Z. I. Grzhebina, Berlin, 1923.

Poliakov, Ia., A. Gen. *Donskie kazaki v bor'be s bol'shevikami.* Munich, no publisher, 1962.

Polotsov, L. V. *Rytsary ternogo ventsa; vospominaniia oi-om Kubanskom pokhode gen. M. V. Alekseeva, L. G. Kornilova, i A. I. Denikina.* Prague, Tip. Griunkhut, 1921.

Power, Rhoda. *Under Cossack and Bolshevik.* London, 1919.

Pronin, Dmitrii. *Sed'maia gaubchnaia, 1918-1921.* New York, no publisher, 1960.

Rabinovich, S. *Bor'ba za armiiu v 1917 g.* Moscow, Gosizdat, 1930.

Radkey, O. H. *The Election to the Russian Constituent Assembly of 1917.* Cambridge, Harvard University Press, 1950.

——. *The Sickle Under the Hammer.* New York, Columbia University Press, 1963.

Raenko, Iafl *Khronika istoricheskikh sobytii na Donu, Kubani i v Cherno-more.* Rostov on the Don, Rostovskoe oblastnoe knigoizdatel'stvo, 1939.

Rafes, M. *Dva goda revoliutsii na Ukraine*. Moscow, Gosizdat, 1920.

Rakovskii, G. N. *V stane belykh: grazhdanskaia voina na iuge Rossii*. Constantinople, Izdat "Pressa," 1920.

Reilly, Sydney. *Britain's Master Spy*. London, Harper and Brothers, 1933.

Reshetar, John S. *The Ukrainian Revolution: A Study in Nationalism, 1917-1920*. Princeton, Princeton University Press, 1952.

Riasianskii, S. N. (ed.). *Ledianoi pokhod: Sbornik*. Izdanie glavnogo pravleniia, New York, 1953.

Rosenberg, W. G. *A. I. Denikin and the Anti-Bolshevik Movement in South Russia*. Amherst, Amherst College Press, Amherst College Honors Thesis No. 7, 1961.

Rosenfeld, Gunther. *Sowjetrussland und Deutschland, 1917-1922*. Berlin, Akademie Verlag, 1960.

Rossiia v mirovoi voine 1914-1918 goda (v tsifrakh). Moscow, Tsentralnoe statisticheskoe upravlenie, 1925.

Saenko, D. P. *Dmitrii Zhloba*. Krasnodar, 1964.

Samoilov, F. *Delo Borisa Savinkova*. Moscow, Gosizdat, 1924.

Savtchenko, I. *La Guerre des Rouges et des Blancs: Les Insurges du Kuban*. Paris, Payot, 1929.

Savinkov, B. V. *Bor'ba s bolshevikami*. Warsaw, Izdanie Russkogo politicheskogo komiteta, 1920.

Sazonov, S. D. *Vospominaniia*. Paris, knigoizdatel'stvo E. Siial'okoi, 1927.

Schapiro, L. B. *The Communist Party of the Soviet Union*. New York, Random House, 1959.

Sergeev, A. *Denikinskaia armiia samo o sebe; po dokumentam sobrannym na boevykh liniakh voennym korrespondentam "Rosta."* Moscow, Gosizdat, 1920.

Shafir, Ia. M. *Grazhdanskaia voina v Rossi i men'shevistskaia Gruziia*. Moscow, Tip "Tsustran," 1921.

Shchagolev, P. E. (ed.). *Frantsuzy v Odesse; iz belykh memuarov Gen A. I. Denikina, M. S. Margulies, M. V. Braikeicha*. Leningrad, Izdatel'stvo "Krasnaia gazeta," 1928.

Shkuro, A. G. *Zapiski belogo partizana*. Buenos Aires, Izdatel'stvo "Seiatel," 1961.

Shliapnikov, A. *Semnadtsatyi god*, 4 vols. Moscow-Petrograd, Gosizdat, 1925.

Shteifon, Gen. M. B. *Krizis dobrovol'chestva*. Belgrad, Russkaia Tip., 1928.

Shulgin, V. V. *Dni*. Belgrad, knigoizdatel'stvo M. A. Suverin i Co. "Novoe vremia," 1925.

Skobtsov, D. E. *Tri goda resoliutsii i grazhdanskoi voiny na Kubani*. Paris, no date.

Sokolov, K. N. *Pravlenie generala Denikina*. Sofia, Rossisko-Bolgarskoe knigoizdatel'stvo, 1921.

Spiridonov, N. *Podpolnaia deiatel'nost' bol'shevikov Kubani v gody grazhdanskoi voiny*. Krasnodar, Krasnodarskoe knizhnoe izdatel'stvo, 1960.

Stalin, J. et al. (eds.). *The History of the Civil War in the USSR*. Vol. 1: *The Prelude of the Great Proletarian Revolution (From the Beginning of the War to the beginning of October 1917)*. London, Lawrence and Wishart, 1937.

Stalin, J. et al. (eds.). *The History of the Civil War*, Vol. 2. Moscow, Foreign Language Publishing House, 1946.

Stankevich, V. B. *Vospominaniia, 1914-1919 g*. Berlin, Izdatel'stvo I. P. Ladyshnikova, 1920.

Stewart, G. *The White Armies of Russia*. New York, Macmillan Co., 1933.

Sukhanov, N. N. *Zapiski o revoliutsii*. 7 vols. Berlin, Petrograd, and Moscow, Z. I. Grzhebin, 1922-1923.

Sukhorukov, V. T. *XI Armiia v boiakh na Severnom Kavkaze i nizhnei Volge*. Moscow, Voennoe izdatel'stvo, 1961.

Suliatinskii, P. P. *Narisi z istorii revoliutsii na Kubani*. Prague, Ukrainskii institut gromadoznavstva v Prazi, 1925.

Suvorin, B. A. *Za rodinoi: geroicheskaia epokha Dobrovol'cheskoi Armii, 1917-1918 gg*. Paris, O. D. i ko., 1922.

Svechin, Mikhail. *Zapiski starogo generala o bylom*. Nice, 1964.

Svechnikov, M. S. *Bor'ba Krasnoi armii na severnom Kavkaze, sentiabr' 1918 aprel' 1919*. Moscow, Gosvoenizdat, 1926.

Tolmachev, I. P. *V stepiakh Donskikh*. Moscow, Voennoe izdatel'stvo, 1959.

Trotsky, Leon. *Between Red and White: A Study of Some Fundamental Questions of Revolution with Particular Reference to Georgia*. London, Communist Party of Great Britain, 1922.

———. *The History of the Russian Revolution*. 3 vols. New York, Simon and Schuster, 1932.

———. *My Life: An Attempt at an Autobiography*. New York, Charles Scribner's, 1930.

Trotskii, L. *Kak vooruzhalas' revoliutsiia*. 5 vols. Moscow, Vysshii voennyi redaktsionnyi sovet, 1923-1925.

Tschebotarioff, G. P. *Russia, My Native Land*. New York, London, and Toronto, McGraw-Hill, 1964.

Turkul, A. V. *Drozdovtsy v ogne*. Munich. Izdatel'stvo Iav i byl, 1948.

Ulam, Adam. *The Bolsheviks*. New York, Macmillan, 1965.

Ul'ianov, I. *Kazachestvo v pervye dni revoliutsii*. Moscow, Gosizdat, 1920.

———. *Dumy vol'nogo kazaka*. Moscow, Gosizdat, 1920.

Ullman, R. H. *Anglo-Soviet Relations, 1917-1921*. Vol. 1: *Intervention and the War*. Princeton, Princeton University Press, 1961.

Val', E. G. *K istorii belogo dvizheniia: deiatel'nost' General-adiutanta Shcherbacheva*. Tallin, Izdanie avtora, 1938.

———. *Prichiny raspadeniia Rossiiskoi imperii i neudachi russkogo natsional'nogo dvizheniia*. 4 vols. in 1 Tallin, Izdanie avtora, 1938.

Vasilevskii, I. M. *Belye memuary*. Izdatel'stvo "Petrograd," Petrograd and Moscow, 1923.

——. *A. I. Denikin i ego memuary*. Berlin, Izdanie "Nakanune," 1924.

Vavrik, V. R. *Karpatorossy v Kornilovskom pokhode i Dobrovol'cheskoi Armii*. Lvov, Izd. Tip. Savropgiiskago instituta, pod upravleniem A. I. Iaskova, 1923.

Vinaver, M. M. *Nashe pravitel'stvo: Krymskie vospominaniia, 1918-1919 gg.* Paris, Izdanie posmertnoe, 1929.

Vladimirova, Vera. *God sluzhby "sotsialistov" kaptitalom*. Moscow, Gosizdat, 1927.

——. *Kontr-revoliutsiia v 1917*. Moscow, Krasnaia Nov', 1924.

Warth, R. D. *The Allies and the Russian Revolution: From the Fall of the Monarchy to the Peace of Brest-Litovsk*. Durham, Duke University Press, 1954.

Wheeler-Bennett, J. W. *The Forgotten Peace: Brest-Litovsk, March 1918*. London, Macmillan and Co., 1938.

Woytinsky, W. S. *Stormy Passage*. New York, the Vanguard Press, 1961.

Wrangel, N. N. *Memoirs*. London, Williams and Norgate Ltd., 1929. (Republished as *Always with Honor*, New York, Robert Speller and Sons, 1957).

Xydias, Jean. *L'intervention francaise en Russie, 1918-1919: souvenirs d'un témoin*. Paris, editions de France, 1927.

Zaitsov, A. A. *1918 god: Ocherki po istorii russkoi grazhdanskoi voiny*. Paris, no publisher, 1934.

Zaporozhets, M. Ia. *Kommunisty Makaevki v bor'be za pobedu i ukreplenie sovetskoi vlasti*. Donskoe knizhnoe izdatel'stvo, 1961.

Zhukov, V. *Chernomorskii flot v revoliutsii 1917-1918 gg*. Moscow, Molodaiia gvardiia, 1932.

Zinkevich, M. M. *Osnovanie i put' Dobrovol'cheskoi Armii 1917-1930*. Sofia, 1930.

Znamenskii, O. N. *Iiul'skii krizis 1917 goda*. Moscow-Leningrad, Nauka, 1964.

ARTICLES

Ascher, Abraham. "The Kornilov Affair," *Russian Review*, Vol. 12, No. 3 (Oct. 1953), pp. 235-252.

Astrov, N. I. "Iasskoe soveshchanie," *Golos Minuvshego Na Chuzhoi Storone*, No. 3 (1926), pp. 39-76.

Baizov, B. "Vospominaniia o revoliutsii v Zakavkaze, 117-1920 gg," *Arkhiv Russkoi Revoliutsii*, Vol. 9 (1923), pp. 91-194.

Balkum, F. "Interventsiia v Odesse, 1918-1919 gg," *Proletarskaia Revoliutsiia*, No. 6-7 (1923), pp. 196-221.

Boyd, J. R. "The Origins of Order No. 1," *Soviet Studies*, Vol. 19 (January 1968), pp. 359-372.

Bradley, J. F. N. "The Allies and Russia in the Light of the French Archives," *Soviet Studies*, vol. 14 (Oct. 1964), pp. 166-185.

Bykadorov, I. F. "Vospominaniia o Voiskovom Atamane Generale A. M. Nazarove," *Donskaia Letopis'*, vol. 2, pp. 209-223.

———. "Zametki k state 'Osvobozhdanie Novocherkasska,' " *Donskaia Letopis'*, vol. 3, pp. 63-67.

Cheriachukin, A. V. "Donskaia delegatsiia na Ukrainu i Berlin v 1918-1919 gg." *Donskaia Letopis'*, vol. 3, pp. 163-231.

Dobrynin, V. V. "Vooruzhennaia bor'ba Dona s bol'shevikami," *Donskaia Letopis'*, vol. 1, pp. 93-130.

Duvakin, N. "Voisko Ataman General A. M. Nazarov," *Donskaia Letopis'*, vol. 2, pp. 223-228.

Elkin, Boris. "The Kerensky Government and its Fate," *Slavic Review*, vol. 23, No. 4 (Dec. 1964), pp. 717-736.

———. "Further Notes on the policies of the Kerensky Government," Slavic Review, Vol. 25, No. 2 (June 1966), pp. 323-332.

Feldman, R. S. "The Russian General Staff and the June 1917 Offensive," *Soviet Studies*, vol. 19 (April, 1968), pp. 526-543.

Filimonov, A. P. "Kubantsy," *Deloe Delo*, vol. 2, pp. 62-107.

———. "Razgrom Kubanskoi rady," *Arkhiv Russkoi Revoliutsii*," vol. 5 (1922), pp. 322-329.

Grekov, A. N. "Soiuz kazachikh voisk v Petrograde v 1917 godu," *Donskaia Letopis'*, vol. 2, pp. 229-283.

Gurko, V. I. "Iz Petrograda cherez Moskvu, Parizh i London v Odessu 1917-1918 gg," *Arkhiv Russkoi Revoliutsii*, vol. 15 (1924), pp. 5-84.

Ianov, G. P. "Don pod bol'shevikami vesnoi 1918 g. i vostanie stanits na Donu," *Donskaia Letopis'*, vol. 3, pp. 12-31.

———. "Donskoe nastroenie ko vremeni revoliutsii," *Donskaia Letopis'*, vol. 1, pp. 61-68.

———. "Osvobozhdenie Novocherkasska i Krug Spasenia Dona," *Donskaia Letopis'*, vol. 3, pp. 32-62.

———. "Paritet," *Donskaia Letopis'*, vol. 2, pp. 170-199.

———. "Revoliutsiia i Donskie kazaki," *Donskaia Letopis'*, vol. 2, pp. 5-39.

Kakliugin, K. P. "M. P. Bogaevskii; Kharakteristika," *Donskaia Letopis'*, vol. 1, pp. 43-60.

———. "Donskoi Ataman P. N. Krasnov i ego vremia," *Donskaia Letopis'*, vol. 3, pp. 68-163.

———. "Organizatsiia vlasti na Donu v nachale revoliutsii," *Donskaia Letopis'*, vol. 2, pp. 63-107.

———. "Stepnoi pokhod v Zadon'e 1918 goda i ego znachenie," *Donskaia Letopis'*, vol. 3, pp. 5-10.

———. "Voiskovoi Ataman A. M. Kaledin i ego vremia," *Donskaia Letopis'*, vol. 2, pp. 108-170.

———. "Voiskovoi Ataman A. M. Nazarov i ego vremia," *Donskaia Letopis'*, vol. 2, pp. 205-209.

Kazanovich, B., "Poezdka iz Dobrovol'cheskoi Armii v Krasnuiu Moskvu", *Arkhiv Russkoi Revoliutsii*. Vol. 7 (1922), pp. 184-202.

Kharlamov, V. A. "Iugo-vostochnyi soiuz v 1917 godu," *Donskaia Letopis'*, vol. 2, pp. 284-292.

Krasnov, P. N. "Na vnutrennem fronte," *Arkhiv Russkoi Revoliutsii*, vol. 5 (1922), pp. 190-321.

Kritskii, M. "Krasnaia armii na iuzhnom fronte v 1918-1920 gg," *Arkhiv Russkoi Revoliutsii*, vol. 18, pp. 254-300.

Leikhtenbergskii, G. (Prince). "Kak nachalas' Iuzhnaia Armiia," *Arkhiv Russkoi Revoliutsii*, vol. 8 (1923), pp. 166-182.

Lukomskii, A. S. "Iz vospominanii," *Arkhiv Russkoi Revoliutsii*, vol. 2 (1921), pp. 14-44; vol. 5 (1922), pp. 107-189; vol. 6 (1922), pp. 81-160.

Makarenko, P. L. "1918 god," *Volnoe Kazachestvo* (March 25), pp. 15-19; Apr. 10, pp. 15-19; Apr. 25, pp. 14-18 (1935).

Mal't, M., "Denikinshchina i krestianstvo," *Proletarskaia Revoliutsiia*, Vol. 24, No. 1 (1924), pp. 140-157.

McNeal, R. H., "The Conference of Jassy: An Early Fiasco of the Anti-Bolshevik Movement," in J. S. Curtiss, ed. *Essays in Russian and Soviet History in Honor of Geroid Tanquary Robinson*, New York, Columbia University Press, 1963. pp. 221-236.

Mel'nikov, N. M., "A. M. Kaledin. Lichnost' i deiatel'nost'," *Donskaia Letopis'*, vol. 1, pp. 15-42.

Miakotin, V. A. "Iz nedalekogo proshlogo," *Na Chuzhoi Storone*, vol. 2 (1923), pp. 178-199.

Miliukov, P. N. "Dnevnik," *Novyi Zhurnal*, No. 66, pp. 173-203; No. 67, pp. 180-218.

Oberlaender, Erwin. "The All-Russian Fascist Party," *International Fascim, 1920-1945* (Walter Laqueur and George L. Mosse, eds.), New York, Harper, 1966.

"Otchet o komandirovke iz Dobrovol'cheskoi Armii v Sibir' v 1918 godu," *Arkhiv Russkoi Revoliutsii*, vol. 9, (1923) pp. 243-304.

Padalkin, A. "Poezdka v Mosku k Leninu s pis'mom Donskogo atamana P. N. Krasnova," *Donskaia Letopis'*, vol. 3, pp. 261-267.

Pokrovskii, M. N. "Memuary tsaria Antona," *Pechat' i Revoliutsiia*, no. 2 (1922), pp. 19-31.

Savinkov, B. "Gen. Kornilov" (Iz vospominanii), *Byloe*, No. 3 (1925), pp. 182-197.

Serezhnikov, K. "Vospominaniia donskogo ofitsera o sluzhebnoi poezdke v Germaniiu; Oseniu 1918 g." *Arkhiv Russkoi Revoliutsii*, vol. 18, pp. 208-236.

Stalinskii, E. "Patriotism i liberalism v belom dvizhenii," *Volia Rossii*, no. 8-9 (May 1924), pp. 140-157.

Stein, Hans-Peter. "Der Offizier des russischen Heeres im Zeitabschnitt zwischen Reform und Revolution, 1861-1905," *Forschungen zur osteuro-*

paeischen Geschichte, Berlin, Osteuropa-Institut an der Freien Universitaet Berlin, vol. 13 (1967), pp. 346-507.

Strakhovskii, L. I. "The Franco-British Plot to Dismember Russia," *Current History*, vol. 33 (March 1931), pp. 839-842.

Treadgold, D. W. "The Ideology of the White Movement: Wrangel's 'Leftist Policy from Rightist Hands,'" *Harvard Slavic Studies*, vol. 4, pp. 481-498.

Thompson, J. M. "Allied and American Intervention in Russia, 1918-1921," *Rewriting Russian History: Soviet Interpretations of Russia's Past* (ed. Cyril E. Black), New York, Praeger, 1956.

Trubetskoi, E. N. "Iz putevykh zametok bezhentsa," *Arkhiv Russkoi Revoliutsii*, vol. 18, pp. 137-207.

Vendziagolskii, K. "Savinkov," *Novyi Zhurnal*, no. 70 (1962), pp. 142-183.

Vishniak, Mark. "A Pamphlet in the Guise of a Review," *Slavic Review*, vol. 25, no. 1 (March 1966), pp. 143-149.

Wade, R. A. "Why October? The Search for Peace in 1917," *Soviet Studies*, vol. 20 (July 1968), pp. 36-45.

Wettig, Gerhard. "Die Rolle der russischen Armee im revolutionaeren Machtkampf, 1917," *Forschungen zur osteuropaeschen Geschichte*, Berlin, Osteuropa-Institut an der Freien Universitaet Berlin, vol. 12 (1967), pp. 46-389.

Zalesskii, P. "Iuzhnaia armiia," *Donskaia Letopis'*, vol. 3, pp. 232-260.

DISSERTATIONS

Brinkley, G. A. "Allied Intervention and the Volunteer Army in South Russia." Columbia University, 1964.

Godwin, R. K. "Russian-Georgian Relations, 1917-1921." Russian Institute Essay, Columbia University, 1951.

Rosenberg, W. G. "Constitutional Democracy and the Russian Civil War." Harvard University, 1967.

Thompson, J. M. "The Russian Problem at the Paris Peace Conference." Columbia University, 1960.

NEWSPAPERS OCCASIONALLY FOUND USEFUL

Golos Kazaka, Hoover Library

Kazach'i Dumy, New York Public Library

Kazachii Nabat, New York Public Library

Kazachii put', New York Public Library

Novoe Vremia, Russian Archives, Columbia University

Poslednie Novosti, New York Public Library

Russkii Invalid, Russian Archives, Columbia University

Slovo, Russian Archives, Columbia University

Signal, Hoover Library

Volia Rossii, New York Public Library

Vozrozhdenie, Harvard.

Index